Resources of the City

Historical Urban Studies

Series Editors: Richard Rodger and Jean-Luc Pinol

Titles in this series include:

Resources of the City

Contributions to an Environmental History of Modern Europe

Edited by

DIETER SCHOTT
BILL LUCKIN
GENEVIÈVE MASSARD-GUILBAUD

ASHGATE

Published by
Ashgate Publishing Limited
Gower House
Croft Road
Aldershot
Hampshire GU11 3HR
England

Ashgate Publishing Company
Suite 420
101 Cherry Street
Burlington, VT 05401-4405
USA

Ashgate website: http://www.ashgate.com

British Library Cataloguing in Publication Data
Resources of the city : contributions to an environmental
   history of modern Europe. – (Historical urban studies)
   1. Urban ecology – Europe – History 2. Cities and towns –
   Europe – History 3. Municipal engineering – Europe – History
   I. Schott, Dieter II. Luckin, Bill III. Massard-Guilbaud, Geneviève
   307.7'6'094

Library of Congress Cataloging-in-Publication Data
Resources of the city : contributions to an environmental history of modern Europe /
edited by Dieter Schott, Bill Luckin and Geneviève Massard-Guilbaud.
      p. cm.—(Historical urban studies)
   Includes index.
   ISBN 0-7546-5081-2 (alk. paper)
   1. Urban ecology—Europe—History. 2. Human ecology—Europe—History. 3.
Cities and towns—Europe—Growth. 4. Cities and towns—Europe—History. 5.
Europe—Environmental conditions. I. Schott, Dieter. II. Luckin, Bill. III.
Massard-Guilbard, Geneviève. IV. Series.

   GF540.R47 2005
   577.5'6'094—dc22

                                                                    2004010927

ISBN 0 7546 5081 2

Printed and bound in Great Britain by Antony Rowe Ltd, Chippenham

Contents

List of Figures

List of Tables

Notes on Contributors

Sabine Barles, Ir Dr, is *Maître de conférences* at the University of Paris 8 and is a researcher at the Laboratoire Théorie des Mutations Urbaines (UMR Architecture, urbanisme, sociétés). Her work is principally concerned with urban environmental history and the history of technology (19th and 20th centuries). In 1999, she published *La ville délétère : médecins et ingénieurs dans l'espace urbain, XVIIIe-XIXe siècles.*

sabine.barles@univ-paris8.fr

Christoph Bernhardt is a senior research fellow at the Leibniz-Institut für Regionalentwicklung und Strukturplanung (IRS) in Erkner near Berlin and co-editor of the German Urban History Journal *Informationen zur Modernen Stadtgeschicht*. Publications, as editor, include *Environmental Problems in European Cities in the Nineteenth and Twentieth Centuries – Umweltprobleme in europäischen Städten des 19. und 20. Jahrhunderts* (2001), and together with Geneviève Massard-Guilbaud: *Le Démon moderne. La pollution dans les sociétés urbaines et industrielles d'Europe / The Modern Demon. Pollution in urban and industrial European societie*s (2002).

bernhardt@irs-net.de

Gabriella Corona is Senior Researcher at the Institute for the Study of Mediterranean Societies of the National Research Council in Naples (CNR-ISSM). Her publications deal with economic, social and environmental history especially in relation to the contemporary history of Italy. Recent publications include 'La propriété collective en Italie', in Marie-Danielle Demelas et Nadine Vivier (sous la direction de), *Les propriétés collectives face aux attaques libérales (1770–1914)*, Presses universitaires de Rennes, 2003; 'Declino dei commons ed equilibri ambientali. Il caso italiano tra Otto e Novecento', in the press at 'Società e storia' (2004).

corona@issm.cnr.it

Michèle Dagenais is Professor of History at the Université de Montréal and co-editor of the Canadian journal *Urban History Review/Revue d'histoire urbaine*. Her main research interest is related to the development of the municipal domain in Canadian cities in comparative perspective. She has recently edited, together with Irene Maver and Pierre Saunier, *Municipal Services and Employees in the Modern City: New Historic Approaches* (2003).

michele.dagenais@umontreal.ca

Jens Ivo Engels was awarded a doctorate on the public perception of the French monarchy in the eighteenth century. Since 2004 he has been Hochschuldozent (associate professor) in the History Department at Freiburg University. Recently he has completed a habilitation thesis on the transformation of the conservation and environmental protection movements in West Germany between 1950 and 1980, forthcoming.

Jens.Ivo.Engels@geschichte.uni-freiburg.de

Nicholas Goddard is Professor of Agrarian and Environmental History at Anglia Polytechnic University, Cambridge. His publications include *Harvests of Change. The Royal Agricultural Society of England 1838–1988* (1989) and contributions to the *Agrarian History of England and Wales VI 1750–1850* (1989) and *VII 1850–1914* (2000). He has written a number of essays on nineteenth century agricultural journalists and scientists for the *New Oxford Dictionary of National Biography*.

n.p.w.goddard@anglia.ac.uk

Ulrich Koppitz is working on his PhD at Muenster University Historical Institute. Since 1996 he has been secretary of the Institute for the History of Medicine at the Heinrich-Heine-University, Duesseldorf. He is also a board member of the European Society for Environmental History.

koppitz@uni-duesseldorf.de

Laurence Lestel, Dr. Ing., *Maître de conférences*, supervises a research group on 'Space, Occupation and Environment' at the Center for the History of Technology (CDHT-CNAM), Paris. She has worked on the environmental impact of increasing nineteenth century industrialization and urbanization in France.

lestel@cnam.fr

Bill Luckin is Research Professor in Urban History at Bolton Institute, U.K. and author of *Pollution and Control: A Social History of the Thames in the Nineteenth Century* (1986) and *Questions of Power: Electricity and Environment in Interwar Britain* (1990). His most recent publication is 'The shaping of a public environmental sphere in late nineteenth century London' in S. Sturdy, ed. *Medicine, Health and the Public Sphere in Britain* (2002). Bill Luckin is currently working on 'the image of the slum' and the ideological shaping of environmental history in Europe and the United States.

bl3@bolton.ac.uk

Clay McShane is Professor of History at Northeastern University in Boston. With Joel Tarr he is working on a history of the urban horse in America. He is the author of *Down the Asphalt Path: American Cities and the Automobile* (New York: Columbia University Press, 1994); 'Surf City: Urban History on the Web', *Urban History Review XXI* (October, 2001) and 'The Origins and Globalization of Traffic Control Signals', *Journal of Urban History* (March, 1999).

c.mcshane@neu.edu

Geneviève Massard-Guilbaud is *Maître de conférences* at Blaise-Pascal University, Clermont-Ferrand. She has recently completed *Une histoire sociale de la pollution industrielle dans les villes françaises, 1789–1914* (forthcoming, éd. Belin). Recent publications include a coedited volume with Christoph Bernhardt, *Le Démon moderne. La pollution dans les sociétés urbaines et industrielles d'Europe / The modern Demon. Pollution in Urban and Industrial European Societies*, (2002), and 'Urban catastrophe: Challenge to the social, economic, and cultural order of the city', in *Cities and Catastrophes: Coping with Emergency in European History. Villes et catastrophes. Réactions face à l'urgence dans l'histoire européenne*) (2002), a volume which she co-edited with Harold Platt and Dieter Schott.

massard.guilbaud@wanadoo.fr

Helen Meller is Professor of Urban History at the University of Nottingham and Director of the Centre of Urban Culture. She has published widely on themes relating to leisure in cities, women and cities, philanthropy and planning. Her previous books include: *Patrick Geddes: social evolutionist and city planner* (1990), *Towns, Plans and Society in Modern Britain* (1997) and *European Cities 1890-1940: history, culture and the built environment* (2001). Her principal research interest is now on green open spaces in European cities in the twentieth century.

Helen.Meller@nottingham.ac.uk

Martin V. Melosi is Distinguished University Professor of History and Director of the Center for Public History at the University of Houston. He also held the Fulbright Chair of American Studies at the University of Southern Denmark. He is the author or editor of ten books, dealing with the urban environment, energy, and public policy.

mmelosi@uh.edu

Simone Neri Serneri is Professor of Contemporary History at the University of Siena, associate editor of *Contemporanea. Rivista di storia dell'800 e del 900*, and a specialist on Italian political and environmental urban history. Recent edited publications include *Storia del territorio e dell'ambiente* (2002), and *Società locale e sviluppo locale. Grosseto e il suo territorio* (2003).

neriserneri@unisi.it

Dieter Schott is Professor for Modern History at Darmstadt University of Technology. He is a member of the editorial boards of the journals *Die Alte Stadt* and *Informationen zur modernen Stadtgeschichte*. Publications include *Die Vernetzung der Stadt. Kommunale Energiepolitik, öffentlicher Nahverkehr und die Produktion der modernen Stadt* (1999) and as editor with Geneviève Massard-Guilbaud and Harold Platt, *Cities and Catastrophes. Coping with Emergency in European History* (2002).

schott@pg.tu-darmstadt.de

Joel A. Tarr is the Richard S. Caliguiri University Professor of History and Policy at Carnegie Mellon University. He has published numerous articles in the fields of urban, environmental and policy history, and has written or edited six books. Most recently, he has been the editor of *Devastation and Renewal: An Environmental History of Pittsburgh and Its Region* (University of Pittsburgh Press, 2004).

jt03@andrew.cmu.edu

Michael Toyka-Seid lives in Königswinter and teaches at the Technical University of Darmstadt. He is currently preparing a habilitation thesis on noise pollution and abatement in nineteenth and twentieth century Germany. Recent publications include 'Mensch und Umwelt in der Geschichte. Neues aus dem produktiven Selbstfindungsprozess der Umweltgeschichte', in *Archiv für Sozialgeschichte* 43 (2003).

toyka-seid@gmx.de

Historical Urban Studies
General Editors' Preface

Density and proximity are two of the defining characteristics of the urban dimension. It is these that identify a place as uniquely urban, though the threshold for such pressure points varies from place to place. What is considered an important cluster in one context may not be considered as urban elsewhere. A third defining characteristic is functionality – the commercial or strategic position of a town or city which conveys an advantage over other places. Over time, these functional advantages may diminish, or the balance of advantage may change within a hierarchy of towns. To understand how the relative importance of towns shifts over time and space is to grasp a set of relationships which is fundamental to the study of urban history.

Towns and cities are products of history, yet have themselves helped to shape history. As the proportion of urban dwellers has increased, so the urban dimension has proved a legitimate unit of analysis through which to understand the spectrum of human experience and to explore the cumulative memory of past generations. Though obscured by layers of economic, social and political change, the study of the urban milieu provides insights into the functioning of human relationships and, if urban historians themselves are not directly concerned with current policy studies, few contemporary concerns can be understood without reference to the historical development of towns and cities.

This longer historical perspective is essential to an understanding of social processes. Crime, housing conditions and property values, health and education, discrimination and deviance, and the formulation of regulations and social policies to deal with them were, and remain, amongst the perennial preoccupations of towns and cities – no historical period has a monopoly of these concerns. They recur in successive generations, albeit in varying mixtures and strengths; the details may differ.

The central forces of class, power and authority in the city remain. If this was the case for different periods, so it was for different geographical entities and cultures. Both scientific knowledge and technical information were available across Europe and showed little respect for frontiers. Yet despite common concerns and access to broadly similar knowledge, different solutions to urban problems were proposed and adopted by towns and cities in different parts of Europe. This comparative dimension informs urban historians as to which were systematic factors and which were of a purely local nature: general and particular forces can be distinguished.

These analytical frameworks, considered in a comparative context, inform the books in this series.

Université de Tours   Jean-Luc Pinol
University of Leicester   Richard Rodger

CHAPTER ONE

Resources of the City: Towards a European Urban Environmental History

Dieter Schott

This book originates in a conference held at the Centre for Urban History at the University of Leicester in June 2002 on 'Urban Environment: Resources, Perceptions, Uses'.[1] Nearly forty scholars from Europe, North America and Japan came to this 'Second Round-Table on Environmental History' which took its place in a – still developing – line of similar events which aim to generate discussion on European environmental history in and related to cities.

One of the steps on the way to the Leicester meeting was a major session on 'Urban Environmental Problems' at the International Conference of Urban History in Venice 1998, organised by Christoph Bernhardt, which resulted in a book comprising contributions from some of the leading scholars in the field.[2] Eleven papers, covering six European countries and the USA, dealt with a wide range of topics relating to the history of the urban environment. From this well-received initiative longer-term cooperation developed in the form of bi-annual round-tables on environmental history.

In May 2000 the first of the round-tables was held in Clermont-Ferrand, France, organised by Geneviève Massard-Guilbaud.[3] The central theme was 'Pollution in Cities' and the papers delivered and the volume in which they were collected[4] demonstrated that urban

---

[1] The author would like to thank his fellow editors, especially Bill Luckin, for valuable comments on earlier drafts of this introduction.

[2] C. Bernhardt (ed.), *Environmental Problems in European Cities in the Nineteenth and Twentieth Centuries/Umweltprobleme in europäischen Städten des 19. und 20. Jahrhunderts*, (Münster/New York et al., 2001).

[3] O. Faure, 'Pour une histoire de l'environnement', *Vingtième siècle, Revue d'histoire*, 70, 2001, 147–78; G. Corona, 'Inquinati e inquinatori nella storia d'Europa', *Meridiana, Rivista di storia e scienze sociali*, 40, 2001, 99–128; B. Luckin, 'European Round Table on Environmental History, Université Blaise-Pascal, Clermont-Ferrand, 4–6 May 2000', *Urban History*, 27, 3 (2000), 397–400.

[4] C. Bernhardt and G. Massard-Guilbaud, eds., *Le Démon Moderne. La pollution dans les sociétés urbaines et industrielles d'Europe/ The Modern*

environmental history is now following a promising trajectory in
Europe. As we shall see, earlier impulses had their origins in the United
States. The leading and inspiring role played by American scholars is
highlighted by the example of Joel Tarr, a pioneer in the field. Based on
a comprehensive state-of-the-art survey of major studies in American
urban and environmental history, Tarr has pointed out how, since the
early 1990s, urban environmental history has emerged in the USA as a
'major sub-field of both urban and environmental history'.[5]

Three influences can be seen as underpinning this process. Firstly,
research into urban technical infrastructures, especially systems of water
provision and sewage, as well as waste collection and disposal, has been
developed by Tarr, Martin Melosi and other scholars since the 1970s.
This research has greatly expanded knowledge of how these systems
were put in place and how perceptions of the problems with which they
were meant to deal governed their design and implementation. Such
contributions had not initially been defined as 'environmental history'
per se, but rather as being situated within the fields of the history of
technology and public works (or public) history.[6]

The second influence can be seen in the seminal work of William
Cronon on Chicago, which conceptualizes the city-hinterland
relationships of that city and demonstrates how crucial Chicago was for
the environmental transformation of the Mid-West and how that city –
in turn – transformed itself and its immediate environment in order
better to fulfil the functions of a 'gateway to the west'.[7]

Current political influences, especially contemporary debate in the
wake of the Rio conference of 1992 on climate change and a generally,
though by no means universally, agreed target to aim for 'sustainable
development', comprised a third influence. This motivated urban
historians to ask themselves to what extent the cities had been
'sustainable' in the past. In addition, these contemporary
developments encouraged scholars to focus on changes and breaks in

Demon. Pollution in urban and industrial European societies (Clermont-
Ferrand, 2002). The 23 papers in the volume deal with the emergence of the
concept of 'pollution', and focus on degradation of water and air, relationships
between town and industry, environmental movements and the issue of
environmental justice.

[5] J.A. Tarr, Urban history and environmental history in the United States:
complementary and overlapping fields, in C. Bernhardt, ed., Environmental
Problems . . ., 25–39, 39.

[6] See J.A. Tarr, The Search for the Ultimate Sink (Akron, 1996),
'introduction' XXIX–XLVII, where Tarr reflects on his own intellectual and
academic development.

[7] W. Cronon, Nature's Metropolis. Chicago and the Great West (New York,
1991).

the ways in which cities managed their environments and used their resources.

From 1993 on, historians such as Melosi, Tarr, Christine Meisner Rosen, Jeffrey Stine, Samuel Hays and others went onto the offensive.[8] In a series of programmatic articles they took their stand against the reduction of environmental history to a 'history of the natural environment', an idea postulated by Donald Worster in 'Transformations of the Earth. Towards an Agro-ecological Perspective in History'.[9]

Melosi broke the ice with his 1993 essay 'The Place of the City . . .' in which he attacked Worster's definition of nature as 'the world we have not in any primary sense created' and which effectively excluded the built environment and the city in general from environmental history. Melosi criticized this position as arbitrary, insisting that the built environment 'is not wholly expressive of culture, since on its creation it is part of the physical world; whether we like it or not, it interacts and sometimes blends with the natural world'.[10] Moreover, such an isolation of the natural world 'denies the powerful holistic quality of environmental history, which demands inclusion more than exclusion, . . .'.[11] Thus Melosi pleads for an urban environmental history which would combine 'the study of the natural history of the city with the history of the city building process and the possible intersections between the two'.[12] Nevertheless, this urban environmental history – he reminds his readers – would need to gain a better foothold in theory and undertake research, which gives more attention to the real functioning of real cities.

Melosi's perspective on urban environmental history as a comprehensive and interdisciplinary field is echoed by Harold Platt, also

---

[8] M.V. Melosi, 'The Place of the City in Environmental History', *Environmental History Review* (Spring 1993), 1–23 (reprinted in idem, *Effluent America. Cities, Industry, Energy and the Environment*, Pittsburgh, 2001, 125–42); C. Meisner Rosen and J.A. Tarr, 'The Importance of an Urban Perspective in Environmental History', *Journal of Urban History* 20 (May 1994), (the special issue edited by Rosen and Tarr contained four other essays focusing on urban environmental issues); J.A. Tarr and J.K. Stine (eds), 'Industry, Pollution, and the Environment', *Environmental History Review* (special issue) 18 (Spring 1994); S.P. Hays, 'The Role of Urbanization in Environmental History', in idem, *Explorations in Environmental History* (Pittsburgh, 1998), 69–100.

[9] D. Worster, Transformations of the Earth. Towards an Agro-ecological Perspective in History, *Journal of American History* 76 (March 1990), 1087–1106.

[10] Melosi, Place of the City . . ., in idem, *Effluent*, 128.

[11] Ibid., 128.

[12] Ibid., 126.

a champion of this relatively new style of history, when he characterizes this scholarship as 'reversing decades of academic fragmentation' and as leading towards 'an integration of the physical and social sciences'.[13]

By 2000 Tarr was able to report on an impressive body of scholarship dealing with urban environmental history, seen by John McNeill as 'the most interesting frontier'. Tarr identified five primary themes in this field:[14]

- the impact of the built environment and human activities in cities on the natural environment
- societal responses to these impacts and efforts to alleviate environmental problems
- exploration of the effect of the natural environment on city life
- the relationship between cities and an ever-widening hinterland
- the role of gender, class and race in regard to environmental issues

European Environmental History: Themes, Questions, Preoccupations

In Europe, environmental history also made strides from the 1970s onwards, although clearly at a slower pace than in the United States and with significant national variations. Perhaps with the exception of some Scandinavian environmental historians,[15] most European scholars had never subscribed to an 'agro-ecological perspective', as the notion of wilderness, of 'untouched nature' held little relevance in a region so thoroughly characterised by the domestication of nature over so many centuries. On the other hand, although many studies of environmental problems had thus far also dealt with pollution in and produced by cities, the urban dimension had in some ways been incidental. Cities were frequently only dealt with as places where pollution occurred, not as actors and shapers of their environments in their own right. Dominant here were studies focusing on the pollution of one environmental medium (air, water, soil) and the history of

---

[13] H.L. Platt, 'The emergence of urban environmental history', *Urban History* 26, 1 (1999), 89–95, 89, 95. John McNeill observes in a recent state-of-the-art survey that the emphasis on 'wilderness and the West remains powerful' in US environmental history, although less so than in the 1980s, J.R. McNeill, 'Observations on the Nature and Culture of Environmental History', *History and Theory*, 42 (2003), 5–43, 11.

[14] Tarr, *Urban History*, 38; McNeill, Observations, 16.

[15] See T. Myllyntaus and M. Saikku, 'Environmental History: A New Discipline with Long Traditions', in idem (eds), *Encountering the Past in Nature. Essays in Environmental History* (Athens/Ohio, 1999), 1–28.

environmental protest, regulation and conflict resolution which centred on degradation of this kind.[16] This was in some ways an academic reflection of the way environmental protection evolved from the 1970s onwards with the passage of specific legislation targeted at individual media.[17] Thus the environmental history of the city is, as Verena Winiwarter observed in 2000, by no means a well-established field of research in Europe.[18]

In Germany environmental history tended to be located within the history of technology, and was stimulated by contemporary problems such as the intense debate over nuclear energy.[19] This provided an impetus for scholars to reflect on the historical genesis of energy systems beyond the threshold of industrialization, on earlier perceived or real

---

[16] See recent surveys for Germany: W. Siemann (ed.), *Umweltgeschichte. Themen und Perspektiven* (Munich, 2003); with a universal and global perspective J. Radkau, *Natur und Macht. Eine Weltgeschichte der Umwelt* (Munich, 2000); F.-J. Brüggemeier, *Tschernobyl, 26. April 1986. Die ökologische Herausforderung* (Munich, 1998). R.-P. Sieferle, *Rückblick auf die Natur. Eine Geschichte des Menschen und seiner Umwelt* (Munich, 1997). For the formation of environmental history in Great Britain see the paper by Bill Luckin in this volume and B. Luckin, 'Pollution in the City', in M. Daunton (ed.), *The Cambridge Urban History of Britain. Vol. III 1840–1950* (Cambridge, 2000), 207–28. For France and French-speaking Europe see G. Massard-Guilbaud, 'De la "part du milieu" à l'histoire de l'environnement', *Le mouvement social* 200 (2002), 64–72; idem, 'La régulation des nuisances industrielles urbaines (1800–1940)', *Vingtième Siècle, Revue d'histoire*, n°64, oct.–déc. 1999, 53–66; Geneviève Massard-Guilbaud has just completed a volume on 'Social History of industrial pollution in nineteenth century French cities' (forthcoming); R. Delort and F. Walter, *Histoire de l'environnement européen* (Paris, 2001). For a general survey on Europe see McNeill, Observations, 19–21.

[17] On air pollution see F.-J. Brüggemeier, *Das unendliche Meer der Lüfte. Luftverschmutzung, Industrialisierung und Risikodebatten im 19. Jahrhundert* (Essen, 1996); A. Andersen, *Historische Technikfolgenabschätzung am Beispiel des Metallhüttenwesens und der Chemieindustrie* (Stuttgart, 1996); on water T. Kluge and E. Schramm, *Wassernöte. Zur Geschichte des Trinkwassers* (2nd edn, Cologne, 1988).

[18] V. Winiwarter criticizes the preponderance of studies following a 'toxicological-hygienic' paradigm and suggests that urban environmental history should be structured around the concept of 'social metabolism'; see V. Winiwarter, 'Umweltgeschichte der Stadt', in idem, *Lebensraum Wien. Machbarkeitsstudie für zwei Bände 'Landschaft und Ökologie' und 'Umweltgeschichte' des Wiener Raumes* (unpublished final report, Vienna, 2000), 42–70, published in ww.oeaw.ac.at/isr/wien_umwelt/public/texte/winiwarter2000.html.

[19] J. Radkau, *Aufstieg und Krise der deutschen Atomwirtschaft 1945–1975. Verdrängte Alternative in der Kerntechnik und der Ursprung der nuklearen Kontroverse* (Reinbek, 1978).

limits to growth set by scarcity of energy resources.[20] As a result of these
debates some protagonists developed a universal model of the
periodization of world history according to dominant energy systems.[21]
The energy issue also provided a field in which urban historians,
historians of technology and environmental historians could develop
shared interests in the role of cities during the formation of network-
bound systems of energy in the late nineteenth century. Inspired by the
ground-breaking work of Thomas P. Hughes and the general debate
over the 'networked city',[22] scholars analysed the choices and decisions
made by municipalities on electrification and the development of gas
works in terms of embarking on different technological pathways which
had at the same time potentially long-term economic, social and
environmental consequences.[23]

Another field in which a close overlap emerged between urban and
environmental history was public health and the creation of the 'sanitary
city'. The focus of earlier research, still inspired by the Whiggish

---

[20] See R.-P. Sieferle, *Der unterirdische Wald. Energiekrise und Industrielle
Revolution* (Munich, 1982) [now also in English: The subterranean forest.
Energy systems and the industrial revolution (Cambridge, 2001)]; an important
debate on whether there was an energy crisis in terms of wood shortage around
1800 developed between Joachim Radkau and Rolf-Jürgen Gleitsmann, see J.
Radkau, 'Zur angeblichen Energiekrise des 18. Jahrhunderts: Revisionistische
Betrachtungen über die "Holznot"', in *Vierteljahrschrift für Sozial- und
Wirtschaftsgeschichte* 73 (1986); R.-J. Gleitsmann, 'Technikhistorische
Erkenntnisse – eine Ressource für Entwicklungsländer? Überlegungen zum
Themenkomplex "Holzsparkünste" zwischen Vergangenheit und Gegenwart', in
P. Leidinger (ed.), *Historische Ökologie und ökologisches Lernen im historisch-
politischen Unterricht* (Paderborn, 1986), 57–78.

[21] R.-P. Sieferle, 'Nachhaltigkeit in universalhistorischer Perspektive', in
Siemann (ed.), *Umweltgeschichte*, 39–60. Christian Pfister has argued that the
1950s form another threshold in terms of energy use due to a massive global
increase in the consumption of fossil fuels, accompanied by a long-term relative
decline in real energy prices, C. Pfister, 'Energiepreis und Umweltbelastung. Zum
Stand der Diskussion über das "1950er Syndrom"', in W. Siemann, ed.,
Umweltgeschichte, 61–86.

[22] T.P. Hughes, *Networks of Power. Electrification in Western Society 1880-
1930* (Baltimore/London, 1983); J.A. Tarr and G. Dupuy, eds, *Technology and
the rise of the networked city in Europe and America* (Philadelphia, 1988).

[23] With a European perspective, D. Schott, ed., *Energie und Stadt in Europa.
/Energy and the city in Europe* (Stuttgart, 1997); a comparison of three German
cities in terms of their electrification and transport development is presented in
D. Schott, *Die Vernetzung der Stadt. Kommunale Energiepolitik, öffentlicher
Nahverkehr und die 'Produktion' der modernen Stadt. Darmstadt – Mannheim
–Mainz 1880–1918*, Darmstadt 1999; on European gas industry see S. Paquier
and J.-P. Williot, eds, *Naissance et développement de l'industrie gazière en
Europe (XIXe–XXe siècles)* (Berne, Berlin, 2005); B. Luckin, *Questions of
Power : Electricity and Environment in Inter-War Britain* (Manchester, 1990).

triumphalism of engineering achievements, had largely been on the beneficial health aspects of sewage systems and municipal health policy.[24] More recent studies have tended to embrace a wider environmental agenda. This has highlighted the damaging effects of displacing residential and industrial waste into rivers and watercourses, which would eventually lead to widespread environmental degradation.[25] The entire complex of urban water cycles has recently attracted significant scholarly attention, as a result of the more obvious direct health relevance of water-borne diseases, which made healthy water a top priority for city governments. The preponderance of public health on municipal agendas during the second half of the nineteenth century, perceived from a Chadwickian perspective, was predicated on an ideology in which a clean urban environment would not only improve the health of urban residents, but also their ability to work and live a moral life.[26] Such notions motivated urban governments to undertake expensive investments in sanitary infrastructure which comprehensively reshaped cities. Bill Luckin claims in his contribution to this volume that in Britain research into place-related and differential mortality and morbidity, under the general rubric of the 'social history of medicine' has to a certain extent played the role developed by urban environmental history in the United States.

The general acceptance of environmental history within mainstream history proceeded in Europe at a slower rate than in America.[27] At the same time the process of institutionalization was significantly delayed. American environmental historians successfully organized themselves into the 'American Society for Environmental History' (ASEH) in 1977. This organization has held well attended conferences since 1982. These have now become annual. Moreover, the ASEH now produces the premier journal in its field, *Environmental History*. In Europe, on the

---

[24] J.v. Simson, *Kanalisation und Städtehygiene im 19. Jahrhundert* (Düsseldorf, 1983).

[25] J. Büschenfeld, *Flüsse und Kloaken. Umweltfragen im Zeitalter der Industrialisierung, 1870–1918* (Stuttgart, 1998); focusing on the Rhine as receptacle of residential and industrial waste water, M. Cioc, *The Rhine. An Eco-Biography, 1815–2000* (Seattle and London, 2002); for British rivers, L. Breeze, *The British Experience with River Pollution, 1865–1876* (New York/Berlin et al., 1993). For a more detailed bibliography see the footnotes in the contribution by Ulrich Koppitz in this volume.

[26] C. Hamlin, *Public Health and Social Justice in the Age of Chadwick: Britain, 1800–54* (Cambridge, 1998).

[27] The enhanced status of environmental history within the historical sciences in general can be judged by the fact that environmental history will constitute a major theme ('Humankind and Nature in History') at the 2005 World Congress of History in Sydney.

other hand, early attempts to establish international cooperation and
discussion, which appeared to have made ground with the publication
of conference proceedings from 1988 in the form of a volume entitled
Silent Countdown[28] and in the establishment of an *Environmental
History Newsletter*, faltered.[29] Only in the late 1990s did conditions
appear ripe for the establishment of the 'European Society for
Environmental History', an equivalent body to the American ASEH.[30]
Following two successful ESEH-conferences (at St. Andrews in 2001
and Prague in 2003), European environmental history has achieved a
much higher profile and now seems to be in a promising position.

The Purpose of the 'Round-Table'

Within this overall context, then, the aim of the 'Round-tables on
Environmental History' has been to create a framework for a more
intensive discussion of urban environmental problems, involving scholars
from a range of fields such as urban history, environmental history,
history of technology and history of planning. It was hoped that these
meetings, involving a limited number of participants, and structured in
sessions around clearly focused themes, would generate deep and well-
informed debate. It was also intended that research and methodological
issues originating in different countries would be related to one another,
thereby opening up a genuinely comparative perspective. These hopes
have to a significant degree been realized. Moreover, interchange between
younger and more senior scholars has also proven rewarding.[31]

At the round-tables we have sought to study cities not simply as
localities, in which pollution occurred, and in which resources were

---

[28] P. Brimblecombe and C. Pfister, eds, *The silent countdown: essays in
European environmental history* (Berlin/Heidelberg, 1990).

[29] The 'Environmental History Newsletter' was published between 1989 and
1993 by the Landesmuseum fuer Technik und Arbeit, Mannheim, but was
discontinued due to lack of funds. 'Environment & History', published by White
Horse Press since 1995 has provided a publication outlet for European
environmental historians. During the first years of its existence, however, this
journal showed little interest in urban-environmental issues.

[30] The ESEH was founded in 1999, the first general assembly took place at
the first conference in St. Andrews in September 2001. Scholars who played a
major role in this development include Christian Pfister of the University of
Berne, Switzerland, and Verena Winiwarter of the University of Vienna.

[31] At the time of writing, the next round-table in Siena in June 2004,
organized by Simone Neri Serneri, promises a continuation of discussions of this
kind and a welcome widening of participants so that southern Europe in
particular is more fully represented.

consumed and waste produced. Cities, it has been agreed, should be analysed as collective social actors engaged in the opening up of resources, in the shaping of technologies implemented to organize the provision of certain resources. And these activities should also be considered in terms of their effects on remodelling urban patterns of behaviour. Such a perspective, it is to be hoped, will challenge the notion of inevitability, that is, that levels of environmental degradation that were actually experienced were the necessary by-products of urban industrialism. Rather, it is intended to isolate and interrogate debates and choices which were involved in shaping the kind of urban environment with which we live today. An urban environmental history of this type will create awareness of the significance of context, and of dialectical relationships between concurrent chains of events in different fields. Concentration on place, not in a merely spatial, geographical sense, but as a constellation of topography, natural resources, social, economic and cultural relationships, might thus produce a multi-layered and more complex narrative of the processes by which cities made use of their environments in the past.

With these ideas in mind the issue of 'resources' was selected as the main theme for the round-table at Leicester in June 2002.[32] Following the meeting in Clermont-Ferrand with its concentration on pollution and the impact of towns and industries through emissions and effluents – the 'output'-side of industrial and urban processes – we wanted to change focus and to reflect upon 'input'. Hence the emphasis in this collection is on how cities have used their natural environments, and how processes of this kind have transformed environments and cities themselves. At the same time, this focus is underwritten by contemporary policy agendas, the target of 'sustainable development', above all the aim to reduce the emission of greenhouse gases. These goals have initiated a fundamental shift in the attitudes towards resource use on the part of urban managers, policy makers and the general public. In the past the focus had been on providing the resources (water, energy, raw materials) essential for urban and demographic growth with little regard for the consequences this provision might have had on the environment. Now the focus is on restricting and possibly reducing resource use, on shrinking rather than enlarging the ecological footprint of cities, in unlinking resource use from human comfort and urban amenities. This shift has promoted a new perspective on the city as an urban metabolism, an approach which embeds cities in their wider natural environment, to analyse the flow of

---

[32] For the 'round-table' in Leicester, the academic committee consisted of Christoph Bernhardt, Geneviève Massard-Guilbaud and Dieter Schott; Dieter Schott was the organizer of this conference.

materials through them.[33] Urban metabolism includes the individual metabolism of urban residents, in terms of food, water, air and basic necessities of life. It also comprises the general functioning of the city as a 'social organism' which is dependent on the provision of water, energy, raw materials, and information. This latter metabolism necessarily encompasses inputs of resources as well as outputs of waste products, which must be expelled in order to render them more or less harmless for urban residents. This 'social metabolism' allows the city to be perceived as a 'quasi-organism'. Equivalents to these concepts were current in the nineteenth century, for instance in Chadwick's models.[34] In the aforementioned programmatic article in 1993 Melosi pointed out how far such metaphors, conceiving the city as some kind of organism, have also been prevalent in modern social scientific ideas about the city, as developed by Spenser Havlick, David Harvey and Manuel Castells.[35] Melosi suggests that cities should be understood as 'open systems' in order to prevent an artificially isolating perspective, and to determine 'how they [cities] interact with, influence or modify the natural world as an animate social/spatial system'.[36]

The concept of 'social metabolism' linked with 'colonization of nature', as developed in a research project directed by Marina Fischer-Kowalski at the University of Vienna, provides a useful framework for a differentiated understanding of every kind of environmental intervention and appears to be particularly relevant at the level of the city. According to Verena Winiwarter, the 'metabolism' of a society is defined as 'the sum of all input and output between the biosphere/geosphere and society'. Colonizing interventions are defined 'as the sum of all purposive changes made in natural systems that aim to render nature more useful for society'.[37]

---

[33] For an example of a policy study on how to achieve more sustainable urban development, using the concept of urban metabolism, see J. Ravetz, *City-Region 2020. Integrated planning for a sustainable environment* (London, 2000), 133. This study analyses which strategies and policies would be required to redirect urban development in the Greater Manchester region towards a more sustainable path by 2020.

[34] See G. Davison, 'The City as a Natural System: Theories of Urban Society in Early Nineteenth Century Britain', in D. Fraser and A. Sutcliffe (eds), *The Pursuit of Urban History* (London, 1983).

[35] Melosi, The place . . ., in idem, *Effluent*, 129–30; S. Havlick, *The urban organism* (New York, 1974); D. Harvey, *Social justice and the city* (Baltimore, 1973); M. Castells, *The City and the Grassroots: A Cross-Cultural Theory of Urban Social Movements* (London, 1983).

[36] Melosi, *The place . . .*, 134.

[37] M. Fischer-Kowalski et al., *Gesellschaftlicher Stoffwechsel und Kolonisierung von Natur. Ein Versuch in Sozialer Ökologie* (Amsterdam, 1997); quotes from V. Winiwarter, 'Where did all the waters go? The introduction of

Such a concept draws attention to the fact that pre-industrial cities were also characterized by social metabolism and thus had to provide resources via 'colonizing' interventions. The systems approach has implication for the 'loose ends' of material flows that sustain social metabolism. Where did required inputs originate from, what consequences did their extraction have for the physical and natural environment? Where did metabolic outputs finish up? Were they re-used, recycled within the limits of the city or disposed of in a different form and/or at a distance? What were the consequences of these forms of disposal for the natural environment as well as for other users of environmental resources downstream and downwind? The advantage of such a 'holistic approach' is that the artificial boundaries between different environmental media drawn by earlier studies of water or air pollution are erased, since all extraction and use of resources constitutes part of the total metabolism. In their analysis of the ways in which societies have coped with environmental problems historians have frequently identified what Joel Tarr has called the 'search for the ultimate sink': the quest for a place or way of disposing of noxious substances, from which they would not return to urban circulation.[38] Tarr shows that one popular method was to transfer pollution from one medium to another in order to comply with new regulations and to prosecution. This, however, produced no solution but simply led to displacement and transfer of the original problem, the effects of which might be felt only decades later through leaking landfills, which slowly poison groundwater streams.

Common Themes and Questions: Infrastructures, Values, and Pathways

The papers assembled here do not all use the 'social metabolism' concept, but it was nevertheless considered useful to introduce it here as a framework within which individual papers might be contextualised. All papers deal with resources, be they material such as water, which plays a prominent role, land or food, or immaterial, such as quiet urban space or intellectual capital directed towards the reduction of environmental degradation.

The articles not only analyse physical change through urban resource use; they also show how 'colonizing interventions', such as the building

sewage systems in urban settlements', in C. Bernhardt, ed., *Environmental problems*, 105–19, 107.
   [38] J.A. Tarr, 'The search of the Ultimate Sink'. Urban Air, Land and Water Pollution in Historical Perspective, in idem, *The Search*, 7–35.

of sewage systems, have resulted from the cultural construction of nature, expressions of particular scientific theories, and social expectations about the beneficial effects of a cleaning up of cities on the character and behaviour of urban residents. Such cultural constructions as, for example, the miasmatic theory of disease, could be and were challenged and falsified. In conflicts over side-effects associated with new systems both scientific accuracy and the reputation and social capital of local experts were at stake.

The use and allocation of resources were contested within cities. Clean air, peace and quiet and green space became increasingly scarce resources during the process of industrialization, leading to attempts to preserve protected enclaves, such as neighbourhoods where industry would be barred, usually as a result of market forces. The latter would be reserved for the more affluent social strata. Within the 'social metabolism' of the whole city, varying quality of resource provision and exposure to environmental hazards could thus lead to radical socio-economic differentiation. As a consequence, the notion of environmental injustice as an important dimension of social inequality must be incorporated into urban environmental history, a process which in Europe, in contrast to the USA, is only just beginning.

Those papers dealing with water illustrate a particular paradox of urban environmental history: infrastructures through which cities coped with environmental crises as represented by waves of epidemic disease. These constitute answers to the construction of specific contemporary problems. However, the solution of one issue invariably created difficulties elsewhere, above all through displacement effects. At the same time we can see that these technologies promoted behavioural changes in cities, rewarding some and penalising other forms of behaviour. Associated with the cleaning up of cities through the construction of sewage systems and water-closets, a range of educational policies and new reforming institutions emerged on the urban scene, geared to remodel urban culture. Therefore, when in recent decades some of the solutions to problems associated with the past have themselves come to be perceived as problems, not only the 'hardware' of pipes and networks was at issue. Just as much the wide-ranging complex of regulations, cultural perceptions and daily practices which had evolved in synchronization with the technical infrastructure came to be seen in a more critical light. While repairing crumbling sewers rather than re-designing new disposal systems, modern urban-industrial society frequently finds itself locked into situations in which earlier decisions, frequently initiated in the nineteenth century, still pre-determine and limit through the inertia of their physical legacy the choice of options available to address problems in the twenty-first century. This can be explained by the sheer scale of physical change that would need to be carried out, but also by the cultural baggage, associated with earlier technology choices.[39] Urban environmental history might find a major function for the rationalization of contemporary policy-making in drawing, by way of historical analogy, attention to the long-term implications of current technology choices. Against quick-fix solutions it could raise the question, as to how and at what monetary, social and environmental costs specific decisions taken today might be revised and modified in 30, 50 or 100 years time.

Although this book cannot cover all resources in equal depth,[40] the editors are confident that the range of papers, the breadth of approach and the inherent structural parallels of the problems analysed will offer readers a stimulating overview of what urban environmental history is seeking to do and has already achieved in Europe.

Metabolism and City-hinterland

The volume opens with two papers representing the aspects of 'metabolism' and of 'city-hinterland' relationships. Sabine Barles' 'metabolic approach to the city' shows how the inputs and outputs of Paris were short-circuited, with wastes becoming resources for other processes, right up until the twentieth century. From a different perspective, Joel Tarr and Clay McShane analyse how 'short-circuits', close symbiotic relationships between the city and its immediate hinterland for horse feed and manure, were slowly being substituted and abandoned in favour of a much wider notion of hinterland towards the end of the nineteenth century.

Barles' *A metabolic approach to the city: nineteenth and twentieth century Paris* takes issue with the popular understanding of the capital as a monstrous parasite feeding on an ever-extending hinterland. She demonstrates that the economy of Paris in the nineteenth and the early twentieth centuries depended on a sophisticated system of recycling 'waste' products. These material cycles were not simply residuals from a pre-industrial economy of scarcity but developed new functions within

---

[39] The concept of 'path dependency' as presented by Martin Melosi in his contribution to this volume is particularly useful here.

[40] For air pollution see S. Mosley, *The Chimney of the World: A History of Smoke Pollution in Victorian and Edwardian Manchester* (Cambridge, 2001); S. Mosley, 'Fresh Air and Foul', *Planning Perspectives*, Vol. 18, 2003, 1–21; B. Luckin, Town, Country and Metropolis: The Formation of an Air Pollution Problem in London, 1800–1870, in D. Schott, ed., *Energie und Stadt in Europa. /Energy and the city in Europe* (Stuttgart, 1997), 77–92.

an evolving industrial economy and the needs this generated. Barles notes
a keen awareness on the part of natural scientists and economists as to
the material value of waste products and an intensive commitment to
reconstitute material cycles, in such a way that waste products would be
fed back into industrial production or used as agricultural fertilizer. This
first phase of urban stability, however, was followed by a growing
'divorce', which resulted from increasing availability of cheap substitutes,
the disappearance of supplies of waste products, or a growing imbalance
between the total volume of sewage to be treated and the area available
for sewage farming. Barles identifies very nearly simultaneous decisions
in the 1930s to use landfill sites rather than recycling or incineration for
urban refuse and to install sewage treatment plants as expressions of a
fundamental change in the perception of waste materials.

The crucial role of horses for urban economies in the nineteenth and
early twentieth centuries is probably one of the most neglected topics in
modern urban history. Joel Tarr and Clay McShane investigate in *Urban
Horses and changing city-hinterland relationships in the United States*,
how growing numbers of horses have been fed and the effects of this
demand on the structure of agriculture as well as methods and
procedures of transportation and marketing. In line with von Thünen's
model of concentric rings around a city, they identify hay growing
regions, together with market gardeners and dairy farmers in the first
belt. This was because hay, a bulky product, could not be transported for
distances of more than 20 or 30 miles. The spread of railways and the
improvement of agricultural technology opened potential new
hinterlands for hay production in the West. Earlier restrictions linking
hay production and marketing to an informal local context, were swept
away by technological innovation and institutionalized marketing
standards. As a result of the decline in prices brought about by cheaper
hay production in an almost continent-wide market, urban transport
costs were also reduced. This ample and cheap supply of hay allowed
former hay-growing regions in the first agricultural belt around large
cities to be transformed into market gardens or suburban housing estates.
It would be revealing to compare and contrast the findings of Tarr and
McShane with the situation in Europe, where as a result of technological
backwardness of the great bulk of the continent such a dispersal of hay
growing regions appears to have been inherently unlikely.

Space as Urban Resource

The following four papers deal with space and nature as urban resources
in different national and temporal contexts . In 'Returning to nature':

Vacation and life style in the Montreal region, Dagenais analyses how selected places in the region of Montreal were transformed in the late nineteenth and early twentieth century by wealthy urbanites in search of more 'natural' surroundings. This process evolved in the form of a gradual metamorphosis of the urban to the suburban, taking its departure from summer homes and residences. The flight from the hot and stinking city of Montreal in the summer brought upper middle-class residents to areas of natural beauty, frequently on the shores of lakes and rivers. As transport connections with the metropolis developed, transitory summer homes were improved into permanent residences, and summer dwellers became year-round commuters. This 'suburbanization', however, involved major interventions into a space that had been intensively and distinctively developed by earlier residents. The newcomers did not simply immerse themselves in the rural landscape. Their notion of 'nature' envisaged a constructed entity containing supposedly 'wild' elements, but also an environment which was not threatening and which was also totally detached from foul rural odours. Suburbanization thus involved social and cultural colonization, pitting newcomers against rural dwellers in conflicts about how to regulate the use of space. Despite the cultural specifics of Montreal as a bilingual and multi-confessional city with a uniquely water-rich topography, Dagenais' focus on the cultural dimension of such suburbanization has resonances with the European context.[41] Urban environmental history needs to conceptualize suburbanization as a multi-layered transformational process, involving conflicts about values, about notions of nature and agricultural practices, and about the use of resources between old and new residents.

Helen Meller takes a different perspective in *Citizens in pursuit of nature: Gardens, allotments and private space in European cities, 1850-2000*, and focuses on the attempts of European urbanites to secure green niches within the city. Initially this had been driven by the fight for survival through the growing of food.[42] Meller identifies an almost subversive urban garden movement. It grew from the bottom upwards and frequently contravened official planning goals. This movement was also a Pan-European one (at least north of the Alps), and strongly allied to various factions within the Labour movement. The fate of these movements and their inner-city allotments fluctuated wildly: highly

---

[41] For the critical role of public transport for early suburbanization, see C. Divall and W. Bond, eds, *Suburbanizing the Masses. Public Transport and Urban Development in Historical Perspective* (Aldershot, 2003).

[42] See also T. Hotaka, 'Civic movements for urban green space. The case of Leipzig, 1871–1918', in C. Bernhardt and G. Massard-Guilbaud (eds), *Le Démon moderne*, 393–407.

valued as a result of their contribution to food supply during times of war, allotment areas came under massive pressure during upswings in the building cycle, especially after the second world war. But in the 'green niches' of allotment gardens and garden colonies on the periphery of cities a new culture could develop, strongly tied to the ideals and values of reform movements striving for a new style of urban existence. This could also maintain a considerable independence in spite of totalitarian pressure.[43] When after the second world war houses with gardens rather than allotments became the general model, gardening gradually lost its subsistence character and increasingly became a leisure pursuit. For urban environmental history the fundamental ambivalence of this elementary desire for a green space within the form and fabric of cities should not be overlooked. The more people could fulfil their suburban dream with a house in a garden, the higher the environmental costs of such an urban model would become in terms of transport, extended networks and transformation of agricultural into residential land.

Gabriella Corona presents in *Sustainable Naples: The disappearance of nature as resource* a story of loss, despoliation and destruction. Her 'nature' is a complex ensemble of factors, indeed, the whole aspect of Naples, so often eulogized in literature and memorialized in paintings. It refers to environmentally unstable or sensitive terrain, the combination of a particular range of natural resources, such as thermal springs and fertile soil, all within a picturesque landscape. Corona points out that Naples' environmental crisis should in the last resort be attributed to a total failure of planning and regulation. A new political constellation at the end of the Second World War vehemently rejected state interventionism as outlined in planning guidelines under the Fascist regime. Supported by lavish subsidies from central government to develop the backward South, the new municipal authority, dominated by developers and speculators, acted in contravention of existing building regulations or environmental protection. A regime of

---

[43] Already before the fascist take-over in Germany, peripheral garden colonies around Berlin provided a refuge for many victims of depression in the early 1930s. They became home to many thousands of victims of unemployment, during a period in which people were ejected from their city flats for defaulting on rent. Many lived in their garden huts and sheds and concentrated on growing food. This is the background to the famous movie by Bertolt Brecht (text), Hanns Eisler (music) and S.Th. Dudow (dir.)'Kuhle Wampe oder Wem gehört die Welt', 1932; see *Bertolt Brecht. Kuhle Wampe. Protokoll des Films und Materialien*, ed. by W. Gersch and W. Hecht (Frankfurt am Main, 1969). See also on peripheral housing estates during the depression T. Harlander et al. *Siedeln in der Not. Umbruch von Wohnungspolitik und Siedlungsbau am Ende der Weimarer Republik* (Hamburg, 1988).

institutionalized corruption dominated by local authorities, the police and the Mafia further contributed to this environmental degradation. The aggregate effects of this uncoordinated development were geological destabilization, a multitude of disastrous landslides and appalling living conditions for the majority of Napolitans in overcrowded, polluted and insanitary houses and streets. Naples thus presents a clear example for the consequences of failed planning, but it is particularly telling in terms of the complex mechanisms of ground-water hydrology and soil stability, which piecemeal and profit-oriented development so severely disrupted.

In Geneviève Massard-Guilbaud's paper *The Struggle for Urban Space: Nantes and Clermont-Ferrand, 1830-1930*, the author analyses how attractive urban spaces became for industry, which massively polluted the environment and at the same time prevented rational urban planning and zoning. In Nantes a significant complex of industries developed on an island, close to the city centre. Although no permission had been granted, the authorities were incapable (or unwilling) to expel these heavily polluting industries. The reasons for this failure are to be found in a lack of planning powers on the part of the municipality, contradictory policies by the prefect, and the vital role the factories played for effective urban metabolic purposes. The second case-study illustrates how in Clermont-Ferrand the all-powerful Michelin company successfully redirected municipal efforts towards comprehensive town planning. Early drafts had envisaged a well-ordered residential townscape on the large open space between the two centres of Clermont and Montferrand. The company, however, through a package of demands and financial incentives, won over a cash-strapped and obedient town administration and left the city with a legacy of chaotic industrial townscape planning which prevented urban integration. Both case studies demonstrate how decisions, or non-decisions, about the use of space can have long-term effects, establish pathways and preclude alternative developments for periods clearly beyond the life-span of individual decision-makers. But Massard-Guilbaud warns against deterministic shortcuts and reminds us of politics and power relations. Industries were not simply located on river islands because that was their optimum location. Somebody allowed this to happen and in repeatedly doing so, created physical conditions which were exceptionally difficult to eradicate.

Taken together these papers demonstrate that urban environmental history must scrutinize decision-making processes, and analyse constellations of social forces in order to understand why things happened the way they did. Cities were structured by social groups with divergent and frequently antagonistic interests. It is important to note that self-perceptions of urban dwellers, and especially elites, frequently precluded solutions which were predicated on alternative developments. Such scenarios were quite simply beyond the ken of collective imagination. A power structure which had evolved in a particular place could thus appear as natural and 'given'.

Water Resources and Systems

Managing water as a multiple resource created the most far-reaching and persistent motives for change in the urban environment. Water also now constitutes almost ninety per cent of total material flow through the European city. As a consequence, the water cycle is 'at the forefront of the theory and practice of sustainable development'.[44] Starting from the usually localized systems of provision as well as disposal, characteristic of European cities in the middle of the nineteenth century, we have now reached a stage at which water resources from a vast hinterland, frequently several hundred kilometres removed from the city itself, are being harnessed to provide drinking water. In addition, we are now well acquainted with almost completely artificial waste- and storm-water collection systems and controls as well as with methods for the discharge and disposal of waste water. As current environmental debates show, this degree of control and domestication is now increasingly critically evaluated. The major role played by water problems within urban environmental history is reflected by the five papers in this volume.

Nicholas Goddard analyses in *Sanitate Crescamus: Water supply, sewage disposal and environmental values in a Victorian Suburb* the small town of Croydon, south of London. Croydon became nationally famous as an example of Edwin Chadwick's sanitary 'system', including his notion of recycling sewage to fertilize land. Water was a contested and potentially scarce resource, and the connections between surface water and groundwater were not fully known and understood. Goddard shows how the new degree of penetration of nature by sinking deeper wells and tapping strata of groundwater gave rise to legal conflicts about 'ownership' of 'common' resources such as groundwater. The ruling of the House of the Lords (the Upper House of the British Parliament) paved the way for almost a century of largely uncontrolled exploitation of groundwater. The predominance of vested interests in social capital tied to distinctive scientific approaches and infrastructures is highlighted when Goddard explains why prominent members of the local board of health adhered to older paradigms such as the miasmatic view of

---

[44] Ravetz, *City-Region 2020*, 133.

disease. Their personal reputation was at stake when typhoid epidemics challenged the purity of the water supply. The Croydon case illuminates how the incremental solution of public health problems created an inextricably interconnected web of water management, generating, despite relative environmental cleanliness within Croydon itself, problematic environmental consequences in terms of resource use and resource pollution.

Ulrich Koppitz develops a different perspective to Goddard in *Constructing Urban Infrastructure for Multiple Resource Management: Sewerage systems in the Industrialization of the Rhineland, Germany.* He questions the established progressivist engineering and public health narrative that urban disease and squalor have been overcome through feats of technical infrastructural engineering. Rather, he places emphasis on what he calls the key urban resource in growing cities, land to be developed and built on. Koppitz argues that the breakthrough of the immensely expensive sewerage systems depended on their use for turning humid and marshy lands into valuable building land, and thereby bringing order and regularity to urban and suburban expansion. Examples from the city of Düsseldorf serve to illustrate the uneven development of its sewerage system, which did not follow functional imperatives but rather the vagaries of the real estate market. This shift of emphasis in the perception as well as functionalization of sewerage systems as instruments of the real estate market rather than the public health domain yet again reminds us how artificial it can be to focus on just one environmental medium. Contemporary decision makers frequently viewed such decisions in the light of a far more comprehensive range of requirements, interests and benefits seeming to be relevant at that time.

The transformation of Milan, Italy's premier industrial city, and its water system is the subject of Simone Neri Serneri's study *Resource management and environmental transformations. Water incorporation at the time of industrialization: Milan, 1880–1940.* The author emphasizes that the industrial period did not 'invent' a man-made technical system of water management. After centuries of persistent 'colonization' and water management, Milan's watercourses permeated the whole city and its region and constituted an almost indistinguishable web of 'natural' and 'artificial' watercourses serving a wide range of different functions. By the 1880s a point of crisis was reached when the traditional system could no longer function adequately. The result of large-scale engineering was in the short term a massively increased throughput of water through Milan's water network and improved public health, but over the coming decades the problems and inconsistencies of the system became more and more apparent, above all at the interfaces between the natural and the artificial elements of the system. With diminishing supplies and rising pollution levels in the canals leading into Milan, the system became too complex and had to serve too many contradictory requirements. Projects developed in response to the new crisis in the late 1930s demonstrated an awareness of the need to develop solutions on the scale of an entire regional watershed. Thus the case of Milan illustrates how the attempt to better exploit urban water resources resulted in a massively increased degree of intervention into natural cycles. It also highlights the limitations of engineering intervention, with the latter eventually reproducing the problems they had been expected to solve, on a higher and greatly extended level.

In his study *Towards the socialist sanitary city: Urban water problems in East German new towns, 1945–1970* Christoph Bernhardt embarks on a new field of research, the environmental history of the former socialist countries. Bernhardt identifies two central processes which both heavily impacted on water regimes: first, industrialization policies, which generated a massive population increase through new heavy industrial and petrochemical combines, mainly in the formerly underdeveloped region along the Oder river. The second process, a massive increase in water consumption, was attributable to the GDR's housing policy, geared as it was towards maintaining mass loyalty through the construction of new flats equipped with modern domestic amenities. Both processes eventually resulted in a hugely increased throughput of water, governed by a reorganized and centralized system of water provision and waste water treatment, which also stripped city governments from exerting control in this field. In terms of resource use the GDR pushed the limits much further than most European countries. The environmental balance of GDR water politics appears ambivalent. Whereas in quantitative terms water provision provided standards broadly in line with western European countries, waste water treatment lagged behind. A serious water crisis in the 1970s demonstrates that the absence of profit as an economic imperative could not by itself guarantee sustainable management of limited natural resources. The all-dominating aim to industrialize, to exploit domestic resources, produced widespread environmental degradation of water resources. This might well have acted as a brake to further economic growth and it did indeed eventually contribute to the de-legitimization and collapse of the regime.

Measuring and assessing the quality of drinking water as a resource was a difficult and contentious issue in the nineteenth century. Laurence Lestel demonstrates in *Experts and water quality in Paris in 1870* that scientific methods of assessing water quality evolved in a gradual manner. The initial grading according to hardness which could be measured chemically, was slowly replaced by more complex parameters indicating biological pollution through measurements of oxygen content. Within a fairly short period after 1850 the throughput of water in Paris increased tenfold compared to the early nineteenth century. With this rapid evolution of the water system, possible health hazards through lead poisoning, caused by the pipes, suddenly moved to the forefront of scientific debate in the 1870s. Lestel analyses how in this debate a selective recourse to ancient authorities, a subtle differentiation of relative exposure to risk depending on chemical qualities of a specific water and practical experiments coalesced to frame a discourse which for a majority of scientific actors sought to disperse public anxiety about possible risks of lead poisoning. For experts whose methods of water analysis were in a process of evolution in reaction to new scientific paradigms, the priority was to convince the public that water supplies were safe and that residual risks could be handled. What lies beyond the scope of this study is why such a debate should have stirred up so much public interest in Paris in the early 1870s, shortly after the Commune, a period of severe social disruption and political instability? Might concern about lead poisoning be interpreted as an early example of increasingly intense environmental panics, which began to haunt western societies during the final third of the twentieth century?[45] We should remember that the installation of a comprehensive technological system of water provision through pipes is a massive cultural challenge to every-day life and routines. Parisians had become used to assessing the quality of their water by sight, smell and taste, but the new danger of lead was invisible and beyond such methods, and therefore all the more disturbing.

Immaterial Resources and Concepts

Most papers discussed so far deal with physical, and in many senses tangible, resources essential to the material reproduction of individual urban residents and of cities as complex social systems and sites of material production. The last group of essays focuses on immaterial resources and looks at the urban environment from a conceptual and political perspective.

Noise as a principal constituent of urban life is analysed by Michael Toyka-Seid in *Noise abatement and the search for quiet space in the*

---

[45] See for environmental panic F.J. Brüggemeier, Le dépérissement de la forêt (Waldsterben): construction et déconstruction d'un problème d'environement, in Bernhardt/ Massard-Guilbaud (eds), *Le Démon moderne*, 75–90; idem, *Tschernobyl*, 214–16.

modern city. The author considers noise as a threat to quietness as a resource and reflects upon the reasons for the relative dearth of research in this area, compared to other environmental issues. In a manner comparable to Lestel's narrative of water analysis, he notes that measuring noise was far from easy. In a first attempt at periodization Toyka-Seid identifies an early period dominated by industrial noise, roughly up to the first world war, followed by a new kind of noise environment, developing in the interwar years. During this latter period noise – or perhaps rather sounds – produced by the individual urban dweller, – 'consumerist noise' through radio, phonograph or motor car – assumed an ever higher significance for the overall 'soundscape' of the city.[46] The protagonists of anti-noise campaigns were – much as in other environmental movements – predominantly members of the middle class who were not exposed to the most damaging levels of noise but nevertheless insisted on spaces of quietness or at least relative absence of unwanted sounds, even within the city. Toyka-Seid notes remarkable differences between anti-noise societies in the USA whose 'economy-oriented approach' proved fairly successful and European associations which were clearly dominated by elitist, conservative values. In the long term Toyka-Seid highlights increasing levels of exposure to noise, especially through-traffic, and identifies the interwar period and the post-war years up to 1970 as periods requiring additional research. Toyka-Seid's paper may also encourage us to reconsider 'greening' of cities as attempts, however unsuccessful, to create oases of relative silence in parks and urban rest areas. Thus there may be clear links between the desire for 'a piece of nature' as emphasized by Helen Meller, the 'return to nature' described by Michelle Dagenais in the rural hinterland of Montreal and the search for the resource of silence.

In his *Environmental Justice, history and the city: The United States and Britain, 1970-2000* Bill Luckin, one of the pioneers of British environmental history,[47] pursues a dual strand in tracing the development of both American and British environmental history. Asking

---

[46] The background of the receding significance of industrial noise can be seen in the fairly successful attempts made by German town planners to spatially limit pollution problems. See F.J. Brüggemeier, Umweltprobleme und Zonenplanung in Deutschland. Der Aufstieg und die Herrschaft eines Konzepts, 1800–1914, in C. Bernhardt, ed., *Environmental problems*, 143–64; D. Schott, 'The formation of an urban industrial policy to counter pollution in German cities (1890–1914)', in C. Bernhardt and G. Massard-Guilbaud, eds, *Le Démon moderne*, 311–32.

[47] B. Luckin, *Pollution and control: a social history of the Thames in the nineteenth century* (Bristol, 1986); idem, *Questions of power: electricity and environment in inter-war Britain* (Manchester, 1990).

how far and from which perspective the urban dimension has been present in these discourses, he detects a more advanced development in American environmental history, especially in relation to the historiographical mainstream, and a greater degree of sophistication and breadth. In Britain, by contrast, he claims that the position of environmental history still seems to be somewhat marginal.[48] Luckin diagnoses a significant change in US environmental history in the 1990s, when – as highlighted earlier – several scholars re-conceptualized their work as urban environmental history and challenged the mainstream notion of environmental history as proposed by Donald Worster and his 'agro-ecological perspective'. What clearly marks out American environmental history compared with its British or – for that matter – continental European counterparts is, however, a growing preoccupation with environmental justice. This concept, devolved from contemporary ideological debate, seeks to establish a clear pattern of differential exposure to pollution and environmental degradation between white and non-white urban residents. This contemporary perspective has inspired historical approaches, which have analysed the urban environment in respect to specific risks according to class, race or gender. Luckin highlights potential pitfalls and particularly the tendency to oversimplify links between present and past for securing victory in contemporary political conflict. On the other hand, the environmental justice paradigm might usefully introduce politics into environmental history, demonstrating that pollution and environmental degradation not only damage 'nature' per se but also and above all the human 'nature' of certain groups of the population. Luckin claims that British environmental history, implicitly imbued in many aspects with the pastoral ideal of the British countryside, still has some way to go towards incorporating this dimension into its agenda. Inspiration, however, might come from the social history of medicine where place-specific exposure to health risks, frequently rooted in the environment, has been studied with great methodological sophistication and spatial intensity.

---

[48] However, in recent times conferences and other activities point to a climate of slow but steady change. In Scotland there is strong focus on environmental history with the AHRB Centre for Environmental History at the Universities of Stirling and St. Andrews, not least as a result of the influence of T.C. Smout. See T.C. Smout, *Nature Contested. Environmental History in Scotland and Northern England since 1600* (Edinburgh, 2000). These developments made it possible to hold the founding conference of the European Society of Environmental History at St. Andrews in September 2001. Over the last two years several conferences in Manchester (2001) Exeter (Sept 2003), Nottingham (Horticulture 2003), and London ('The Big Smoke: Fifty years after the 1952 London Smog – A commemorative conference', 12/2002), have pointed to significant improvement.

Environmental protest and the formation of environmental movements are central to Jens Ivo Engels' *'In Stadt und Land'. Differences and convergence between urban and local environmentalism in West Germany, 1950–1980.* Engels claims that environmental protest was not only present in the city but was also increasingly in evidence in the countryside. His research points towards a convergence of 'urban' and 'local' environmentalism, where 'local' (sometimes also called 'provincial') is not necessarily associated with rural, but rather denotes settlements of a smaller size, including small towns at some distance from larger cities. This convergence is said to be rooted in a general 'urbanization' of the countryside through the relative decline of agriculture, the rise of the motorized society and the ubiquitous diffusion of modern means of communication.[49] Tracing the roots of environmental protest back to the 1950s, Engels observes a tendency within conservation associations to revise their former ideological anti-urban and anti-industrial stance[50] and to include human quality of life, embracing a wider agenda of environmental improvement. It may be no mere matter of coincidence that the 'Green Charter of the Mainau', a central document for environmental protest in Germany, was released almost at the same time as Rachel Carson's 'Silent Spring'. For the early 1970s Engels observes differences between urban and rural environmental protest in terms of the extent to which each became associated with a rapidly developing alternative sub-culture. Whereas urban movements frequently found it easier to gather a critical mass of activists, to set up regular newsletters and maintain formal structures of communication, local movements had to make use of existing social networks and political structures and mobilize them for specific local issues. The convergence on overarching environmental themes such as nuclear energy and traffic was further promoted by a new organizational culture in new less hierarchical environmental organizations. Engels, while rejecting a simple 'centre-versus-periphery' model, admits, however, that key activities such as the build-up of scientific counter-expertise in environmental groups did in fact originate in cities, mostly university towns. Thus, despite clear tendencies towards

---

[49] See on the cultural 'urbanization' of the countryside as a general postwar phenomenon, J. Reulecke, *Geschichte der Urbanisierung in Deutschland* (Frankfurt a.M., 1985), 147–69; C. Zimmermann, ed., *Dorf und Stadt* (Frankfurt a.M., 2001).

[50] See on the traditions of conservation movements in Germany, R. Koshar, *Germany's transient pasts: preservation and national memory in the twentieth century* (Chapel Hill, 1998); T. Rohkrämer, *Eine andere Moderne?: Zivilisationskritik, Natur und Technik in Deutschland 1880–1933* (Paderborn, 1999).

convergence, the city nevertheless still seems to offer a more fertile breeding ground for protest movements.

In his paper *Path dependence and urban history: Is a marriage possible?* Martin Melosi discusses potential contributions of this concept to urban history. The passion involved in the debate over 'path dependence' within economics derives from its implicit challenging of the foundations of neoclassical theory. Path dependence theory claims that the adoption of a specific technology in a specific situation can 'lock' this technology in and prevent or make nearly impossible the later abandonment of such a technology and transfer to another which is now deemed superior. Drawing on his own work on sanitary infrastructure, the author illustrates the potential of this concept within urban and environmental history. It might provide a framework to understand why American (and for that matter also European) cities have adopted a specific set of technologies from the middle of the nineteenth century onwards to cope with serious health and environmental problems. Thus, a combination of maturing engineering know-how in constructing pipes and designing networks, acquired through river engineering and railway construction, together with the miasmatic theory championed by Edwin Chadwick and his followers to address the problem of mass poverty, coalesced to form a complex of engineering and institutional solutions to a problem that had been conceptualized in a specific way. Paradoxically, Melosi argues, 'bad science had led to relatively effective technology' at least in reducing certain diseases and cleaning up the urban environment, while pollution was externalized and new resource conflicts with other users generated. Path dependence might now help us to understand, why – despite new scientific insights into the causation of disease and despite recognition of an increasing range of negative environmental impacts – those long-established systems continue to predominate and spread. Only adaptations, such as filters, and waste water treatment plants have been added to the end of the pipe. Options that might have fundamentally altered networks were too expensive. Similar aspects and effects can be traced in other complex technologies, especially those with a network character, where the setting of central parameters, such as the gauge of railway systems, would be fundamental for the functioning and performance of the system as a whole, even if original parameters might come to be considered sub-optimal later on.[51]

---

[51] For the field of energy systems this been extensively analysed by Hughes, *Networks*. Hughes does not speak of path dependence but of 'momentum' and emphasizes that technical systems also incorporate non-technical cultural elements. In the history of technology 'social constructivism' implies a similar concept: the choice of a particular technology does not follow a 'natural selection' of the optimal variant but rather is shaped by a discursive process

New Horizons

Since all the contributions in this volume, while sharing a common interest in the city and its natural environment, originate from particular traditions of research and pursue a range of methodological approaches, it would be unhelpful to reduce them to a common denominator. Instead I want here to revisit Tarr's five primary themes of urban environmental history, outlined in his contribution to the volume 'Environmental problems'.[52] Tarr described these as 1) the impact of the built environment and human activities in cities on the natural environment; 2) societal responses to these impacts and efforts to alleviate environmental problems; 3) the effect of the natural environment on city life; 4) city-hinterland relationship; and 5) role of gender, class and race in relation to environmental issues. Most of the contributions certainly address the first two themes when discussing the setting up of water and waste water systems. In tracing the evolution of these systems they show how an ever-widening hinterland gradually became drawn into these technical systems. Thus the natural hydrology of river basins was partially replaced by an artificial water regime with clearly one-sided orientation towards improving public health within cities. At the same time, increasing pollution of water, soil and air outside of cities, inevitably causing problems in densely populated countries like Great Britain or Italy between upstream and downstream users, continued to be tolerated. It has been demonstrated that the concepts of social metabolism – especially from the resource perspective – and path dependency can be usefully applied to contextualize individual studies within a common conceptual framework which helps to clarify different aspects of the environmental impact of cities and their interpenetrations. Tarr's third theme, the effect of the natural environment on city life, has been investigated in this volume in relation to the presence of 'nature', green spaces within cities and the cultural desire for access to natural environments among the first generation of Montreal's suburbanizers. The city-hinterland relationship is present in papers dealing with material flows between city and countryside. The general tendency of subsuming ever-larger territories to the resource needs of the city while breaking up earlier mutual exchange relationships (food / fertilizer) has been forcefully demonstrated. Tarr's last theme, the role of gender, class

---

involving not only designers and engineers, but also marketing experts, consumers and politicians; see W. Bijker/T.P. Hughes and T. Pinch, eds, *The Social Construction of technological* Systems (Cambridge/London, 1987; W. Bijker/J. Law, eds, *Shaping Technology/Building Society. Studies in Sociotechnical change* (Cambridge, Mass./London, 1992).

[52] Tarr, *Urban History*, 38.

and race in regard to environmental issues, is probably the least explored in this volume – apart from Bill Luckin's paper – and in European environmental history in general. However, several contributions clearly point towards the political implications of environmental degradation and differential exposure to environmental risk.

Environmental injustice will certainly be a major field deserving more research and debate in the future within urban environmental history in Europe. The 'Round-Table on Urban Environmental History' in Siena, June 2004, addressed this issue and embraced topics not covered at Leicester, such as motor traffic and energy systems. Furthermore, as a result of discussions at the Leicester Round-Table, the issue of practical regulation and policing of urban pollution and environmental degradation, of measuring and setting environmental standards, will receive greater attention. In the light of the more enabling than enforcing nature of much national environmental legislation prior to 1970, the question will be how far and under which circumstances could and did cities make maximum use of room for manoeuvre. In addition, future research and discussion may well elucidate what this might mean for twenty-first century attempts to move towards more sustainable urban development. To a significant degree, these themes will take the debate away from the nineteenth century, the rise of urban-industrial pollution and resource use, to the twentieth century, an era in which the historian and social scientist is concerned with motor traffic, the transfer to oil and gas as major fuels and the chemicalization of new forms of environmental hazard.

CHAPTER TWO

A Metabolic Approach to the City: Nineteenth and Twentieth Century Paris

Sabine Barles

Introduction

The negative impact of large conurbations on the environment, through their rupturing of biogeochemical cycles and unbalancing of the biosphere as a whole, is already the subject of a wide debate. Cities are represented as systems wholly dependent on external resources while at the same time being largely to blame for their depletion, sustaining themselves only by importing vast amounts of material and energy, and – equally damagingly – by exporting a host of different pollutants and waste products. This analysis, issuing from industrial and urban ecology as constituted and formalized since the 1960s, appears to rest on the assumption that such squandering is now part and parcel of industrialization, after two centuries in which urban policy has contributed nothing towards combating the causes and effects of the former, while hygienism, having greatly contributed to the pressures on areas adjacent to cities, has remained oblivious to the impact of the techniques it has adopted.

It is this monotone[1] view of the relationships between societies and their environment as they have developed over two centuries that we shall be questioning here, by placing greater emphasis on a qualitative approach to urban metabolism, in other words by concerning ourselves with the materials which it mobilizes and with what becomes of them.[2] We shall also be concerned with the attitude towards them adopted by key persons in cities – councillors, engineers, scientists – taking as our particular case the French capital. Thus, we shall see how the last two centuries can be divided into two or perhaps three periods in regard to

---

[1] In the sense that the trend remained the same during the last two centuries: increasing pressure, increasing deterioration, etc.

[2] We shall not here be addressing the question of energy, which merits separate in-depth study.

the very diverse relationships that unite the city with its environment. The first period corresponds to the first phase of industrialization, in which a complex of ties bound together city, industry and countryside, and in which, as a result, the generation of waste and the rupturing of biogeochemical cycles was limited. In the second period, the boundaries of which are extremely difficult to determine, the very reverse applies: city, industry, and countryside are divorced from one another, we see the 'creation' of urban refuse and waste, and the rupturing of natural cycles is widespread. Finally, the third period, which would correspond to the last few years, and which has probably not yet started in Paris, would be characterized as a challenge to the second phase and as the search for a new form of complementarity with the aim of limiting practices which squander materials and by so doing limiting also the pressure on resources and the generation of useless waste products.

The City Comes to the Aid of Industry

Anyone seeking to understand the metabolism of early nineteenth century Paris will immediately note that the city and its industry are spatially inseparable. In 1823 for example, there were 102 factories and businesses on the banks of the Bièvre in the Seine department, 90 of these within Paris itself;[3] industry was also developing at the gateways through the capital's boundaries and downstream along the Seine.[4] Thus a full account of the city's metabolism must take into consideration the impact of handicrafts and industries as well as that of households. But spatial proximity is not the only reason for this choice: examination of the different reagents and materials used by the then booming chemical industry shows how these comprised what we have chosen to call 'urban raw materials', many of which in cities nowadays simply amass as refuse.

The reuse by industry of the city's own products is not new. Take, for example, saltpetre, the raw materials for whose production were obtained in the eighteenth century by scraping damp walls and by collecting ash, in most cases after it had been used by laundries.[5] Early in the following century the practice of scraping gave way to the use of rubble from Paris, from which 450 tonnes of powder were produced in

---

[3] *Recherches statistiques sur la ville de Paris et le département de la Seine* (Paris, 1823), vol. 2, table 8.

[4] A. Guillerme, A.C. Lefort and G. Jigaudon, *Dangereux, insalubres et incommodes: paysages industriels en banlieue parisienne; XIXe–XXe siècles* (Seyssel, 2004).

[5] A.L. de Lavoisier, 'Expériences sur la cendre qu'emploient les Salpêtriers de Paris (. . .)', *Mémoires de l'Académie royale des sciences pour 1777*, 123–36.

1824 in the Seine department (in which there were 25 saltpetre works, 24 of them in Paris).[6] This was despite the slump in urban saltpetre attributable to competition from the imported product. Rags began to be employed in the production of paper in the late middle ages, and yet there was no paper production in Paris and hardly any in France under the Ancien Régime.[7] As to rag collecting, this 'was not an industry from which those engaged in it could earn a living. This remained so until the Revolution.'[8]

The nineteenth century was marked by increased reliance on urban raw materials. These alone could enable the capital's newly established industries to expand and to meet demand from its dense and burgeoning population, a well-known illustration[9] being the trade in rags of vegetable origin: for unless men and women clothed themselves, unless used cloth existed, paper could not be produced. The industrialization and mechanization of papermaking[10] – allowing for recycling of increasingly abundant cotton in addition to hemp and linen fabrics – combined with growing consumption of paper[11] and diversification of its uses to inflate the price of rags, which eventually accounted for half the cost of production,[12] some 1.5 kg of rags being needed to make 1 kg of paper.[13] According to Louis André, one result of the mechanization of papermaking was the reorganization of the rag merchants' trade; as Paris remained central both to the consumption of paper and to the production of rags, numerous merchants would establish depots there.

A less well-known yet highly significant example is that of bone. This raw material was not only anthropogenic, in the sense that stock-rearing

---

[6] *Recherches statistiques sur la ville de Paris et le département de la Seine* (Paris, 1826), vol. 3, plate 105. At the time of the Revolution, 300 tonnes per year were produced in Paris. *Mémoire pour les salpêtriers de Paris (. . .) contre les ci-devant fermiers & commissaire général des Poudres & Salpêtres (. . .)* (179.), 22.

[7] Cf. L. André, *Machines à papier. Innovations et transformations dans l'industrie papetière en France, 1798–1860* (Paris 1996).

[8] J. Barberet, *Le travail en France. Monographies professionnelles* (Paris, 1887), vol. 4, 60. Translated by the author, as later quotes.

[9] There was so much at stake that the export of rags was banned between 1771 and 1863; customs duty was imposed on them up to 1881.

[10] National production increased fivefold between 1812 and 1860. André, *Machines à papier*, 413.

[11] Less than 1.5 kg per inhabitant in France in 1850, it exceeded 3 kg per inhabitant per year in the 1870s. A. Payen, *Précis de chimie industrielle* (6th edn, Paris, 1877–78), vol. 2, 660.

[12] André, *Machines à papier*.

[13] A. Firmin-Didot, 'XVIIe jury. Imprimerie, librairie, papeterie et industries auxiliaires', in *Exposition universelle de 1851. Travaux de la commission française sur l'industrie des nations* (Paris, 1854), vol. 5, 83.

Table 2.1   Urban raw materials: A first inventory, first half of the twentieth century (provisional assessment, not including metals)

Material	Industrial use	Agricultural use
Meat and slaughterhouse by-products	Tallow Inlaid goods Glue and gelatine Sulphate of ammonia (alum) Various ammonia products Blood (sugar refining) Animal charcoal (sugar refining)	Glue mark Sulphate of ammonia Dried blood Compound fertiliser Animal charcoal (after 1822)
Old shoes Woollen rags	Cloth manufacture (unravelling) Potassium cyanoferrate Paper (small quantities)	Fertiliser (direct use)
Hemp, linen, and cotton rags	Paper	
Old paper	Cardboard	
Broken glass	Glass	
Ash	Potassium substitute Laundry Soap works Saltpetre	Laundry or lye ash
Demolition materials	Refining of town gas	
Sludge and night-soil		Green/black sludge
Human and animal urine and excrement	Sulphate of ammonia and various ammonia products	Dried sewage sludge Manure Urate Compound fertilisers Sulphate of ammonia
Manufacturing by-products of town gas	Ammonia Tar Coke	

is a human activity, but also urban, in that most abattoirs were in towns or cities until the 1960s and that in the nineteenth century most bones were collected in urban areas – either from abattoirs, butchers' shops or private households. Bones make up twenty per cent or so of an animal's weight.[14] The larger ones were used in the production of fancy goods; 'very thin and spongy bones from the heads, from inside the horns etc'[15] were destined for gelatine or glue; while tallow was extracted from dry bones, and also from fatty and moist ones left over by butchers. From the first decades of the nineteenth century onwards these uses intensified: Darcet promoted the use of gelatine as a food ingredient at a time when shortages were feared due to the Blockade; gelatine had a bright future ahead of it with the later emergence of photography. A huge variety of fancy goods made of bones also proved seductive to the populace. Next came phosphorus, which had been produced from bones ever since the 1770s, but found a new industrial market in the 1830s, when the phosphorus-tipped match was first marketed. By the late 1850s 1,500 persons were employed in Paris, and between 800 and 1,000 elsewhere in France, producing matches.[16]

But the industrial boom in bone came from another source. At the very beginning of the nineteenth century, pharmacist Pierre Figuier had shown that animal charcoal was superior to vegetable charcoal in respect of its 'singular property of fully absorbing the colour of a wide range of solutions of vegetable or animal origin, and of rendering perfectly clear and colourless the water laden therewith'.[17] How did he prepare his charcoal? 'By roasting the bones of sheep and cattle in a closed pot.'[18] This process caught on immediately in the very small world of French domestic sugar production at a time when the Blockade cut off any supplies from the colonies. Limouzin, pharmacist in Albi, used animal charcoal for 'the decolourising of grape syrup, which at this point in time served as a substitute for cane sugar';[19] from 1813 onwards, Derosne and Payen used the product in their beet sugar works in Grenelle, as did Pluvinet in his in Clichy.[20] The use of bone charcoal became common practice, boosting the domestic production of sugar, the price of which fell from 12 fr/kg in 1813 to 1.40 fr/kg in 1815.[21] It subsequently proved

---

[14] Payen, *Précis de chimie industrielle* (4th edn), vol. 2, 488.

[15] Ibid.

[16] Ibid., 562.

[17] J.B. Dumas, *Traité de chimie appliquée aux arts* (Paris, 1828–33), vol. 1, 448.

[18] L. Figuier, *Les merveilles de l'industrie* (Paris, [1873]), vol. 2, 22.

[19] Ibid., 23.

[20] Payen, *Précis de chimie industrielle* (4th edn), vol. 2, 487.

[21] Figuier, *Les merveilles de l'industrie*, vol. 2, 26.

equally useful in the extraction and refining of raw sugar – whether domestic or colonial in origin – following the former's temporary decline. For this purpose it was used together with a coagulant, oxblood, which had previously been used on its own, and when the latter was unavailable, eggs were 'used rarely on account of their high price'.[22] Its production was perfected (charcoal in powder form) and was for a long time linked with that of ammonium salts, in part destined for the production of alum. As demand for sugar soared – France experienced a fivefold increase between 1788 and 1887[23] – so did that for bones.

The market for sugar was primarily urban: during the 1850s, consumption in France as a whole averaged five kg per person per year, as against eleven kg per person per year in Paris,[24] and since bone similarly met a chiefly urban demand, most bone charcoal factories and sugar refineries were established on the outskirts of cities, in Paris and other cities, chiefly seaports.[25] Out of a total of 64 bone charcoal factories throughout France in the 1850s, 31 were situated in Paris:[26] 'a large proportion of the bone charcoal consumed in France and in our colonies was produced in the department of Seine – understandably so, given that the raw material is more abundant here than anywhere else'.[27] The siting of these industries (animal charcoal *and* sugar) resulted not only from the well-known fact that the city presents a concentration of labour, consumption and distribution, but also from the specifically urban origin of part of the raw material.

'To gain an impression of the importance of this product, think of each kilogram of refined sugar that leaves the factory as representing one kilogram of charcoal.'[28] The incessant demand for bones also largely explains why the Paris rag collecting trade was then in its golden age. Indeed, rags and bones were originally its staple sources of income before numerous others were added. Woollen rags, virtually useless in papermaking, found a ready market in agriculture,[29] and subsequently

---

[22] M. Orfila, *Éléments de chimie appliqués à la médecine et aux arts* (5th edn, Paris, 1831), vol. 2, 22; Payen, *Précis de chimie industrielle* (4th ed.), vol. 2, 249.

[23] Payen, *Précis de chimie industrielle* (4th edn), vol. 2, 176–7; A. de Foville, *La France économique. Statistique raisonnée et comparative. Année 1889* (Paris, 1890), 246.

[24] Payen, *Précis de chimie industrielle* (4th edn), vol. 2, 177.

[25] See Geneviève Massard-Guilbaud's paper in this volume.

[26] A. Moreau de Jonnès, *Statistique de l'industrie de la France (. . .)* (Paris, 1856), 305.

[27] Payen, *Précis de chimie industrielle* (4th ed.), vol. 2, 487.

[28] C.L. Barreswil, A. Girard, *Dictionnaire de chimie industrielle* (Paris, 1861–1862), vol. 2, 458.

[29] L.C. Caillat, 'Engrais', in L. Rénier, ed., *Encyclopédie moderne (. . .)* (new edition. Paris, 1865–1867), vol. 14, col. 135.

in industry too, bought by factories unravelling or pulling it for re-use
in the production of new fabric.[30] Waste paper emerged as a commodity
in much the same way, its primary use being for the production of new
paper: if printed, it was never worth much, and was mostly used for
packaging, but if white it could be used to make new paper, albeit of
lesser quality, and cardboard, for which there was a fast growing
market. Along with the canning of food in the 1850s, there emerged the
new activity of desoldering: separating the solder, tin, from the can's
sheet iron, both of which were saleable materials. The trade was still
carried on in 1902 at 12 plants in the department of Seine with a
combined workforce of over 150.[31] In the early 1880s, some 2,000
workers in Paris were recycling old cork stoppers into new products;[32]
used sardine cans, unless melted, were used by toymakers.[33] Oyster
shells were also collected, Louis Figuier noting in 1873 that this activity
had been going on 'for a number of years [. . .]. This debris from our
tables, when granulated, serves to enrich our fields with the plant
nutrient calcium phosphate, of which it is composed'[34] – more than
fifteen million oysters a year were consumed in Paris at the time. 'Even
mussel shells get collected for some industrial purpose, the nature of
which remains secret', adds Figuier.[35]

Giving Back to the Earth . . .

But then another imperative surfaced, this time concerning food.
France's population was growing, urbanization proceeding apace; all
these people had to be fed, in particular the newcomers to the cities.
This pressure in turn created the need, asserting itself again and again,
to improve crop yields, notably through better fertilization of the soil.
As Nathalie Jas emphasizes, 'in the 1820s, well in advance of any
scientific understanding of plant nutrition, a veritable "manure rush"
was taking shape'.[36] And the city was soon to become its chief mine, at
least in people's minds if not in actual fact, and Paris was the biggest of
these.

---

[30] A. Fontaine, *L'industrie du chiffon à Paris* (Paris 1903), 60.

[31] Ibid., 98.

[32] *Bulletin municipal officiel de la ville de Paris*, 7 February 1884,
supplement, 'Compte rendu analytique de la séance du 6 févr. 1884', 174.

[33] Ibid., 192.

[34] Figuier, *Les merveilles de l'industrie*, vol. 2, 214.

[35] Ibid.

[36] N. Jas, *Au carrefour de la chimie et de l'agriculture: les sciences
agronomiques en France et en Allemagne, 1840–1914* (Paris, 2001), 59.

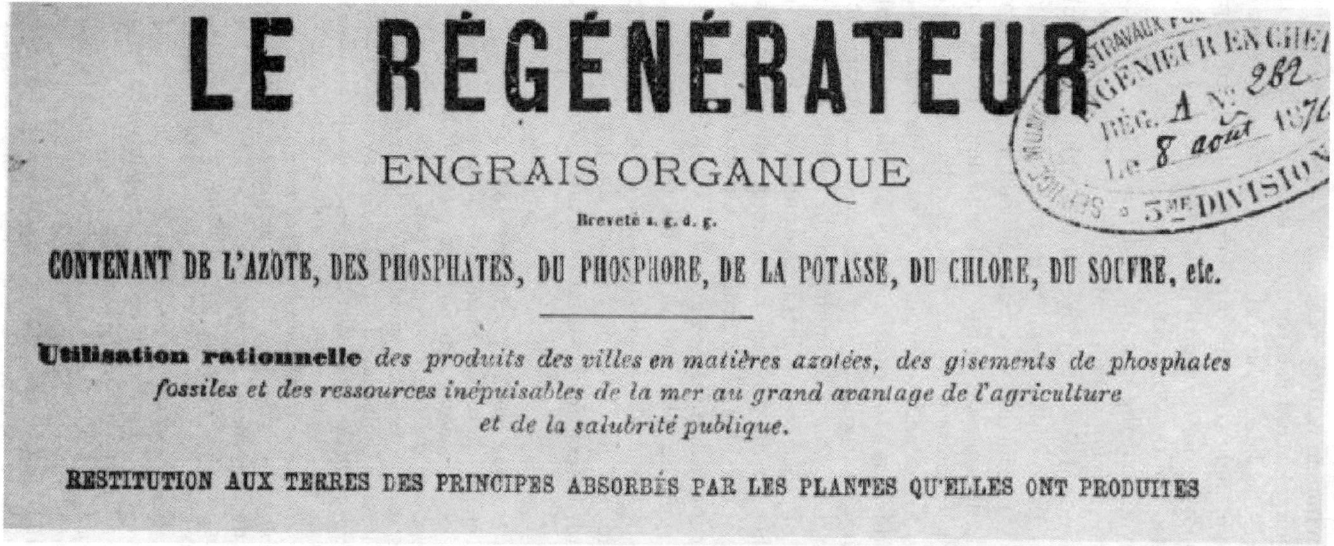

Figure 2.1 'The Regenerator': organic fertilizer. Paris Archive, VO3 163

Manure from human waste[37] has long been a subject of debate.[38] The practice of bringing faeces to surrounding fields goes back to the Middle Ages, and since the late eighteenth century, manure from dried and pulverized human night soil (called *poudrette*) had been prepared. This made sewage into a source of profit, not only for traders who emptied cesspits, but also for the contractor in charge of the night soil tip at Montfaucon, who sold the manure, and finally for the city, which by charging rent to such contractors earned for itself 'a not inconsiderable revenue'.[39] Pulverized sewage sludge proved highly successful, but also had its drawbacks: it took several years to prepare, its active nutrient content was low, production was made difficult as relatively more water was consumed, diluting the waste and impeding the drying process, which gained the reputation of a 'detestable, indeed *barbarous* method'.[40] The search was on for 'another product, more recent, sourced more from industry [. . .]: this was a salt of ammonium.'[41] Ammonium sulphate was extracted from urine collected by the waste disposal contractor in Montfaucon in the 1830s;[42] beginning in the 1850s, fertilizer producers, using a variety of processes, proliferated around Paris, and investors vied with one another for the privilege of collecting the capital's sewage. To take but one example, in 1872 a British firm even offered to pay the city a fee of 6.07 fr for each m³ of sewage, and thereby won the concession, unlike its forerunners, who had never offered so much as a franc.[43] Predictably, the British firm soon found itself 'completely insolvent',[44] but this setback did not deter its competitors; the prefecture of Seine was bombarded with letters, memos and brochures from firms offering to

---

[37] M. Paulet, *L'engrais humain (. . .)* (Paris, 1853).

[38] For more details, see: Barles, 'Entre artisanat et industrie: l'engrais humain XIXe siècle', in N. Coquery, L. Hilaire-Pérez et al. (eds), *Artisans, industrie: Nouvelles revolutions du Moyen Age à nos jours* (Paris, 2005); Barles, 'L'invention des eaux usées: L'assainissement de Paris (1780–1930)', in C. Bernhardt, G. Massard-Guilbaud, eds, *The Modern Demon. Pollution in Urban and Industrial European Societies* (Clermont-Ferrand, 2002), 129–56.

[39] P.S. Girard, 'Du déplacement de la voirie de Montfaucon', *Annales d'hygiène publique et de médecine légale*, 9, 1833, 64.

[40] Paulet, *L'engrais humain*, 265. He complained of the huge loss of gaseous nitrogen due to the slow manufacturing process.

[41] 'Déposition de M. Peauger, représentant la Compagnie Richer', in Commission des Engrais, *Enquête sur les engrais industriels* (Paris, 1865–66), vol. 1, 42.

[42] At first an ancillary product, it became the main source of revenue for the Bondy waste disposal business in the 1890s.

[43] Archives of Paris (AP), VO3 437, letter from A. de Mattos, a member of the company, to the prefect of Seine, 20 June 1876.

[44] AP, VO3 163, Direction des eaux et des égouts de la ville de Paris, Rapport de l'ingénieur ordinaire sur la proposition du Sr Kail, 18 February 1878.

dispose of the capital's sewage, all employing the same sales pitch: namely that the solution offered was in accord with the public interest – both in a salubrious city and in support for agriculture – as well as being highly profitable. Jostling crowds of competing bidders made their way from the postal clerk's office for Loire-Inférieure to the great chemicals producer Solvay.[45] Another alternative to pulverization of sewage and other transformation processes was the Flemish method, which was simply to spread fresh human excreta on the fields, and which proved temporarily attractive to the railway companies, since 'consignments of this kind provided trains with loads, which they invariably lacked when departing from cities'.[46]

Table 2.2   Fertilizers used in the Department of Seine (1892)

Sludge (t)	223,760
Bedding manure (t)	576,425
Sewer water (m³)	37,125,162
Mineral fertiliser (t)	598
Sewage from cesspits (t)	1,995
Dried sewage sludge (t)	21

Source: P. Vincey, *Les gadoues de Paris et l'agriculture du département de la Seine* (Paris, 1896), 37.

In these conditions, one might think that the integrated sewerage system conflicted with the complementarity between city and agriculture. The project, brought to completion by Adolphe Auguste Mille and Alfred Durand-Claye in the 1860s, was well matched to the extensive networking of the capital, but was also inextricably linked to the irrigation of cultivated land with sewage. Engineers from the public sector pursued goals not essentially different from those of private enterprise: they would certainly not allow these materials to be squandered, for 'one tonne of sewage is worth 0.10 fr, or in other words would cost 0.10 fr to manufacture, this representing no more than the cost of purchasing the raw material'.[47] The means employed

---

[45] AP, VO3 163.

[46] 'Déposition de M. Gargan, entrepreneur de matériel de chemin de fer à La Villette, Paris', in Commission des Engrais, *Enquête sur les engrais industriels*, vol. 1, 515.

[47] A.A. Mille, A. Durand-Claye, *Compte rendu des essais d'irrigation et d'épuration* (Paris, 1869), 10.

was, however, different: lavatory water draining into the sewers enabled vast areas of land to be irrigated with water rich in organic, fertilizing matter, but sufficiently diluted. They could thus claim that Parisians' excrement was now exploited commercially by a direct and fully sanitized route, obviating the need for the laborious collection of night soil, and transferring the economic benefits of the material to the city of Paris. The project progressively won the support of the engineering community, Eugène Belgrand came on board in 1871,[48] connection to mains sewerage was optional in 1885, became compulsory in 1894, and by 1900 5,100 ha of land were used for sewage treatment purposes.

At the same time, street sludge, which was all that was left of household refuse and municipal waste after rags and bones removal, became a matter of growing interest, as rich in organic matter, especially, but not only, because of horse manure.[49] The issue of municipal cleansing, much discussed during the nineteenth century, was once again associated with that of agriculture. Although its quality was disputed, sludge contributed greatly to food production in the city's outskirts. In 1830 F. Julliot maintained that 'much of the detritus is removed in the early morning by country folk';[50] this possibly amounted to half of the total. The remainder was taken to dumps where it coalesced and ripened, green sludge turning into black sludge, which was put to many uses by growers. After public and urban refuse tipping was prohibited in 1831, sludge was transported directly to its users: in 1850, of the 356 voies (700 m³) removed daily from Paris, 353 were delivered to farmers.[51] Sludge was to gain in importance during the Second Empire, Bouchardat writing in 1876: 'This mode of operation, truly a work of genius, safeguards public health while providing an inexpensive means of fertilising the poorest land, making it yield as many as six harvests per year of young fruit and vegetables, and should not be abandoned.'[52] The projects of prefect Eugène Poubelle,[53] while aiming to rationalize the depositing of refuse on the streets, as well as its collection and removal from the city, posed no threat to the improvement of

---

[48] E. Belgrand, *Les travaux souterrains de Paris*, vol. 5, *Les égouts. Les vidanges* (Paris, 1888), 319–65.

[49] See Joel Tarr's paper in this volume.

[50] F. Julliot, *Notice sur le nettoiement des rues de Paris* (Paris, 1830), 11.

[51] H. Darcy, 'Rapport à M. le ministre des travaux publics, sur le pavage et le macadamisage des chaussées de Londres et de Paris', *Annales des ponts et chaussées*, Semester 2. 1850, 214.

[52] Bouchardat, *Rapport présenté par M. le docteur Bouchardat au nom de la sous-commission du chiffonnage* (Paris, 1876), 4.

[53] J.H. Jugie, *Poubelle-Paris (1883–1896): la collecte des ordures ménagères à la fin du XIXe siècle* (Paris, 1993).

agriculture: by the end of the nineteenth century, the total area of land under cultivation in the department of Seine had reached 28,000 ha, of which 17,000 ha (sixty per cent) were fertilized with the sludge, any residue being exported to the neighbouring departments.[54] 'This explains why, at a distance of about 25 kilometres from Paris, rent charged for cultivable land with sandy soil doubled over a period of fifteen years',[55] wrote Arthur Fontaine in 1903, adding that where formerly forty hectares were needed for a family to earn a living, a mere eight would now suffice, thanks to sludge.

The Integration of Activities

Quite apart from what the city provided for industry on the one hand and for agriculture on the other, the complex ties binding together city, industry and agriculture continued to strengthen. To return briefly to bones and animal charcoal, as Camille Vincent points out in 1878:

> In the first few years in which refineries used finely ground bone charcoal and oxblood to decolourise and clarify syrups, the residue from this operation, a mixture of carbon from bone and coagulated blood, amassed in the sugar factories and refineries before being transported to public refuse tips. In 1822, following a competition in which Payen had demonstrated the still new application, which in 1820 and 1821 had been used successfully on land recently cleared for cultivation, these residues were tried out as fertilisers; the results were so promising that refiners were soon able to sell the material, the price of which has gradually increased, and today often exceeds that of finely ground bone charcoal.[56]

Its quality resulted from the very fact that it combined carbonized bones, rich in phosphorus, with coagulated blood, rich in nitrogen: used bone charcoal made better fertilizer than new.

The progressive improvement in material flows was thus not confined to vertical integration and increased productivity, very real advances though these were.[57] The complementarity between city, industry and countryside translated not into the deliberate rupturing of biogeochemical cycles, but rather into an endeavour towards the closing of loops, particularly where organic materials were concerned. It is, moreover, astonishing how in some cases manufacture supplanted

---

[54] P. Vincey, *Les gadoues de Paris et l'agriculture du département de la Seine* (Paris, 1896), 40.

[55] Fontaine, *L'industrie du chiffon*, 74.

[56] Payen, *Précis de chimie industrielle* (6th ed.), vol. 2., p. 706–707.

[57] To be convinced, reading successive editions of *Précis de chimie industrielle* of Payen is enough.

Table 2.3   Statistics on the principle of agricultural fertility, Paris, 1895 (kilograms)

	Nitrogen	Phosphoric acid	Potassium
Supply			
Animal	6,828,516	2,182,839	3,655,609
Human	16,626,460	6,078,457	5,596,455
Removal			
Sludge	2,166,129	1,767,105	1,197,071
Manure	3,917,631	2,508,491	1,197,321
Cesspits	3,981,204	452,409	193,889
Sewer water	13,174,179	3,445,576	5,934,047

Source: P. Vincey, *Projet de régime nouveau pour les ordures ménagères de Paris* (Paris, 1901), plate.

extraction.[58] Nor was it solely a legacy from pre-industrial times, but was one of the defining features of this 'first' industrialization; the city did not foist its residues upon agriculture and industry: these latter created the intense demand themselves.[59]

It could be argued that this complementary relationship was not striven for, but that it developed in a more or less unconscious way, or was dictated by the workings of the market. One constantly finds that certain materials capable of being used as high quality fertilizers were not put to this use because they were too expensive as a result of industrial demand. A case in point was fresh ash, as Caillat observed in 1866: 'Despite its effectiveness as an enriching agent, its use in agriculture is restricted; ash has a fairly high value, because of the many uses made of it in the arts, for laundry, in soap works, etc.';[60] from this viewpoint, the use of laundry ash would appear to have been a stopgap. Caillat nevertheless noted that ash from soap works gave good results 'because, besides the addition of lime, it might be mixed with a certain amount of fat or other animal content'.[61] Laundry ash would ultimately be to fresh ash what used animal charcoal was to fresh animal charcoal: a better fertilizer.

[58] With thanks to Laurence Lestel, who provided me with useful details on this point.
[59] This does not mean that the inhabitants accepted the activities in question.
[60] Caillat, 'Amendements', in L. Rénier, ed., *Encyclopédie moderne*, t. 2, col. 438–9.
[61] Ibid., col. 440.

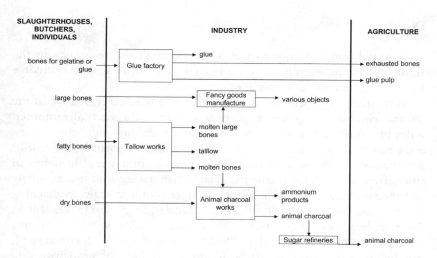

Figure 2.2 Life cycle of bones, Paris in the 1820s

The closing of materials' cycles[62] also emerged with increasing intentionality in the nineteenth century as an urban management issue, ranking alongside health and hygiene. Many were the scientists and intellectuals who campaigned for the return of these 'materials which the cities owe to the earth',[63] namely human urine and excrement. The title of the article published by Durand-Claye in 1872 is revealing in this sense: 'Municipal cleansing: the quantity of nitrogenous matter removed from Paris every day'.[64] This was not merely descriptive; Durand-Claye also gave thought to how the nitrogen cycle could be completed; a great deal was at stake, since the closing of this particular loop was seen as critical to the capacity to feed a booming population. In the same way, when Vincey drew up his *Statistique des principes de la fertilité agricole* for Paris, he was drawing up nothing less than a balance sheet of matter – in brief, an urban metabolism.

---

[62] The notion of a cycle of material appeared in the eighteenth century, notably in Lavoisier. Cf. J. M. Drouin, *réinventer la nature: L'écologie et son histoire* (Paris, 1991); Barles, *La ville délétère: médecins et ingénieurs dans l'espace urbain, XVIIIe–XIXe siècle* (Seyssel, 1999), 63 sq.

[63] Dumas, 'Rapport conclusif', in Commission des Engrais, *Enquête sur les engrais industriels*, vol. 2, xxxi.

[64] Durand-Claye, 'Assainissement municipal: quantité de matière azotée expulsée chaque jour de Paris', *Annales des ponts et chaussées*, Semester 1 1872, 410–12.

Divorce

This equilibrium was not to last long, although the resistance to the rupturing of these cycles was prolonged and the date of the divorce varied from one sector to another.

In the case of paper, the turning point was reached in France in the 1860s, with the emergence of substitutes for rags. Rags actually imposed a double constraint on the paper industry: on the one hand the reasons were economic as the cost of rags formed a large element in the cost of production. On the other hand, the logic was quantitative: 'the debris of fibres from the various textile materials becomes less and less adequate as time passes, as the consumption of paper grows in scale, as teaching spreads and the growth of advertising accelerates',[65] wrote Vincent in 1878. Substitutes, sought since the eighteenth century, finally became industrially competitive in the 1860s,[66] and in the 1870s 'neither linen, nor hemp, nor cotton are to be found in the bulk of newsprint and medium-quality paper, but only straw, esparto, and wood', while 'the use of rags, due to its high cost, tends to be increasingly restricted to the manufacture of fine paper'.[67]

Competition also arose between raw materials of plant and animal origin, resulting in the elimination of the 'urban stage' from the production chain. One example was animal charcoal, which was progressively supplanted by activated charcoal produced by partial combustion of wood, olive stones, coconut shells, peat, wood pulp, etc.[68] Another was glue: starch, starch flour and dextrin (obtained by hydrolysis of starch) being required for its production in the twentieth century,[69] before the development of synthetic products. As a result, even though the production of gelatine continued, as did that of tallow, the main markets for slaughterhouse by-products changed radically in the twentieth century, with a reorientation towards animal fodder. Meanwhile, abattoirs were relocated from the cities to the stock-rearing centres, and thus their by-products, although still correctly classified as 'anthropogenic raw materials', were no longer urban. Similarly, 'Paris bone',[70] highly prized for decorative wares in the nineteenth century, was

---

[65] Payen, *Précis de chimie industrielle* (6th edn), vol. 2, 605. At the time 3.15 kg per person per year of paper and cardboard were consumed in France (ibid., 660), as compared to 180 kg per person per year in 1999.

[66] André, *Machines à papier*, 417 sq.

[67] Payen, *Précis de chimie industrielle* (6th edn), vol. 2, 608.

[68] We are not yet able to specify the circumstances in which this change occurred.

[69] Casein-based glues did not need to pass through the city.

[70] Fontaine, *L'industrie du chiffon*, 58.

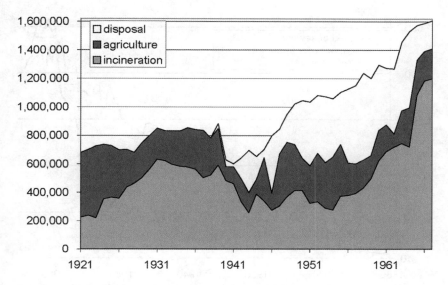

Figure 2.3   Treatment of household waste, Paris and its suburbs, 1921–1967 (tonnes)
The number of municipalities involved rose from 21 to 50 between 1921 and 1967. *Annuaires statistiques de la ville de Paris.*

dethroned by foreign canneries, which were more rural than urban, then by celluloid and bakelite.

This loss of interest in urban raw materials hurt first and foremost Paris' rag and bones trade. Adding to the hardship inflicted on it through the ubiquitous use of dustbins, the 'industry' was in crisis from the late nineteenth century onwards. The 1862 municipal commission on household refuse had concluded: 'This trade, whose mode of operation is distasteful, should be encouraged in view of the useful products that it provides for the manufacture of paper, cardboard, and animal charcoal'.[71] No longer spoken of in such utilitarian terms at the end of the nineteenth century, rag and bone collection had become a social issue: it was better to have rag and bone men than idlers and thieves.

The break-up of city and industry was therefore doubly consummated: not only had part of the activity moved away from the

---

[71] Quoted in *Bulletin municipal officiel de la ville de Paris*, 7 févr. 1884, supplement, 'Compte rendu analytique de la séance du 6 févr. 1884', 171.

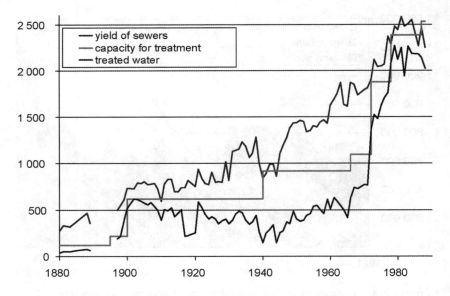

Figure 2.4   **Yield of sewers, capacity for treatment, treated water, Paris conurbation, 1880–1988 (thousand cubic metres per day)** *Annuaires statistiques de la ville de Paris,* Syndicat Interdépartemental d'Assainissement de l'Agglomération Parisienne.

cities but, more importantly, the chemical industry now looked to other sources for its raw materials. The only significant exception was probably glass manufacture, which continued to rely on the use of recycled glass (cullet).

The break-up of town and country was equally significant and contributed to the introduction of two new categories, urban waste and waste water: terms that never occur in the nineteenth-century French literature. In the case of Paris, resistance was prolonged, and it was not until the interwar years that city and agriculture finally separated. The rising population, the expansion of the Paris conurbation, the general availability of mains water and, more gradually, of access to the sewerage system, the changing lifestyles and patterns of consumption, contributed to a continuous increase in the generation of urban excreta, slowed down only temporarily by the two wars. Paris and its suburbs generated household refuse and residual water in increasing quantities and, what is more, continually, whereas agriculture, whose demand was seasonal, moved further away from the capital (land under cultivation in the Department of Seine fell to 14,000 hectares in 1929, and 7,000 hectares in 1952[72]).

Initially, the city authorities endeavoured to adjust to these constraints: not only did they attempt to industrialize the rag collecting trade and rationalize the sorting of refuse in processing plants brought into operation from 1896 on; they also tried to find new markets for sludge. The incineration of household refuse, which aroused the opposition of agronomists such as Vincey, was tried experimentally, beginning in the 1890s. Yet another economic benefit gained official blessing with the rapid introduction of energy recovery from waste. 'The principle is most alluring: rubbish itself generates the energy needed for its removal.'[73] It was loaded onto dumper trucks powered by electricity generated at the incineration plants themselves, while the residual clinker was used as infill or for brick manufacture. In short, as late as 1923 it was contended that 'the problem, expressed in the most general terms, consists in extracting as many *marketable* sub-products as possible'.[74] But in the 1930s the amount of household refuse began to outstrip incineration capacity and agricultural demand, and in 1938 landfill operations commenced.

The situation of the sewerage system was no better. It soon became apparent that there was insufficient land available for sewage treatment, and in the 1920s the idea of irrigating and fertilizing the poor and war-ravished region of Champagne was considered, but never realized[75] and from the 1930s on, the Seine Department's masterplan of its sewerage system formally adopted the principle that a treatment plant would be included; the first phase of the plant at Achères came into operation in 1940. The proximity of the dates concerning landfill and sewage treatment plant is far from coincidental.

Moreover, the market for fertilizers had been evolving. Newer, more convenient and more reliable products were entering the market; the competition to manure of human or urban waste was all the more intense, given the ever increasing supplies of fertilizer needed to improve

---

[72] Ministry of Agriculture, *Monographies agricoles départementales: La Seine* (Paris, 1960), 16.

[73] L.N. Girard, 'L'enlèvement des ordures ménagères de l'agglomération parisienne', in *Où en est l'urbanisme en France et à l'étranger?* (Paris, 1923), 359. The process, tried between 1914 and 1920, was abandoned on account of the high cost of electric traction, but the energy return remained for other uses.

[74] L. Pautot, 'Le problème des ordures ménagères. Leur collecte et leur traitement', in *Où en est l'urbanisme*, 345.

[75] The cost of investment was considerable, while the accounts of the Paris sewage farms showed that profits were far from those expected from agricultural production.

yields. Some of these new products were from natural mineral deposits (superphosphates, developed in Britain in the 1840s and first produced in France in the 1860s; extraction of potassium salts in Germany from the 1860s onwards and imported by France from 1880[76]); some were recovered from industrial processes (dephosphorization slag in the late nineteenth century; ammonium sulphate from coke ovens, also in the late nineteenth century); others were synthesized (ammonia from 1905).[77] In the inter-war period, fertilizers of urban origin shrank to insignificance, apart from ammonium sulphate, although that disappeared from cities once coal gas was abandoned. The city was no longer a mine for fertilizers.

These ruptures had a significant impact on the environment. The management of excreta had been for the sake of the economy, industry and the food supply, not merely of salubrity. Once these motives vanished, it came to be seen as 'an ineluctable burden'[78] the sole purpose of which was to preserve the health of the inhabitants and the cleanliness of the city; efforts to reduce the generation of sewage slackened, and the capacity of the treatment infrastructure was in constant shortfall. This is why discharges proliferated and why the Seine was sacrificed.

Conclusion

Our approach to the metabolism of Paris and to the interconnections between city, industry and agriculture has been essentially qualitative. Further research to quantify the exchanges of materials is needed, and would probably show what a number of exploratory studies have already suggested, namely that metabolic improvement in the nineteenth century – a subject of intense study – was indeed effective but did not produce all the expected effects. More specifically, it is clear that the city ultimately gives very little to the countryside and that industry, although improving its output, squanders a great deal, if only because of increasing flows of materials, resulting in the predictable environmental impact in the city and its outskirts.[79]

---

[76] A. Daujat, '200 ans d'évolution de la fertilité de la terre en France', *Chambres d'agriculture*, suppl. to No. 15, 1 January 1957, 8–10.

[77] C. Matignon, 'Les progrès réalisés par l'industrie chimique dans le dernier demi-siècle', *Chimie et industrie*, 26(2), August 1931, 255–72.

[78] A. Joulot, *Les ordures ménagères* (Paris, 1946), 175.

[79] This work is in progress within the 'retrospective' research path of the PIREN-Seine research group. See Barles, 'L'invention des eaux usées: L'assainissement de Paris (1780–1930)', 129–56.

There is a further question to do with the typicality of the city of Paris. Compared to other French cities, the capital was the place where the most recycling and commercial exploitation of waste has taken place, being the largest and densest deposit of urban raw materials and being the city where the imperatives of public health, industry, agriculture, food supply, economics and politics have been most intense. This is why the 'divorce' was longer delayed here, other cities having abandoned the utilization of excreta much earlier. In Nice between the wars 'rubbish was collected every two days with the aid of a barge towed by a small tug along some 8 kilometres of seafront. But the waste often drifted back towards the coast of the Baie des Anges along the Promenade des Anglais.'[80] Marseille discharged its sewage '12 km from the city, behind a hill at a depth of 30 to 60 m into offshore currents'.[81] Many cities discharged into rivers and lakes. Here the shifting of the nuisance from inner city to outskirts is a stark reality, salubrity for the former being provided at the expense of the latter.

The subjects of debate in Paris are, however, to a great extent international or becoming so, as in the case of the nineteenth-century market in urban raw materials. This is evident from similarities in the literature on recycling in France, Germany and Britain[82] and the techniques adopted (irrigation with sewage[83]). It is also evident from experiments conducted in other countries when the divorce of city, industry and agriculture is imminent (incineration of household refuse with energy recovery).

Furthermore, as we hinted at the beginning, a third period seems to be approaching. Pressure from cities on resources and environments has been lamented since the 1960s, and the need to redress it has meanwhile progressively penetrated the political arena. Although for the Île de France region and for Paris this has brought about a marked improvement in the management of sewage and refuse over the past fifteen years, the biogeochemical cycles remain largely disrupted and their eventual restoration seems a matter of pure conjecture.

---

[80] J. Courmont, *Précis d'hygiène* (4th edn, Paris, 1932), 350. The same was true of New York and Liverpool.

[81] Ibid., 378. This was to be the case up to 1989. Sea disposal was envisaged for Paris in the last third of the nineteenth century.

[82] E. Mårald, 'Everything circulates: Agricultural chemistry and re-cycling theories in the second half of the 19th century', *Environment and History*, 8, 2002, 65–84.

[83] J.A. Tarr, 'Sewerage and the Development of the Networked City in the United States, 1850–1930', in Tarr and G. Dupuy, eds., *Technology and the Rise of the Networked City in Europe and America* (Philadelphia, 1988), 159–85; N. Goddard, J. Sheail, 'Victorian sanitary reform: where were the innovators?', in C. Bernhardt, ed., *Environmental Problems in European Cities in the 19th and 20th Centuries* (Münster/New York, 2001), 87–103.

CHAPTER THREE

Urban Horses and Changing City-Hinterland Relationships in the United States

Joel A. Tarr and Clay McShane

In *Nature's Metropolis*, historian William Cronon illuminated the tight relationship between cities and their hinterlands when market relations mediated flows of products between them. Thus, he notes, a 'rural landscape which omits the city and an urban landscape which omits the country are radically incomplete as portraits of their shared world'.[1] Nineteenth century cities drew heavily on their hinterlands for food to feed their human populations. The same hinterlands, however, also provided the flow of hay, oats and corn to feed the city's horse population, without which cities could not function. And, over the course of the century, just as food production for human populations in the largest cities shifted further and further west, so did the growth of feed for their horse populations.

Thus, the same improvements in agricultural technology and the growth of the national railroad network that made it possible for more people to live in cities also helped meet the food needs of a growing urban horse population.

The United States experienced great urban growth in the nineteenth century. From 1790-1900, the urban population grew from approximately 202,000 to over 25 million. In 1790 there was no city with a population over 50,000; in 1870, there were 25 that exceeded that figure, with three over 300,000 and one close to a million. By 1900, 38 cities had over 100,000 population, 8 were between 300,000 and 600,000, and three had a million or more.

Nineteenth century cities required sizeable horse populations in order to function. In 1870 the Census counted 8,690,219 horses in the United States, with 1,547,370 categorized as 'Not on farms.' By 1900, the total horse population had grown to 24,148,530, with just under 3 million in cities. In that year, cities with over 100,000 population averaged roughly

---

[1] W. Cronon, *Nature's Metropolis: Chicago and the Great West* (New York, 1991), 48–54.

one horse for every fifteen people, although there were wide variations. Kansas City, for instance, had one horse per 7.4 persons, Memphis, one per 17 persons, and New York City one to 26.4 persons.

Cities depended on horses for internal freight movement, for powering public transportation (until late in the century), for private travel and for emergency services. One source estimates that in 1850 animal sources of energy (horses and mules) in US cities constituted about one quarter of the total work output, or 2.8 billion horsepower-hours.[2] In order to generate this energy, horses needed feed. This feed became part of a complex ecological system of exchange, as the fertility of rural land often depended on the application of urban wastes – both horse and human – to the soil. Thus, cities and their hinterlands developed a vital feedback mechanism that insured reciprocal relationships.[3]

The classic von Thunen rent model of agricultural activity suggests how rural hinterlands organized agricultural production in relation to an urban center. According to his model, farmers would produce the highest value and most perishable goods, as well as bulky goods, on farms nearest the urban market in order to keep transport costs low. More distant farmers would grow crops that had less value or keep land in products such as timber or grasses for grazing livestock. The model suggests that farmers nearest the city would specialize in high bulk goods such as hay as well as garden and dairy products, while farmers further from the city might produce wheat and raise cattle. Various studies of agricultural regions and their hinterlands have confirmed the general validity of the von Thunen thesis for nineteenth century American cities, although changes in technology and transportation capabilities caused alterations of patterns from his 'ideal state'.[4]

---

[2] J. Frederic Dewhurst and Associates, *America's Needs and Resources: A New Survey* (New York, 1955), 908–909, 113, 1108–109. These estimates of total horsepower in the economy ignore the growth in horse size during the century and the much longer work schedules of city horses compared to rural. See also, D. Greenberg, 'Energy Flow in a Changing Economy, 1815–1880,' in J.R. Frese and J. Judd, eds., *An Emerging Independent American Economy 1815–1875* (Tarrytown, New York, 1980), 35.

[3] J.A. Tarr, 'From City to Farm: Urban Wastes and the American Farmer,' *Agricultural History*, 49, 1975, 598–612.

[4] For discussions of the von Thunen model in relationship to American cities and towns see Cronon, *Nature's Metropolis*; D. Lindstrom, *Economic Development in the Philadelphia Region, 1810–1850* (New York, 1978); D. Block and E.M. Dupuis, 'Making the Country Work for the City: Von Thunen's Ideas in Geography, Agricultural Economics and the Sociology of Agriculture,' *American Journal of Economics and Sociology*, 60, 2001, 1–15; and, J.R. Peet, 'The Spatial Expansion of Commercial Agriculture in the Nineteenth Century: A von Thunen Interpretation,' ibid., 45, 2000, 283–301.

Farmers produced hay and oats first to feed their own horses (needed for power on the farm) and other livestock, and then for export. A market mentality on the part of some American farmers – that is, an inclination to raise crops for potential profit as well as for local use – developed in the late-eighteenth and early nineteenth century, and farmers who had access to urban markets often produced surpluses for sale. The growth of cities and towns with expanding horse populations for transport and power provided a major market.[5]

Growing Hay for Horses

When cities first developed in North America along the Eastern coast, colonists provided hay for urban horses by farming saltwater marshes and freshwater meadows to provide salt hay (*Spartina patens*) for their livestock. In the early nineteenth century, in areas within reasonable shipping distance of towns, farmers began to cultivate non-native grasses imported from Europe such as bluegrass, orchard grass, alfalfa, timothy, and white and red clovers.[6]

In New England, farmers near urban markets began cropping their land in order to produce several crops of hay per season. New England became a great hay growing region both because of its growing urban network and because hay could be grown on the region's less than ideal soils.[7]

Hay growing areas developed throughout rural America but with concentration near urban markets. Both New York City and Philadelphia, for instance, provided large markets for hay. Hay production gradually declined in the home counties of each city as the built environment extended, but expanded in close-in counties in the urban hinterland. The regions around the cities were marked by a series of zones, with the initial zones reserved for market gardens, dairying, livestock, and hay production. Thus, agricultural production

---

[5] W.B. Rothenberg, *From Market-Places to a Market Economy: The Transformation of Rural Massachusetts, 1750–1850* (Chicago, 1992); D.H. Parkerson, *The Agricultural Transition in New York State: Markets and Migration in Mid-Nineteenth-Century America* (Ames, 1995), 79–102.

[6] G.G. Whitney, *From Coastal Wilderness to Fruited Plain: A History of Environmental Change in Temperate North America 1500 to the Present* (New York, 1994), 250–55; D. Vickers, *Farmers & Fishermen: Two Centuries of Work in Essex County, Massachusetts, 1630–1850* (Chapel Hill, 1994), 295–6.

[7] W.W. Cochrane, *The Development of American Agriculture: A Historical Analysis* (Minneapolis, 1993, 2nd edn), 73–7; Vickers, *Farmers & Fishermen*, 295–6; and, H.S. Russell, *A Long, Deep Furrow: Three Centuries of Farming in New England* (Hanover, NH, 1976), 367.

organized itself as 'rings of lowering production intensity around central cities'.[8]

Lands near cities were frequently enriched by the application of urban manure and other fertilizing material. Farmers often contracted to gather this manure from livery stables and city streets. In Kings County, New York (Brooklyn), for instance, in the middle and late nineteenth century, regional farmers purchased large amounts of manure, both human and equine, street sweepings, and lime and ashes from the city to fertilize their land, increasing their production of hay and oats, as well as garden crops, for the urban market. Manure was especially important for the growing of vegetables, and Kings County, a relatively small county in terms of area, was the twelfth largest user of fertilizers in the nation in 1880. Other cities such as Baltimore, Boston, and Philadelphia also developed this type of recycling relationship.[9]

During the period after 1840, American agriculture increasingly replaced human agricultural labor with horse-powered machines, making possible the expansion of land for the growing of increased amounts of hay and also expanding the demand for horses. The major steps in the haymaking process offering the possibility of replacing labor with capital were cutting, raking, and loading and baling. The horse rake was the critical innovation, and farmers with the potential to increase their markets proved willing to expend the capital to purchase them. Between 1850 and 1870 the horse rake, in both the revolving type and sulky types, had become a 'standard implement' among market-oriented farmers in regions where hay was an important cash crop, such as the urban hinterlands. In the same period, superior mowers appeared on the market and, as prices declined, mowers became common farm machines in gathering the grass.[10]

The ability of the farmer to make a profit on the production of hay also depended on the costs of shipping hay to market, which included loading, storing, and bundling as well as actual transport.[11] Transporting hay to market in the nineteenth century was cumbersome and expensive

---

[8] Block and Dupuis, 'Making the country work for the city', 1; Lindstrom, *Economic Development in the Philadelphia Region*, 140–45, 182.

[9] M. Linder and L.S. Zacharias, *Of Cabbages and Kings County: Agriculture and the Formation of Modern Brooklyn* (Iowa City, 1999). 33, 39–41, 259; Tarr, 'From city to farm', 602–605; and, R.A. Wines, *Fertilizer in America: From Waste Recycling to Resource Exploitation* (Philadelphia, 1985), 8–20.

[10] C.H. Danhof, 'Gathering the Grass', *Agricultural History*, 30, 1956, 231–43; Danhof, *Change in Agriculture*, 228–49; and, R.L. Jones, *History of Agriculture in Ohio to 1880* (Kent, Ohio, 1983), 274–4. For an insightful study of the cultivation of hay in different generations, see S.R. Hoffbeck, *The Haymakers: A Chronicle of Five Farm Families* (Minneapolis, 2000).

[11] Gates, *The Farmer's Age*, 251.

and transportation costs restricted hay sales to markets within twenty to thirty miles. Farmers commonly transported hay to market in their own wagons or sold it 'at the barn', where the buyer assumed the hauling costs. Migratory commission merchants then assumed the responsibility for transport as well as baling.[12] Teamsters also transported hay in large freight wagons on major east-west roads for longer distances.[13]

Regardless of the transport method followed, any technique that would reduce the bulk of the hay would reduce costs. The major technological advance in hay baling was the haypress. As early as 1836 agricultural machinery houses were advertizing large horse-powered haypresses operated by three men that would press five or six tons of hay a day.[14] In the 1850s, numerous manufacturers of agricultural equipment made hay presses and competition drove prices down. Some presses were operated by hand, while a horse-powered capstan drove others. Most balers were stationary and the hay had to be hauled to them and then removed after baling. Often the size of a bale and ease of handling determined the popularity of a press. By 1912, more than seventy makes of hay presses were on the market.[15]

Only farmers with considerable acreage could afford the price of a press, although farming cooperatives occasionally purchased them. Hay merchants frequently operated presses at railroad depots and boat landings where they would purchase hay from farmers and ship it. Larger shipping concerns sent 'drummers' into the countryside, buying and baling hay and pushing the small shippers out of the market.[16]

---

[12] H.B. McClure, *Market Hay*, Farmers' Bulletin 508, U.S. Dept. of Agriculture (Washington, 1912); Rothenberg, *From Market-Places to a Market Economy*, 85–95.

[13] D.E. Schob, *Hired Hands and Plowboys: Farm Labor in the Midwest, 1815–60* (Urbana, Il, 1975), 43–58.

[13] Russell, *A Long, Deep Furrow*, 131–2; A. Todd, 'Hay Trade from a Shipper's Standpoint', *Report of the Seventh Annual Meeting of The National Hay Association* (Chicago, 1900), 188-9

[14] G.S. Blakeslee, 'The National Hay Association', *Report of the Sixth Annual Meeting of The National Hay Association Held At Detroit, Michigan, Aug. 8, 9, 10, 1899* (Cincinnati, 1899), 57; Gates, *The Farmer's Age*, 252; W.E. Roberts, 'An Early Hay Press and Barn on the Ohio River', *Material Culture* 25, 1993, 29–35.

[15] Jones, *History of Agriculture in Ohio*, 276–7; Nourse, Mason & Co., *Descriptive and Illustrated Catalogue of Plows and Other Agricultural and Horticultural Implements and Machines* (Worcester, MA, 1857), 14–15; C.V. Piper, *Growing Hay in the South for Market*, Farmers' Bulletin 677, U.S. Department of (Washington, DC, June 16, 1915), 16; and, McClure, *Market Hay*, 17–22.

[16] Piper, *Growing Hay in the South for Market*, 17; Jones, *Agriculture in Ohio*, 278; C.H. Bates, 'Business Methods Regarding Shippers and Receivers',

By the late nineteenth century, expansion into improved soils, the use of heavier fertilizers, and improved varieties of hay had increased hay production from approximately one ton per acre to an average of almost a ton and a half, although some states produced as much as three tons per acre. In addition, the development of the haypress and the growth of railroads greatly facilitated the transport of hay from farm to city and sharply reduced shipping costs from road transport. In 1899, one hay expert estimated that about 27.5 per cent of hay harvested was shipped out of the county in which it was grown. In that year, the five leading cities for hay receipts were New York, 411,374 tons; Chicago, 197,778 tons; Boston, 184,510 tons; St. Louis, 176,820 tons; and Cincinnati, 102,717 tons.[17]

Between 1879 and 1909, national hay production increased from approximately 35 million tons to over 97 million tons. Increased demand from growing urban horse populations and growing domestic herds of livestock drove the rise. On the supply side, farmers increased output through the greater use of leguminous forage plants and a rise in fertilizer use that enabled them to produce heavier annual yields per acre. In 1879, farmers grew hay on 10.8 per cent of the nation's improved land, and in 1889 they produced hay on 14.8 per cent; it remained at approximately this level through 1909. New England had the highest percentage of land devoted to hay, raising from 32.4 per cent in 1879 to 52.3 per cent in 1909, a substantial amount of which went to urban markets. However, New England's share of the nation's hay production dropped from 20.2 per cent in 1859 to 4.8 percent in 1909. The Middle Atlantic States also lost position, dropping from 33.2 per cent in 1859 to 11.6 percent in 1909. In contrast, the West North Central states increased from 7.7 per cent to 37.3 per cent in the same period.[18] The leading hay growing states in 1909 were New York, Iowa and Kansas. New York and Iowa each had approximately 5 million acres in hay and forage crops while Kansas had over 4 million.

Report of the Seventh Annual Meeting of The National Hay Association, 1900, 68–75; and, E.C. Parker, *High-grade Alfalfa Hay: Methods of Producing, Baling, and Loading for Market* (Washington, DC, 1929), Bulletin #1539, 21–4.

[17] The Paris, France omnibus company began to bale its hay in 1877 and reported that it had reduced the bulk of hay by two-thirds, saving fifty per cent in transport costs. See, G. Bouchet, *Le Cheval A Paris, de 1850 a 1914* (Geneve, 1993), 106. See also, A. Patriarche, 'The Transportation of Hay', *Report of the Seventh Annual Meeting of The National Hay Association, Aug. 14–16, 1900* (Chicago, 1900), 172–5; 'Hay Statistics', *Report of the Seventh Annual Meeting of The National Hay Association*, Baltimore, Md., Aug. 14, 15, 16, 1900 (Chicago, 1900), 48.

[18] J.M. Berry, '*Marketing Oats in the United States*', University of Cincinnati, unpublished B.S. thesis, 1926, 4, 55–6.

Figure 3.1   Dederick's Patent Parallel Lever Hay Press

While hay provided the main food for horses, oats were the primary feed grain. Oats were high in fiber and protein and suited to the horse's sensitive digestive system. Historically, farmers grew oats in conjunction with corn, devoting land to oats early in the spring before corn and harvesting it by midsummer (oats matured within ninety days), again before corn. From approximately 1840 through 1870, New York, Pennsylvania, and Ohio led in oats production. After 1870, however, Midwestern states like Illinois, Indiana, Iowa, Minnesota and Wisconsin with high yields increasingly out-produced eastern states.[18]

The growing of oats also benefited from farm mechanization using horse-powered technology.[19] Production increased greatly, requiring new technologies and techniques to ship and process grain. Up to mid-century, farmers usually shipped grain, whether oats or wheat or barley, in sacks and by water. Sacks were fitted to this form of transport because they could be easily loaded in holds and transferred from boats to piers, and then on to wagons. The sack also provided a convenient method of buying and selling, with each sack maintaining its ownership character.[20] The railroad, however, changed these patterns, opening up new regions, lowering transportation costs, and driving greater production of wheat, oats, and other grains. In order to accommodate and store the vast new flow of grains, another new technology, the steam-powered (but originally horse-powered) grain elevator was devised. First used in Chicago, the efficiency of the city's grain-processing technology rested upon removing grain from its sacks and moving it in a continuous stream by the railroad carload. To fully implement this process, however, required a new administrative technique – the development of standardized grades of inspection, weight and quality for grain.

Markets and Standards for Hay

The increased transport of hay to markets distant from producers drove improvements in inspection methods, standardized ways of weighing and pricing, and the development of an organization of specialized commodity merchants. Before the coming of the railroad, local farmers would haul hay into cities on wagons, boats, and sleds and sell it in locations usually called 'The Hay Market'. Municipal governments regulated the location and operation of the markets, carefully monitoring weights, indicating how important it was to the urban economy. The

---

[19] Hurt, *American Farm Tools*, 69–76; Danhof, *Change in Agriculture*, 221–7.

[20] Cronon, *Nature's Metropolis*, 104–109.

weighers had the obligation to furnish themselves with 'proper scales' inspected and tested every three months by the city sealer of weights and measures. In Chicago, for example, weighers or weighmasters, as well as those in other cities, had to provide sellers with a certificate; persons selling or purchasing hay without a certificate were subject to a fine.[21]

As hay increasingly became a commodity in interstate commerce, however, the need for the development of a more organized market with quality standards increased. Boards of trade in various port and river cities such as Buffalo, Chicago, New York, and Philadelphia had already taken this step in the grain markets by mid-century. Standards for hay came somewhat later because it remained a locally produced commodity for a longer period than wheat and oats.

The Chicago Board of Trade set the first standards for hay in 1877. Other markets slowly followed. The New York hay market, for instance, was plagued by problems of poorly compressed bales, grading, and storage. *The American Grocer* observed in 1882 that the city's hay 'trade' was hampered by 'the lack of system in gathering statistical information, the absence of a recognized standard of grade, such as obtains in Chicago, and the need for rules to induce growers to properly cure and prepare the hay for market'. However, it took until 1883 for the New York Produce Exchange to establish the Manhattan Hay and Produce Exchange (later the New York Hay and Straw Exchange) with 'Rules Regulating the Hay and Straw Trade Among Members of the New York Produce Exchange'.[22] Seven more years went by before the members of the Hay and Straw Exchange established standards for uniform price quotations and for grading hay, and then grading only took place at the request and expense of shippers.[23]

---

[21] See *Laws and Ordinances Governing the City of Chicago*, Jan. 1, 1866, 248–50; *The Charter and Ordinances of the City of Battle Creek* (Battle Creek, 1861), 101–104; *Revised Charter and Ordinances of the City of Detroit*, 182; *Revised Ordinances of the City of Galesburg [Illinois]* (Galesburg, 1863), 52–153; W.W. Thomson comp., *A Digest of the Acts of Assembly Relating To, and The General Ordinances of the City of Pittsburgh From 1804 to Sept. 1, 1886* (Harrisburg, 1887), 353; and, D.J. Sweeney, comp., *Ordinances of the City of Buffalo* (Buffalo, 1920), 224. A good description of a municipal hay market can be found in M. Tuthill Bly, 'The hay market', in E.R. Foreman. comp. and ed., *Centennial History of Rochester, New York* Vol. III: *Expansion* (Rochester, 1933), 127–9

[22] CBT, *Twentieth Annual Report, 1877*, lxxxiii–lxxxiv; Edwards, ed., *New York Produce Exchange*, 49. New York standards, however, were somewhat different from those of the National Hay Association, especially in regard to clover hay. See, comments of J.D. Carscallen in *Report of the Seventh Annual Meeting of The National Hay Association*, 115–17; Todd, 'Hay trade from a shipper's standpoint,' 188–92; and, Boyle, *Marketing of Agricultural Products*, 308–309.

The national market for hay was plagued by the problems that came with many small sellers and buyers. Local markets enabled shippers and consignees to have personal knowledge of each other and their products but long distance contracts often resulted in clashes over grade.[24] Such conditions required 'an interconnecting body of independent middlemen', and in 1895 a group of hay merchants and shippers founded the National Hay Association. The association established a set of rules for grading hay similar to those adopted by the CBT and the New York Produce Exchange and also regulating agreements between buyers and sellers. It created an arbitration committee and a committee on legislation and transportation. In 1899, the Chicago Board of Trade *Annual Report* noted that 'much improvement is observed in the care and uniformity with which hay is loaded and shipped from the west, which is largely the results of the National Hay Association, which is one of the most important commercial organizations of the country . . .' Eventually, these grading standards spread to most locations in the United States.[25]

The National Hay Association served as a 'facilitative organization' that aided middlemen in performing their operations by establishing the 'rules of the game', including grading and standards, and gathering and disseminating relevant information. The organization also represented hay shippers in opposing increases in railroad rates.[26] By the first decade of the twentieth century exchanges in 24 cities had adopted National Hay Association standard grades for timothy, clover, prairie hay, straw, mixed hay, and alfalfa.

Generally, city hay was required to be higher in quality than that kept for use on the farm or sold in the locality. In terms of bulk, hay furnished

---

[23] 'Grades of Hay', *New York Times* (*NYT*), 22 Apr. 1882, 13 Sept. 1889. Other cities also suffered from hay trade problems. See CBT, *Thirty-fifth Annual Report*, 1892, xl; Todd, 'Hay trade from a shipper's standpoint 188–92; Boyle, *Marketing of Agricultural Products*, 308–309; n.a., *The National Hay Association*, 1; and 'The Hay Trade,' *Report of the U.S. Industrial Commission*, 415. 'The Hay Trade,' in *Report of the Industrial Commission on the Distribution of Farm Products*, vol. VI (Washington, 1901), 417; J.E. Boyle, *Marketing of Agricultural Products* (New York, 1925), 309; and, *NYT*, 18 Mar. 18, 1875.

[24] G. Porter and H. C. Livesay, *Merchants and Manufacturers: Studies in the Changing Structure of Nineteenth-Century Marketing* (Baltimore, 1971), 198, 214–15; and McClure, *Market Hay*, 29–30.

[25] *The National Hay Association*, 2, 12–13, 23–4; CBT, *42nd Annual Report* (Dec. 31, 1899), lxi; and McClure, *Market Hay*, 23–4.

[26] R.L. Kohls, *Marketing of Agricultural Products* (New York, 1955), 24–6; 'National Hay Association vs. L.D.&M.S.R.R. et al., 'Report of the Interstate Commerce Commission', in *Report of the Ninth Annual Convention*, The National Hay Association (Chicago, 1902), 133–42.

the largest volume of feed received in the city. Once urban merchants received a load of hay, they marketed it in three ways: directly from railroad cars; from terminal-warehouse companies, railroad warehouses and holding yards; and from warehouses where the hay would be inspected and graded by type and sold in lots of uniform grade. These methods of sale contrasted with the earlier, more casual period when local farmers sold directly from their wagons, as commented on by the *New York Times* in 1900: the 'old-style load of loose hay, which wound its picturesque way through the city, is no longer seen. . . . The hay received in the city is all baled . . .'.[27]

Hay, oats and other feed for horses were sold in cities by feed stores, by livery stables, and occasionally by grocery stores. In 1876, for instance, Pittsburgh, with a population of about 150,000, had 64 'flour, grain & feed' establishments; sixteen years later the Steel City had 63 retail flour, grain & feed establishments and 18 wholesale establishments. The retail businesses were scattered throughout the city, while the wholesale businesses were concentrated in the so-called 'strip' district along Liberty Avenue adjacent to the tracks of the Pennsylvania Railroad. This location pointed to the importance of the railroad as a transporter of hay into the city and was typical of wholesale markets in other cities.[28]

Because of their small stomachs, horses ate and drank five times a day. Depending on the type of work, horses required daily caloric intake that varied from 9,000 to nearly 30,000 calories (16 to 47 pounds).[29] If a horse worked a full eight or ten hour shift, its teamster would frequently have to feed and water it on the streets. Drivers either carried feed with them or bought small quantities from local livery stables or grocery stores. Usually, drivers held a feedbag over the horse's head, although sometimes they threw hay on the street. Teamsters usually carried water, although philanthropic groups and city governments began to build water fountains in the 1860s. The ASPCA built the first fountain in Union Square, New York City in 1867. Such fountains and troughs could be a source of sickness, especially hoof and mouth disease, a zoonose for which humans were the reservoir. Wells Fargo banned its drivers from using them and the veterinary profession recommended their elimination.

---

[27] McClure, *Market Hay,* 25–36; Balas and Bayor, eds, *Haymaker's Handbook,* 174; and *NYT,* Mar. 4, 1900.

[28] G.H. Thurston, *Pittsburgh As It Is* (Pittsburgh, 1857), 183.

[29] S. Budiansky, *The Nature of Horses: Exploring Equine Evolution, Intelligence and Behavior* (New York, 1997), 15; W.H. Jordan, 'The Feeding of Animals', 56–103, in L.H. Bailey, ed., *Cyclopedia of American Agriculture: A Popular Survey of Agricultural Conditions, Practices and Ideals in the United States and Canada* (4 vols, New York, 1908), III, 78–87.

New York City's Board of Health, which was concerned with equine, as well as human health, removed them in 1910.[30]

Prices for feed affected the diet of horses. An 1859 stable manual noted that a carthorse could only eat 'as much as his owner could afford'. Even after the railroad network was created, a combination of an imperfect national transportation system and an imperfect market led to wild fluctuations in grain prices both seasonally, annually and by location. The extreme seasonality of urban economies also exacerbated the problem. Owners cut back the rations of urban animals in the winter, not just because animals worked less, but also because revenues declined significantly and food prices rose.[31]

Because of a combination of better management, improved transportation and more productive farming, hay and oats prices declined by half between 1867 and 1897. Since feeding was the highest daily expense of urban transportation firms, cheaper food undoubtedly played a major role in the extraordinary growth of urban cavalries. Lower prices meant that horses were better fed and perhaps not worked as hard. Rising prices for hay and oats after 1900, however, probably accelerated the decline of the horse in the face of growing competition from the electric streetcar, the automobile and the motor truck.[32]

A better understanding of nutrition, as well as the increase in the supply of food, also improved the quality of the urban horse. Most stable owners likely defined their interest in animals as did Robert Bakewell, the great eighteenth century British agricultural reformer, when he said that he 'sought to discover the animal which was the best machine for turning food into money'. Urban stable owners sought to find the least expensive, but still adequate feed for their 'machines'. The literature for horse breeders and owners paid constant attention to the science of nutrition then emerging in Europe.[33]

---

[30] I.S. Lyon, *Recollections of An Old Cartman* (New York, 1984, reprint of 1872 edition). A few ornamental trough/fountains remain. For water fountains, see ASPCA Archives, File 1; and Wells Fargo & Co. Express, *Rules and Instructions* (San Francisco, 1914), leaflet at the Wells-Fargo archives, San Francisco.

[31] J. Stewart, *The Stable Book* (New York, 1859), 225; N. Rector, 'Where the Draft Horse Excels and Pays', 134–50; *Annual Report of the State Board of Agriculture of Ohio* (1891), 152; J.H.S. Johnstone, *The Horse Book: A Practical Treatise on the American Horse Breeding Industry as Allied to the Farm* (Chicago, 1908), 56; and *Street Railway Journal* II (May, 1888), 245.

[32] J.H.S. Johnstone, *The Horse Book: A Practical Treatise on the American Horse Breeding Industry as Allied to the Farm* (Chicago, 1908), 56.

[33] As quoted in Rowland Ernie, *English Farming: Past and Present* (London, 1936 edn), 185. John H. Klippert, Secretary of the State Board of Agriculture of Ohio, translated and printed the leading works of German and French scholarship in its widely circulated *Annual Report* and made numerous research

Stable owners often followed changes in scientific knowledge about horse food requirements. Nutritional science had its roots in Lavoisier's discovery of the chemical basis for respiration and metabolism in the 1770s. In 1842 Joseph Liebig's widely read *Animal Chemistry* laid the groundwork for scientific nutritional studies by discovering (or publicizing) the existence of carbohydrates, nitrogen and protein as basic foodstuffs. European agricultural reformers (and the owners of large urban stables, including omnibus companies in both London and Paris) conducted controlled experiments (for Paris, 20,000 of them!) in food equivalencies. Their object was not just to define optimum nutritional requirements, but also to find the cheapest food that would satisfy draft animals ('least cost rations'). Horse owners sought to substitute other commodities such as corn for relatively expensive oats and to chop their grain and mix it with warm water.[34]

Long-term benefits flowed from nutritional experimentation. By 1908, nutritionists had worked out precise, money-saving diets based on horse size, weather and workload. Increasingly, urban horses lived in larger herds whose owners had the capital resources to follow an appropriate nutritional regime and to avoid winter feeding crises. The decline in seasonal variations in the economy helped this process, since fewer owners faced a slack season, with the temptation to skimp on feed. They also knew that some animals, frequently called 'easy keepers', were better (i.e. less costly) feeders, with Percherons being especially valued for that reason.[35]

---

trips to England and the continent. Accounts of European research also appeared in official (or quasi-official) agricultural reports of New York and Massachusetts, two states that were among the leading users of urban draft animals, and in veterinary and street railway periodicals. See J.H. Klippert, 'Report of an Agricultural Tour in Europe', in State Board of Agriculture of Ohio, *Annual Report* 1867, 173–367.

[34] J.K. Loosli, 'History of the Development of Animal Nutrition', in P.A. Putnam, ed., *Handbook of Animal Science* (New York, 1991), 32; W. Coleman *Biology in the Nineteenth Century: Problems of Form, Function and Transformation* (New York, 1971), 131. When wheat prices fell it was often substituted for oats. See, for example, 'Grain Feeding of Young Horses vs. Starving as a Means of Toughening', and G.E. Morrow, 'Economical Feeding', in Ohio State Agricultural Board, *Annual Report*, (1891), 151–4 and (1894), 567.

[35] *National Livestock Journal* XI (12–80), 'Feeding Animals-Horses,' 508–10; *Annual Report of the State Board of Agriculture of Ohio* 1863; J. Stonehenge, 'Theory and Practice of Feeding', 182–96; R.L. Jones, 'The Horse and Mule Industry in Ohio to 1865' *Mississippi Valley Historical Review*, 1933, 65–8; 'Stables and Care of Horses,' *American Veterinary Review*; R. Kay, 'Railroad Horses: Their Selection, Management, Some of Their Diseases and Treatment', 207–13, 210; Bouchet, *Le Cheval A Paris*, 105–37; and, N.

Conclusions

This article has dealt primarily with the relationship between the urban hinterland and the city in terms of flows of hay as feed (or fuel) for horses. American cities during the nineteenth century and well into the twentieth were closely dependent on the horse for a variety of services and functions. This dependence resulted in the evolution of a critical relationship between the urban hinterland and the city itself, involving food for urban horses, such as hay, oats and corn, as well as the provision of a supply of city workhorses. For much of the century this link also included the collection and application of manure from urban horses to land in close in hinterland farms.

Feed was the highest item in a stable's budget and at mid-century often amounted to more than half of expenses, although prices declined later in the century. Reducing feeding costs for horses depended on farm productivity and on the economics of packing and transporting hay and oats over distances. Critical production innovations included improvements in agricultural technologies such as raking, mowing and reaping grasses while the hay press dramatically increased the efficiency of baling and lowered transport costs. When the railroad network penetrated new agricultural areas in the Midwest, farmers increased their hay production, aiming at urban markets. Hay increasingly ceased to be a commodity grown locally and became an element in interstate commerce.

Just as with other commodities, these production increases and entrance into long distance transport caused major market changes. A more formal and organized market evolved to replace the informal ones that had existed for much of the nineteenth century. This market featured the development of grading standards, the formulation of more uniform methods of buying and selling the product, the gathering of statistics and a national trade association. By the turn of the twentieth century the production, transportation, and marketing of hay for horses had become much more systematic, although still characterized, as were markets for other agricultural commodities, by numerous inefficiencies.

Beginning in the 1890s, but accelerating during the first quarter of the twentieth century, changes in urban transport – particularly the coming of the electric streetcar, the automobile and the motor truck – altered many aspects of this relationship. Dissatisfaction with the nuisances produced by horse manure, urine, and dead horses also helped drive the

Papayanis, *The Coachmen of Twentieth Century Paris: Service Workers and Class Consciousness* (Baton Rouge, 1993), 2. Proper feeding practices required avoidance of specific diseases. Colic was the leading and frequently fatal symptom of a number of illnesses.

transition. The growing acceptance by public health officials of the bacterial theory of disease and the identification of flies, which bred in manure heaps, as prime carriers of various acute diseases also added a medical factor to the drive to replace the horse.[36] Horses began to disappear from city streets and the need for horse feed was sharply reduced. By 1920, the total number of urban horses had dropped to 1.7 million from about 3 million in 1910; by 1930, the number had shrunk to under a million. Increasingly, land formerly devoted to growing feed for horses was shifted to other crops or even urbanized. One agricultural researcher estimated that in 1910 16 million out of 325 million acres of harvested cropland were devoted to producing feed for urban horses – now this total was greatly reduced. Some of this freed-up land was located in the contiguous urban hinterland, while the remainder was in more distant growing areas.[39]

Thus, on the demand side, the changing character of urban transportation and its fuel needs after about 1890 drove major changes in the crops grown in the urban hinterland and in more distant production areas. City and hinterland relationships remained intimate and intertwined, but increasingly in the twentieth century horses had become less and less important in the equation.

[36] H. Bolce, 'The Horse vs. Health', *The Review of Reviews*, 47, May, 1908, 623–4. The flow of manure from the city into the countryside also came close to an end, although its use had been affected earlier by the availability of artificial fertilizers.

Acknowledgements
We are grateful to David R. Meyer, Ronald Dale Karr, James Corbett, Jr., and James J. Corbett, D.V.M., for reading and commenting on the paper. John E. Baylor and Paul S. Fischbeck provided helpful information about issues relating to hay and oats.

CHAPTER FOUR

'Returning to Nature': Vacation and Life Style in the Montréal Region[1]

Michèle Dagenais

At the heart of the debate surrounding the development of cities in the nineteenth and twentieth centuries lies the resource and fundamental dimension of the urban environment, open space, its definitions and its uses. The pressures accompanying the advent of the industrialized city and the increasing urbanization of society gave rise to a large-scale reconsideration of the question of the organization of the urban landscape. These pressures were also at the heart of the tendency of members of the urban elite to distance themselves from the city centre and move towards the outskirts.[2] Inspired by the desire to get closer to nature, this relocation on the part of elite groups disrupted the periphery surrounding the city and significantly transformed it. The definition of space on the fringes of the urban milieu, along with what constitutes nature and what use to put it to, would become major issues that would bring 'colonizing' elites into conflict with the largely rural populations that were already in situ.

The desire to return to nature arose primarily within the framework of holiday and leisure activities that were expanding rapidly during the second half of the nineteenth century. But rather than merely changing their surroundings, the upper classes who had embraced the idea of the holiday sought to transform the locations they now coveted. Thus, when they moved from the city, these groups brought with them ideas about nature and the environment that they wished to transport to their newly

---

[1] This article has been translated by Yvonne M. Klein. It is part of a larger regional history project entitled 'Montréal, ville-région d'Amérique'. I should like to thank Harold Bérubé who first examined the local history monographs for the Montréal region that have been an essential source for the information contained in this text. I should also like to thank Geneviève Massard-Guilbaud for her rigorous and stimulating reading of the first draft of this paper and for her comments that have guided me in its revision.

[2] K.T. Jackson, *Crabgrass frontier. The suburbanization of the United States* (New York, Oxford University Press 1985), 18–19.

chosen surroundings.[3] The encounter between the urban elite and local residents who were already there occurred as a colonization of the outskirts by the town and gave rise to numerous tensions. At the centre of these debates were questions concerning the definition of nature, the reshaping of the landscape, and the utilization of natural settings for various purposes, which were sometimes connected to leisure and recreational pursuits, sometimes to economic activities related to making a living, notably, in this instance, farming. In the end, this dynamic would transform outlying areas of North American cities, originally almost exclusively given over to agriculture, into giant suburbs.

This essay will endeavour to analyse this process as it relates to the Montréal archipelago, an area favourable to the development of summer cottage communities as it comprises numerous waterfront properties, particularly prized by those in search of holiday homes. Stress will be placed on the role played by the middle classes and their life styles in the transformation of the urban environment, understood in this case as the environment in close proximity to the city. We shall analyse how their conception of this environment and what they did to reshape its landscape and localities would lead to the urbanization of the Montréal periphery. Confident that they could adapt their surroundings to suit their requirements and proud of their ability to manage this change, the middle classes set to work to develop these spaces. We shall examine the procedures they adopted to transform visions into reality, the strategies they employed, and the mechanisms they used.

In the course of time, summer visitors decided to move permanently to their new environment, a choice that was facilitated by the development of communications and transportation between the city and the outlying areas. What then were the models that were developed? To what ideal visions were they responding? What sort of life style were they seeking to espouse? There is also the question of uncovering tensions generated by outsiders moving in and the conflicts that arose with local populations. This colonization did not take place without difficulty. In moving to the countryside, the urban middle classes had to come to terms with the population that already lived there. If, for country people, the arrival of city-dwellers might at times prove a source of profit, more often it gave rise to changes in their environments and way of life that threatened their very survival. The various relationships between these groups and the manner in which they evolved reveal what

---

[3] J.A. Crets, 'The land of a million smiles: Urban tourism and the commodification of the Missouri Ozarks, 1900–1940', in A. Hurley, dir. *Common Fields. An Environmental History of St.Louis* (St. Louis, Missouri Historical Society Press, 1997), 176–98.

processes were at work and what upheavals resulted from this urban colonization of the outlying regions. After a brief sketch of the Montréal natural environment, we shall turn to a discussion of overall progress of the holiday movement in the region from the middle of the nineteenth century until the 1930s. We shall then examine in greater detail the development of three localities that illustrate different aspects of this phenomenon – the criteria operating in the choice of vacation areas, transformations imposed on sites as vacationers moved in, the most prominent models of urbanization and life style, and finally, resulting confrontations with local populations.

The Montréal Archipelago

It is customary, when speaking of the history of a city, to remark upon the positive effects of its site in the development of its resources, communications, and trade. It is all the more commonplace since cities are usually located as a consequence of quality of site. Montréal is no exception to the rule and no study that has appeared in the past century has missed the opportunity to celebrate the qualities and attractiveness of its situation, which are outstanding.[4] Montréal sits on a archipelago formed of a number of islands, the largest of which are the islands of Montréal and Jésus and is surrounded by the Saint Lawrence River, Lac Saint-Louis, Lac des Deux-Montagnes, Rivière des Prairies.[5]

Central to the history of Montréal, water has played a determining role in its ascent as a Canadian metropolis. Thanks to its situation at the Lachine rapids, Montréal rapidly became the linchpin of international trade between Canada, parts of the United States, and the United Kingdom, and one of the great North American ports. The power

---

[4] This is especially true until the 1950s, a decade that marked a turning point in its history. After that, those natural qualities which had been a matter of congratulation for Montréal in the past no longer appeared to be so markedly in its favour. This period also saw the beginning of the removal of economic activities into the surrounding suburbs, a shift that would become more marked in the following decade. Thus, in view of this sprawl, natural assets, especially those involving bodies of water, tended to be seen as an obstacle to the free flow of traffic among the various constituents of the Montréal archipelago. It is only with increased awareness in very recent decades that regional developers, disturbed at the damage inflicted on the area, have once again become interested in the natural environment of the city and its suburbs. H. Bérubé, *Les différents visages de Montréal*, (Montréal, INRS-Urbanisation, Culture et Société 2002), 93.

[5] G. Sénécal et al., *Le portrait environnemental de l'île de Montréal* (Montréal, INRS-Urbanisation, 2000), 19p.

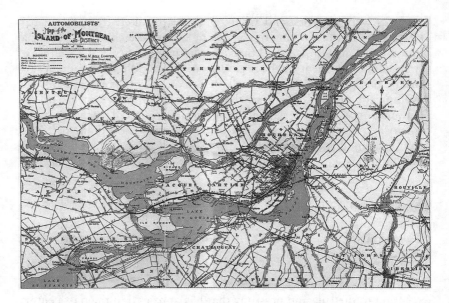

**Figure 4.1   Main railways and roads networks in the region of
Montréal in the 1920s**

generated by the Lachine rapids would in turn be channeled and utilized
in the industrial era, making Montréal one of the great centres of
production in North America.

If all these environmental advantages that Montréal enjoys have been
regularly portrayed in many studies of the city,[6] the connection between
these features and leisure activities they have permitted since the
nineteenth century has been much more rarely established.[7] It was only
in the 1960s and 70s, when holidays became a mass activity, that its
impact began to arouse systematic interest and analysis. By this period,
however, the structured holiday was already a hundred years old and for
many years the wealthy and powerful of Montréal had been flocking to
the numerous riversides and hills of the Montérégie, to the south and
west of the city.

---

[6] Bérubé, 'Les différents visages'.

[7] A notable exception is M. Samson, *La résidence secondaire et la région
métropolitaine de Montréal* (Université de Droit, d'Économie et des Sciences
d'Aix-Marseille PhD thesis, 1988).

The Colonization of the Shores

The rapid urbanization of Montréal around the middle of the nineteenth century is to a large degree responsible for the desire on the part of the urban elite to move towards the fringes of the island and even beyond. On the one hand, the increasing density of the Montréal urban fabric at a time when the local authorities were still almost powerless to control the problems of lack of hygiene and sanitation, ill health, and other threats to welfare occasioned by the rapid increase in the population pushed the upper classes here, as elsewhere, to flee from the ugliness of the city and to move into a rural setting. The crushing heat of the Montréal summer made it even harder to put up with the terrible odours rising from horse-droppings and household garbage and the inconvenience of roads that were alternatively muddy and dusty. Furthermore, the desire for social exclusiveness and an ability to choose one's own neighbours, not to mention increasing enthusiasm on the part of the upper middle-classes for sport and leisure, also contributed to the creation of separate spheres of places of day-to-day activity and places of leisure.[8] In this context, the movement away from the city centre took on an elite patina, since up until this point, the outlying areas had been largely reserved for those too poor to afford a place to live inside the city limits.

With the development of suburban railway lines, the settlement of the outlying areas of Montréal by summer residents rapidly developed.[9] From the 1880s onward, suburban train lines, in part following the routes of the freight lines developed several decades earlier, ran along the shores of the island of Montréal and linked it to Île Jésus and to the mainland at various points. In this initial phase, the development of summer homes in the Montréal region followed models of social and ethnic segregation that were more or less parallel to those already woven into the Montréal city fabric, which was itself segmented.[10] Thus, to the west of the island, and especially in Pointe-Claire, were to be found members of the prosperous anglophone community, who had progressively moved in, at first as summer residents. On Île Jésus, francophone vacationers transformed

---

[8] J.M. Mayo, *The American country club. Its origins and development* (New Brunswick, Rutgers University Press, 1998). See also C.S. Aron, *Working at play. A history of vacations in the United States* (New York, Oxford University Press, 1999).

[9] D.B. Hanna, 'Les réseaux de transport et leur rôle dans l'étalement urbain de Montréal', in H. Capel and P-A. Linteau, eds., *Barcelona-Montréal. Desarrollo urbano comparado/ Développement urbain comparé* (Barcelona, Publicacions de la Universitad de Barcelona 1998), 117–32.

[10] C. McNicoll, *Montréal. Une société multiculturelle* (Paris, Belin, 1993).

themselves into suburbanites in a matter of a few years.[11] On the mainland itself, Boucherville, just across from Montréal, represented the acme of the holiday resort for the francophone elite:

> You board one of the steamers that travel between Montréal and Boucherville. . . . With waves to gently rock you, the breeze to caress you, and conversation to charm your ear, the splendid panorama of the banks of the Saint Lawrence unfolds before your delighted eyes. . . . We wend our way through the gracious maze that is the emerald islands of the Saint Lawrence, the precious jewels of this great river. . . . We greet as we pass . . . 'La Broquerie' . . . the superb edifice that houses M. Carmel. . . . With its lovely veranda, M. Jos Tarte's villa would satisfy all the dreams of any poet. . . . Here we are, at the end of our voyage, and we now set foot on the enchanted soil of Boucherville. . . .[12]

Not far from Montréal, this time to the north, the lower Laurentian region was also rapidly invaded by summer visitors. In the area of Terrebonne Heights, the land 'is studded with little English and Jewish cottages', while further west, the summer homes of francophones lined the banks of the Mille-Iles river.[13] We could provide endless examples of summer colonies organized according to ethnic and social origins.[14] By and large, however, the summer colony movement remained relatively exclusive and was primarily the province of wealthy Anglo-Protestant Montréalers.

This first wave of territorial expansion was followed by a second, in the 1920s, when a number of main roads and several bridges were being built around the island. The resulting multiplication of exits from the island permitted new automobile owners access to a variety of destinations and thus encouraged urban sprawl. This second stage was characterized by a diversification of the social origins of the vacationers. Expanded access to a countryside dominated by the architectural qualities of the cottage was expressed in the appearance of a different kind of construction that added more modest structures in the shape of cottages and summer camps to the lavish villas of the first phase.[15] In

[11] P. Dauphinais et al., *De la seigneurie à la banlieue: l'histoire de Laval-des-Rapides des origines à la fusion* (Montréal, 1984).

[12] G. Pépin, ed., *La belle époque de la villégiature à Boucherville* (Boucherville, Société d'histoire des Îles Percées, 1999), 36. All French quotes translated by the author.

[13] S. Laurin, *Histoire des Laurentides* (Québec, Institut québécois de recherche sur la culture, 1995), 353p.

[14] Samson, *La résidence secondaire*, 69–70.

[15] Marcel Samson provides a useful explanation of the relation between this type of second home and the 'bungalow', a word used to signify 'a small, lightly-built house erected in a natural surrounding for temporary stays'. The bungalow would become the dominant type of residential construction in the various suburbs that sprang up after 1945. Samson, *La résidence secondaire*, 74–5.

the Montréal area, numerous properties along the banks of various watercourses remained the terrain of choice for summer holiday-makers, who tended to cluster according to ethnic, though not social, origins. Of course, the development of the suburban tramway system that took place on the eve of the first world war permitted Montréalers of more modest circumstance a chance to get out to the periphery.[16] Confronted by this broadening of the social origins of the holiday population, a good many members of the elite upper classes moved ever further out into the countryside in order the better to achieve their aim of getting 'back to nature'.

Enchanted Sites, in Need of Some Improvement

The nature that all the vacationers were seeking could be found, first and foremost, along the various shores of the island of Montréal and the mainland surrounding it. Because of the natural attractions of Pointe-Claire, situated on the shores of Lac Saint-Louis, a group of wealthy Montréal businessmen began to build summer homes there at the beginning of the nineteenth century. The decisive movement into the area occurred around the middle of the century, when the Grand Trunk Railway company built a line in 1855, followed by a second line in 1887, constructed by Canadian Pacific. During this era, summer residents and vacationers who flooded in were Anglo-Protestant. They set about transforming a part of Pointe-Claire, then largely composed of French Catholic farmers, into a huge summer playground. In the beginning, the wealthier summer people acquired land along the shores of Lac Saint-Louis where they built themselves sumptuous dwellings. Others opted to rent farmhouses for the summer while farmers took the opportunity to make money by living out behind their homes for a few months.[17] Several excellent hotels were also built to accommodate summer visitors staying only briefly or for those awaiting the completion of their own homes. All these people chose Pointe-Claire for much the same reasons – to pursue yachting, golf, and horseback riding.

Private clubs and associations were rapidly formed to organize all these leisure activities. Because joining these clubs and associations, which required the purchase of shares or the payment of dues, demanded a certain level of affluence, it was easy to restrict them to

---

[16] Hanna, 'Les réseaux de transport', 120–23.

[17] In other areas, summer residents might also 'rent a farmer's house who would then live in his barn for the summer season'. (R. Viau, *Le tourisme dans les Laurentides* Université de Montréal Master's thesis, 1957, 26, cited in Samson, 65).

members of those classes that had both the money and the time to take advantage of the activities they offered. These organizations also played a role in the spread of cultural activities like theatre, the cinema, and, through the establishment of bookstores and libraries, of reading. To the colonization of the land itself through the development parks, marinas, or sports grounds must be added a kind of cultural and social colonization through which urban activities were disseminated, although these were not, in the beginning, available to the original inhabitants and farmers of the area.

Carved out from the same area – the old parish of Saint-Martin – the second locality under study is the municipality of Laval-des-Rapides, which a group of summer colonizers created in 1912. This group had had access to the area since 1876, when a wooden bridge connecting Île Jésus with the island of Montréal was built with the aim of extending one of the regional railway lines towards the north.[18] At that time, 'the landscape was dominated by the concession and the shape of the rural settlement that it established. In truth, these concessions all ran perpendicular to the river and the farmers' houses were all built at one end of the site, on the riverbank.'[19] Very quickly, lots along the river were separated from the fields to be sold off to wealthy Montréalers who seized this chance to set themselves up on extensive properties. There they built second homes, originally intended as summer residences. Then, in 1887, the construction of a new and sturdier metal bridge allowed for a regular rail service between Montréal and Île Jésus. This safer and more reliable transport encouraged more and more vacationers to settle beside the Rivière des Prairies and eventually to transform their summer homes into year-round residences. Thus we may observe an influx of city-dwellers from a broader social base.[20] If land generally in this area was acquired by individuals, sometimes small businessmen bought property, divided it into lots, and then sold the lots, not bothering to improve access roads unless they were also building houses.[21] At Laval-des-Rapides, the changeover from a vacation landscape to suburbia took place more quickly than in Pointe-Claire, probably because of its greater proximity to Montréal.

[18] Dauphinais, *De la seigneurie à la banlieue.*
[19] Ibid., 32.
[20] The authors mention the arrival of skilled workers, tradesmen, and 'professionals' [sic] without, however, providing details about the social origins of the summer residents. (Ibid., 37).
[21] This type of development was most common in the period preceding the second world war. Numerous instances are noted in *La Belle époque de la villégiature à Boucherville*, 33ff and in S. Plante, *Ville de deux-Montagnes, 1804–1994* (Deux-Montagnes, Ville de deux-Montagnes 1993) 40ff.

'To establish a beautiful town' while radically transforming its setting and completely changing its structure – here in brief are encapsulated the objectives of the founders of the third locality under study, the town of Laval-sur-le-Lac, objectives that were in every way analogous to those of the promoters of the neighbouring area of Laval-des-Rapides. At the beginning of this town are found a couple of land developers who were 'seduced by the beauty of this enchanted site', who proposed to acquire all the land and properties at the tip of Île Jésus, a magnificent site 'bounded on three sides by the Rivière des Mille-Iles, Lac des Deux-Montagnes and Rivière des Prairies'. Delighted to discover so picturesque a site on the point, the summer home developers immediately turned to the government to obtain permission to create a municipality, as was the case with Laval-des-Rapides, to be carved from the same rural parish lands. Laval-sur-le-Lac was born in 1915, only a few years after its site was 'discovered'. Once the promoters had acquired the land from farmers, they re-sold it to a group of small businessmen who founded the 'Compagnie des terrains de Laval' and proceeded to develop it. This company utterly transformed a site where there 'once had been a few half-cleared acres . . . and . . . now we have caused a charming city to spring up'.[22]

Civilizing Selected Settings

If the procedures for securing desired transformations were not the same in the three localities, the patterns we can discern nevertheless have very strong similarities. Sometimes quickly, sometimes more gradually, the summer colonists established themselves in the outskirts of Montréal and set to work to urbanize their new surroundings. These generally lacked the public services that were available in urban centres during the same period. This alteration of the environment was managed by various groups of holiday cottage owners, who now organized themselves into residents' associations. In Laval-des-Rapides, the new inhabitants proposed to form an association in order to bring about the incorporation of the areas into a municipality.[23] This was in order to obtain the same services as in an urban setting, services they

---

[22] Es.-L. Patenaude, *Laval-sur-le-Lac* (Montréal, 1967), 14.
[23] 'Every Sunday after mass in the chapel of the Moulin du Crochet, Napoléon Rochon, insurance broker and ardent promoter of this innovation, invited his friends round to his porch. This group discussed plans for local autonomy . . . their immediate aim being to supply the proposed modern municipality with "macadamized" roads, and water, lighting, and sewer systems' (Dauphinais et al., *De la seigneurie à la banlieue*, 42).

deemed essential – running water, a sewerage system, lighting, and paved roads.

This was also true of the Valois Citizen Association, named for the section of Pointe-Claire in which its members lived. This group worked to develop infrastructure and services that the new residents felt they needed – highways, water mains, sewers, and the like. Much the same can be said of the members of a golf club who formed themselves into the Pointe-Claire Lighting Company in order to arrange lighting for the area abutting on to the golf course before the municipality finally took the service over.

In Pointe-Claire, a different initiative was undertaken by the Canadian Nursery Company, Ltd. Founded in 1904, this group bought up agricultural land, sub-divided it, and built houses on it that they sold as part of a regulated model housing estate. Conceived by the highly-regarded landscape architect, Frederick Todd,[24] who was closely allied to the City Beautiful movement, the scheme developed rapidly into a series of homes inspired specifically by the English Garden City movement, although only some of its principles were retained. Thus, the Pointe-Claire developers were not motivated by the ideals of justice or social equality that were part of the urban projects of Ebenezer Howard, but rather by the desire to create a setting in which the advantages of both town and country might be found.[25] Each house was individually designed, incorporating standards of modern convenience while retaining contact with nature. This link to a nature that was in large part constructed sought to satisfy the need to commune with an authentic universe, at least in ways accessible in the urban, modern world of the early twentieth century. At the same time, there was the aim of achieving the creation of an exclusive and protected community, developed within an environment that preserved some aspects of untamed, yet benign nature: 'the best of country living with the convenience of modern technology'.[26]

---

[24] This architect trained with the Olmsted brothers in Massachusetts. For the role played by Frederick Todd in Canadian urban development and the influence of the City Beautiful Movement, see Walter Van Nuss, 'The Fate of City Beautiful Thought in Canada, 1893–1930', in Gilbert A. Stelter and Alan F.J. Artibise, eds, *The Canadian City, Essays in Urban and Social History* (Ottawa: Carleton University Press, 1984), 167–86.

[25] On city gardens: Helen Meller, *Towns, Plans, and Society in Modern Britain* (Cambridge, Cambridge University Press, 1997), 35–8; for specific application in Montréal, Paul-André Linteau, *Histoire de Montréal depuis la Confédération* (Montréal, Boréal, 1992), 366–8.

[26] B.R. Matthews, *A History of Pointe-Claire* (Pointe-Claire, Brianor Ltd., 1985), 136.

In addition to its efforts to promote an authentic character to the estate, the Canadian Nursery Company, Ltd. encouraged a milieu dominated by greenery, imparting to the new residential area an atmosphere that epitomized recreation and leisure. The houses were set in a circle surrounding a park, reminiscent in some ways of eighteenth century Clapham, in London. If each residence was a private home, it was no less a part of the aesthetic continuity of the whole housing estate, which gave it the attraction of a large park dotted with houses.[27] Being so close to the park provided easy access to a variety of sports like lawn bowls and tennis. This space was reserved for the exclusive use of the residents of the estate, which was, incidentally, known as the 'Bowling Green'. A specific association was formed to oversee the preservation of the original (pristine) character of the place and further to establish a club that was responsible for organizing social activities for residents. Although this development was conceived and designed by a privileged group of urban Montréalers, its much sought-after leisured quality helped mark it out as distinct from the urban setting. It underlined the selective, elite appearance of the estate at a time when engaging in leisure activities constituted a distinctive mark of upper middle-class status[28] and was still the privilege of the affluent.

In Laval-sur-le-Lac, there was the same close link between residential development and the provision of recreational opportunities. The 'Compagnie des Terrains de Laval' set about improving the area so that where 'There had been neither paved road nor water main, nor even a rural postal service . . . now a modern town had been brought into being, with its boulevard and streets, its water mains, its electric light, its post office, its train stations and every means of communication', as one of the proud city fathers observed on the occasion of its fiftieth anniversary.[29] For their part, the new residents were to 'erect attractive homes, plant ornamental trees and establish flower gardens. . . .'

Once the town was founded, a plan was set on foot to develop recreational facilities, and particularly a golf course, conceived as the jewel in the city's crown. The project was directed by a club formed expressly for that purpose, which it was possible to join by buying shares that cost $100 each, an amount that represented the equivalent of one-fifth of the annual salary of an office clerk. What made this development appear all the more exclusive was that a recreational

---

[27] As Robert Fishman explains in his book: 'Each property is private, but each contributes to the total landscape of *houses in a park*', *Bourgeois Utopias: The Rise and Fall of Suburbia* (New York: Basic Books, 1987), 55.

[28] Crets, 'The land of a million smiles', 190–91.

[29] Patenaude, *Laval-sur-le-Lac*, 21–2.

opportunity was not provided for the whole population of Laval-sur-le-Lac but only to those who had joined the club. As soon as it was founded, the Laval-sur-le-Lac Club rented lands in the vicinity of the development company that owned the entire area with the intention of constructing a golf course and clubhouse. A titanic effort was required in order to accomplish the labour of transforming the land, commensurate with the scale of the task of cultivation to which the promoters of the project committed themselves. As the commemorative booklet issued for the municipality's fiftieth birthday observed, these men 'transformed a "miserable patch of land"' into one of the most beautiful golf courses in the province, if not the country:

> We found swamps and bogs which had to be got rid of and which we had to replace with ponds and little lakes. . . . We also took advantage of the opportunity to erect a beautiful cedar hedge. . . . While we were ploughing to get rid of the stones, we worked the earth deeply so as to make it fit for a golf course. We bought and had brought in thousands of loads of earth, sand, and manure. . . . As the work proceeded, we came across a large number of trees, the best of which we preserved. . . .[30]

Different Relationships to the Environment: a Source of Conflict

With the arrival of city people, two categories of residents appeared who were relatively impervious to each other and who conceived of the environment and their situation within it in very different ways. Thus, in Pointe-Claire, the Anglo-Protestant urban elite developed without making any real contact with the Franco-Catholic population who were less well-off. For the former group, Pointe-Claire represented a playground and a setting for an idealized life, one that could be improved according to taste. For the others, the area had never been anything other than the place they lived and worked. Perhaps because of the social distance between the two communities, a function of the barriers of language and religion, there is no record of major conflict.[31] This absence of conflict might also be explained by the fact that the farmers got something out of the presence of the newcomers, even if they did not share their ideas about local development. We have already seen that certain farmers profited from the holiday-makers who were in

---

[30] Ibid., 38–9.

[31] Or so it would appear from the monograph by B. Matthews, *A History of Pointe-Claire*. A more extensive search of municipal archives, for example, might reveal the existence of tensions among the various groups of inhabitants of this locality.

Pointe-Claire for the summer by renting them their houses. Presumably, the summer people also bought local farm produce. Despite these advantages, the examples that follow suggest that the summer people or suburbanites and the farmers more often than not ran into difficulty when attempting to 'share' the neighbourhood.[32]

In Laval-des-Rapides, the division between the two groups was openly expressed. From the moment that local farmers heard about the plan of elite migrants from the city to establish a municipality, they went into action. Fearing that the project, if realized, would lead to an accompanying development of public services that would bring about a rise in taxes, local farmers,[33] through the intervention of the Saint-Martin Parish Council, approached the provincial government to express their opposition to the development. The government, however, decided to support the project by creating the new municipality, and in 1912, the area that the 'additions', as the locals called the newcomers, shared with the farmers was incorporated under the name Laval-des-Rapides.

Dispersed as they were among several electoral constituencies, the farmers were able to take control of city hall in the first elections, while newly arrived city people, who were concentrated in two districts along the river, had fewer seats on the municipal council. From this point onwards, politics in Laval-des-Rapides was dominated by confrontations between the farmers and 'newcomers'. In order to assert their point of view, the newcomers formed a Citizens' Committee in the mid-1920s[34] that undertook to oversee the city council and propose various reforms. Every initiative on the part of the city council automatically became subject to debate between the two interest groups, from rates of taxation on agricultural land to divergent proposals for the development of the region. One of these disputes precisely illustrates problems that arose out of the differing interests of the newcomers and the farmers.

The decision of the new city council to authorize the establishment of fox farms within municipal boundaries in order to provide a second source of income for farmers would be the centre of dispute for a number of years. These farms, which raised and butchered foxes for their pelts, emitted foul odours emanating from decay and urine which '. . . annoyed the commuters all the more since they, working in Montréal as they did, lived in Laval-des-Rapides in order to enjoy the

---

[32] In the absence of specific studies of this subject, closer investigation of the situation of farmers in the Montréal region during the first decades of the twentieth century should be undertaken.

[33] On this issue, see T. Loo, 'Making a modern wilderness: Conserving wildlife in twentieth-century Canada', *Canadian Historical Review*, 82, 1, March 2001, 99–102.

[34] Dauphinais et al., *De la seigneurie à la banlieue*, 71–72.

pure air and the natural surroundings'.[35] The newcomers deplored this nuisance and exerted pressure throughout the decade to obtain the closure of these enterprises, which provided local inhabitants with their first paid employment outside the family farm. The Great Depression finally got the better of the fox farmers, but interminable political conflicts arising from confrontations between the two groups concerned clearly illustrate how their respective interests resonated on local life.

Moreover, in Laval-sur-le-Lac, the gulf separating country people from new arrivals from the city was deepened by the different purposes to which the two groups devoted their property, and the perceptions each side had of the other. In struggling to protect their property and way of life, the farmers were also committed to promoting an environment based on the exploitation of local resources. For their part, middle-class city people considered the farmers' life style to be an anachronism and were therefore convinced of the need to transform the countryside. Assured of the correctness both of their perceptions and their aims, they considered their proposals to develop an enchanting version of 'nature' to be legitimate, since it had till now rested in the hands of a population unequipped to appreciate the richness of the natural scene and to take advantage of it as they rightly ought. This perception, expressed by a resident of the new estate in Laval-sur-le-Lac, stands as an eloquent testimony to this point of view:

> Round about 1910, the tip of Île Jésus was hardly settled at all. There was barely anything connecting the tip of the island to Montréal save the original road and the old bridge. . . . The children went to a little school until they were about twelve to learn a smattering of reading, writing, and arithmetic. People's lives were simple and humble. They were living in an enchanted land without being altogether aware of it, and who could imagine that within the space of a single generation, a beautiful town and a splendid golf course could be built there.[36]

These remarks reveal the state of mind of developers who were ready to redesign the countryside from top to bottom and take active pride in it. Here, as before, we can identify the perception they had of their undertaking as intended not merely to adorn and improve the landscape, but also to 'civilize' it. This description expresses clearly the distance separating city from country dwellers, a distance that the newcomers had no intention of bridging. Indeed, precisely the opposite was the case as they settled on the outskirts of the town. In this context, the development of a new suburban setting corresponds to the

---

[35] Ibid., 74.
[36] Patenaude, *Laval-sur-le-Lac*, 14.

establishment of a separate territory, cut off from the rest of the area and isolated from the local population. The following description of the work undertaken to mark out a golf course could just as well be applied to the residential development as a whole: 'We wanted to feel completely at home as soon as possible. We fenced in our property and planted 3000 poplars around it. At the same time, we were protecting ourselves from the smoke coming from the railway and from the weed seeds that the wind might blow onto our side of the barrier.'[37] This interference with the natural environment indicates moreover a contemporary state of mind, optimistically ready to shape and rearrange various elements in accordance with immediate requirements. Nature is thus seen as something to be modeled and perfected. At the same time, the ability to transform, shape, and domesticate nature was celebrated.[38]

The Great Depression would undermine such optimism and significantly slow down suburban development. As the primary reason for these first garden city schemes was not so much profit as to appropriate desirable sites on which select, protected environments could be made to blossom, a number of these projects, especially that in Pointe-Claire, were not able to survive the Depression. When the movement to build in the outlying districts resurfaced after the second world war, in a period of economic prosperity, it unfolded on a broader scale and in areas further removed from Montréal. Moreover, studies of Pointe-Claire and Laval-des-Rapides reveal that both of these municipalities participated in this period of massive suburbanization, now orchestrated by property developers.[39] It was the same for localities located in proximity to Montréal, each of which came to be transformed.[40] The landscape of the Montréal area was profoundly altered once again, this time to be changed into a vast and increasingly uniform suburb. A new spate of highway improvement, starting in the late 1950s and continuing until the 1970s, aided this metamorphosis. The construction of freeways around Montréal stimulated a wholesale and anarchic development of land both in and beyond the original area of development within an ever-widening radius.[41]

---

[37] Ibid., 39-40.

[38] Patricia Jasen has studied this process whereby tourist development provoked the domestication of nature: *Wild things: Nature, culture and tourism in Ontario, 1790–1914* (Toronto, University of Toronto Press 1995).

[39] For a consideration of the environmental dimensions of this phenomenon, see A.W. Rome, 'Building on the land. Toward an environmental history of residential development in American cities and suburbs, 1870–1990', *Journal of Urban History*, 20, 3, May 1994, 415 ff.

[40] Samson, *La résidence secondaire*, chapter 3.

[41] 'The link between commuters and summer people, observed in the age of the railway, repeats itself. The freeway emerges as an incomparable tool toward

Conclusion

A review of the upheavals and reorganizations occasioned by the suburbanization of the Montréal region provides an excellent illustration of the importance of open space as a resource in the urban environment. It also attests to the existence of a connection to nature itself, in this period influenced by the advent of a society that was predominantly urban. This context, closely related to a need to return to nature, is also characterized by important advances in the realm of technology that confirmed urban elites in their ability to shape and dominate the environment.

Thus the motives that nourished this need on the part of the upper classes to return to nature cannot simply be explained by a desire to commune with nature itself. The whole movement towards such a return proceeded as much if not more from an instrumental vision of nature, exploited in order to realize projects that were developed in response to specific social and cultural aspirations. Nature appeared to be the means through which a new framework and idealized setting might take shape at the fringe of the city. To succeed in their ambitions, the privileged classes had to conquer and appropriate spaces that were already occupied by a rural population. The improvements they accomplished and the models on which they were based would contribute to the redefinition of those spaces according to a set of characteristics essentially opposite to those prevailing in an urban milieu. The suburb that emerged was composed of airy and spacious areas, in contrast to the congested city. It represented a way of life that was private and intimate as opposed to the 'promiscuity' within which urban life unfolded. It was characterized by the social uniformity of its inhabitants, unlike the mixture of populations typical of an urban setting. The suburb made healthy sports and leisure activities possible, in contrast to supposedly unhealthy pursuits in towns. It is this model of suburban life, forged in large part out of the habits and hopes of holiday-makers at the end of the nineteenth century and in the first decades of the succeeding century, that would be the source of the representation of the 'ideal' suburb and that would influence the process of suburbanization, especially in North America and Great Britain. Even if it has not yet found full expression in the various types of suburbs now in existence, this model of the leafy suburb nevertheless continues to make its presence felt, and particularly in aesthetically attractive areas.

---

the development of the suburb and of the summer colony. . . . In short, everything that the railway and the suburban tram had previously done, the freeway magnified', Hanna, 'Les réseaux de transport', 126.

Thus the connection to nature and to the environment is revealed as fundamentally cultural and proceeds through a range of negotiations. It exists, is worked out, and is expressed through considerations that relate to the representations of a specific environment, the values that attach to it, and the formulation of specific requirements and projects. In the final analysis very few of these elements can be said to be integrally related to an actual 'nature', even though such a connection would seem to be central to their formulation.

CHAPTER FIVE

Citizens in Pursuit of Nature: Gardens, Allotments and Private Space in European Cities, 1850–2000

Helen Meller

The history of urban planning in European cities in the modern period has always been written from the 'top down'.[1] Planning means control over space and the built environment. From the mid-nineteenth century onwards, as the management of cities became an ever-greater issue for local and central governments, for public health officials, for architects and planners committed to preventing unplanned urban sprawl, control over urban space has become a matter of political significance. Exerting any kind of control over space in the public interest was, and is, extremely difficult. It has to be exerted against the two strongest forces in the urban arena: the rights of private property and dynamic change produced by market forces. On the side of those wishing to establish control, the strongest tools for the job have been the growing body of legislation relating to public health and the needs of modern transportation and communication.[2] Over the past 150 years, the majority of every European nation, one after another, has become urbanized.[3] The scale of the challenge for city authorities and the results

---

[1] There are a great many volumes on the history of planning which illustrate this. I will confine myself to two on European cities: K. Bosma, and H. Hellinga, eds. *Mastering the City: North European city planning 1900–2000 Vols I and II* (Rotterdam/The Hague, 1997); E. Blau and M. Platzer, eds, *Shaping the Great City: Modern Architecture in Central Europe 1890–1937* (Munich/London/New York, 1999).

[2] A. Sutcliffe, *Towards the Planned City: Germany, Britain, the United States and France, 1780–1914* (Oxford, 1981); J. Reulecke, *Geschichte der Urbanisierung in Deutschland*, (Frankfurt am Main, 1985); C. Topalov, ed., *Laboratoires du nouveau siècle: la nébuleuse réformatrice et ses réseaux en France 1880–1914* (Paris, 1999).

[3] A.F. Weber, *The Growth of Cities in the Nineteenth Century* (Ithaca, New York, 1899; reprinted 1963); P.M. Hohenburg, and L. Hollen Lees, *The Making of Urban Europe, 1000–1950* (Cambridge, Mass., 1985).

of their actions for the health and well-being of future generations has very properly been the subject of historical study. What has received less attention has been the way newly urbanizing populations themselves have made use of space in the city. The very processes of expanding city boundaries and changing the way land is used in city centres, have created opportunities for citizens to exert considerable influence from 'the bottom up'.

This chapter is concerned with their efforts to bring nature into the city. It is not about planned urban space but the ways in which people have used and adapted space in cities for their own purposes. It has three interconnecting themes, related to widespread social and cultural changes that have deeply influenced generations of urban dwellers in every European country. The first is concerned with poverty and survival – especially in terms of food – problems that greatly exercised the first generation of urban dwellers and became more widespread at exceptional times such as the two world wars. The second is more a cultural construct. Over most of the period between 1850 to 2000, an ideal of domesticity prevailed in which the reward for the successful male wage earner increasingly became a modern home and garden and an intense family life, built on the freely given labour of his wife.[4] The prime demand for such a life-style was private space, both interior and exterior. The third is more difficult to pin down because it is multi-layered and is concerned with community issues, especially since the second world war. It concerns the efforts of citizens in many different urban contexts who, since the second world war, have sought to 'reclaim' space in the city for themselves. It includes those who have fought against local authorities and urban planners for what they want rather than what is decreed by others to be necessary. It includes those who have become politicized in the process of fighting to keep 'natural influences' within the urban environment.

All the various elements contained in this last issue have been ones which have existed over the whole period and fed into all the others. At heart they radiate from two centres: the desire to preserve and enhance one's own use of space, be it private or public space; the other, to redefine the relationship between town and country, between the influences of

---

[4] L. Davidoff, M. Doolittle, J. Fink, and K. Holden, *The Family Story: blood, contract and intimacy, 1830–1960* (London and New York, 1999); Jane Lewis, Jane, ed., (1986) *Labour and Love: women's experience of home and family 1850–1940* (Oxford, 1986); T. Hareven, 'The history of the family and the complexity of social change', *American Historical Review*, 96, 1, 1991; L.A. Tilly and J.W. Scott, *Women, work and the family* (New York, 1989); B.S. Anderson and J. Zinsser, *A history of their own: Women in Europe from Prehistory to the Present Vol II* (New York, 1988).

nature and the man-made built environment. Problems of definition abound. What is private space in the city? Eschewing the complicated and sophisticated, private space in this paper will be defined as outside open space where people could grow things of their choice and which could also be used for private and family recreation. Such space in the expanding provincial cities of Europe came in two forms: as pockets of land used for gardens unconnected with residence or as gardens attached to residential properties. After the second world war, there was also an increasing movement to use spare parcels of land for semi-private community projects with educational and therapeutic objectives. Urban farms, hospital gardens, communal gardens on public housing estates fall into this category. All these developments are indications of the huge shifts in the perception of the use of 'green' urban space. The history of modern urban planning is full of references to the ways in which planners tried to relate town and country in the context of modern developments. Meanwhile, under their noses, it was happening anyway!

Green Open Space and the Urban Working Classes

A review of the first theme, poverty and survival, illustrates this point very clearly. Many of the poorest immigrants in European cities in the twentieth century came from rural backgrounds. Even Britain, the most urbanized nation in the world before the first world war, was still receiving rural immigrants from Ireland. Dublin at the time was packed with exceptionally poor landless labourers.[5] Between 1850–1950 and frequently beyond, France, Italy and Spain and the Nordic countries, all had peasants from areas peripheral to the industrialized regions, moving to the cities. Germany and Central Europe experienced a constant stream of immigrants from more rural areas into their cities. Most of these rural workers had never enjoyed reasonable wages. In the second half of the nineteenth century, some from Eastern Europe may have been the children or grandchildren of serfs. In rural areas, they survived by growing their own food and when they first came to the city, they did the same. A classic example of an unplanned interaction between pioneer modern town planners and the people can be found in Barcelona. Ilfonso Cerdà's dramatic gridiron extension of the city took more than half a century to develop fully.[6] Begun finally after an edict

---

[5] F.H.A. Aalen and K. Whelan, eds, *Dublin City and County: from prehistory to the present* (Dublin 1992); M.J. Bannon, ed., *Planning: the Irish Experience 1920–88* (Dublin, 1989).

[6] V.M. Lampugnani, 'Cerdà's Plan or progressive urbanism', in *Contemporary Barcelona, 1856–1999* Catalogue of Exhibition, (Barcelona, 1996).

from Madrid in the 1870s, it was barely complete at the outbreak of the civil war. Meanwhile, generations of families had used the undeveloped plots for vegetable gardens and recreation. In the shanty towns which grew up on the outskirts of Barcelona before the first world war, the very poor survived by growing their own food.[7]

This kind of activity had happened on such a scale that it had not escaped the notice of philanthropists and governments. Equally, aspects of this activity – the greater independence it gave to workers and the communal issues surrounding the acquisition of land – meant that it also became part of the working class labour movement across Europe. Gardening, it seems, could encompass the extremes of Right and Left wing politics! From both directions, there was a thrust to organize land and its cultivation which marks the beginning of an attempt to control space in the city on behalf of the people. One example will suffice to illustrate the political polarities of early efforts to organize gardens for the workers. Denmark still had an economy based on production of primary produce before the first world war and yet its towns were also growing. In Alborg, the very first organization of workers' gardens in Europe was set up by socialist organizations in 1884.[8] In Copenhagen, however, it was a right-wing movement, the Workers' Defence League, which pioneered there. The League gained two allotment areas but soon fell out with the chair of the association set up to manage the gardens. He left and set up the Copenhagen Garden Society in 1892 as a private company without politics. The gardeners bought shares in the company which then apportioned them land, though the land itself was still in public ownership which made the question of distribution of the company profits a matter of debate. Eventually, an Allotment Garden Federation was organized in Copenhagen in 1908 which rented land from the state and from municipalities. During the first world war, the Federation spread to the rest of the country as the provision of food for the towns and cities became a matter of urgency.

This example is useful for illustrating key facets of the early urban garden movement. As well as the varied political motives of the organizers of city gardens, there was always the endless problem of securing land for such purposes. However, the huge impact of the two

---

[7] In the early days of the ill-fated Republic of 1931, the President, Francesc Macia ensured that every child in a Catalan public school had a little book. The title was *La Caseta i l'hort* which is Catalan for *The Little House and Garden*. The message was that every Catalan had a right to private space as part of an idealized heritage when mass urbanization had been unknown and national values had been based on a rural society.

[8] Niels Jenson, *Allotment Guide: Copenhagen and Surroundings* (1996) extracts published on the web, http://www.cityfarmer.org/DenmarkHistory.html.

world wars was to ensure that finding resolutions to these problems was a matter of crucial importance. Every European country experienced an urban garden movement before the first world war, though each with individual variations, including the three most industrialized: Britain, Germany and France. This movement, supported by philanthropists, governments, capital and labour, was separate from, though inevitably linked to, the nascent town planning movement. Since the earliest days of the Industrial Revolution, the relationship between city and country had been in a process of constant redefinition. Early factory masters had seized on the idea that offering homes with gardens was an excellent method of both recruiting and taming labour, giving the carrot of a comfortable home life as compensation for introducing new working conditions. In the late nineteenth century, the efforts of large businessmen in Britain and Germany contributed to a new kind of built environment in which nature played a greater part. George Cadbury, founder of Bournville, built the settlement around a park system so his workers could walk through parks to work. He also provided each worker's cottage with a garden with a fruit tree. In Germany, the Krupp firm in Essen created the most famous example of a new style of workers' community, with single family homes with gardens.[9] These developments may have been techniques for managing labour but by this time they were also realizations of a new ideal of urban living, made possible by industrialization.

Since the early nineteenth century, France had also had its philosophers and thinkers on these issues, such as Charles Fourier (1772–1837), who had come up with the idea of le phalanstère. This was a specially planned industrial settlement whose objective was to achieve the kind of harmony which was only possible when enlightened humanity was at peace with a larger cosmology, through the orderly control of nurture and nature, manufacturing and the natural environment. The mid-century experiment at Mulhouse to realise these ideas reverberated around other parts of Europe where conditions were favourable.[10] It was an influential idea which reached its culmination in the work of the Englishman, Ebenezer Howard, who interpreted it idiosyncratically in his text, *To-morrow: A Peaceful Path to Real Reform* (1898). Real reform was deemed possible because, in the Garden City, the people would live in harmony with their environment and thus with themselves. The garden city ideal had an international impact in Europe and beyond, especially in the first half

---

    [9] F. Bollerey, G. Fehl, and K. Hartmann, eds, *Im Grünen wohnen- im Blauen planen: ein Lesebuch zur Gartenstadt* (Delft, 1986).
    [10] O. Söderstrom, ed., *L'Industriel,L'Architecte et le Phalanstère:invention et usages de la citéd'enterprise d'Ugine* (Paris and Montreal, 1997).

of the twentieth century.[11] But demands for gardens and private open
space extended well beyond the province of the modern town planning
movement. In Britain, the government had been supporting the idea of
gardens for the poor since the Poor Law had first reached the statute
book in 1603. Growing your own food was a way of encouraging the
able-bodied to be self-supporting. In 1908, the year that Lloyd George
at the Exchequer provided money for the first Old Age Pensions (one
of the first planks in a system of state welfare in Britain), a Small
Holdings and Allotments Act was passed which obliged municipalities
to make land available for allotments on demand. It was the solution
to poverty for the able-bodied that had been used for generations in
rural areas where the workers were paid very low wages, transposed
to an urban context. By 1913, the best estimates are that around half
a million urban allotments had come into existence.[12]

In Germany, established traditions relating to the provision of private
gardens were urban as well as rural with, by the turn of the nineteenth
century, added cultural dimensions of a national fervour for 'Heimat'
and an idealized view of the past. Dr Schreber of Leipzig (1808–61), a
physician concerned with the health of children, is credited with
pioneering the idea of organizing small gardens for recreation and play.[13]
Soon such organizations spread to other cities, notably Berlin and
Hannover. But *Schrebergärten*, as they were called, soon ceased to be
only playgrounds for children and became family-centred, including
plots for growing vegetables. These philanthropic ventures were varied.
Another example was that of the Red Cross inspired *Kleingartenanlagen*
– small garden sites – based on older philanthropic traditions of
providing *Armengarten* for the poor. However, philanthropy was soon
matched in the large cities by workers' associations, mostly left-wing,
organizing their own gardens. In Berlin between 1890 and 1910, there
were about 40,000 worker-planters (*Pflanzer*) using land owned by the
city. The Social Democratic Party, however, which was strong in most
industrial cities, encouraged its members to work small gardens as part
of its project to provide a total political and cultural context for the
workers apart from bourgeois influences.[14] The first world war, of

[11] H. Meller, *European Cities 1890–1930s: history, culture and the built
environment* (Chicester and New York, 2001), Chapter 3 'European responses
to the Garden City ideal'.
[12] C. Ward and D. Crouch, *The Allotment: its Landscape and Culture*
(London, 1988), 70.
[13] Birgit Wahmann, 'Allotments and Schrebergarten in Germany', in M.
Mosser and G. Teyssot, *The History of Garden Design: the western tradition
from the Renaissance to the Present Day* (London, 1991) 451–4.
[14] Dick Geary, 'Socialism and the German Working Class', in Dick Geary, ed.,
Labour and Socialist Movements in Europe before 1914 (Oxford, 1989), 101–36.

course, made the produce of these gardens a vital element in the struggle
to survive the Allied blockade.

The French took their own individual path in developing a garden
movement, becoming leaders in the first three decades of the twentieth
century in developing it on an international scale. The famous figure is
that of Abbé Lemire, founder of the *Ligue française du coin de terre et
du foyer* in 1896, dedicated to developing workers' gardens.[15] This,
however, did not mean domination by the Catholic Church. The French
process of urbanization had been slower than in Britain and Germany.
Traditions of the '*jardin potager*' had survived in many places and were
supported by many different groups: private gardeners, politicians and
workers. Socialist deputies were vigorous in introducing the idea of
workers' gardens in places such as St-Etienne, Valenciennes, Le Puy,
Millau. Two factors, one intellectual, the other practical, were
particularly helpful. The intellectual element was provided by the great
exponent, in the mid-nineteenth century, of social reform based on social
science, Frédéric Le Play. His influence on the organization of the great
International Expositions in Paris, especially between 1867 and 1889,
was particularly concentrated in the pavilions devoted to Social Peace.
Here were to be found models of ideal homes for workers, each replete
with gardens and the means for supplementing family incomes.[16] After
his death, Le Play was made into an icon of the far right and taken up
by *Action Française*. But his support for homes and gardens for the
workers as a measure of social progress was far more widely accepted.[17]

The practical element was the introduction of new government policy.
Like elsewhere, better housing for the workers was a favoured political
option and the method adopted in France, the combination of public
and private enterprise known as the HBM (*Habitations bon marché* –
low-rent housing), was particularly well suited to helping workers to
gain land for gardens. Under the rules governing the HBM system, land
could be purchased by loans from government-accredited companies
who were providing the capital for the housing.[18] In this way, some of
the French garden associations were able, eventually, to secure their land
through the collection of rents. These associations were in a minority
but they nevertheless gave the French small garden movement a degree
of stability which enabled it to lead the rest of Europe. These advantages

---

[15] B. Cabedoce and P. Pierson, eds, *Cent ans d'histoire du jardins ouvriers
1896–1996: la Ligue française du coin de terre et du foyer* (Grâne, 1996).

[16] H. Meller, *Patrick Geddes: social evolutionist and city planner* (London,
1990).

[17] C. Bauer, *Modern Housing* (Boston and New York, 1934).

[18] This was regularized in a law of 1922. Cabedoce and Pierson, *Cent ans
d'histoire,* 198–200.

became a matter of law in 1921, after the small gardeners had proved their worth during the first world war. The League had just made itself the *Fédération nationale des jardins ouvriers* in all France. It was poised, too, to head the campaign for an international movement. As early as 1903, the First International Congress devoted to Workers' Gardens was held in Paris, even before the society of Workers Gardens was set up for Paris and its suburbs, which took place a year later. In 1926, the *Ligue du coin de terre et du foyer* celebrated its thirtieth birthday with great celebrations in Luxembourg when 82 delegations and 6000 gardeners with all the local dignitaries marched through the gardens of Luxembourg. A couple of months later, a meeting of workers' garden associations from Germany, Britain, Austria, Belgium and obviously France and Luxembourg (since the meeting was held there) formed the International Office of the Federations of Workers' Gardens which is still in existence.[19]

The importance of all these organizations, apart from the fact that they were all voluntary and that they covered a wide spectrum of political views, was that they offered individuals a means for fighting other interest groups over the use of space in the city. Apart from the two world wars, the movement reached its heyday in the 1930s when Europe was obsessed with campaigns for fresh air, health and a vigorous outdoor life style.[20] In northern, central and eastern Europe especially, but also to be found elsewhere, allotment plots were developed as recreational centres with little cabins and summer houses. Families moved to live on them in the summer months.[21] The key fact about a vegetable garden was that it had to be within easy access of the permanent home of the gardener, who usually had nothing more sophisticated than a bicycle to get there. So plots, even on the outskirts of cities, were never far away. With cabins and weekend cottages and the family commitment this entailed, the rights of allotment holders became a vexed issue. Generally, legislation in most countries insisted on municipalities or the state supplying land, but security of tenure for any particular plot was not guaranteed. Gardeners could lose their plots when land was developed. There were, though, three factors which

---

[19] Ibid., 127–30.

[20] T. Harlander, ed., *Villa und Eigenheim:Suburbaner Städtebau in Deutschland* (Stuttgart, 2001).

[21] These features give a significant indication of the social class of allotment gardeners. They were not able to purchase second homes but they were not the poorest either. They were mostly modest people in work who could at least support the development of their allotment as a leisure resource. T. Harlander et al., *Siedeln in der Not. Umbruch von Wohnungspolitik und Siedlungsbau am Ende der Weimarer Republik* (Hamburg, 1988).

helped allotment holders hang onto their land. The first was that no country in Europe could operate a comprehensive land use policy which could leave established allotments undisturbed. Second, the allotment holders occupied the high moral ground in view of their contribution to feeding civilian populations during the Great War; and finally, in the 1930s, the effect of the Great Depression slowed down the demand for land.

They also had their organizations and federations which were a force to be reckoned with. The Nazis recognized this and insisted in 1933 that the chair of the German Federation must follow Nazi policy, banning any Jews or those of non-Aryan descent from holding gardening plots. He refused and was immediately removed from office.[22] The Federation was taken over by the Nazis but individual plot holders fought back by hiding Jews and other wanted people in their allotment huts, often at great risk to themselves. Gardeners' associations, even in the interwar years, might have been representative of only a minority of citizens. The very fact that they were organized, however, and were cultivating green spaces within the city environment, gave them a higher profile than their numbers warranted. They offered a people-centred framework for bringing nature into the city that even had an impact on the public park movement, until the end of the 19th century the major force bringing nature into the cities. In many industrial cities, parks may have been introduced to provide space and air – the 'city's lungs' – as a public health measure. But what to do with the space provided was another matter. Parks as a force for civilization, in the aesthetic pleasure of landscaped gardens, in the control of social behaviour of park users, in the provision of innocent recreation and pleasure facilities, had always been a 'top down' activity and was largely to remain so for most of the 20th century.[23]

Yet in Germany, in the early years of the century and to a lesser extent elsewhere, aesthetically unpleasing but socially rewarding, allotment gardens began to be seen as a possible adjunct to park development. Fritz Schumacher, founder member of the Werkbund and first architect planner in Hamburg, built his great park in the city with the people in mind.[24] He was still doing grand designs but other architects and landscape designers such as Migge and Lesser were pioneers of parks

---

[22] G. Gröning, 'Politics of Community Gardening', paper presented at the 1996 Annual Conference of the *American Community Gardening Association* http://www.cityfarmer.org/german99.html.

[23] A. Tate, *Great City Parks* (London, 2000).

[24] He outlined his beliefs in many publications and summed them up in his autobiography, F. Schumacher, *Stufen des Lebens: Erinnerungen eines Baumeister* (Stuttgart, 1935).

designed for the masses which included areas for private cultivation. Their work was result of a debate on the reform of the urban park. As De Michelis suggests, it was a debate

> fuelled by the arguments not dissimilar from those that, in the same period, helped to change the landscape of German cultural reform: the spread of new standards of hygiene and eugenetics (*sic*), of better nourishment and medical facilities; criticism levelled at city housing conditions, and the conflict between the town and country which produced initiatives such as *Siedlung*, (new housing schemes and garden cities); the search for a 'third way' between capitalism and socialism, capable of alleviating the class war; the need for a 'new style' to give form and expression to the modern industrial world, which was dominated by the machine.[25]

For a brief while, architects and landscape architects were prepared to work with the people. This was most markedly the case in Vienna, a city which had had a particularly harrowing experience of starvation during the first world war and the produce from allotments had often meant the difference between life and death. In the immediate postwar years, the allotment gardeners of Vienna had greater political influence than ever before or since. Their organizations were to commission Adolf Loos and other town planners of his stature to prepare new plans for the city which took on board the need to provide for gardens.[26] It was a rare instance of planners having direct communication with those for whom they planned.[27]

The Allotment Movement after the Second World War

It was a hopeful beginning that was brought to an abrupt end after the second world war. Allotment gardeners played their vital role again in this war. A recent study of the contribution of urban gardeners in Britain during the war suggests that, in 1944, allotment gardens provided 10 per cent of all the food produced in Great Britain and about 50 per cent of national requirements in fruit and vegetables.[28] In France the number of workers' gardens and industrial gardens increased rapidly to about a

---

[25] Marco De Michelis, 'The Green Revolution: Leberecht Migge and the Reform of the Garden in Modernist Germany', in Mosser and Teyssot, eds, op. cit., 409.

[26] E. Blau, 'Vienna 1919–34, Großstadt and proletariat in Red Vienna', in Blau and Platzer, eds, *Shaping the Great City*, 205–14.

[27] Though the experiments at building garden suburbs were swiftly curtailed because of costs. H. Weihsman, *Das Rote Wien* (Wien, 1985), 175–9.

[28] T. Garnett, *Growing food in cities: a report to highlight and promote the benefits of urban agriculture in the UK* (London, 1996).

million in 1943.[29] The postwar world, however, was to prove a nadir for the movement. Strong forces at every level militated against it. All European nations started the task of rebuilding bombed cities or developing their economies with a new framework of planning legislation.[30] The heyday of centralized planning in the 1940s and 50s was the death knell of the compromises that had existed over land-use issues in the prewar years. The crucial element was land-zoning. The separation of land into zones for different purposes effectively put many allotment gardens at risk since they were often located by industrial developments or wherever small pockets of land had been left free by all kinds of other development activities. However, it was not just the legal, political and economic context which was threatening allotment gardens. Now the demand for such gardens from the people themselves was falling away. The increasing momentum of the private housing market was gaining strength and private housing tended to have gardens large enough for use as fruit and vegetable gardens.

Family Homes with Gardens: the Twentieth Century Ideal

This element introduces the second major theme of this chapter: the cultural revolution in domestic life which was transforming patterns of marriage and the raising of children and the context within which this was accomplished. There is no doubt that the period between the 1880s and the end of the second world war witnessed a dramatic change in the personal aspirations of most Europeans. Surveying the enormous changes that took place in European housing for the majority in the period 1889–1930, Pooley suggests that 'the major change which affected most European countries was a gradual transformation from a relatively public life in which many everyday aspects of living were shared with the family, neighbours and workmates to a more private existence based around the nuclear family'.[31] All countries of Europe

---

[29] J.-J. Gouguet, 'Jardins familiaux, croissance urbaine et insertion sociale: une analyse économique' in G. Monediaire, ed., *Agricultures urbaines et ville durable européenne : droits et politiques du jardinage familial urbain en Europe* (Limoges, 1999), 247–8.

[30] Germany had the least centralized system of planning after the war. As Diefendorf has pointed out: 'urban planning and reconstruction in post-war Germany was the responsibility of the towns. There was no national government until 1949 and no national building law until 1960'. J. Diefendorf, 'Urban reconstruction and traffic planning in post-war Germany', *Journal of Urban History* 15, 1989, 131–58.

[31] C. Pooley, 'Housing strategies in Europe, 1880–1930: towards a comparative perspective', in C. Pooley, ed., *Housing Strategies in Europe 1880–1930* (Leicester, 1992), 337.

had taken on board some element of the idea of the house and garden, or the *cité-jardin* ideal, as a norm. When Tomáš Bat´a, the Czech shoe magnate, built his ideal town around his shoe factory in Zlín, 100 kilometres from Brno, he built thousands of single family homes, each set in their own garden, as the epitome of the most up-to-date design for modern living.[32] The private sector market everywhere was to continue this trend ever more widely after the second world war. Such developments demanded more space, and private sector building burst beyond city boundaries, sustained by the now more widely available means of transport brought by the motor car. Villages close to cities became accessible for development as dormitory suburbs.

All this development of housing with gardens had already created a new kind of urban environment within the public sector by the second world war. The British low-rise public housing schemes such as the 15 major estates built around the city of Birmingham, which added a third to the total size of the city, had a major impact on bringing natural influences into the city.[33] While social housing estates had been built by the local authority, a multitude of small builders had also moved out from the city centre, usually along the major road routes, building single family, semi-detached homes with gardens in those areas left untouched by social housing schemes. Birmingham may have been exceptional in the vigour of its housing policies and the buoyancy of the private house building market in the interwar years because of its relative prosperity during the Great Depression compared with elsewhere. But there was not a city in Britain which did not experience this phenomenon in some degree.[34] After the second world war, despite the initial controls exercized by the Labour Government over the private housing sector because of the shortages of building materials and the needs of the public sector, Britain still remained ahead of its continental neighbours in suburban development. But by the late 1950s, this was no longer the case. Demand for the private single family home with a garden had become a European-wide phenomenon.

By the 1960s, new biotechnology revolutionizing the propagation of plants, and the potential of new commercial ventures promoting gardening as a mass consumer activity were being realised. In her pathbreaking book on the English domestic environment in the twentieth century, Alison Ravetz has emphasized how the use of gardens changed in the postwar period, aided and abetted by these

---

[32] H. Meller, *European Cities 1890–1930s*, Chapter 3.
[33] Ibid., Chapter 6.
[34] M. Clapson, *Invincible Green Suburbs, Brave New Towns: social change and urban dispersal* (Manchester, 1998).

developments.[35] The back garden was ceasing to be a place for growing vegetables and hanging out the washing and instead was becoming more used for pleasure and recreation, as an additional 'personal space' outside the home. 'Cheap plastics', she writes, 'which became widely available in the 1960s, were ideally suited to use in the garden. The durable plant pot and plastic seats and tables were the most important of the resulting products'.[36] Micropropagation techniques opened up the possibility of the mass production of plants, and 'garden centres' replaced, to a large extent, old-fashioned plant 'nurseries' as the places where a car-owning public could purchase cheaply the accoutrements of the newest fashions in the use of garden space.

Historical studies in the changing patterns of social relationships, especially marriage, have tended to be focused on specific issues such as attitudes to birth control or the relationship between different kinds of employment and their social consequences.[37] The relationship between changing social environments and marriage patterns is harder to pin down. Work on the different social context of public housing tends to get bogged down in the contrasting cultural priorities of those who planned and built the housing and those expected to live there.[38] In the private sector, that ambivalence tends to disappear as the element of choice increases. But as choice increases so do the difficulties of finding hard evidence about the impact of domestic environments on the life they encompass. Increasing means of communication continually expand the cultural context of everyday life. However, in the context of bringing the influence of nature into the city, one thing remains clear. Private gardens became a European norm and one that was ever more widely sought in the postwar decades of rising living standards. So, indirectly through market forces, the more affluent sectors of society have profoundly influenced the quality of the urban environment with their demands for private space.

---

[35] A. Ravetz with R. Turkington, *The Place of Home: English Domestic Environments, 1914–2000* (London, 1995).

[36] Ibid., 194.

[37] D. Gittens, *Fair Sex: family size and structure* (London 1982); M. Glucksmann, *Women assembly workers: women workers and the new industries in inter-war Britain* (London, 1990).

[38] For example, in Britain, there are a number of studies on the social impact of public housing which uses information from surveys taken during the 1930s, e.g. J. Greatorex, and S. Clarke, *Looking back at Wythenshawe* (Timperley, 1984), which assesses the conditions in Manchester's 'flagship' public housing estate, Wythenshawe.

Citizens' Rights and Private Space

Surprisingly, over the last three decades, demand for private space not attached to housing has also increased, in defiance of all the obstacles to the maintenance of such spaces. The nadir of the family garden movement came swiftly after the second world war. Just to cite one example from West Berlin in the 1950s, the area of Berlin-Charlottenburg had 15,000 allotment gardens at the end of the war. Within a decade 12,000 had been lost and the remaining 3,000 were under extreme pressure from all kinds of demand. Land from the 12,000 lost allotments was used for new residential areas, Berlin's wholesale market, a prison for women, a fire station, a high school, several industrial premises and road improvements, especially the road to Tegel airport.[39] In all countries, allotment gardeners faced similar problems. Yet the movement did not entirely die out, for a number of reasons. The tenacity of its organizations remained, the International Office of the Federation of Workers' Garden Associations regrouped in 1948. The French Federation even managed to get a law passed in 1952 which 'guaranteed' the rights of gardeners to have a garden, but crucially, there was still no guarantee of a particular location.[40] This was the key problem and yet the erstwhile adversaries of the gardeners, the new planning professionals, were finding that they had difficulties controlling land use despite their government-given powers.

By the early 1970s, a more holistic approach to cities and their environment had begun to emerge. A number of countries, including Britain, established new government Ministries for the Environment, to be followed shortly by the European Union. Such a broadening of terminology reflected a widening range of references for measuring the quality of an urban environment.[41] In France, some of the first Ministers for the Environment, such as Robert Poujade, mayor of Dijon, and Michel Crépeau, mayor of La Rochelle, had been involved with the family garden movement in their home towns.[42] It was a link which was

---

[39] Berlin was a special case. In the 1950s, there was very little room for suburban expansion thus the pressure on allotment gardens was particularly severe. Gröning, op. cit., 6.

[40] A. Vaut, 'Contribution à une geo-histoire (1) des "jardins ouvriers stéphanois"', *Cahier 4* UER Sciences de l'homme et de son environnement, Centre de recherches sur l'environnement géographique et social (Lyons, 1977).

[41] In France, President Georges Pompidou took a personal interest in introducing what he saw as a new political initiative. M. Flonneau, 'Entre morale et politique, l'invention du 'Ministère de l'Impossible', in C. Bernhardt and G. Massard-Guilbaud, *Le Démon Moderne: La pollution dans les sociétés urbaines et industrielles d'Europe* (Clermont-Ferrand, 2002), 109–25.

[42] F. Dubost, 'Les jardins ouvriers : un patrimoine culturel' in Cabedoce and Pierson, eds, *Cent ans d'histoire*, 201.

strengthened by the developments in planning practices, involving greater community participation in developments, in 'greening' city spaces and in thinking of city resources in terms of 'sustainability'. All these changes gave renewed strength to the family garden movements. From the mid 1970s, there is a new crop of academic studies about allotment gardens. One produced by the Centre de recherches sur l'environnement géographique et social at the University Lyon II in 1977, chronicles in minute detail the fortunes of the gardens in each arrondissement of the city and the continued strength of the organizational framework of the movement despite the loss of many gardens.[43] In Germany, there has been a veritable academic industry devoted to family gardens – at least 20 PhD theses during the twentieth century.[44] In 1983, West Germany went as far as to pass a law to protect all existing gardens. The pulling down of the Berlin Wall and reunification provided an ultimate testing ground. There were at least three times as many allotment gardens still surviving in the East in relation to population, compared to the West. The new Germany cast its vote for the gardeners with a further piece of legislation in 1994, guaranteeing the rights of gardeners to their land more irrevocably than at any time in their past history.[45]

With the resurgence of the allotment movement has come a new reassessment of the relationship between town and country. In Britain, a movement was started to introduce town children to an understanding of plants and animals in a non-formal environment, which became known as the city farms movement. The experience of evacuation of school children during the war had highlighted the total lack of knowledge of country lore among young city children. Starting in 1973 in London, in Kentish Town and Kings Cross, waste land was occupied and used productively for plants and animals. In London and Bristol, which was to become the centre for the National Federation of City Farms, formed in 1979, the farms often existed alongside or displaced the rag-and-bone men, who sold scrap metal and kept horses, pigs, chickens and goats in the city and had done so for generations.[46] By the 1980s, ideas of community gardening as a way of encouraging a

---

[43] See fn. 40 above for publication details.

[44] G. Gröning, 'Politics of community gardening', 12.

[45] Denmark followed this example even more dramatically in 2001, passing a law securing current gardens and making existing gardens permanent – or at least they cannot be closed down without alternative plots being provided at least one month before closure. The Danish Minister for the Environment has had his speech on the subject posted on the web in the Urban Agriculture Notes 1-4 http://www.cityfarmer.org/denmark.html.

[46] Information from Dr Katherine Holden who was a pioneer in this work.

communal spirit on social housing estates was being widely advocated. For enthusiasts, the Internet has provided a means of communication for kinds of schemes promoting gardens and gardening. At the University of Nottingham in 2001, an international conference was held on 'People, Land and Sustainability: a global view of community gardening' part funded by the Co-operative Society, the University and the City of Nottingham. People came from all over Europe as well as many other parts of the world.[47]

What has taken place is the growth of a passion for the natural world amongst the inhabitants of large cities all over Europe. Owners of small private gardens have developed their passion for gardens and gardening into a major leisure activity. Caring for the home and garden became the shared context for marriage and family life in the late twentieth century. This development has fundamentally altered the morphology of the modern European cities. Currently, the most expensive housing is to be found on city perimeters where space is adequate to provide suburban dwellings with large gardens in low-density developments. Such gardens are used mostly for ornament rather than food production and an entire industry has grown up to serve this consumer market.[48] Paradoxically, the greater interest in private gardening has been paralleled with increasing public support for private organizations devoted to preserving 'natural' influences in the city. National organizations devoted to promoting gardening, horticulture and the preservation of rare species have gained a new lease of life, far exceeding the original impetus usually dating from the nineteenth century which created them in the first place. To look at France for example, *La Societé nationale d'horticulture de France* has enjoyed growing mass support. Another organization, *L'Association des parcs et jardins botaniques de France*, has over one million members.[49] There are regional associations devoted to saving and caring for remarkable gardens, some of which are to be found in urban areas. Whether gardens are in cities or attached to country houses now matters less.

In conclusion, it is possible to say that this is one movement that has not emanated exclusively from architects and planners in shaping the modern urban environment. There is an historical continuity in many different towns and cities of Europe between the rural immigrants into large cities in the nineteenth century and their gardening descendants.

---

[47] Communal editorial, *People, Land and Sustainability: a global view of community gardening* (Nottingham, 2001).

[48] See fn. 35.

[49] C. De Fleurieu, 'Histoire et actualité des jardins botaniques de France: des examples en Beaujolais', *Chronique du pays beaujolais* Bulletin no 17, Académie de Villefranche-en-Beaujolais, 1993, 14.

The extraordinary variety of organizations that were set up in virtually every city to try to help people have access to private land has been both a weakness and a strength. A weakness, because the fragmented nature of these kinds of activities, despite national and international federations, have left them no match for the forces ranged against them when fighting for their land. A strength, in that gardening, by its very nature, is local and place-centred and thus can demand loyalties and support from individuals which could be sustained over very long periods of time. Above all, the development of private space for all in the city was one of the strongest factors changing the quality of the built environment of towns and cities everywhere. The blurring of the urban and the rural in the second half of the twentieth century, as city boundaries extend ever further into rural hinterlands, can be seen, at least partly, as an achievement of the small garden movement. In terms of the encouragement of urban sprawl, though, it has had some negative effects on the quality of urban life and the rural environment. The passion of small gardeners has influenced the property market and has contributed both directly and indirectly to a rethinking of the priorities of urban planners in terms of transport, conservation and sustainability. The physical and cultural split between town and country, which had been so clear in the mid-nineteenth century, has disappeared. Globalization has brought environmental issues to the fore in ways empowering those with concerns about nature, gardens and human interaction with the natural world. When urban planners envisage new developments or the renovation of the old, these are the concerns which are currently dominant. It may be the only instance in the history of European urban planning, of ideas sustained and developed from 'the bottom up'.

CHAPTER SIX

Sustainable Naples:
The Disappearance of Nature
as Resource[*]

Gabriella Corona

The Historical Characteristics of the Environmental Context

According to Raffaele La Capria there is no city in the world, apart from perhaps Rio De Janeiro, which 'contains more nature' than Naples.[1] A well-known literary, iconographic and historiographical tradition dating back to the eighteenth century discovered and depicted nature in the Neapolitan urban context as an element which both embellished and nourished the city. It constituted an attraction of continual and renewable sustenance. This representation of Naples traditionally highlighted aspects of extraordinary natural beauty (the sea, the hills, Vesuvius), the wealth of fountains and gardens, woods and mountains, the fertile soil, the mild climate, its famous works of art and tradition of folklore, the beneficial effects of the thermal springs and sea-bathing. This combination of resources, moreover, not only contributed to support a commonly accepted view of the landscape and construct an artificial image, but was also an important founding element both at the economic and social level. At the beginning of the 1900s, economic and working practices closely linked to the natural resources – mining, fishing and mineral waters, agriculture, animal rearing and tourism – were important sources of employment and revenue which, at the same time, impressed upon vast urban spaces a strong social and cultural identity and even characterized the actual typology and form of housing.[2]

---

[*] Translation by Sharon Gleave
[1] Reference is to R. La Capria, *L'occhio di Napoli* (Mondadori, 1994). The citation is not first-hand, but taken from the first chapter of the Naples City Council town-planning department's *Proposta di variante per la zona nord-occidentale*, (ESI, 1997), 13, written by Giovanni Disposto and Laura Travaglini, to whom I apologize.
[2] Cf. G. Corona, 'Risorse nella città. Natura e territorio a Napoli tra Otto e Novecento', in P. Bevilacqua and G. Corona, eds, *Ambiente e risorse nel Mezzogiorno contemporaneo*, (Meridiana Libri, 2000), 191–208.

The Naples depicted in these images is no longer recognizable. Instead, the city appears disfigured by a destructive process. On the basis of a law n°349 of the Ministry of Environment dated 8th July 1986, Naples was declared an area at considerable environmental risk. In the last decade various problems of sustainability have developed, all of which derive from a lack of consideration of physical laws and of the logic of the regenerative capacity of natural resources.[3] Among these the following should be mentioned: pollution in the gulf; the effects of unauthorized building on the quality of natural resources (water, air, soil, sea, woods) and problems associated with underground strata; the consequences of establishing factories in densely populated areas. In addition to these problems it is possible to remember also the effects of the drastic reduction of agricultural land and urban parks on the quality of environment and resources and difficulties inherent in the allocation of waste material; and the worsening of urban traffic congestion due to the increased number of vehicles.

However, in order to examine problems of sustainability beyond a simple descriptive analysis, we must determine the historical reasons and the fundamental logic which have governed the underlying mechanisms of the process of material and social construction of urban space. And yet, what is environmental history if not an historical reading of today's environmental and social problems? For this reason, it is necessary to look back to the nineteenth century when urban changes began to impose a new imprint, compared to the past, on the problems of sustainability. This imprint, although manifesting different forms and entities, continued throughout the whole of the twentieth century.

There are three questions which seem to give direction to an historical analysis. First, within what system of relations between structural factors and dynamics of change were problems of sustainability formed as we know them today? Second, how has the relationship between real change and government policy towards urban territory been shaped? Finally, to what extent is Naples a representative case of other urban realities, or to what extent does it present peculiar characteristics?

An analysis of the problems of urban sustainability therefore requires a return to the consideration of the city as a place of both natural and

---

[3] For the concept of sustainability, reference is made to a general bibliography: H.E. Daly, *Lo stato stazionario* (Sansoni, 1981); N. Georgescu-Roegen, *Energia e miti economici* (Boringhieri, 1982); R. Costanza, *Ecological Economics: The Science and Management of Sustainability* (Columbia University Press, 1991); Enzo Tiezzi-Nadia Marchettini, *Che cos'è lo sviluppo sostenibile? Le basi scientifiche della sostenibilità e i guasti del pensiero unico* (Donzelli Editore, 1999). For urban sustainability, see V. Bettini, *Elementi di ecologia urbana* (Einaudi, 1996).

human resources, and a place where social, economic and demographic phenomena interact with the geographical space in which they occur. Let us consider here two historical features which have for some time played a central role in the shaping of environmental problems in Naples; first, the morphology of territory. Naples is not situated amid expanses of open fields and regular plains. On the contrary, it is surrounded to the northwest by extended upland and valleys, by the sea to the west – enclosed to the north-west by islands (Capri, Ischia, Procida) – and by Vesuvius to the south. The entire urban area has sections of irregular territory, valleys and hills.[4] Since ancient times there has been a particular relationship with the surrounding countryside where the rapport between highly cultivated agricultural districts and the coastal city resembles that of conditions in the mountain-plain. Furthermore, the morphology of this territory has favoured the development of a Mediterranean agrarian landscape, terraced hill slopes and dry walls providing a home for groves and orchards.[5] In addition to these structural features lie that of great demographic pressure which Pasquale Villani has defined as one of the elements that Naples has inherited from the past.[6] This pressure has continued to increase in the modern period; it grew from the 1880s up to the first world war and during the period between the two wars, and then there was a further increase in the decades following the second world war.[7] Between 1951 and 1981 the population of the province increased by 43 per cent. By 1981 half of the population of the region was concentrated in this area, approximately 550 per thousand.

The problems of sustainability in Naples have been shaped historically by the way in which processes of environmental change in western cities have been linked to two structural features: *the morphology of the territory* and *strong demographic pressure*. As far as general dynamics of change are concerned, a particular historical moment may be defined which affected the modern city from an environmental point of view. It concerned a phase of change characterized by the environmental implications of processes affecting the city, and proved to be the turning point which would mark a particular environmental period in Naples' history.

---

[4] Naples City Council town-planning department, *Proposta di variante*, 13–36.

[5] Ibid.

[6] P. Villani, 'L'eredità storica e la società rurale', in *Storia d'Italia. Le regioni dall'Unità ad oggi, La Campania* (Einaudi, 1990), 80. For demographic matters in modern Naples, see in the same volume G. Montroni, 'Popolazione e insediamenti in Campania (1861–1981)', 263–315. See also the classic work of G. Galasso, 'Lo sviluppo demografico del Mezzogiorno prima e dopo l'unità', in Id., *Mezzogiorno medievale e moderno* (Einaudi, 1975).

[7] P. Villani, *L'eredità storica*, 87.

In this phase, the city underwent an extraordinary increase in the consumption of energy and natural resources, and saw the transformation of the use of nature as a resource to that of inert material. It is what might be defined as the *thermic city* in reference to that type of energy which the system can no longer re-use.[8] It is the consequence of a major process which led to the creation of the city-metropolis, a city with immense suburbs whose base was excessively enlarged. Martin Melosi has defined this phase as 'the urban crisis in the age of ecology'. It was this very phase that began in the United States in 1945 when the whole sanitary infrastructure previously set up was severely tested.[9] Even though this phase began in Naples in the 1950s, it was only from the 1960s onwards that it actually unfolded.

Hygienic Changes

Under the powerful push of the population explosion, and the development of the industrial city, local administrations which aspired to progressive and modern ideals adopted measures designed to resolve the problems of hygiene and to change the image of the city according to criteria elaborated by the 'hygienic' approach. In this phase, the question of the environment in an urban context dominated public debate and the politics of intervention as a question of hygiene-cum-sanitation. Thus elements of nature were seen and conceived in relation to human health and its problems. There were three environmental consequences:

First, the breakdown of the metabolic circle of country-city-country, whereby human waste was no longer returned to agriculture. Agriculture, in turn, by adopting the widespread use of chemical fertilizers, ceased to be a self-sufficient and self-reproducing sector: 'The cities separate', as Piero Bevilacqua has written, 'they lose their connection as reproducers with the country'.[10] A new process took over, whereby 'refuse' ceased to be a resource and became one of the principal factors of pollution and environmental imbalance. One entered totally into what Guido Viale has defined as 'a disposable, throw-away world'.[11]

---

[8] V. Bettini, 'La città come sistema dissipativo', in Id., ed., *Elementi di ecologia urbana* (Einaudi, 1996), 39–57.

[9] M.V. Melosi, *The sanitary city, Urban infrastructure in America from colonial times to the present* (The Johns Hopkins University Press, 2000), 283–95.

[10] P. Bevilacqua, 'Il secolo planetario. Tempi e scansioni per una storia dell'ambiente', in C. Pavone, ed., *'900. I tempi della storia* (Donzelli editore, 1997), p.128.

[11] G. Viale, *Un mondo usa e getta* (Feltrinelli, 1995).

Second, an extraordinary growth in the demand for water for domestic use (the construction of aqueducts and sewers for human waste) and therefore also a rise in the human demand for water resources.

Finally, the need to find an outlet for liquid effluent, with a consequent increase in the pollution of wells (in the case of land outlets), and of the sea and rivers, a problem which was resolved by enlarging the areas of outflow. The most damaging effects of these changes in urban growth would be felt in Naples during the second half of the twentieth century.

From the point of view of changes in hygiene-cum-sanitation in this period, Naples was not only in line with other cities in the western world,[12] but was also a leader among Italian cities. And even though the desired results were not always attained, Naples became a role model for the whole of Italy, flying the flag for national hygiene.[13] However, as in the case of a majority of western cities, while the improvement in hygiene brought about better conditions in the city, at the same time it caused an enormous environmental change, destined to have unforeseeable and ever-more imposing consequences.

In this phase, the virtuous circle that had set population and resources in a complementary relationship began to break. This triggered in the second half of the eighteenth century an extensive development process of areas around Naples, a process which would continue up until the early decades of the twentieth century. 'The creative force of the Neapolitan market',[14] was how Pietro Tinto defined it, speaking enthusiastically of the blossom seen on the outskirts of the city with an agriculture rich in orchards, orange groves and market gardens. The exchange mainly came about at the level of fertilization of the soil, whereby the city fertilized the countryside with its human waste products.[15]

To speak of 'sanitary' changes, however, does not involve only actual interventions, such as aqueducts or sewers or drainage systems, but to a phase in which hygiene would direct social change in the city. This is an

---

[12] J.R. McNeill, *Qualcosa di nuovo sotto il sole. Storia dell'ambiente nel XX secolo*, (Einaudi, 2000), 343–76. According to this author, the main hygienic-sanitary changes in the city took place in Europe, Japan and North America between 1870 and 1920.

[13] C. Giovannini, *Risanare la città. L'utopia igienista di fine Ottocento* (Franco Angeli, 1996), 14–17.

[14] P. Tino, *Campania felice? Territorio e agricolture prima della 'grande trasformazione'* (Meridiana Libri, 1997), 48.

[15] Ibid., 20. Pietro Tino returns many times to this exchange, citing among others a famous passage by Goethe in his *Viaggio in Italia*.

important element. Let us consider, for example, just how long this phase lasted: the establishment of the eastern area as an industrial zone;[16] the 'invention' (here I have borrowed Alain Corbin's famous title[17]) of thermal springs and sea-bathing in the city area; the substitution of social values by aesthetic ones in the structuring of the city's open spaces; the social redefinition of urban space;[18] the projects of creating an infrastructure arising out of the plans for urban renewal; and finally, the great question of the old, run-down quarters of Naples.

In the famous debate on the historic centre of Naples,[19] the description of the pollution of the districts and the horrendous living conditions of the very poor was combined with an extraordinarily powerful ideological denunciation of social problems which, as is well known, for a long time strongly influenced the image of 'a great city divided between an immense mass of dangerous plebeians and a small, cultured and aristocratic elite'.[20] Such a description echoes the contemporary description of the London smoke fogs elaborated by British reformers in the nineteenth century, in which pollution became a great metaphor of the moral and material decay of the nineteenth century city, thereby offering an opportunity to deal with the problem of the metropolis as an important social question.[21]

The Thermic City

It was the city, as previously mentioned, which caused an enormous increase in the consumption of energy and resources, and through which Naples lost its hinterland as its support base by expanding the territorial map from which energy sources and agricultural products had been

[16] See R. Parisi, *Lo spazio della produzione a Napoli: la periferia orientale* (Edizioni Athena, 1998), 74–5.

[17] A. Corbin, *L'invenzione del mare* (Marsilio Editori, 1990).

[18] See G. Saredo, A. Leris, A. Rossi, F. Nuscianisi, A. Sinigaglia, *Relazione della R.Commissione d'Inchiesta istituita con R: Decreto 8 novembre 1900* (Forzani e C., Tipografi del Senato, 1901), volume I, 436.

[19] For the works of individual authors, see once again G. Russo, *Napoli come città* (ESI, 1966), 250–59.

[20] The citation is taken from G. Gribaudi, 'Familismo e famiglia a Napoli e nel Mezzogiorno', *Meridiana. Rivista di storia e scienze sociali*, 17, 1993, 23.

[21] For London smoke fogs, see B. Luckin, 'Demographic, social and cultural parameters of environmental crisis: the great London smoke fogs in the late 19th and early 20th centuries', in C. Bernhardt and G. Massard-Guilbaud, eds, *Le démon moderne. La pollution dans les sociétés urbaines et industrielles d'Europe/ The modern Demon. Pollution in Urban and Industrial European Societies* (Clermont-Ferrand Presses de l'UBP, collection Histoires croisées, 2001), 199.238.

derived. The city's boundaries greatly expanded, engulfing areas both near and far which supported mechanisms through which its continued survival was assured.

The process which characterized this phase reached its highest point in Naples in the 1950s and 1960s. These were the years of the population explosion, during which a large number of inhabitants were attracted to Naples from the south and from inland regions.[22] Population increase, in turn, led to a strong demand for housing, dramatically amplified by the after-effects of the war. These years saw the end of farming communities and the decline of the agrarian sector. It was the phase of the great conurbation[23] and the construction of exceptionally large suburbs. In this phase the environmental change process, previously initiated, affected the positive relationship between population and resources, and emerged as a relationship which was highly wasteful of natural resources and extremely destructive to the environment.

There are four main environmental implications linked to the way in which the construction of the thermic city took place in Naples. First, the l960s represented a great historical break, the years in which the conflict between diverse and contrasting utilization of resources was at its height, when their auto-reproductive capacities were reduced and sources of pollution were greatly increased. This was the beginning of the period when nature ceased to be a resource, in that the earth became soil to be built on, the sea mainly an area destined to host urban waste products (domestic and industrial waste and sewage), and the areas designated for swimming and thermal baths were cancelled out by urban and industrial expansion.[24] In addition, agricultural areas which, at the beginning of the 1960s, still represented four-fifths[25] of the provincial territory were reduced during a decade or so to two-

[22] The population in the province rose by 43 per cent between 1951 and 1981. See G. Montroni, *Popolazione e insediamenti in Campania (1861–1981)*, 248.251.

[23] It is important not to forget the historical origins of the formation process of a metropolitan area as we know it today, for which we need to go back to the decades bridging the nineteenth and twentieth centuries when the industrial sector was strengthened and the transport network expanded, for this, see G. Montroni, 'Popolazione e insediamenti in Campania (1860–1981)', 236–7.

[24] The Council decided that from 1966, the authorization for Bagnoli's bathing establishments to operate during the summer would no longer be granted. S. Ascione, G.Corona, 'Activités humaines et ressources naturelles à Naples au XXème siècle: l'exemple du complexe industriel de Bagnoli', in C. Bernhardt and G. Massard-Guilbaud, eds, *Le démon moderne*, 351–74.

[25] F. Ceci, D. Lepore, *Arcipelago Vesuviano. Percorsi e ragionamenti intorno a Napoli* (Argo, 1997), 16.

fifths.[26] Building construction became one of the largest industries authorized by public authorities,[27] thereby determining the economic hegemony of constructors so frequently recorded by Ada Becchi.[28] But it was from this very private, uncontrolled, public-supported activity[29] that were spawned a series of problems linked to total lack of governance within this territory.

Second, the entropic quality of the city as an ecosystem of in-flow and out-flow reached its peak. The city resorted to taking resources from distant territories, even from a distance of a thousand kilometres. In this way, the urban ecological footprint of the city was enlarged.[30] According to Biagio Cillo, Naples, covering an area of approximately 120 square kilometres and with a million inhabitants, requires for its food consumption an agricultural area equal to three times the size of the province. Moreover, most of the urbanized areas are concentrated on soil of volcanic origin, and therefore very fertile, with a consequent loss of terrain of particularly high productive value.[31]

Finally, with an increase in demographic pressure, the consequences of hygienic change became increasingly serious. The first and most obvious effect was the pollution of gulf waters, which became a major problem for a city considered as a dissipative system whose role was principal out-flow point. The out-flow area tended to expand during the twentieth century. This expansion was brought about by the fact that polluted waters coming from coastal towns were mixed with those of internal areas flowing into the gulf, as well as those associated with maritime activity. Waters coming from a wide hydrographic range flowed into the gulf, including territories belonging to the provinces of Salerno and Avellino. According to data from the 1970s, 6.4 per cent of

---

[26] Taken from data of June 2001 and collected by the Chamber of Commerce, on line, *www.na.camcom.it*. The agricultural area is 460 sq.km out of a total in the province of 1,171 sq.km.

[27] For the process of destruction of the southern territories as occurred after the second world war, see the introduction to the interview 'Napoli, il Sud e la "rivoluzione comunale". Conversazione con Antonio Bassolino', in *Meridiana. Rivista di storia e scienze sociali*, n.26–7, 203–46. For Naples in particular, this process is explained by A. Dal Piaz, *Napoli 1945–1985*.

[28] A. Becchi, 'Napoli contro Napoli. Città come economia e città come potere', in *Meridiana. Rivista di storia e scienze sociali*, n.5, 143–67.

[29] See once again the introductory notes to 'Napoli, il Sud e la "rivoluzione comunale"', 207.

[30] Reference is made to one of the principal measures of sustainability: urban ecological footprint. See W. Rees, 'Ecological footprints and appropriated carrying capacity: what urban economics leaves out', *Environment and urbanization*, IV, 2, 1992.

[31] B. Cillo, G. Solera, eds, *Sviluppo sostenibile e città. Ragionamento sul futuro di Napoli* (Clean Edizioni, 1997), 61.

the region, namely that part descending towards the gulf of Naples, received the discharge waters of 46.5 per cent of the population.[32]

Only from the 1960s did Neapolitan technicians begin to perceive the combined environmental effects of the ways in which the city had been constructed during the previous decades. Above all, the problem was the ever-increasing load of water consumption for domestic use compared with that used for industry, public services and agriculture.[33] In addition, there was growing water pollution both of land and sea water caused mainly by the fact that purification plants had not been built in line with the sewerage network.[34] This meant that the interpretation of the general situation in Italy outlined by Simone Neri Serneri was also valid for Naples. This thesis states that a hygienic approach to the problem of pollution, based on the protection of the health of the population, was incapable of identifying a series of problems because it ignored environmental consequences, and not only those that were concerned with public health, in relation to the use of water.[35]

Finally, it is in this context that the morphology of the territory, the geographic layout, that particular incline of the resource-bearing terrain which contributed to the construction of the artificial image of the landscape, came to define the limited spatial dimension of the territory. Moreover, it became an obstacle to the development of human initiatives and a physical limitation to the explosive expansion of the city, with hills and valleys both to north and south, the sea to the west and the volcano to the south. Many of these limitations have been taken to the extreme, as in the case of dense housing along the slopes of Vesuvius, in spite of the very serious risks that this entailed; or in the case of the enormous housing expansion in the hills followed by the dramatic consequences of hydrological imbalance. Such limitations have strongly influenced choice of sites for industries which, unlike in other cities, have had to

---

[32] Ibid., 8. The data refers to 1961.

[33] E. d'Elia e A. Ippolito, 'Considerazioni sui consumi idrici della città di Napoli', paper given at 4th National Congress of Aziende Municipalizzate, Viareggio 2-3-4 maggio 1974; A. Saturnino, 'Stima del fabbisogno idrico della Regione Campania. Notazioni metodologiche e principali risultati', *TEAM Territorio Ambiente*, Series Abstracts, 2, 1990.

[34] L. Mendia, E. d'Elia, G. d'Antonio, *Sul problema dell'inquinamento del Golfo di Napoli* (Stabilimento tipografico G. Genovese, 1973), 5. See also B. Angelillo, G.C.De Riu, G.Renga, *Studio longitudinale sullo stato di inquinamento delle acque di mare costiere del litorale napoletano* (Stabilimento Tipografico G. Genovese, 1973).

[35] S. Neri Serneri, 'Water pollution in Italy, the failure of the hygienic approach (1890–1960)', in C. Bernhardt and G. Massard-Guilbaud, eds, *Le démon moderne*, 157–78.

move away from not only the local territory, but even from the province itself.[36]

A Question of Governance

With regard to the rapid development of the city, with its serious and unprecedented consequences upon the environment, Naples may be considered in line with other western cities. According to John R. McNeill, in the period after 1950 all cities in the western world progressively expanded outwards to their surrounding territories, and urban development began to have serious repercussions on natural resources.[37] Among the main characteristics of the modern period were the social and environmental effects of sanitary change and the emergence of the thermic city. What needs to be examined, however, is why in Naples the process took such an extreme form. It was during this phase that the gravity of its environmental problems singled out Naples from Italian and other western cities.

However, can the ways in which change of this kind associated with the emergence of the modern city, and linked to the specific morphology of its territory and high demographic density, explain problems of sustainability in the period between the second world war and today? Could Naples have been different, or was it 'condemned' by its peculiar characteristics to be an unmanageable network of urban chaos, a place of wasted environmental resources and social degradation?

It is true that the duty of the historian is not to argue in hypothetical terms. The task, rather, is to analyse the past and explain its underlying dynamic and logic. It is nevertheless the case that if the functioning of sustainability is to be historiographically examined, we need to ask whether or not this could have been possible, above all in the modern world? In order to do this, it is essential to identify the threshold decided upon by scientific inquiry and the political-institutional debate at a given point in time. This will make it possible to formulate the nature of relationships between productive activity and environmental resources, to control the unceasing reproduction of these resources, and guarantee their utilization in the least dissipative manner.

And yet, a 'less unsustainable' Naples could have existed. It was part of the 1939 plan which, far from being the most reactionary of Fascist measures, represented an interesting product of the urban culture of that

---

[36] For this, see Naples City Council, town-planning department's *Proposta di variante per la zona nord-occidentale di Napoli*, 141.

[37] R. McNeill, *Qualcosa di nuovo sotto il sole*, 371.

epoch. It provided for a great expansion in which built-up areas would be interspersed with open areas and parks. The plan's designers were conscious of the need to reconcile residential and occupational needs with the functioning of an overall urban ecosystem, providing large, open spaces which would by 1989 have created 16.4 sq. metres of non-agricultural land per inhabitant.[38] Against ideas of this kind, however, a series of spontaneous dynamics came into play. They could not be regulated by population movement, or levels of congestion in a specific area. But is this what really happened? Did spontaneous dynamics bring about demographic overcrowding in a province of more than half the population of the whole region, with some areas reaching a population density of 35,000 inhabitants per sq. km?[39] Or was it the case that rather than placing urban expansion within the realm of regional organization, a location hierarchy was selected, whereby Naples would become the largest attraction for heavy investment in various sectors, thus providing the greatest profits. During the post-second world war period, estate agents, professionals, business people, bureaucrats and politicians began to express intolerance towards any constraint or plan which limited the expansion of the city; rather, they promoted and supported permissive development programmes.

It was the 1950s onwards, with the constitution of the 'city-building coalition' formed by centre-right political forces and by a group of landowners and building entrepreneurs, which saw the beginning of a period in which municipal policy supported the various pressures coming from land and building speculation. Assisted by a contradiction between laws governing building regulations, this speculation supported continuous high-density urban growth, leaving no space between each development. Every corner became occupied, including the area between the historic city and the surrounding municipalities, areas which the 1939 plan had designated for public parks and agricultural land. Here began the saturation of the hill areas, including illegal construction facilitated by the adoption of changes to the proposed plan. The result was that areas designated for agriculture and public parks, or classified as 'beauty spots' soon came to be built on.[40] This transformation of nature into inert material, providing an opportunity for economic investment and rapid profit, was a process which took place throughout the whole of Italy. This was the triumph of the new entrepreneur,

---

[38] De Lucia-Iannello, 'L'urbanistica a Napoli dal dopoguerra ad oggi: note e documenti', *Urbanistica*, 65, 7.

[39] See B. Cillo, 'Aspetti urbanistici della città di Napoli', *Atlante degli uccelli nidificanti e svernanti nella città di Napoli* (Electa, 1995), 43.

[40] A. Dal Piaz, *Napoli 1945–1985. Quarant'anni di urbanistica* (Franco Angeli, 1985), 27–34.

masterfully described by Italo Calvino in his 1957 novel dedicated to building speculation.[41] Nevertheless, in Naples this phenomenon was aggravated by the fact that because of the existence of a poor productive network, construction, with the help of public authorities, became one of the main industries. Those involved were not so much true entrepreneurs, but rather bricklayers, amateur builders, technicians who were able to obtain part of the allocation of buildings damaged during the war, thus intercepting state funding. By means of a series of false survey reports, they managed to keep for themselves and their firms high profit margins. They were free to operate without any controls, and systematically violated the town-planning and construction laws in force. In this way they were able to build two or three floors higher and increase the number of apartments and rooms without meeting any institutional barriers. On the other hand, their actions were not only approved at the local level, but also by national controlling bodies, such as the Council of State, which declared legal construction licences which went against urban policy.

This model gained support in sections of Neapolitan society reaching far beyond the business circle. The construction industry provided an opportunity for development, employment and profit for the urban 'bourgeoisie' and a large section of the subproletariat. Left-wing political and trade union opposition was weak, as well as that of local information bodies.

Naples, was not the only large Italian city to be affected by intense speculation. In the post-second world war period Rome also, experienced great urban development of a speculative and destructive nature.[42] As well as its peculiar characteristics and the prevailing economic interests of the 'city-building coalition' there was also a series of factors associated with Naples and its position in southern Italy. This consisted in Naples being allocated huge financial resources from 'the southern Italy fund' and from state and corporate intervention at the national level to carry out public works and set up infrastructure and urban developments. With the initial aim of bringing southern regions in line with more developed areas, such interventions resulted in highly destructive processes.[43] Lack of sustainability lay in the actual logic of the mechanisms which justified its existence, in the reason for the work as it was perceived during these years. Public works were instrumental in promoting a system of patronage between politicians, planners and

---

[41] I. Calvino, *La speculazione edilizia*. One of the last editions is that of 1994 with Oscar Mondadori.

[42] V. De Lucia, *Se questa è una città* (Editori Riuniti, 1992), 16–21.

[43] A. Becchi, 'Opere pubbliche', *Meridiana. Rivista di storia e scienze sociali*, 9, 1990, 223–43.

builders. Their objective was not to produce something functional but rather to establish relationships that would make it easier to attain consensus. Paradoxically, the work did not have to be carried out. Interventions of this sort have left the city of Naples with a large road network, two large state housing developments in Secondigliano and Ponticelli, and the *Centro Direzionale* (Business Centre). Such great works did not take into account any damage to the environment or the countryside, nor the need for mobility and transportation or accessibility to the areas concerned. The reconstruction phase which followed the 1980 earthquake provided a further opportunity to gain access to financial resources and the multiplication of investments intended for public works of a structural nature as previously described. Also in these years the local Mafia (*Camorra*) infiltration became more apparent. In the construction sector, the direct presence of clan organizations in the bid for tenders for public works grew considerably.

It is necessary to identify from the inextricable combination of peculiar characteristics and the effects of local and national policy towards the territory, the reasons for the destructive process which led to the province becoming an area of great environmental risk. It is therefore not just a question of the effects of modernization and of the development process which have affected cities around the western world, particularly during the second half of the twentieth century. The greatest environmental damage to Naples in terms of the city that it actually became, compared to the city that it might have been, stems from the destruction of the relationship between nature and artefact, in that the environmental consequences of the construction of the city were never taken into account. The major factors contributing to the pollution of the province have resulted from the saturation of mechanisms regulating the outflow of the urban ecosystem which include domestic and industrial drainage systems, the disposal of solid waste, and traffic. It would be easy to place the blame on a general lack of infrastructure and a poorly modernized urban system. It is worth noting, however, that Naples ranks among the first cities in Italy in terms of the quality of transport infrastructure, road network and drainage system for effluents.[44]

Similarly, it would be easy to arrive at the conclusion that the traffic problem and its most serious implications are linked to the increased number of vehicles in relation to the size of the territory. Naples, however, has a per capita car ratio lower than the national average. The factors which make traffic one of the most serious problems in terms of

---

[44] R. Giannì, 'Illegalità e disordine urbanistico a Napoli negli anni '80', *La città nuova*, 3–4, 1993, 28–9.

sustainability for the city lie in the manner in which the urban structure took shape during the period of intense motorization: a poor road network, combined with inadequate public transport and limited extension of the urban rail network. All this resulted in an over-stretched, unplanned urban network.

The violation of building and hygienic plans and regulations led to construction on inclines which were too steep, to buildings that were too high and too close and serviced by an insufficient number of streets. The height of buildings, incommensurate with the width of the roads and limited number of open squares, makes the breakdown of toxic car fumes more difficult. Furthermore, as a result the level of background noise and the average temperature are heightened.[45] Environmental problems are exacerbated by reduced park areas which, according to data referring to the last ten years, amount to as little as 1.4 sq. metres per inhabitant, and the over-filling with cement of underground strata The latter causes serious interruptions in the water cycle, leading to a set of problems associated with natural causes – floods and overflows, water shortages and limited saturation of the water table, the bursting of covered channels and of the drainage system.[46]

And yet, it is impossible to separate the destructive impact on the natural environment from the social context. The sustainability of the urban configuration is strongly conditioned by the concept of a city in which nature's existence is profoundly linked to society. This is the concept of resources as commons,[47] whereby the private interest must be limited and reconciled with collective interest. This implies both a broad vision which should take external matters into consideration and a long-term vision of development which should take account of the well-being of future generations.[48] This certainly was not the idea of

[45] Ufficio tecnico Pser, 'La riqualificazione dell'area metropolitana di Napoli', *Urbanistica informazioni*, 116–17, 125.

[46] L.Postiglione, 'I rischi naturali e l'impatto antropico visti da un agronomo', in G. Barone and G. Graziano, eds, *Rischi naturali ed impatto antropico nell'area metropolitana napoletana* (Guida, 1994), 68–9.

[47] The discussion on natural resources as commons gave rise to intense debate following G. Hardin's 'The tragedy of the commons', *Science*, 1968. From the vast literature, I refer to: A. Alchian and H. Demsetz, 'The property rights paradigm', *The Journal of Economic History*, March 1973, 16–27; S.V. Ciriacy-Wantrup, R.C. Bishop, '"Common property" as a concept in natural resource policy', *Natural Resources Journal*, October 1975, 713–27; *Proceedings of the conference on common property resource management* (National Academy Press, 1986).

[48] A well structured and more complex reasoning related to the concept of development deriving from the consideration of natural resources as commons can be found in P. Dasgupta, *The control of resources* (Harvard University Press, 1982).

urban expansion which prevailed between the political and municipal powers governing the city between the 1950s and 1980s. Naples is a case of outright denial in the most profound meaning of Garrett Hardin's 'Tragedy of the Commons'.[49] As Adam Smith noted: the free pursuit of private interests does not lead to the protection of common property, but to its destruction. It leads to disastrous results which swallow up, destroy, kill, and which in Naples have led to a list of foreseeable tragedies. 'Unnatural catastrophes' have followed one after the other at an unrelenting pace over the last few decades (4,000 landslides between 1966-69) and others which more recently have caused substantial suffering and even death.[50]

At the beginning of the 1990s, there was a reversal in municipal policy regarding the relationship between the city and its natural resources. This policy reversal, despite having been mooted ten years earlier, was not to come fully into force until the 1990s. It is important to remember here that policy was changed from an instrument which gave full support to private speculation, totally dismissing the relationship between nature and society, to one which organized urban development in a way which would minimize the destruction of both the territory and its natural resources. Taken together, such policies constitute a plan of urban and ecological renewal for the whole of the city of Naples, with a view to facing not only the problems of renewal and development of open spaces, but more generally those of the quality of the environment and the physical integrity of the territory, including pollution of the air, water and underground strata, waste management, and control of hydrogeological decline.[51] What was intended were not grandiose works, but rather the setting of objectives which would return normal conditions of efficiency to the city: urban renewal, development of services, restructuring of public rail transport, conservation of public parks. The greatest innovation, however, remains that of conserving those remaining areas which have not been built upon, amounting to nearly 4,000 hectares of uncultivated agricultural land.

Returning to the questions raised earlier, there is no doubt that problems originating from the particular morphology of the territory and high demographic density cannot explain the reasons for the process through which Naples was transformed from a place once blessed with resources of extraordinary environmental value to an area of high environmental risk. Even though structural factors made the expansion process extremely complex, they did not wholly determine it. The main

---

[49] Reference here is to G. Hardin, *The tragedy of the commons*, 1244–5.

[50] Eleonora Puntillo, *Le catastrofi innaturali* (Tullio Pironti editore 2001).

[51] Naples City Council, *Indirizzi per la pianificazione urbanistica*, Napoli, 19 giugno 1994, 10.

reasons lie in an absence of territorial governance. In the period since the 1950s, the growth of the city was managed without considering possible, and serious, environmental consequences. Instead of dedicating itself to the conservation of public property, municipal policy favoured private interests. And while in the last ten years things have certainly changed, the past cannot be wiped out. It will continue to produce broad and long-term consequences which run against the social and collective value of natural resources.

CHAPTER SEVEN

The Struggle for Urban Space: Nantes and Clermont-Ferrand, 1830–1930[1]

Geneviève Massard-Guilbaud

On September 21, 2001, when the world was still traumatized by the attacks on the twin towers in New York, 330,000 tonnes of ammonium nitrate exploded at the AZF plant in Toulouse. This industrial catastrophe, the most serious in Western Europe since the end of the second world war, killed thirty people, injured several thousand and destroyed innumerable buildings. People lost their homes, children found themselves without schools and wage-earners were deprived of work. The site of the explosion itself resembled a devastated battlefield. When the official investigation began, observers emphasized how outrageous it was that a factory of this kind should have been located at the very heart of so densely populated an area. Thirty thousand people lived within the immediate vicinity of AZF – a plant belonging to the Total-Fina-Elf group – and its two neighbours, the Société Nationale des Poudres et Explosifs, which manufactured gunpowder and explosives, and Tolochimie. It had long been known precisely how dangerous these enterprises were. Indeed, each factory had been submitted to stringent national security standards, known as 'Seveso 2'.

A central and underlying question generated by these tragic events is how any society can evaluate and then set about coping with the risks that it generates, not least since the idea of a totally risk-free society is wholly illusory. However, following the catastrophe in Toulouse, a majority of observers simply wanted to know how it was that a potentially threatening plant of this kind could have been allowed to be constructed so close to residential dwellings. Historians could have explained that precisely the opposite occurred: it was *residential houses* that had gradually been built in ever larger numbers in the immediate vicinity of highly dangerous factories. The catastrophe was not

[1] I am very grateful to my fellow editors: Bill Luckin, for the patience with which he edited this paper from the rather approximate English in which it was originally written, and Dieter Schott for his careful reading and comments. Needless to say, all the mistakes which remain are my own.

fortuitous, its origins could be clearly detected and a similar kind of tragedy might at any moment afflict other centres in urban France.

Indeed, debate over this issue began as early as the end of the eighteenth century. A law of 1810, modified in 1917 and 1976, stated that dangerous or unhealthy plants must not be located close to dwellings. Nonetheless, as the cities sprawled, larger numbers of houses were erected closer to, and almost surrounded, the potentially life-threatening plants. Very frequently, public authorities themselves failed in their duty and allowed (by way of official planning maps – *plans d'occupation des sols*) dwellings, infrastructure and amenities to merge with dangerous industrial plant. We then need to ask why these regulations have come to be so freely ignored. Was the law itself inadequate? Have policy-makers failed to comprehend the need to introduce spatial restrictions? Have good intentions been outweighed by the increasing power of vested interests? In a word, who have held responsibility for the construction and protection of urban, public and residential space?

This contribution seeks to show how situations of this kind have come into existence and perpetuated themselves. It also attempts to provide an overview of the vested power of industry and the margin for manoeuvre possessed by public authorities. The paper comprises two case-studies, Nantes and Clermont-Ferrand. These examples cannot, of course, lay claim to universality. However, in both instances, the plants in question possessed major importance within their respective cities. Indeed, in Clermont-Ferrand, they continue to do so at the beginning of the twenty-first century. The first case-study concerns the Prairie-aux-Ducs (The Duke Meadows), an island at the heart of Nantes, a large port city at the mouth of the Loire. The second case-study focuses on the multinational, though still privately owned, corporation of Michelin, in Clermont-Ferrand. This enterprise has long dominated the industrial and residential infrastructure of the town and exerted a massive influence over the lives of its inhabitants. Following the logic of globalization, in recent years Michelin has expanded outwards into the developing world. Yet the company still owns and operates factories at the very heart of residential areas in Clermont.

Nantes: City Against Industry

Throughout July 1883 Nantes experienced a terrible stench. Inhabitants had frequently complained about this recurrent nuisance but, on this occasion, it had become unendurable. Unaware of the discoveries of the new microbiology, many feared that the stink would trigger a cholera

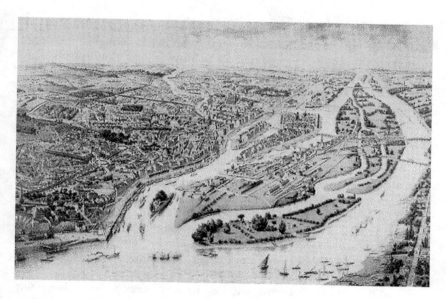

Figure 7.1   Nantes seen from South-West. Engraving 1888. Cliché
Ville de Nantes. By permission of Musée du Château des
Ducs de Bretagne. The second island from the bottom of
the picture is the Prairie-aux-Ducs. The factories, canals,
railway station we are evoking below are visible.

epidemic. Some claimed that the odour could be traced back to the
production of ammonia sulphate in the Prairie-aux-Ducs[2] (see Figure 7.1).
   Pressurized by local inhabitants, the head of the *conseil central
d'hygiène et de salubrité* – a departmental board of health with
consultative powers – sought prefectorial power to investigate the
factories. Receiving a positive response, the *conseil* established a
commission which concluded that twenty-eight factories on the island
were ill-administered and 'notoriously unhealthy and insalubrious'.[3]
Only three had obtained a legal right to begin operations and the
manufacturing processes that were being used were clearly capable of
creating the stink that now afflicted the city. The *préfet* was advised that
any plant that had failed to gain prior authorization would be expelled.

---

[2] All information on the Prairie-aux-Ducs history can be found in Archives
Départementales de Loire-Atlantique, (ADLA) série 1M, and especially 1M
2901 et 1M 1550.
[3] All translations are by the author.

However, each would be given a year in which to find an alternative site, and in the interim, required to implement basic hygienic measures. However, the question remained as to how it was that twenty-eight plants, which were patently in breach of the law, and following highly insalubrious production practices, could have survived without having been noticed or reprimanded by the authorities. In fact, the enterprises had gradually insinuated themselves onto the island and transformed an area in which cattle had quietly grazed at the beginning of the century into a large industrial quarter with close links to maritime commerce. Actually, we can detect a degree of hypocrisy in the prefect's 'discovery' that a number of factories had established themselves. A glance at the map indicates the wide range of buildings that had been put up on the island. It reveals several streets and squares, and a railway track and station, as well as four canals running into one of the many tributaries of the Loire (see Figure 7.2). How could all this have been established on the island without the authorities knowing about it or even complicity with what had been done?

To understand these events, we need to move back to an earlier point in the century. The first factory had opened its doors in 1836. By 1855 there were thirteen and twenty-eight in 1883. Each of these businesses specialized in the production of chemicals. They also treated sewage. The liquid element was transformed into ammonia sulphate and solids into a fertilizer called poudrette. Animal charcoal, transported from every part of the country, was stored here before being delivered to sugar refineries on the north bank of the river, where it was used for the purification of sugar or coagulated and dried to produce fertilizer. Guano and seaweed were imported, and so were mountains of lime sulphate which, reacting with sulphuric acid, were transformed into superphosphates, highly valued by farmers. Horn, bones, scraps of leather from slaughterhouse, fish remains from canning factories – very nearly everything associated with the old chemical order were treated in the Prairie-aux-Ducs. The organic chemical revolution of the late-nineteenth century had yet to make its presence felt.

During the official investigation which followed a request for the opening of the first factory, the city had reacted positively. But the municipal council then changed its mind and rejected succeeding applications in the hope that the island might develop into a luxurious residential district. The municipal council only possessed advisory and consultative powers in relation to the establishment of a new factory, and its opinion could be ignored by the *préfet*. Moreover, the criteria which had to be applied – would the factory constitute a nuisance vis-à-vis already existing neighbours? – prevented him from expressing a view on what, from the perspective of zoning, should be

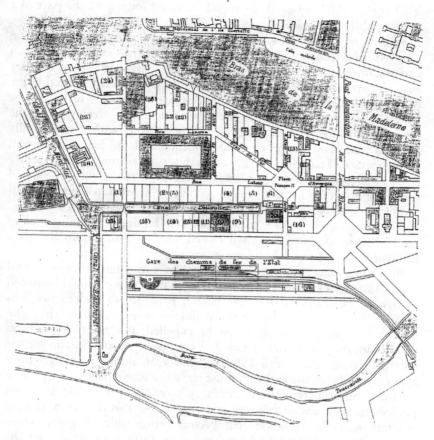

Figure 7.2   The Prairie aux-Ducs in 1883 (part of), scale 0.0002 m.
Archives départementales de Loire-Atlantique, 1M 1550

allowed to be erected in a specific location. Nevertheless, in arriving
at a negative view in relation to the opening of factories, the mayor
attempted to make partial use of planning powers that the law had
effectively denied him. In the early 1840s, the *préfecture* adopted an
ambiguous   attitude   towards   the   issue   of   authorization.
Notwithstanding the repeated complaints of the municipality, the
préfet reacted passively and turned a blind eye to the new factories,
which were tolerated 'at their own risk'. In other words, formal
permission would not be required. The works would easily be
expelled when it became absolutely essential to do so – at least, that

is what the *préfet* believed. Strange behaviour indeed on the part of a vested public authority!

Several of the factories which had applied for a licence having received negative response, newly arrived enterprises evaded regulation and began operations without obtaining permission to do so. Protests ensued, particularly on the part of a middle-class element located in the expensive tenements built during the eighteenth century on the embankment which faced the island to the north. Nevertheless, the Prairie-aux-Ducs was soon transformed into a home for the most foully noxious industries in the city. Convenience and the fact that several unauthorized factories were successfully operating there clearly constituted major incentives. Officially unknown to the authorities, and therefore exempt from a need to adopt salubrious methods of production, most of the works operated in appalling conditions. Perishable goods were kept for far too long. Drying was undertaken in the open air. Open rather than closed vessels were habitually used. Effluent went untreated into canals.

In 1855, following yet another public campaign, the municipal council attempted to persuade the *préfet* that an order should be issued to banish the factories from the island. Evidence of malpractice was presented and there was now widespread expectation that the insalubrious works would at last be expelled. But the final decision rested with the *préfet*, and he failed to act. As a consequence, no further measures were taken until 1883. In that year, public protesters once again insisted that the factories must leave the island. The citizenry was inflamed but the republican *préfet* behaved no differently than his predecessors. A new survey was undertaken, but this did no more than reiterate that the situation had become intolerable. The *préfecture* ignored the new set of findings, preferring instead to argue that the works must seek legal authorization. Twenty-two 'clandestine' factories did so. Five of the most insalubrious were requested to leave the locality within three months. The mayor was to be responsible for the implementation of the decision. Legally, this was correct. Every mayor during our period had wanted to banish the factories but had been prevented from doing so by the absence of prefectoral confirmation. When the order was finally given, the municipality tried to find alternative sites for displaced works, since the work that they undertook was vital for the city. They collected sewage, treated slaughterhouse waste, disposed of every kind of foul matter requiring immediate extrusion from residential districts and furnished other manufacturers with much-needed raw materials. But the mayor failed to find adequate new sites, not least as a result of the fact that, when approached, neighbouring municipalities refused to cooperate. As for the *conseil d'hygiène*, it repeatedly insisted that it must advise where factories *should not* be located, not where they *should*.

Had it not been tinged with tragedy, the narrative of Nantes might well have been comic. In order to prevent the spread of pollution, it was suggested that the canals into which manufacturers had long been dumping waste should be filled in. But these waterways – and notably the Pelloutier canal – which had been illegally dug, could not claim a legal existence. As a result it was unclear who should pay the costs for remedial action of this kind. Plans for the construction of water and sewage disposal systems were also discussed, but to little avail. The construction of a sewerage system might have provided a solution, but only if it directed sewage and waste water from the factories to a treatment plant or if the works themselves purified their own effluent. But none of these possibilities was contemplated. In August 1900 – seventeen years after the first decision to expel the factories from the island – the works were still there, and the *préfet* framed a new decree to compel them to leave. However, in November he granted yet another delay. And here the evidence runs out. Over a period of sixty years nobody had been able to prevent the establishment and day-to-day operation of foul-smelling factories at the very heart of one of the largest cities in France. We do not know what happened after 1900, but the much-debated island continued to be dominated by industry until deindustrialization set in during the 1970s and 1980s.

What lessons can be learnt from this narrative? First, as early as the 1830s the city government envisaged a future very different from that which actually came into being. It hoped to encourage the development of a residential area on unspoilt and picturesque land, and in doing so demonstrated that it possessed a sense of how to plan and zone.

Second, successive *préfets*, powerful representatives of the central state, repeatedly broke the law. This happened within a context in which the medical police responsible for the inspection of polluting factories and workshops worked well and effectively in other parts of the city throughout the nineteenth century.[4] One is therefore forced to conclude that the *préfecture* endorsed two quite different policies. Attitudes towards small and isolated enterprises tended to be severe but socially powerful undertakings were leniently treated. The factories described in this paper were either small or medium-sized. However, they derived their power from the fact that their urban waste disposal activities were central to the healthiness of the city as a whole. The successive *préfets* believed that, *in extremis*, it would indeed be possible to banish the factories, but this proved inaccurate. The issue of corruption should also

---

[4] See ADLA 1M.

be raised – it almost certainly played a role. But here the archives provide only hints and allusions.

Next, there was the issue of the extraordinary complexity of the administrative process. Thus the *conseil d'hygiène*, the best informed body, or rather, the body which should have been best informed, was concerned with evaluation and advice but deprived of power.[5] The *conseil de préfecture* acted as an advisory committee for the *préfet*, who took the decisions but played no part in their implementation. And finally, the mayor and municipal council, who were required to enforce prefectoral decisions, only rarely appeared to agree with them.

We may now return, by way of conclusion, to the question posed in the introduction to this paper – the balance between industrialists and public authorities in relation to the use of public urban space. This first case-study indicates that in Nantes it was impossible to enforce a law forbidding the interpenetration of industrial and residential zones. When the 'dirty' manufacturing interest had fully imbedded itself within the city, the potential of regulatory control became ever weaker. As in every other urban centre, Nantes generated waste products which had to be removed from the inner core. Disposal had to be undertaken rapidly and in close proximity to the city itself: factory-owners who claimed that their enterprises would cease to be profitable if plant had to be resited to remote locations were simply telling the truth. This was the vicious circle that neutralized the implementation of regulations that would have separated residential from manufacturing space.

Clermont-Ferrand: Industry Against Urban Planning

In terms of chronology, our second case-study is very different from the first, since it is located in the period between the two world wars. Clermont-Ferrand, at the dead centre of France, remained under-industrialized until the beginning of the twentieth century. At this date, the Michelin company, which was to become an overwhelmingly dominant manufacturing presence, began operation. This company has always and continues to be perceived as central to the development of the city. Indeed, the tyre-producing giant became known for the range of facilities that it provided – housing, social amenities and clubs, schools,

---

[5] For a considerable period – despite laboratory breakthroughs in bacteriology – they continued to adhere to the idea that infections were transmitted by miasmas generated by putrefaction rather than via the media of polluted water. On this subject, see the case of Croydon, observed by Nicholas Goddard in this book.

a cooperative shop. Not only has Michelin long been acknowledged as a positive force for the development of the city in which it is located, but it has also been widely perceived as distancing itself from local politics: no member of the family ever sat on the municipal council or stood for the mayoralty. Nevertheless, and as this section seeks to demonstrate, the company affected the city in every conceivable way – social, economic, environmental and cultural. Michelin not only employed thousands of workers but wholly controlled the construction of urban space. This was to the detriment of the community at large: early twentieth century Clermont-Ferrand was shaped according to a plan which served the interests of its largest employer rather than the residential needs of its inhabitants.

In order to better understand this argument, we need to say rather more about geography and history. The city of Clermont-Ferrand originally comprised two towns separated by a distance of three kilometers. Clermont was the larger and older. Montferrand was a medieval bastide which reached its peak of glory in the later middle ages and then declined into a sleepy wine-growing community. The towns had been joined by royal decree in 1630, a decision long opposed by the inhabitants of Montferrand. By the beginning of the twentieth century, the latter still hankered after independence and in 1911 vigorously demonstrated against inclusion within the *octroi*, the limit within which it was compulsory for outsiders to pay taxes on goods in order to allow them to enter the city. Montferrand looked upon itself as a poor relation – a 'despised suburb' – to their larger neighbour. The first world war seemed to reduce animosity. However, in 1919 the inhabitants of Montferrand presented their own independent list for the municipal elections of that year and in 1926 initiated a new campaign for full independence.[6] The problem was central to local politics.

After having stagnated for most of the nineteenth century, Clermont-Ferrand now entered a period of very rapid demographic growth. The population reached 53,000 in 1901, 65,000 in 1911 and no fewer than 111,000 in 1926. The increase was mainly attributable to the expansion of the rubber industry and more specifically to the growth of Michelin, which made great strides during the war.[7] The city suffered from a severe housing shortage and grave sanitary deficiencies – there was no adequate public water supply system and the disposal and treatment of sewage was rather archaic. The death-rate remained unacceptably high

---

[6] P. Chirac, *Le séparatisme montferrandais*, mémoire de maîtrise, dir. Massard-Guilbaud (Clermont-Ferrand, 1996).

[7] A. Moulin-Bourret, *Guerre et industrie, Clermont-Ferrand 1912–1922: la victoire du pneu*, 2 vols (Clermont-Ferrand, 1997).

at 22.5 per thousand population.[8] Clearly, the city needed to cleanse and modernize the urban core and construct, as rapidly as possible, extensive suburban districts.

Despite the efforts of the Musée Social, a Parisian group concerned with propaganda on behalf of urban and sanitary planning, to develop new attitudes towards town planning, France remained backward in this area until the end of the first world war. Ten years after the seminal British Town Planning Act of 1909, a key piece of legislation, the *loi Cornudet* was passed by parliament. It obliged cities with populations of more than ten thousand – as well as centres dependent on tourism – to draw up development and improvement plans.[9] However, this law, which was strengthened in 1924, was only very partially implemented. By 1931 approximately three hundred out of the 1,600 centres which should have complied, had in fact produced relevant documentation. Of these, only very few had transformed plan into reality.[10]

Clermont-Ferrand prepared its plan. Rather than consult experts, the municipal council 'entrust[ed] people who had known the city and its needs for a long time'. A team, including the chief engineer, city architect and highways officer, was entrusted with the work. In addition, an extra-municipal commission, containing members of the council and coopted representatives, was appointed.[11] The mayor informed the council that the plan 'aimed to prevent the development of irrational buildings'. It would be 'based on big ideas [and include] streets, boulevards and open spaces of such grace and size that there would be no regrets in the future'. 'The city', he continued, 'which is now entering a new phase of development, will possess streets and gardens worthy of its prosperity and the beauty of the landscape which surrounds it'.[12] Given the many problems by which Clermont-Ferrand found itself confronted, the work of the planning team was crucially important. However, as the mayor's words indicate, practicalities were sacrificed on the altar of civic glory.

---

[8] Ph. Arbos, *Etude de géographie urbaine: Clermont-Ferrand* (Clermont-Ferrand, 1930), 127. See also Ch. Genaud, *La question de l'eau à Clermont-Ferrand, 1850–1914*, and B. Rispal, *La naissance de l'hygiène, Les Conseils d'hygiène et de salubrité du Puy-de-Dôme 1848–1930*, mémoires de maîtrise, dir. Massard-Guilbaud (Clermont-Ferrand, 1997 and 2003).

[9] A. Sutcliffe, ed., *The rise of the modern urban planning, 1800–1914* (London, 1980). A. Sutcliffe, ed., *Towards the planned city, Germany, Britain, the United States, 1780–1914* (Oxford, 1981). J.-P. Gaudin, *L'Avenir en Plan. Technique et politique dans la prévision urbaine, 1900–1930* (Seyssel, 1985).

[10] G. Monnier (dir.), *L'architecture moderne en France*, tome 1, *1889–1940* (Paris, 1997), 144. See also G. Bardet, *L'urbanisme* (Paris, 1945), 28.

[11] *Bulletin municipal de Clermont-Ferrand (BMCF)*, April 16th, 1920.

[12] Ibid.

The historian can try to evaluate what priorities might have served the interests of the inhabitants of Clermont-Ferrand better that this rhetoric. First, it would have been essential to reduce over-crowding in the urban core. Second, the planners were now in a position to give high priority to narrowing the spatial and, as a consequence, the social gap between Clermont and Montferrand. In terms of this second task, at the end of the first world war, the large area that separated the two centres continued to lack anything remotely approaching adequate residential provision, even though the Michelin company had established its first housing estate at the foot of the medieval walls of Montferrand (see Figure 7.3). In the remainder of this area, there was a cemetery, slaughterhouse, gas works, and a massive barracks. However, as has already been noted, the bulk of the area remained free of buildings at a time when it was clearly ripe for increased urbanization. In other geographical directions topography worked against coherent expansion. To the west, Clermont abutted on to neighbouring towns, while to the north-east and south a steep incline and railway tracks blocked coordinated development (in due course a huge viaduct would be constructed to improve access to the plateau that edged the city to the south). The north-eastern plain separating Clermont from Montferrand was clearly the place where new building demanded to be undertaken.

Before considering how the municipality confronted this problem, we need to say rather more about the principal though 'uninvited' actor in this complex narrative – the Michelin company. Founded in 1889, the enterprise expanded rapidly and in rhythm with burgeoning demand for automobile tyres. Michelin originally established itself at the northern limit of Clermont on the banks of the river Tiretaine, a small waterway with an irregular and foully polluted flow which would prove a convenient stream in which to dump waste water and all other kinds of industrial effluent. Between 1889 and 1919, the area occupied by this first plant increased from 12,380 to 100,000 square metres. The growth in number of employees was equally remarkable – from 182 in 1892 to no fewer than ten thousand in 1919.[13] Hardly surprisingly, in 1913 a second site, which would be used as a stockyard, was acquired next to the railway track.[14] At the end of hostilities the demand for tyres increased even more rapidly and as a consequence Michelin needed to find another site and build housing estates to attract migrants from the countryside. Important land purchases had already been made in the

---

[13] These figures were gathered by L. Dumont, in A. Gueslin (dir.), *Michelin, Les hommes du pneu tome 1, 1889–1940* (Paris, 1993), 54. We know very little about Michelin, since the company has never allowed historians to examine its archives.

[14] Ibid., p. 50.

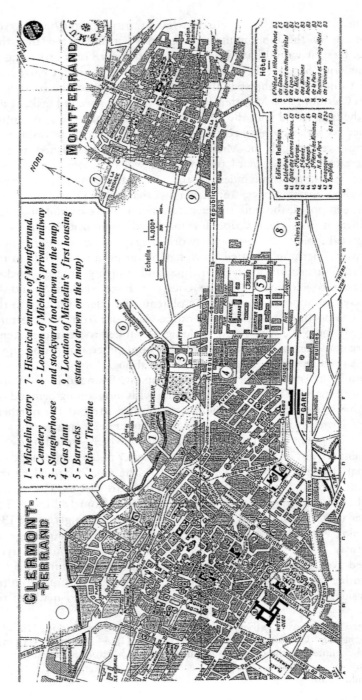

Figure 7.3   Clermont-Ferrand in 1918. In *Guide pratique Pol Clermont-Ferrand-Royat, 1918*

under-developed area between the two cities. It was precisely at this juncture that Michelin began to play a major role in the planning process.

In fact, not one but two successive and quite different planning maps were drawn up in order to fulfil the demands of the law of 1919. The first was produced in 1921 but then abandoned. This map is reproduced in this article for the first time (Figure 7.4).[15] The second was prepared in 1925, adopted by the council and forwarded to the central authority which, despite making substantial criticisms, granted its approval (Figure 7.5). In comparing the maps, we shall concentrate on the problematic area separating the two centres. According to the 1921 version, Michelin had already acquired a large portion of land to the west of Montferrand. Housing estates began to stretch along the road that runs from one city to the other. In the space that was left, the planners foresaw the development of streets, which would prepare the way for much needed residential provision, and squares. One of the latter was to be located in the space formerly occupied by the slaughterhouse, which would be moved elsewhere. The design combined a grid formation with a far less regular pattern. Overall, there was a degree of balance.

We may now compare this first tentative plan with the final version. The space controlled by Michelin now amounted to an extraordinarily large area: indeed, the three factories, excluding the housing estates, now covered 420 ha., a space approximately equivalent to that occupied by the 'old' Clermont.[16] Streets and squares had disappeared and the space had been appropriated by a company which was now invading yet additional land to the north of Montferrand. A nightmarish landscape of the future had already been etched in – tall smoke stacks, railway tracks, aerial pipes, thirty metre high tyre testing apparatus and electric cables – would soon separate the two towns.

It is possible to reconstruct the manner in which the company pressurized and then out-manoeuvred the mayor and the council in order to obtain this result. First, Michelin needed more land. After preliminary negotiations the company presented the mayor, a *radical-socialiste* doctor, a comprehensive package of measures. On March 12 1920, the council was asked to approve an agreement that had been prepared on the basis of these Michelin proposals.[17] This long text favoured the eradication of two existing streets which, in the light of

---

[15] I was extremely surprised to discover the second map while gathering material for this article. No existing work on the history of the city even hints of its existence.

[16] M. Couret-Le Guédard, *Le développement urbain de Clermont de 1900 à 1925*, mémoire de maîtrise, dir. Gille (Clermont-Ferrand, 1972).

[17] *BMCF*, March 12th, 1920.

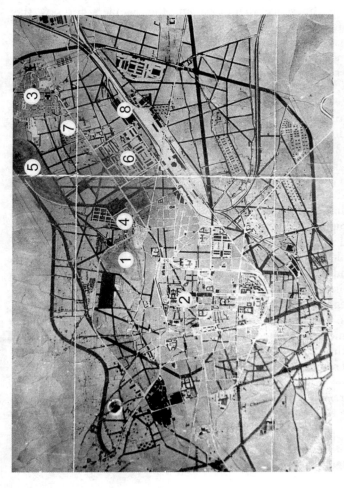

Figure 7.4 First enlargement project for Clermont-Ferrand, 1921. All the streets drawn in black are projected ones. 1- Michelin factory, 2- Clermont, 3- Montferrand, 4- Cemetery, 5- 'New Michelin factory', 6- Barracks, 7- First Michelin housing estate, 8- Michelin private railway and stockyard. (Archives des services techniques de la ville de Clermont-Ferrand)

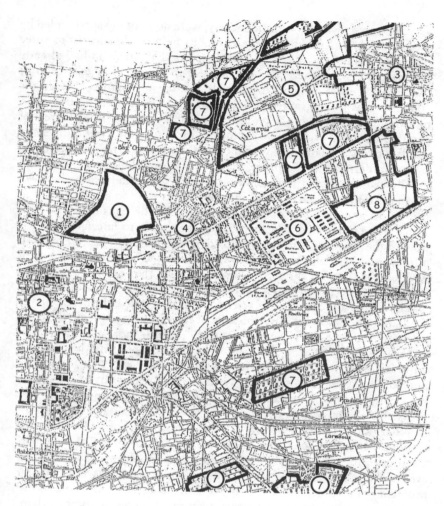

Figure 7.5 Enlargement project for Clermont-Ferrand, 1925, adopted
by ministerial decree 1926. All the areas circled with black
lines are Michelin properties. 1- Michelin factory, 2-
Clermont, 3- Montferrand, 4- Cemetery, 5- 'New Michelin
factory', 6- Barracks, 7- Michelin housing estates, 8-
Michelin private railway and stockyard. (Archives des
services techniques de la ville de Clermont-Ferrand)

successive expansions of the old factory, were now totally surrounded by industrial plant. In addition, there was to be an 'adjustment' to three other thoroughfares which cut into the plots that Michelin had already purchased.[18] Next, there was the issue of the creation or extension of two other streets which would link factory to factory. Third, the company was to be granted the right to install additional equipment – pipes and cables – across public rights of way. As if that were not enough, Michelin would also be allowed to build a private railway to connect plant to plant: this would cross the wide street which stretched from Monferrand to Clermont, which was currently served by a tram. Finally, the filthy river Tiretaine would be deepened in the area between the old and the new factory. All these measures were to be carried out at Michelin's expense. The municipality accepted the package. Only two demands were rejected. The city lacked the power to interfere with the flow of the Tiretaine – in which the company wanted to install pipes. It also refused Michelin a right of way through the cemetery. The mayor was satisfied, and expressed himself amazed that such a wonderful bargain had been struck. He stated that he 'dare[d] not use the word "sacrifice" to describe the expenses the powerful Michelin Company [had imposed] upon itself for the sake of the city'. Aggregating the costs of the proposed works, he presented the total – more than a million francs – as a *saving*. The company was certainly spending this sum but only in order to maximize profits from the land that had been purchased. Needless to say, the city had not in reality saved a centime. In addition, the municipality agreed to 'all the arrangements that [Michelin] might need in the future'.

What kind of explanation can the historian provide for such seemingly senseless behaviour on the part of the mayor and the council? Of course, the expansion of industrial plants would provide work for ever-larger numbers of workers. But unemployment was not a major problem at this time, and certainly not a major concern for the city. But the mayor wished to see his city transformed into a modern, urban-industrial centre, based on a new and dynamic manufacturing enterprise. But, in succumbing to this temptation, the municipality renounced an opportunity to take control of its most valuable asset – space.

The municipality had been both misguided and not a little dishonest. Michelin had probably spent very large sums to convince the owners of numerous parcels of land that they needed that it would be in their best interests to sell. Some resisted. To get round this problem the mayor deployed powers of expropriation, claiming that such action was in the

---

BMCF, April 16th, 1920.

public interest. In due course, the land that had been compulsorily purchased was passed on to Michelin. This occurred in 1920 and again in 1922: fifteen lots required to widen the street linking the main entries of the old and the new factory were made subject to compulsory purchase orders.[19] Expropriation was justified on the grounds that it was essential to undertake street widening, but the real motive was Michelin's determination to extend a private railway line to their original factory. The 'need' was not in fact 'public'. The expropriation cost the city almost 154,000 francs, 50 per cent more than the hundred thousand francs that Michelin had recently offered the city to finance sanitary reform.[20]

The company may not have needed authorization to purchase land but it did require permission to construct and open a new factory. In this respect, it is genuinely surprising that the *préfet* should have granted permission, since zoning – in practice, though not as a legal requirement – was becoming more prominent in urban France at this time.[21] However, we do not know if and when this permission had, if ever, been granted: there is no 'Michelin' entry in the 'rubber' file of the official archives. Who knows when and why these records disappeared?

The conclusion that can be drawn from this second case-study is clear enough. A key tract of urban space should have been used to improve the lot of the community as a whole, to develop and make more airy a city that was metaphorically suffocating within its traditional bounds. But this area was appropriated by an all-powerful company which exchanged the promise of work and civic prestige for what would rapidly degenerate into an environmentally and visually degraded cityscape. Decisions taken during this period inhibited the possibility of coherent town planning for many years to come. This is confirmed by the fact that, as you enter the early twenty-first century city from the north, you will be astonished by the sight of cathedral spires framed by two massive factory chimneys. Municipal politicians possessing the power to act in the interests of the community to which they were responsible had been willing to barter the future for a right to accommodate the massively successful company that fate had brought to its gates. And as if this were not enough, the tyre test apparatus built in the 1920s, but no longer used, has recently been declared a 'national heritage'. Even were the mighty Michelin to close or go elsewhere, it would leave its mark on the landscape for a very long time.

[19] *BMCF*, November 24th, 1922.
[20] *BMCF*, March 6th, 1922.
[21] This only became compulsory with the passing of legislation on April 20, 1932.

Conclusion

Although these two case studies deal with two cities of a rather different kind, and at different times, they give us a first insight into the variety of ways industry could interfere within the urban development and prevent the use of urban planning as a tool in the service of a whole community. These interferences are all the more serious for their long-term effects, as is often the case in environmental matters. In both the cases we examined, the consequences of the policies followed, in the nineteenth century for the first, in the 1920s for the latter, are still visible today in the cityscape, and their social effects still vivid.

Nantes is, by many aspects, a beautiful city: the medieval fabric of the urban centre still in situ, many historical monuments as important as the gothic cathedral or the Renaissance castle (Château des Ducs de Bretagne), beautiful *hôtels* built in local yellow limestone by wealthy ship constructors, superb eighteenth century estates to the west of city, interesting achievements of the nineteenth century, too. Nobody would assert that the industrialization of the Prairie-aux-Ducs totally spoiled a city which has many other assets and charms. But Nantes' mayor was not mistaken when he claimed, in the 1830s, that this island was wonderfully situated to welcome a nice residential neighbourhood. Given the time he said that, he probably did not think of a public utility, more of a middle class estate development. A determinist history or geography, the kind we all learnt at school some decades ago, would have considered it 'natural' that industry had settled near the river which made transport easy. The same would find it 'natural' as well that it has become an ugly industrial wasteland by the end of the twentieth century. But let us imagine, looking back at the engraving shown above, how appropriate the place would have been to establish a great public garden all along the several arms of the river and just in front of the spectacle of the port, a park that the lower classes living above the port, in Chantenay, could have easily enjoyed?[22] Historians are not supposed to write counterfactual history. But the understanding that landscapes are anything but 'natural', that there are constructions which change according to the balance of social forces, requires the ability to imagine alternative paths.

The case of Clermont is much worse, as the impact of Michelin is still greater, and happened in a city which was far from having the presence of Nantes. The settlement of the company between the two historical parts of the city not only prevented their unification into a continuous

---

[22] The city needed one: it would buy, in 1913, the beautiful but until then private Parc de Procé, situated at the west of the city.

urban fabric and the building of well-situated new healthy neighbourhoods. It desperately spoiled the visual cityscape. But you may need to be an outsider to realize the extent of the despoliation. The conviction that Michelin brought wealth, prosperity and even fame to the city (however shaken by the thousands of redundancies of the last decades) seems to make locals blind to the urbanistic mess they are living in because of the presence, right in the middle of the city, of such huge factories, surrounded by their long and sad walls and topped by high chimney stacks, big tanks and so on. Being myself struck by this chaotic landscape, I was still more upset by the answer I often got from the Clermontois when I challenged the beauty of their city: why should the city be beautiful? Haven't you seen the wonderful countryside we have? This is generally being said with a nod toward the volcanoes, and namely the highest of them, the puy de Dôme. This state of mind often made me think that in spite of the age of this city, most of its inhabitants still see themselves as rurals, who flocked in the city only to earn their living and eager to leave it as soon as they can – which they massively do during the weekends. As if the offspring of the migrants from the beginning of the twentieth century, drained from the countryside by Michelin, were still resisting their cultural urbanization, and did not care about the looks of their city. . . .

Other case studies will be needed to generalize about the ways industry interfered in the use of urban space. But we shall probably find out that the process usually rested, as is the case in these two examples, on local characteristics and customs, on social stratification, on the demographic, geographic and environmental conditions, and therefore produced a wide range of outcomes.

CHAPTER EIGHT

Sanitate Crescamus:
Water Supply, Sewage Disposal and Environmental Values in a Victorian Suburb

Nicholas Goddard

'The History of Croydon is but the History of the World'[1]

The Public Health Act of 1848 was the culmination of what A. S. Wohl has termed the 'first stage' in the British public health movement which followed the publication in 1842 of Edwin Chadwick's famous *Report on the Sanitary Conditions of the Labouring Population of Great Britain*. The Act not only established a General Board of Health but also had provisions for local authorities to form local boards of health with extensive powers over town infrastructure, including the management of water supply and sewage disposal, and the regulation and control of offensive trades, unfit habitations, and 'nuisance' removal. Establishment of local boards was initially slow as the clauses that provided for them were permissive rather than mandatory, and although the General Board could impose them on districts where the death rate exceeded 23:1000 these powers were rarely enacted.[2] Paradoxically, it was the smaller towns which enjoyed relatively salubrious living conditions which evinced most enthusiasm for adopting the Act. Thus the average population of the first fifteen places to petition for a local board of health consisted of less than 18,000 inhabitants.[3] Foremost amongst these pioneers was the town of Croydon, located about twelve miles south of London and with a mid-nineteenth century population of about 20,000. Its local board was the first to install a continuous piped water supply and sewage removal

---

[1] Comment in *Croydon Chronicle* (CC) 13 Apr. 1867.

[2] A.S. Wohl, *Endangered Lives. Public Health in Victorian Britain* (London, 1983), 149–50. For a recent re-evaluation of Chadwick's work see C. Hamlin, *Public Health and Social Justice in the Age of Chadwick* (Cambridge, 1998).

[3] N. Goddard and J. Sheail, 'Victorian sanitary reform; where were the innovators?' in C. Bernhardt, ed., *Environmental Problems in European Cities in the 19th and 20th Centuries* (Münster, 2001), 88.

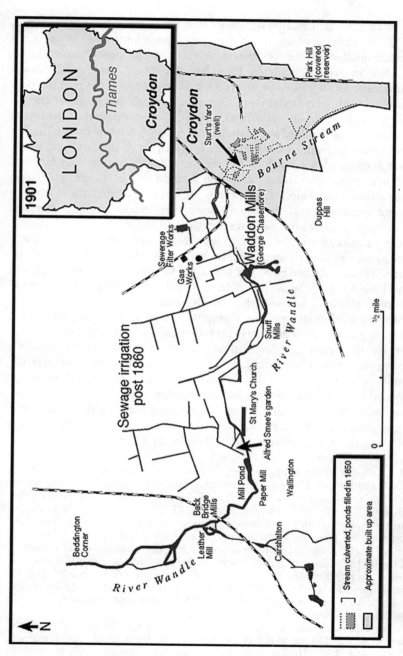

Figure 8.1   Map of Early Victorian Croydon and the Wandle

system on the Chadwickian principles that the General Board prescribed, and it is the purpose of this paper to examine the unexpected environmental consequences that resulted from the board's activities in this area in some detail, as they had far more than merely local significance. As an innovator, the town's successes and failures in the field of public health were under constant public scrutiny and its experience in dealing with complex and unanticipated environmental problems assumed national, indeed international, attention. Case law from Croydon in the 1850s determined the principles of the rights to underground water which became also guidelines for the rest of the century and beyond. Evidence from the town was also sought by a range of Royal Commissions and Select Committees which investigated the Victorian 'sewage question', and the town's sewage treatment grounds featured prominently in later texts on sewage disposal.[4]

Croydon is situated at the base of the dip slope of the chalk North Downs, on the upper reaches of the River Wandle, there known as the Bourne (Figure 8.1). Above the town the stream was intermittent and only flowed when the water table was high after wetter than normal seasons, a reflection of the permeable character of the local geology. This phenomenon, known as 'the rising of the bourne', was one which attracted great interest and was carefully studied.[5] Crucially in the local context, it served to demonstrate a general connection between underground water levels and the river flow. Despite its small size the Wandle was an important local resource. Its clear alkaline water provided downstream of Croydon an excellent environment for brown trout, and the sport-fishing that it provided was highly valued and strictly preserved. The amenity value of the river and its surroundings was also prized. According to John Ruskin, in 1850

---

[4] J.S. Will, 'Underground water', *Transactions of the Surveyors Institute*, XXXII, 1899–1900, 256–60. Parliamentary Papers (PP) XIV, 1862, *First Report from Select Committee on Sewage of Towns*, 106–107 (index of Croydon evidence); XXVII, 1865, *Third Report* 51, 71, 202–203; XIV, 1864, *Report from the Select Committee on Sewage (Metropolis)* 520–21; XXXIII, 1866, *First Report of the Commissioners appointed to Inquire into the Best Means of Preventing the Pollution of Rivers*, Vol. 1, 328 (index to Croydon evidence); XXXVIII, 1876, *Report of a Committee appointed by the Local Government Board to Inquire into the Several Modes of Treating Town Sewage* 96–100; W. Santo Crimp, *Sewage Disposal Works*, 2nd edn (London, 1894), 168–73; G.B. Kershaw, *Modern Methods of Sewage Purification and Disposal*, 2nd edn (Cambridge, 1925), 150, 161–2, 197, 203–204.

[5] For a contemporary account see F. Braithwaite, 'On the rise and fall of the River Wandle', *Minutes of the Proceedings of the Institute of Civil Engineers*, XX, 1860–61, 191–210. The term 'bourne' was (and is) used widely in southern England to denote an intermittent stream as well as being a common river name. See also B. Latham, *Croydon Bourne Flows* (Croydon, 1904).

... there was no lovelier piece of lowland scenery in South England, nor any more pathetic, in the world, by its expression of sweet human character and life, than that immediately bordering on the sources of the Wandel (sic) ... and the villages of Beddington and Carshalton, with their pools and streams.[6]

The fall of the river below Croydon and the reliability, after augmentation by springs and tributaries, of its flow additionally made the Wandle a valuable industrial resource. It was intensively utilized by a series of mills which ground not only corn but also snuff and lavender, which was grown locally. Additionally, there were numerous tanneries, silk works, and print and paper manufactures situated on its banks. Before the local board commenced its activities these potentially antagonistic activities, in that the acquatic life of the river could be damaged by harmful industrial discharges, appear to have coexisted in reasonably harmonious equilibrium, but from the start the local board seemed hostile to both the amenity and industrial users of the key local resource. To the Croydon local board, the groundwater which sustained the river was seen as a source of pure water for the town's residents, while the Wandle itself was viewed as a convenient receptacle for its sewage. These conflicting assessments of an urban environmental resource soon led to the local board being embroiled in a linked series of unforeseen environmental disputes. Abstraction of the groundwater diminished the flow of the river to the detriment of the milling interests and opened up the issue of subsurface water ownership rights. Discharge of sewage polluted the river, killed the trout and silted the millponds. The local board was soon caught up in numerous legal actions which ultimately questioned the viability of its public health initiatives and the sustainability of urban living.

'Earthly Waters . . . not only a Temporal but a Spiritual Blessing'?

Shortly after its establishment in August 1849 the Croydon local board of health embarked upon an ambitious programme of environmental improvements in the central part of the town where there were various contaminated ponds and areas prone to flooding.[7] No action was taken to address the question of overcrowded and substandard habitations;

---

[6] J. Ruskin, *The Crown of Wild Olive* (London, 1873), 1.

[7] For a general account, see D.W. Blackmore, 'The rebirth of Croydon in 1851', *Proceedings of the Croydon Natural History and Scientific Society*, 12, 1952, 95–114 and R. Savage, 'Croydon's local board of health in the early 1850s', Ibid., 16, 1973, 455–8. For a highly detailed account of the early activities of the board see B. Lancaster, 'The "Croydon Case": dirty old town to model town', Ibid., 18, (7), 2001, 145–206.

most importance was attached to the installation of a comprehensive system of piped water supply and sewage disposal systems.[8] In 1850 a surveyor/engineer, Thomas Cox, was appointed, comprehensive surveys were carried out, and plans drawn up for a piped water supply and sewage disposal system utilizing small bore pipes promoted by Chadwick. A covered reservoir was constructed on high ground (Park Hill) adjacent to the town and a well sunk in the lower old central part of Croydon (Sturt's Yard), to tap the groundwater from the underlying chalk aquifer (Figure 1). A Cornish beam engine was installed to pump the water to the storage reservoir and individual homes were supplied by gravity feed. A scale of water charges was drawn up in November 1851 based upon the poor rate. More than half of the houses were supplied at 1d. per week and the charges were considerably less than those levied by the metropolitan water companies to the north. The quality of the water was also seen to be superior to that drawn from the Thames, for at mid-century contaminated water was increasingly linked with diseases such as cholera and enteric fever (typhoid) even if there was no consensus about the causative agent.[9] Thus, when the continuous water supply was inaugurated by the Archbishop of Canterbury at the end of the year, his hope that the 'earthly waters' would prove to be 'not only a temporal but a spiritual blessing' imbued the Croydon supply with a symbolic significance – health was linked with moral as well as physical cleanliness.[10]

The immediate outcome was the opposite of what was intended; early in 1853 the town experienced 'an epidemic of a very serious and distressing character not withstanding the extensive works of the board for improving sewerage and drainage': 1,800 cases of (typhoid) fever occurred with 60 deaths and a mortality rate of 28.57 per 1,000 was recorded, significantly above the 23 per 1000 threshold for the establishment of a local board.[11] The irony was not lost of

> Such events occurring in a place like Croydon, with an intelligent Local Board of honourable men eager to perform any amount of gratuitous service which promised advantage to their town and who were near to the Central Board in London, for easy conferences.[12]

---

[8] On the built environment of Victorian Croydon see R.C.W. Cox, 'The old centre of Croydon: Victorian decay and redevelopment', in A. Everitt, ed., *Perspectives in Urban History* (London, 1973), 184–212.

[9] On nineteenth-century ideas on the links between water quality and health see C. Hamlin, *A Science of Impurity: Water Analysis in Nineteenth Century Britain* (Bristol, 1990).

[10] *Illustrated London News*, 20 Dec.1851, 725–6.

[11] Croydon local board of health minute book, 11 Jan.1853.

[12] PP, XCVI, 1852-3, *Reports on an Inquiry relative to Prevalence of Disease at Croydon, and to Plan of Sewerage; with abstract of Evidence,* 'Medical report' by Dr. Arnott, 7.

The subsequent investigation noted the extensive clearance of cesspools over land, a large number of blockages and breakages of sewerage pipes, and an absence of ventilation, which was held to allow a build-up of sewer gas. The incident provided abundant ammunition for those who were hostile to sanitary improvements both locally and nationally and certainly put members of the local board on the defensive.[13] Significantly, Cuthbert Johnson, the board's first chairman, was not re-elected in 1853.[14] It was essential, in order to justify their individual positions and the large financial outlay on urban infrastructure to which the town was committed, that no blame be attached to the water supply in relation to the epidemic that had taken place. The chemist J.T. Way was able to present 'scientific' evidence to legitimize the board's position in that he was unable to detect more than a minute trace of organic matter in samples of the Croydon water that he analysed.[15] The 'sewer gas' theory of disease which drew upon the widely held 'miasmatic' explanation for the spread of infection offered a convenient way out for the local board in that it provided an easy remedy to avoid repetitions – improved ventilation in order to prevent concentrations of noxious sewer gas occurring in the future. It also claimed that Croydon mortality had been exaggerated in newspaper reports.[16]

From the 1850s onwards the population of Croydon expanded rapidly – it approached 80,000 by 1881. Even if it was recognized that the town could never be 'another Leamington or Tunbridge Wells' (two minor spa resorts with pretensions to salubrity), the perceived superior water supply, sewage disposal arrangements and associated healthiness, once the 1853 epidemic had been overcome, were seen as major selling points making Croydon attractive to developers.[17] In the cholera year of 1866, for example, the town was described as 'an oasis in a desert of fear',[18] but the precocious growth, which was partly accounted for by its reputation for superior sanitary arrangements, together with

---

[13] For the broader significance of this episode in the context of Chadwick's agenda see C. Hamlin, 'Edwin Chadwick and the engineers, 1842–1854: systems and antisystems in the pipe-and-brick sewers war', *Technology and Culture*, 33 1992, 680–709. See also *Public Health*, especially chapter 10 'Lost in the pipes', 324–8.

[14] C.W. Johnson (1799–1878) was a barrister, agricultural writer, and authority on fertilizers. He had campaigned for the 1848 Act and published an annotated guide to its provisions, C.W. Johnson, *The Acts for Promoting the Public Health 1848 to 1851* (London, 1852). For a memoir see 'Noteworthy agriculturists: C.W. Johnson', *Agricultural Gazette*, 29 May 1875.

[15] Croydon local board of health minute book, 18 Jun. 1853.

[16] Ibid., 27 Jun. 1853.

[17] Comment in *CC*, 16 Mar. 1861.

[18] Ibid., 18 Aug. 1866.

abundant rail connections to London, contributed to the environmental problems of the board; there was constant pressure on the water supply while the sewage treatment grounds established in 1860 were barely able to keep up with the demands put upon them.

The leading advocates of public health intervention in Croydon, such as the physicians Alfred Carpenter and E. Westall, were under constant pressure to justify the board's expenditure in the light of sometimes contradictory evidence on the links between health and public investment, as exemplified by the events of 1852–53. Carpenter, who started to practise in the town in the early 1850s and was to become one of Croydon's most fervent, if controversial, publicists appealed to the notion of preventive medicine. In the year 1859 – when the local board was coming under increasing attack – he recognized that the increase of rates that infrastructure investment required was likely to retard the progress of sanitary science, but it was 'far more profitable and glorious . . . to prevent the development of disease than to cure it when developed'.[19] Westall, who came to Croydon in 1831 and published quarterly mortality tables in the *Croydon Chronicle*, also recognized that health legislation was not popular because it interfered with the liberty of the subject, but nevertheless vigorously defended the successes of the board.[20] In his presidential address to the Society of Engineers in 1868 Baldwin Latham, who had been appointed as the Croydon local board's engineer five years previously, presented statistics that attributed a mortality fall of twenty-two per cent directly to the construction of the board's various works. However, as Latham was himself later to point out, this line of reasoning was flawed as the mortality rate might have been expected to decline on account of the immigration of a young and mostly affluent population. Nevertheless, expenditure on sanitary works brought, according to Latham, numerous benefits; although he admitted that life itself was 'priceless', money savings in terms of the cost of sickness prevented, the additional value of labour through longer life expectancy, and even the reduction of expenditure on funerals were shown, by way of elaborate calculations, to have exceeded the board's contested outlay of £195,000 by the late 1860s by thirty-five per cent.[21]

---

[19] A. Carpenter, *The History of Sanitary Progress in Croydon* (Croydon, 1859) 2,5; See also A. Carpenter, 'Croydon the past and present successes and failures of the local board', in J. Hitchman, ed., *The Sewage of Towns* (Leamington, 1866) 126–37 for a typically robust defence.

[20] E. Westall, *On the Advantages to be derived from the Adoption of the Local Government Act as exemplified in Croydon* (Croydon, 1865), 6.

[21] B. Latham, 'Inaugural address', *Transactions of the Society of Engineers* 1868, 6–8. For Latham's later comment see *Sanitary Engineering* 2nd edn (1878), 6, and 'A chapter in the history of Croydon', *Proceedings of the Croydon Natural History and Scientific Society*, 6, 1907–08, clvi. Baldwin Latham (1836–1917) had an extensive private practice as a sanitary engineering consultant.

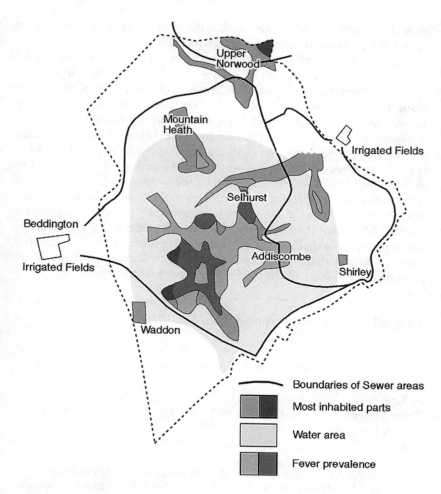

Figure 8.2   Map showing the prevalence of typhoid in Croydon, 1875

Despite Latham's claim that the incidence of typhoid had declined by sixty-three per cent after the completion of the water and sewerage scheme, it appears to have been rarely absent and another severe outbreak was recorded in 1875, this time with 1,200 individual cases and 90 deaths.[22] On this occasion epidemiological analysis appeared to

[22] *Reports of the Medical Officer of the Privy Council and Local Government Board NS, VII:* PP XXXVIII, 1876. No. 5, 'Report on an epidemic of enteric fever at Croydon 1875', by Dr. Buchanan, 41–2.

provide incontrovertible evidence that the water supply was implicated (Table 8.1), especially when viewed cartographically (Figure 8.2).

As in 1853 there was every incentive to avoid any damaging connections between the water supply and typhoid incidence. In the face of a concerted onslaught on their reputations members of the board clung to the Chadwickian miasmatic theory, and the official report by George Buchanan largely vindicated them. This dismissed the Croydon water as a causative agent because of the number of analyses which consistently stressed its *chemical* purity. Typhoid, it was held, was spread by escapes of sewer gas which could build-up in voids in water system pipes at times of interruption to the supply. Anecdotal evidence was given more weight than epidemiological data, as in the alleged case of evidence of foul air in the water pipes at a Croydon school: 'Here's a jolly stink!' one of the boys was heard to say while waiting to wash in the morning, 'We shall be having the water come now'.[23] The essential point made was that of the contamination of a local service, not of an unwholesome quality in the total water supply of the town.

Table 8.1   Incidence of typhoid, Croydon 1875

	Number of houses	Fever incidence	Per 1000 houses	Deaths	Per 1000 houses
Homes supplied by Croydon Water System	9,039	942	104	83	9.1
Not on Croydon's System	2,487	17	7	7	2.8

Source: PP, XXXVIII, 1876, *Reports of the Medical Officer of the Privy Council and Local Government Board*, NS, VII, No.5 'Report on an epidemic of enteric fever at Croydon 1875, by Dr Buchanan', 41–2.

An increasing number of Croydon residents found, however, the board's position to be untenable. They gained a powerful advocate in Baldwin Latham who, although he had ceased to act as the board's official engineer, remained as an elected member and local resident. Although in the late 1860s Latham had adhered to the generally held view that the epidemic of 1852–53 was due to lack of sewer ventilation and restated this position in the first edition of his influential *Sanitary*

---

[23] Ibid., 53–4.

Engineering (1873), the evidence of the 1875 outbreak led him to abandon the 'sewer air theory' as being an essential cause of disease.[24] A report by the chemist J.A. Wanklyn (29 November 1875) cast some suspicion on the source of the Croydon water because although the well itself was pronounced pure, Wanklyn had found samples of subsurface water to be charged with sewage. Although the general paradigm of self-purification could be appealed to and it was maintained that this subsoil seepage was insignificant, the caveat was entered that it was 'not known how far a very large dilution with pure water will render sewage containing the excreta of typhoid patients innocuous'.[25]

Whether the sources of Croydon's water were safe, especially in the context of the need to meet expanding demand by sinking new wells, became a matter of the utmost controversy. In the face of continuous onslaughts, Carpenter steadfastly denied any link between the quality of the Croydon water and typhoid incidence and dismissed the theory that an epidemic could be traced to water which had been repeatedly declared chemically pure. The link demonstrated between the incidence of diseases – diphtheria and infantile diarrhoea as well as typhoid – to the area served by the Croydon water district not only questioned the reputation of members of the local board, such as Johnson and Carpenter, which had been built up over a quarter of a century, but also threatened the very prosperity of the town itself, for the supposed purity of its water was seen as Croydon's greatest asset. The sewer gas explanation remained the most plausible way to preserve the integrity of the water, especially when germ theory itself was seen as pressing the boundaries of credulity:

> . . . that we who have subdued so many of the forces of nature to our uses should leave ourselves at the mercy of these ignoble things that kill our children is an antithesis too absurd to be endured.[26]

By 1878, however, Latham had come to the conclusion that Croydon's sanitary works had not been so successful in terms of mortality reduction as they should have been. This he attributed to the contamination of the well which had been sunk in the lower part of old central Croydon. He

---

[24] B. Latham, *Report on the Permanent Sanitary Works and their cost executed in the Parish of Croydon* (Croydon, 1868), 11; *Sanitary Engineering* (London, 1873), 198; see letter in CC, 18 Aug. 1877 as an example of his changing viewpoint.

[25] CC 18 Dec. 1875. On the theory of self-purification see C. Hamlin, *What Becomes of Pollution: Adversary Science and the Controversy on the Self-Purification of Rivers in Britain 1850–1900*, (New York, 1987). On Wanklyn's approach to water analysis and pollution see *A Science of Impurity*, 184–90.

[26] CC, 4 Mar. 1876. See also 'Fever in Croydon', CC, 1 Apr. 1876 for a statement of Latham's opposition.

even went so far as to present data which purported to show that the
neighbouring district of Norwood, supplied with Thames water by the
Lambeth company, enjoyed better overall health. There could not, he
claimed, remain a shadow of doubt that the epidemic of enteric fever in
Croydon was due to unwholesome water rather than sewer air, which he
dismissed as a significant causative agent. Disease was caused by 'living
microscopic germs' that could not be detected by chemical analysis.[27] It
is difficult to overstate the vehemence of the local debate over the safety
of water in Croydon in the late 1870s, especially as it was clear that new
sources would have to be exploited in order to meet the ever-rising
demand. Latham orchestrated a campaign against proposals to sink
further wells in the central area because of the suspected contamination.
This brought him to a head-on collision with the majority of the local
board who accused him of blackening Croydon's name for electoral
purposes. Yielding to pressure to sink wells on the chalk downs away
from the town would be seen as an admission that the existing supply
was suspect, and the board was wary that if the water supply could be
proven to be connected with typhoid incidence, they might open
themselves to legal action by Croydon householders.[28]

The long debate over the safety or otherwise of the Croydon water
was but one problem encountered by the local board on the supply side.
As early as 1850 it had been threatened with legal action by powerful
milling interests along the Wandle who feared that the river's flow would
be diminished by the board's intended abstraction. Four years later an
action was started by George Chasemore, the occupier of a large corn
mill, the substance of which was that the board's well had lowered the
flow of the Wandle and so interfered with the efficient operation of the
mill. The significance of this development was that if the case were lost
by the board, it would render invalid the expenditure that had been
invested in the supply system. The position of Chasemore and other
mill-owners appeared to be supported by the case of *Dickenson* v. *Gt.
Junction Canal Company* (1852); in the Croydon case the issue revolved
around the ownership rights of groundwater as opposed to water
flowing in defined channels. The dispute was first heard in the nearby
Kingston assizes, and after numerous appeals and counter appeals was
only finally resolved in the board's favour by the House of Lords in
1859.[29] This judgment vindicated the board's position and it must have

---

[27] *Sanitary Engineering*, 2nd edn, 13–16 (note) and 311.
[28] This was a matter of continuous attack and counter-attack. For examples,
see 'Enteric fever and water', CC, 27 May 1876, and letters from Latham in CC,
18 Aug. and 1 Sep. 1877.
[29] Croydon local board of health minutes 1854–61; J.S. Will, 'Underground
water', 260.

been with great satisfaction that Johnston reported that percolating water was held not to have the same degree of protection as that in rivers: it was considered to be 'one of the most important questions that ever came under the consideration of a court of justice'.[30] The case was to have profound longer term ecological consequences. It allowed for the largely uncontrolled exploitation of groundwater resources around London and elsewhere until 1963 when the Water Resources Act brought in a system of regulation and licensing.[31] In the neighbouring county of Kent (to the east of Surrey) groundwater abstraction varied between 78,583 m^3 day^{-1} and 99,492 m^3 day^{-1} during the last three decades of the nineteenth century, with adverse environmental effects, while Sheail has reported acute resource conflicts in Hertfordshire, to the north of London, again due to uncontrolled groundwater exploitation that was legitimised by *Chasemore v. Richards*.[32]

The demands that would be put on local water resources were hugely underestimated at the time of the board's initial planning. This was partly because of the unforeseen rate of increase in Croydon's population but also because of changing consumption patterns. Soon after the supply was inaugurated, members of the local board were shocked to find that the precious groundwater was being applied to domestic gardens and lawns. This prompted consideration of restrictions on hosepipe usage (reminiscent of 'hosepipe bans' familiar to UK householders during the dry summers of the 1990s!) and the levying of additional hosepipe charges. This latter measure proved ineffectual as once a payment was made the Croydon householders were all the more determined to use the water for which they had paid. Another matter of consumption was the increased demand for industrial use, which was never envisaged in the early 1850s.[33]

---

[30] C.W. Johnson, 'The right to underground water', *Farmer's Magazine*, 3rd ser., XVI, 1859, 185, quoting Lord Kingsdown, one of the appeal judges.

[31] J. Hassan, *A History of Water in Modern England and Wales* (Manchester, 1998), 104.

[32] H.F. Cook, 'Groundwater development in England', *Environment and History*, 5, 1999, 83; J. Sheail, 'Underground water abstraction: indirect effects of urbanisation upon the countryside', *Journal of Historical Geography*, 8, (4), 1982, 394–408. Richards was clerk to the board.

[33] The theme of excessive usage and waste of water is one which runs continually through the Croydon board's proceedings. Discussions reported in CC, 12 Feb. 1859 and 31 Mar. 1860 are typical of many such debates that were had by the board's members.

'An *Irrigatingly* Sewaged Town'

If the supply of water to Croydon posed a series of interrelated and unsuspected environmental problems, then the disposal of sewage posed still more conundrums. The early failure of part of the sewerage system largely because of the smallness of the bore of the pipes has already been noted – much of the system had to be relaid and repairs were ongoing. Little thought was initially given to the disposal of the sewage although Cuthbert Johnson was aware of its theoretical value as a fertilizer. Indeed, he applied his own domestic sewage to his garden, a practice which gave rise to considerable complaints by his neighbours in the Waldrons – a superior housing development – by the 1870s. A filter house for Croydon's sewage was constructed in 1852 to separate out the solid material from the liquid, which was then discharged into the Wandle and various ditches. A very limited amount of irrigation was carried out but space for this mode of treatment was initially restricted. The Wandle outfall soon gave rise to complaint and by 1853 there were numerous notices of actions to restrain the board from polluting the river. Not only did riparian owners allege fish mortality as a result of the board's activities, but the mill owners also held that the discharge of sewage silted up their millponds. In the year 1859 the members of the local board came very close to imprisonment on account of their inability to comply with a range of injunctions that had been issued. Numerous methods of chemical treatment were employed and all were found, predictably, to be deficient. The situation of the board in this respect was eased when the 1858 Local Government Act permitted land to be taken for sewage irrigation (which was then the treatment method most capable of yielding a tolerable effluent) in an area beyond the board's immediate jurisdiction. Ground also became available on the nearby Carew estate and this was the origin of the Beddington irrigation grounds – where the sewage of Croydon is still treated.[34] From limited beginnings, by the early 1880s some 540 acres were utilized with a separate site dealing with the Norwood district to the north-east of Croydon which had undergone rapid residential expansion. Initially there were high expectations that farming of the land irrigated would generate enough revenue to meet the costs of treatment and disposal but

---

[34] Detail on the local board's problems of water pollution is provided in the minutes between 1852 and 1859. Reporters were first admitted to meetings on 9 June 1857 after which there is extensive coverage, and comment on, the board's proceedings in the *Croydon Chronicle*. Writs were served on the board for contempt of court in April 1859 (CC 16 Apr. 1859). The Croydon Local Board was the first to take advantage of the provisions of the 1858 Act for sewage treatment.

such hopes were never realized. Indeed, the management of the farm and the appropriate farming methods were, like so many of the board's environmental activities, the subject of continual controversy. Extensive harvests of rye grass and other crops were achieved, but the financial results were found to be disappointing: sewage farming, it was concluded, resembled the produce of private gardens 'in which every cabbage cost a shilling', a conclusion which reflected a more general disillusionment with sewage recycling in the 1870s.[35]

While irrigation had its limitations, not least because the amount of land available did not keep pace with the increase of population, the number of legal actions decreased in the 1860s, although the board continued to deal with a range of complaints. One of the last major actions against it was that launched by George Parker Bidder which held the board to account for a major pollution incident on his Ravensbury estate downstream at Morden.[36] This was traced to a discharge from the Croydon gas works for which the board disclaimed liability. It also found it difficult to accept that such waste was harmful given that 'coal tar' was used as a disinfectant and was beneficial to health and, by extension, could therefore not harm aquatic life.[37]

The condition of the Beddington irrigation grounds was a matter of vigorous debate. Part of the board's difficulty in this respect was that, as previously noted, the Croydon population expanded faster than the amount of land available to treat the sewage. Owners of land that could be added to the existing irrigation area were fully aware of the board's predicament over the matter of effective sewage treatment and could thus inflate the sale or rental value of suitable land. The nuisance of the Beddington grounds was difficult to establish with objectivity and also varied with prevailing climatic conditions. Although opinion in the town was initially generally supportive of the board's treatment project as the solution to a problem which had in the late 1850s threatened the very continuation of sewage disposal by water carriage in Croydon, residents were only too aware of the proximity of the sewage farm in warm summers. In 1868, for example, the *Croydon Chronicle* questioned whether the proximity of the treatment area to the town itself posed a health hazard:

> We should be glad to know whether these filter beds, these huge
> receptacles of sewage, steaming and vomiting forth in the blazing

---

[35] Comment in *CC*, 19 Jun. 1875; see also N. Goddard, '"A mine of wealth"? The Victorians and the agricultural value of sewage', *Journal of Historical Geography*, 22, (3), 1996, 274–90.

[36] G.P. Bidder (1806–78) was a leading civil engineer; for a life see S.E.F. Clark, *George Parker Bidder. The Calculating Boy* (Bedford, 1983).

[37] Report of the board's proceedings in *CC*, 29 Dec. 1860.

sun vapours of disease and floating globules of malaria, are innocuous?

Croydon, indeed, was an *irrigatingly* sewaged town.[38]

Not only did some local residents downstream of Croydon resent the expansion of the sewage irrigation area as it impinged on their amenities, but at the national level there were vested interests eager to seize on accounts of their alleged 'pestilential' condition as a rationale for not installing expensive water disposal sewerage systems elsewhere in large urban areas of low rateable value.[39] A particularly forthright attack was launched at a meeting of the Society of Arts in 1875 by Alfred Smee who established a famous garden on the Wandle between Beddington and Wallington (Figure 8.1).[40] Smee had been a leading instigator of the actions against the board over the matter of the destruction of fish in the late 1850s and although an uneasy truce between him and the board had been established following the improved effluent that resulted from the establishment of irrigation, the expansion of the irrigation area gave rise to increased complaint. According to Smee 'Croydon cleanses itself, but pollutes Beddington. Croydon has no interest but to save expense to itself, whilst Beddington has to suffer from the parishioners of Croydon', and his 'Proposed Heads of Legislation for the Regulation of Sewage-Grounds' not only advocated stringent controls on sewage-farming activities – including the sale of sewage-irrigated produce – but a scale of penalties for infringements which amounted to an early statement of the 'polluter pays' principle.[41]

A particular point of interest in Smee's criticisms of the Beddington grounds was the way in which he drew attention to the large amount of 'inorganic poisonous matter' that sewage contained. The prevailing general concern was with decaying organic matter, which was widely held to be linked to the 'cause' of disease and which was the basic rationale for the removal of sewage from habitations by water-carriage. Hamlin has demonstrated how Carpenter rationalized the wholesomeness of the Beddington grounds even when complaints of nuisance frequently suggested the contrary; in the late 1870s he told his St. Thomas's Hospital students that plants grown on the irrigation farm

---

[38] Comment in CC, 12 Sep. 1868.

[39] For example, adverse comment in Henry Letherby, *The Sewage Question* (London, 1872), 22.

[40] Alfred Smee (1816–77) was medical consultant to the Bank of England and writer on scientific and botanical topics. See A. Smee, *My Garden* (London, 1872), and *Alfred Smee. A Memoir.* By his daughter (London, 1878).

[41] A. Smee, 'Proposed heads of legislation for the regulation of sewage-grounds', *Journal of the Society of Arts*, 24, 1875–76, 39–40.

had an appetite for animal albuminoids like 'the Venus fly-trap'.[42] The alleged accumulation of 'various metallic poisons from the electro-chemical works, the fluid residue of various manufactures, disinfecting solutions etc.' raised the spectre of a new category of contamination, which was dismissed as inconsequential at the time but in the late twentieth century it was the concern about the heavy metal content of sewage which gave rise to particular caution about its deployment as a fertilizer.[43]

Although Smee, Bidder and numerous other riparian owners had legitimate grounds for complaints about the loss of amenity occasioned by the board of health's activities, these had to be set against the benefits that accrued to the town. Further, some deleterious ecological changes in the Wandle could be attributed to their own activities. The sporting press criticized Smee and others for overstocking the river with trout and introducing inappropriate exotic species of fish.[44] Bidder also commented on the spread of a new water weed thought to have come from America (almost certainly *elodea canadensis*, 'Canadian pondweed') which encouraged siltation to the detriment of the health of the river.[45]

An 'Almost Sensational' History

By the early 1880s the meetings of the Croydon board of health had become increasingly ill-tempered – 'miserable bear gardens and nursery squabbles'[46] – as its members were under constant attack over the cost of the sewage farm and the associated expenses of sewage treatment and the quality and reliability of the water supply. The complexity of the unsuspected environmental health issues encountered over the previous thirty years dominated their proceedings and were a matter of continual public criticism. There were also other environmental resource issues outside of the scope of this chapter, not least the arrangement for the collection of household waste, the propriety of the board's acquisition of open space for public amenity use, and questions surrounding the

---

[42] C. Hamlin, 'Providence and putrefaction. Victorian sanitarians and the natural theology of disease and decay', *Victorian Studies*, 28, (3), 1985, 406–409. Comments reported in *CC*, 23 Jun. 1876.

[43] Smee, 'Proposed heads of legislation', 37, and Baldwin Latham in discussion of Smee's paper, 153.

[44] See, for example, comment in the *Field*, 2 & 9 May 1863.

[45] In discussion of Braithwaite's paper on 'The rise and the fall of the river Wandle'; see also E. Salisbury, *Weeds and Aliens* (London, 1964), 78.

[46] Comment in *CC*, 3 Feb. 1883.

redevelopment of old central parts of the town. If much had been achieved by the board, this had been at the cost of the personal reputations of many of the prime instigators of public health reform, not least those of Johnson and Carpenter.

The proceedings of the board were terminated when Croydon was incorporated as a County Borough in 1883. Opinions as to the board's achievement in public and environmental health differed. To the *Croydon Chronicle,* the history of water in the district had been 'interesting and almost sensational'.[47] Corbet Anderson, a member of the board in its later years and local historian considered that since 1850 Croydon had been

> Transformed from an undrained district, surrounded by every kind
> of filth tending to generate disease of the worst description into one
> of the dryest, cleanest and healthiest towns in England.[48]

Baldwin Latham's conclusion was that the early actions of the board were 'proper and praiseworthy but results differed from what was anticipated on all hands'.[49] However, despite the contradictory and ambiguous attitudes often directed towards the Croydon board of health's activities there was also a considerable amount of civic pride invested in its achievements. Thus the new borough's coat of arms, which was adopted in 1886, incorporated two bunches of rye grass to give recognition to the fame of the Beddington irrigation grounds, together with the motto *Sanitate Crescamus* – 'Let us grow in health'.

As for the Wandle, which was the environmental resource around which so much Croydon controversy was directly or indirectly connected, by the early twentieth century its general condition gave rise to significant environmental concern; trout fishing along the river was a fading memory and pollution and neglect typified much of its course.[50]

---

[47] Ibid., 23 Oct. 1879.

[48] J. Corbet Anderson, *A Short Chronicle concerning the Parish of Croydon* (Croydon, 1882), 237.

[49] 'A chapter in the history of Croydon', cxliv.

[50] Thomas Bentham, *A History of Beddington* (1923), 16; *River Wandle. Report of the County Medical Officer of Health* (Surrey County Council, 1923).

Acknowledgements
The author is grateful for use of the resources in the Croydon Library Local Studies Centre, John Walsh for drawing the figures and to Helen Humphrys and Claire Santo for assistance in producing the text.

CHAPTER NINE

Resource Management and Environmental Transformations. Water Incorporation at the Time of Industrialization: Milan, 1880–1940

Simone Neri Serneri

1880–1940: Development and Resources

From the 1880s on Italy underwent gradual but significant urbanization. The causes lay principally in population growth, the agrarian crisis brought on by the 'Great Depression', and the first phase of industrialization. In 1871 15.3 per cent of Italy's population lived in urban centres with more than 20,000 inhabitants. By 1921 this had risen to 33.3 per cent and ten years later to 35.1 per cent. In the years between 1902 and 1911 Northern Italy urbanized faster than it was to do until the massive economic expansion of the 1950s. At the same time, from the end of the 1880s, GNP growth-rates rose significantly and performed best in the years 1896–1913. The average annual growth rate of the industrial sector between 1881 and 1913 is estimated at between 3.8 and 4.2 per cent. The industrial workforce numbered 2,180,627 in 1911 and rose to 4,445,757 by 1938. This synchronization of growth in population, urbanization and industrialization was not occurring in the whole of Italy but, in the years spanning the turn of the twentieth century, was certainly visible in the north west, that is the areas that were in general equivalent to the regions of Piedmont, Lombardy and Liguria. In particular, in these areas, and in their three major urbanized centres, Turin, Genoa, Milan, as they were to do in all of Italy's cities to a lesser or greater extent, rising population and the requirements of new economic activities revealed the ancien régime character of Italian cities as well as their inadequacy in terms of housing, streets, water provision and sewage disposal, urban space and public buildings.

In the 1880s the return of cholera provoked a heated and intense public debate leading to the passing of a new health act in 1888 and a

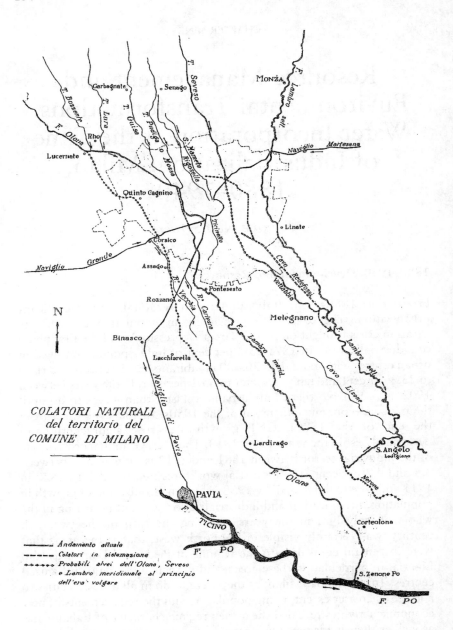

Figure 9.1   Watercourses and canals around Milan about 1890

few years later to a set of regulations that, beginning with the dramatic case of the city of Naples, aimed at urban improvement in terms of infrastructure and hygiene as well as in industrial development. In fact, this legislation responded to the need to modernize the entire urban system, and, from the point of view of the environment, to the need to redefine the ways in which natural resources – water and soil – could be incorporated within that system to ensure an adequate supply and function that would respect new ways of living and producing now also developing in Italian cities too.

At least two aspects of this legislation need highlighting. The first concerns its approach; it was orientated towards regulating private activity in order to safeguard its freedom of action but at the same time to constrain it to the common good. Thus, for example, we witness the establishment of the principle of public hygiene management, the pressure on municipal governments to provide for the construction of aqueducts and sewers, the provision of (totally inadequate, it must be said) government funding for these works, the obligation to issue municipal regulations for construction and hygiene. The second aspect that needs highlighting is that this legislation not only conditioned urban transformation in its totality, but also included a set of norms that were specifically directed towards protecting the quality of some natural resources from possible pollution. In particular, it stated that the most polluting factories should be away from the urban centre and adopted special safeguarding measures for other productive activities and, as far as water was concerned, affirmed the general principle of the protection of drinking water, forcing sewers that would avoid its contamination to be built and required that any potential disposal of factory waste water into the sewerage system should have prior authorization. Although the vagueness of the regulations, the weakness of local authorities and complex infrastructural problems rendered much of this legislation a dead letter, it remained true that in Italy too the construction of an urban-industrial environment[1] on the basis of the dominant hygienic outlook was now finally under way.[2]

---

[1] As M.V. Melosi conceptualized this in *Effluent America. Cities, Industry, Energy, and the Environment* (Pittsburgh, 2001), 143 ff., and described it in *The Sanitary City. Urban Infrastructure from Colonial Times to the Present* (Baltimore, 2000). See also J.A. Tarr and G. Depuy, eds, *Technology and the Rise of the Networked City in Europe and America* (Philadelphia, 1988).

[2] Cf. S. Neri Serneri, 'Industrial pollution and urbanisation. Ancient and new industrial areas in the early 20th century Italy', in C. Bernhardt, ed., *Environmental Problems in European Cities in the 19th and 20th Centuries* (Münster, 2001); S. Neri Serneri, 'Water pollution in Italy: the failure of the hygienic approach, 1890s–1960s', in C. Bernhardt and G. Massard-Guilbaud, eds, *The Modern Demon. Pollution in urban and industrial Societies* (Clermont-Ferrand, 2002).

The years between 1880 and 1940 were in fact also the period in which the construction of Italy's most important infrastructures took place: whilst the railway network reached completion and the road system underwent substantial modernization, the foundations of the system for the collection, distribution and disposal of natural resources, in particular water, were also being laid via the construction of rural and urban aqueducts, sewerage systems, irrigation canals, collection basins, pipe-lines and hydro-electric power stations. The scale of these works can be understood by the fact that in 1899 only 3,361 of the 8,262 communes were provided with some sort of aqueduct whilst in 1951 57.1 per cent of the 2,3716 'inhabited places' were provided with an acqueduct.[3] The situation for sewers was even more dramatic and was to remain so, even though in completely changed terms, until the end of the 1940s. In fact, it should be remembered that in this span of time the construction of 'modern' infrastructures was dictated by the dual need to respond to growth in demand for water and, at the same time, to tackle the collapse of 'traditional' infrastructures caused by the increased mobilization of natural resources. It was therefore necessary to expand the infrastructural network as well as to adapt it to totally new needs. This led to a marked and completely new integration between the hygienist and productive dimension. The progress of hygiene was a result of the new requirements of urban development. That is to say, over and above progressive and hygienist ideologies, infrastructural and therefore environmental transformations were primarily aimed at the development of the urban-industrial system and only secondarily at improvement in public hygiene.

Milan, Water and Men

The most conspicuous and most interesting case of the construction of an urban-industrial environment was certainly Milan. Its interest lies in the fact that in that city most of the questions posed and choices made were to be taken up or adopted by other Italian cities later on. Its conspicuousness stems from the fact that it became Italy's most populous city (overtaking Naples in 1931) as well as its most important industrial centre, and because this involved, among other things, the

---

[3] Ministero dell'interno, Direzione generale della sanità pubblica (MI DGSP), *Inchiesta sulle acque potabili nei comuni del regno al 31 dicembre 1903. Vol. I. Relazione generale. Acquedotti* (Rome, 1906), XVII–XX; Istat, *Rilevazione statistica sull'approvvigionamento idrico in Italia. I. Sistemi di approvvigionamento al 31 dicembre 1951* (Rome, 1954).

profound transformation of the ways in which water resources were incorporated into its urban system. This is not surprising considering the particular location of the city. Milan, in fact, lies in a position a little higher than the centre of the northern half of a section of a plain which is slightly inclined from north to south and which is delimited in its northern boundary by the pre-Alpine hills; its longitudinal boundaries are respectively the river Ticino, which issues from lake Maggiore, and the river Adda which issues from lake Garda, both affluents of the Po, the east to west flowing river that closes the southern part of the square surrounding Milan. The plain is cut from north to south with a large number of waterways, of varying dimensions, that issue from the Alpine valleys and the pre-Alpine hills, and by a dense network of man-made canals, the so-called *fontanili*, which are fed by the large number of outflows of North-South flowing underground – sometimes no more than a few metres below the soil – rivers.

The history and the fortunes of Milan have been largely determined by its central location in this delicate and complex territorial and hydraulic system (see Figure 9.1). This system was the product of centuries of reclamation which, beginning in the early middle-ages, has integrated natural and 'artificial' watercourses in a mesh so intricate as to often render the former indistinguishable from the latter. A circuit of hydro-resources was created for transporting goods, producing energy, irrigating farm land and paddy fields, providing drinking water for animals and men, embellishing villas, and dispersing waste. From time immemorial this network of waterways penetrated the urban structure (see Figure 9.2) and even in the 1880s Milan was criss-crossed by canals called *navigli*, which were supplied by the rivers that from the west (Olona and Nirone) and from the east (Lambro and Seveso) flowed near the city. Of these canals, the most important were the *Naviglio Grande*, the *Naviglio di Bereguardo* and the *Naviglio di Pavia* to the east, the *Naviglio della Martesana* to the north and the east. Also towards the north and east flowed the *Canale Villoresi* (completed in 1891) and the *Canale Muzza* which were given over solely to irrigation. The *Naviglio della Martesana* fed the roughly five kilometre long *Naviglio interno* (also known as the *Fossa interna*) which encircled on three sides the oldest quarter of the city. Because of this course, the *Naviglio interno* acted as a canal for the transport of a whole variety of goods but also as the collector of the waste water that issued from a tight mesh of minor, and in part underground, canals. In particular, the canals used as sewers were the *Redefossi* canal, the canal *del Castello*, the *Civico*, the *Vettabbia*, the *Balossa*, and the *Acqualunga Fontanile*. The principal outlet of the system was the *Vettabbia* which for centuries brought sewage water to irrigate the *marcite* (water-meadows) which were located to the south of the city. Thereafter, purified water flowed into the river Lambro.[4]

This set-up was about to be transformed by intense demographic and economic growth. In 1873 the commune of Milan incorporated the commune of the *Corpi Santi* which circled the city and whose population was made up of market gardeners and stockbreeders who lived on the *marcite*, and artisans, industrial workers, and people employed in small commercial activities. The expansion of the city's urban and industrial areas destroyed, even in administrative terms, the old delimitation between the urban nucleus and its surrounding (and dependent) countryside. In the decades that followed the population grew considerably inside and outside the old border of the city and by 1901 the majority (294,028 out of 539,596) lived outside what had once been considered the perimeter of the city. After further expansion of the commune's territory in 1923, the population grew from 858,808 in 1924 to 974,115 in 1930 and to 1,202,000 in 1938. The built-up area grew at a similarly rapid rate: between 1859 and 1921 the built-up area grew from 3,950,000 square metres to 16,145,754 (out of a total communal area of 77,970,366), and after the expansion of 1923, from 21,500,000 square metres in 1926 to 41,289,300 in 1933, the total area of the commune now standing at 182,990,000.

To a significant degree, the city's expansion can be put down to industrial development as well as to related commercial activities and management. The somewhat unreliable statistics for the 1870s show that there were roughly 110,000 people employed by 3,244 factories and 7,342 workshops. However, the more reliable statistics for the early 1890s which show 50,561 people employed in 1,564 plants are a better base upon which to measure industrial growth before 1911, by which time Milan was indisputably Italy's most important industrial city. It counted 153,165 (6.6 per cent of the total for the whole of Italy) workers in 8,238 plants distributed throughout the city's territories. Demonstrating the connection between industrialization and urbanization, at the beginning of the twentieth century, 56.6 per cent of the city's population were members of the working-class and half of these had lived in Milan for less than ten years. Such a rate of growth is confirmed by figures for 1927 which show 192,410 workers in 19,588 industrial firms, excluding the building and energy industry, and for 1937 where the figures stand respectively at 277,316 and 24,332, excluding the printing industry too.

---

[4] E. Bignami Sormani, 'Milano idrografica', in *Mediolanum* (Vallardi, 1881).

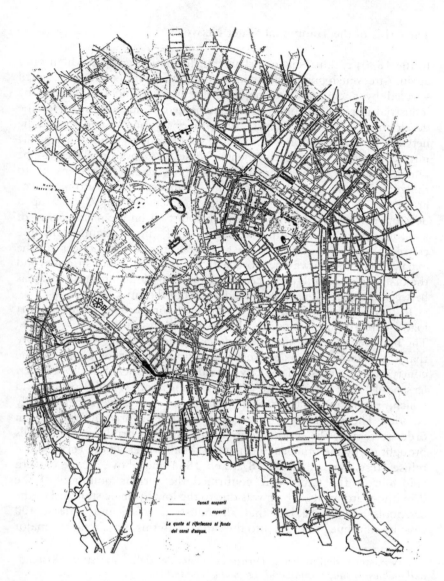

Figure 9.2   Superficial and underground watercourses in Milan about
1888

The Crisis of the Traditional Water Network

In the 1880s enthusiasm for urban transformation gripped Milan once again. After much public debate inside and outside the communal council – ruled by a conservative majority that was strongly influenced by industrial intrerests – three priorities emerged: to identify areas for the development of housing, industry and offices; to improve and expand the network for the transport of goods and people; and to adapt the hygienic infrastructure to new developments. These three priorities were to be pursued together as they were all closely connected and indispensable to the growth of the city and its economic primacy. The 'Beruto plan' was approved in 1889 and, summing up prevalent attitudes, drew up a development project for the city that based itself on the maintenance of a monocentric and radial structure and, in particular, on the concentration of offices and the tertiary sector in the city-centre, the expansion of the railway network with the moving of industries beyond the first ring-road and the succeeding saturation of the intermediate areas between the radial links that spread out from the city-centre.

In this new context, the city's water network revealed itself in part inadequate and in part useless. It was based on two large sub-circuits. The first was the domestic one and was made up of the wells (no more than six or seven metres deep) used for drinking water to be found in the courtyards of almost all the city's buildings, and the 15,000 *pozzi neri* (cesspools) that served about 7,000 buildings and 300,000 people and which, producing 900,000 litres of waste a day, were periodically emptied. The use of cesspools had developed in the preceding decades in order to remedy the serious contamination of the drinking-water wells brought on by the practice of using the canals to get rid of every kind of refuse. Tests carried out in 1876 and 1884 and above all the cholera epidemic of the latter year confirmed the serious pollution of the drinking-water wells, which was due to the low hygienic standard of the cesspools and to the fact that all industrial waste and at least 400 cesspits continued to drain into the canals.[5] In this sub-circuit the major

---

[5] Ministero dell'interno, Direzione generale della statistica, *Risultati dell'inchiesta sulle condizioni igieniche e sanitarie nei comuni del regno. Relazione generale* (Rome, 1886), 28–30; A. Cantalupi, *Della costruzione dei canali di fognatura e dei diversi mezzi impiegati per tradurre all'esterno le acque lorde e le dejezioni* (Milan, 1890), 149 ff.; A. Cantalupi, *L'igiene delle città. Dell'acqua potabile* (Milan, 1891), 170; F. Poggi, *Le fognature di Milano. Studio generale delle canalizzazioni urbane con speciale applicazione alla rete di Milano* (Milan, 1913), 28 ff.; cf. A. Galbani, 'L'Ufficio tecnico municipale da Domenico Cesa Bianchi a Giovanni Manera', in R. Rozzi, ed., *La Milano del piano Beruto (1884–1889). Società, urbanistica e architettura nella seconda metà dell'Ottocento* (Milan, 1992), 181–4.

problem remained the inadequate quality of water provision which had been brought on by the fact that the traditional system of splintered and local water collection and drainage no longer guaranteed hygienic conditions that were acceptable in the new situation of growing population density, the rapid expansion of built-up areas and where demand for water was on the increase due to the growing number of private toilets and bathrooms.

The second sub-circuit, that of the *Navigli*, hinged on the *Naviglio interno* which circled nearly the whole of the old city and which connected part of the covered and uncovered canal network in the city with the larger network of irrigation and navigable canals of the region. Thus the *Fossa interna* connected the city, by water, to the whole territory between the Ticino, the Adda and the Po, and at the same time contributed to the complex system for the control of flooding in that area. It also drained the rainwater of the city, parts of its sewerage and, no less important, the waste of numerous industries including dye-works, distilleries, and chemical plants etc. Subject of repeated complaints since the 1870s, the presence of various chemical residues in the *Naviglio Grande* and in other canals had caused such damage to agriculture, to laundries and to residents that at the end of the 1880s a municipal commission was set up to tackle the problem. It proposed, probably for the first time in Italy, that maximum levels for polluting substances should be established. In fact it was thought impossible to purify waste water before it entered the *Naviglio* system, but also awkward to raise the quantity of water within it because this would have altered the established way of providing for irrigation and dealing with floods.[6]

It was obvious that the delicate balance between the different functions of the water-circuit was changing rapidly. The canals' military uses were now defunct while their importance for navigation and economic activities – building, timber-transport and so on – as well as for irrigation had developed rapidly in the course of the nineteenth century. But the canals themselves now experienced strong competition from the railways, whilst in the city the demand for a new and bigger road network had developed.[7] At the same time, the worsening of the hygienic condition of the water and the continual rise of industrial and rain discharge into them seemed to indicate the inadequacy of the *Fossa*

---

[6] Archivio comunale di Milano, Acque (ACM Ac), II, c. 14, n. 47344; Comune di Milano and G. Codara, *La situazione della fognatura cittadina* (Milan, 1924).

[7] F. Reggiori, *Milano 1800-1943. Itinerario urbanistico-edilizio* (Milan, 1947), 292–3.

interna to carry out even its traditional function as the principal collector of the city's waste water.

A variety of plans and projects for reclaiming, but also for a substantial restructuring of the *Naviglio interno* was put forward. Ever since the 1860s the main proposal had been to cover the canal in order to improve the hygiene and the value of the buildings next to it, and possibly build a railway on the new surface and to dig new canals outside the city in order to keep the water and navigation system functioning. Nevertheless, perplexity as to the hygienic effectiveness of the covering and the legal implications that this would have entailed for Milan, central government, and other cities involved in the running of the canal led to abandonment of any projects and to a provision merely that, after 1881, the canals would be paved, periodically cleaned and covered only in a small section that was not navigable.

Debate was sparked immediately precisely by the 'Beruto plan' which envisaged covering the whole of the *Naviglio interno* in order to use it exclusively as a sewer and to provide the city with a wide ring-road around its centre. In addition, the respected Milanese '*Consiglio degli ingegneri e degli architetti*' (Council of engineers and architects) approved the plan to cover the canal because it was considered suitable from the hygienic point of view and because it favoured the affirmation, in the city, of road transport over water transport. Once again, however, the high costs and uncertain results of these projects caused them to be shelved and the choice was made to restore the existing canals.[8]

However, the development of road transport, of building and industrialization continued to put the existing water circuit under inordinate pressure. As early as 1861 the construction of a separate collecting system for rainwater had got under way in order to facilitate road-traffic: indeed, rainwater volumes were rapidly increasing as more roads were paved and given a convex instead of concave surface. Thus twenty years later large sections of the 'new' network for the collection of rainwater needed to be restored and rationalized. In addition, the separate channeling of rainwater avoided the overburdening of the sewerage canals only within the circle of the *Navigli*, outside of which the waste-water drained into the multifunctional water system described above.

At the end of the 1880s four different needs came together: first, to reorder the separate system within the circle of the *Navigli*; second, to reorganize the 124 open canals in the external area that were used for irrigation, for collecting road drainage, as actual sewers and which had been encapsulated by the growth of the city; third, to collect sewage and

---

[8] A. Galbani, 'L'Ufficio tecnico', 177–8.

rainwater in the areas that had recently been built up; and finally to bring it to the network of more external canals (the *Redefossi*, the *Naviglio Grande*, the *Pavia* and their linked canals). This would avoid pollution and flooding in those areas or, alternatively, in the countryside, get rid of industrial waste water. In other words, the changed ways in which water was incorporated necessitated the reorganization of the sequence of functions of the use-cycle of the water, and of devising a new way to drain the growing quantities of water used in the city.[9]

New Ways of Incorporation: The Aqueduct and the Sewer

As in many other cities, the construction of Milan's new water system was the result of the interaction of a whole set of geographical, social, technological and financial variables.[10] As early as 1847 and again in 1856 plans had been made to combat the pollution of drinking water wells by digging new wells in the nearby commune of Sesto San Giovanni or in other areas of the city. In 1880, instead, the growing need for water had given rise to a project that would use a much more substantial source: water from the Val Brembana – over 70 km from Milan. But within a few years this project had also come to naught due to, among other things, the serious protests of the valley's inhabitants. The criterion of using water from Alpine valleys or lakes or from underground, in all cases from a considerable distance, was also the key theme in projects formulated in 1887. These projects, however, were not implemented because they were considered technically inadequate.[11] In sum, the possibility of tackling the crisis of the traditional water network by using new ways of getting water seemed to be floundering due to inertia and uncertainty, perhaps because the most urgent problem was quality rather than quantity.

The municipal commissions set up between 1885 and 1886 to tackle the question considered the problem of waste water as much more urgent. They verified that the separate systems for collecting rainwater

---

[9] For a quantitative approach to the urban water system, see: S. Barles, 'Umwelt und Städtebautechniken. Der Pariser Boden im 19. Jahrhundert', in Bernhardt, ed., *Environmental Problems*.

[10] See considerations on this by B. Luckin, 'Pollution in the city', in M. Daunton, ed., *The Cambridge Urban History. III: 1840–1950* (Cambridge, 2000), 213–15.

[11] Cantalupi, *L'igiene delle città*, 136 ff.; cf. also V. Motta, *L'acquedotto di Milano* (Milan, 1981), 121 ff.; C. Morandi, 'L'adeguamento del sistema infrastrutturale di Milano tra l'Unità e la fine del secolo', in Rozzi, ed., *Milano del piano Beruto*, I, 204–205; T. Isenburg, 'L'acquedotto di Milano', *Storia urbana*, 93, 2000, 19–29.

and domestic waste that had been built in the town centre from 1868 were inadequate; that the domestic sewers were hygienically risky and difficult to maintain; and that in the city's new quarters effluents were insufficient both for rain and waste water. They therefore proposed to give the whole city (apart from those areas where a separate system existed already) a combined continuous channel sewerage system, the so called *tout a l'égout*, down which would flow both rain and waste water. At the time, evaluations of the combined system were controversial and Milan was one of the first Italian cities which adopted it. The hypothesis of keeping the channeling separate remained a minority view because it was believed it would have been less hygienically reliable, more expensive and technically complex. The combined system was considered better suited to the established practice of the city to drain into the irrigation canals instead of rivers, and, in general, for the reestablishment of the relationship between the town and the surrounding countryside, seeing as all the water would continue to drain into the *marcite*.[12]

The combined system offered a single and adequate solution for the whole area covered by the 'Beruto plan' because it connected the zones on both sides of the *Naviglio interno*, preserved the latter by the use of more external collectors, and with its technical simplicity favoured the expansion of the road system. It was also quickly adopted because the new quarters being built as a continuation of the monumental centre of the city, the *Foro Bonaparte*, needed sewers. Finally, a combined system acted as a catalyst for the reorganization of the internal water circuit because it needed an adequate amount of water and this induced the digging of some new and deeper than usual wells in the *Arena* zone in the centre of the city. The very positive outcome of this led to the choice of providing the aqueduct with water taken from beneath the city via wells 25 to 80 metres deep. These provided plenty of safe drinking water.

This solution allowed the Milanese aqueduct – municipally owned like the sewerage system throughout this period – to develop and keep abreast of demographic and urban growth whilst at the same time providing for increasing consumption: if in 1905 five plants provided around 1,000 litres a second (roughly 86,400 a day), serving 6000 houses and three fifths of the population, in 1909 we find 9 plants and

---

[12] Poggi, *Le fognature*, 46 ff.; Galbani, 'L'Ufficio tecnico', 181 ff. On the contemporary debate between supporters of the combined or separate system in the USA see J. Tarr, *The Search for the Ultimate Sink. Urban Pollution in Historical Perspective* (Akron, Ohio, 1996), 111–58, and in Germany, see J. Büschenfeld, *Flüsse und Kloaken. Umweltfragen im Zeitalter der Industrialisierung (1870–1918)* (Stuttgart, 1997) 101 ff.

73 wells, providing 2,290 litres a second, whilst the distributive network was 256 km long, serving 8,460 users. In 1927 plants had grown to 21 and wells to 336, their capacity to 5,919 litres a second. In 1940 the 38 plants could count on roughly 514 wells providing more than 11,000 litres a second via a network 820 km long for the benefit of 34,509 users.[13] The growth of per capita daily consumption was also important: in 1900 this stood at something like 50 litres and reliable data show that consumption steadied at 270 litres after 1913. The relative simplicity and cost-effectiveness of this system of collecting water, that used underground sources and avoided competing functions, had made the Milanese aqueduct one of Italy's best both in terms of absolute quantities and in terms of average consumption.[14] Not surprisingly, the underground water supply was to be quickly resorted to by many other cities.

The sewerage network also developed rapidly due to the simplicity of constructing a combined system, the availability of the water necessary for its efficient running, and the possibility of adequately draining away the considerable volume of water produced by this kind of complex. In 1905 a 140 km long sewer served 4,200 houses out of a total of 10,500; in 1910 the network had grown to 250 km and the houses served to 6,500; in 1923 there were over 11,000 houses served and 620 km, which had reached 760 km by 1942.[15] This constantly expanding system gathered together sewage, water from the roads, and rainwater in a 'natural' biological purification basin made up of 10–12,000 hectares of farmland which produced good harvests of rice and forage: in the 1930s around 220 million cubic metres of sewage were pumped onto this land per year, without a single case of proven damage to

---

[13] MI DGSP, *Risanamenti urbani. Miglioramenti edilizi e sanitarii dal 1885 al 1905* (Rome 1908); C. Capacci, *Acquedotti e acque potabili* (Milan 1918); A. Belloni, *L'acquedotto milanese. L'approvvigionamento idrico della città di Milano dal 1892 al 1951* (Milan, 1952); Motta, *L'acquedotto di Milano*, 17 and table 22.

[14] A. Cecchi, *Il continuo incremento del fabbisogno idrico potabile nei grandi centri urbani in rapporto alle nostre disponibilità idriche*, in *Atti del VII congresso nazionale delle acque (Bari, 1933)* (Pisa, 1935).

[15] MI DGSP, *Risanamenti urbani*; F. Poggi, 'Cenni sui lavori di fognatura della città di Milano', *Rivista di Ingegneria Sanitaria*, 1908, 12; Poggi, *Le fognature*, 667; Reggiori, *Milano*, 496–7; G. Baselli, 'Notizie sulla rete di fognatura della città di Milano', in Sindacato provinciale fascista ingegneri di Milano, *Atti del convegno interprovinciale dei gruppi acquedotti e fognature dei sindacati fascisti ingegneri della Liguria-Lombardia-Piemonte* (Milan, 1934); Reggenza nazionale dei gruppi di acquedotti e fognature del sindacato nazionale fascista degli ingegneri, *Acquedotti e fognature in Italia, nell'impero nei possidimenti dell'Egeo e nell'Albania. Rassegna descrittiva e statistica* (Rome, 1940), I.

drinking-water of the area.[16] This purification system was very nearly unique in Europe for its size and effectiveness but it was also highly unusual in Italy. Its efficiency and profitability depended on the coming together of many factors. The peculiar make-up of the Milanese water catchment area, the distance from the city, the extent of irrigable land and the slight inclination of the land-surface allowed for a considerable diluting of sewage as well as the maintenance of the water's flow. In this way the depositing on the land of organic material and the concentration there of fertilizing substances were drastically reduced. These risks were in any case also lessened by the singular characteristics of the poor soil and the practice of farmers to periodically lower the level of the *marcite* to remove excess material. Finally, the possibility of growing rice and vegetables meant that the purification basin was exploited to its utmost.[17]

The City and Territorial Circuit

New ways of incorporating water had allowed the enormous growth of water available to the industrial-urban system of Milan. This was due, on the one hand, to the fact that the collecting circuit was not limited by the competition of other uses (drinking, industrial or electro-irrigational) and only, it appeared, by the technologies to obtain it. On the other hand, it was related to the fact that the construction of the network of drainage of the growing quantities of waste water present in the urban territory had derived advantage largely from the complexity of the territorial water system. However, the centre of gravity of the system had moved outwards and its functionality and its environmental implications depended on the quality and quantities of water incorporated in the urban-industrial circuit, and, just as important, on the connections and balances between urban and the larger territorial circuit. In turn, the latter was itself affected by the changing environment and by man.

Already in the period considered here the new system showed some weaknesses if not obvious imbalances. It is important to notice that

---

[16] D. Spataro, *Ingegneria sanitaria. Provvista dell'acqua e risanamento dell'abitato* (Milan, 1909), 403 ff.; B. Bernardi, 'Ricerche sulle acque di fognatura di Milano', *Reale istituto lombardo di scienze e lettere. Rendiconti*, 53, 1920; Baselli, 'Notizie sulla rete'; Eger, 'La depurazione agricola delle acque cloacali di Milano', *Monitore tecnico*, 1938, 11; C. Antoniani, *Sommario di chimica pedologica* (Milan, 1945), 118–19.

[17] This problem is tackled, with reference to the British case, in J. Sheail, 'Town wastes, agricultural sustainability and Victorian sewage', *Urban History*, 23, 1996, 189–210.

these weaknesses tended to be located at the points in which the 'natural' and 'artificial' segments of the circuit met, or between different circuits using water resources. An example of the first case is provided by the tendency to dig ever-deeper wells in order to get better and more water, and by the fact that the level of water in the aquifer began to go down by a few centimetres a year until 1920, by 14 centimetres in the next 25 years, all of which heralded the subsequent and far more drastic lowering of the water level. An example of the second case was the failure of the reorganization of the system of internal navigation: the *Naviglio interno* was practically completely covered in 1928–30, favouring housing and road-transport interests over the aesthetics of the city and the by now marginal water-transport sector. The project to link the city with the great lakes and the Po by building a new river port succumbed to economic and infrastructural necessities dictated now by the railways and hydro-electricity infrastructures. It should also be stressed that there was substantial continuity between the main options taken up and criteria used by the fascist central and local authorities and earlier administrations.

Undoubtedly the most pressing and direct weakness of the system was the interface between the sewers and the surface water regimen. The principal connection between them was the Vettabbia canal, which had been transformed into a final collector thanks to the renewed deal between the commune of Milan and the consortium that used the sewage for irrigation and that cultivated land to the south of the city. However, the project to transform the Redefossi canal into an eastern sewer was never implemented because this canal already acted as an outlet (draining into the Southern Lambro) for the Villoresi and Seveso canals when they were in flood. In these areas the height from the ground of the minor irrigation canals did not allow for their transformation into sewage canals that were needed for new areas of the city recently built.[18] The project for the transformation of the so called Southern Lambro into a collector for the western side of the city, which had been considered since 1890, was never implemented. The users of this canal firmly opposed the plan, because it would have collected both sewage and rainwater from a huge and ever-more built-up area, and the floodwater of the Olona, which was notoriously polluted by industrial waste. An increase in its capacity and a lowering of the quality of its water would have definitely altered the delicate balance of the Southern Lambro and its wanton use as outlet for

---

[18] Poggi, *Le fognature*, 52, 219–39, Reggiori, *Milano*, 497; U. Massari, 'Il canale "Emissario a Redefossi"', *Milano*, 1928, 6; G. Baselli, 'Le opere del comune inaugurate nella giornata del XXVIII ottobre', ibid., 1928, 10; G. Michetti, 'Il collettore della zona di ampliamento est', ibid., 1929, 10.

irrigation and industrial waste.[19] It was evident that the more the city expanded the more the complexity of the 'modern' water circuit reduced its own efficiency and, above all, compelled the renunciation of combined watercourse usage.

The tension between the combined system of the city and the territorial water system emerged plainly in the 1930s. Urban expansion and growth in production, the expansion of the built-up areas and the still unresolved problem of industrial waste weighed heavily on the first of these by loading it with ever-increasing quantities of unpurified domestic and industrial waste and rainwater. The second was adversely affected by the expansion of demand for water, strongly motivated by the fascist regime, for irrigation needs and the increase in the amount of waste produced by numerous urban industrial nuclei particularly to the north of the city. This tension highlighted the difficulty of managing a water-system which was now very integrated, but overburdened, quantitatively unstable and qualitatively modified, as is demonstrated respectively by recurring floods, bacterial and, above all, industrial contamination of the water. It was obvious that the goal of greater urban hygiene did not coincide with the goal of cleaner and better water, and in fact the former had often been achieved at the expense of the latter.[20]

Moreover, unified channeling amplified the effect of floods and industrial pollution. Indeed, the issue of industrial waste water had become ever more pressing but was largely ignored.[21] The legal obligation to purify industrial waste before draining it into the sewer had remained a dead letter and the illegal and legal ('in exceptional circumstances') discharge of waste prevailed. Nor had, at the beginning of the twentieth century, the proposal to place two collectors exclusively for industrial waste inside the *Naviglio grande* and the Redefossi, appeared a possible and viable solution to the wide distribution of industrial complexes throughout the territory. Rather, and this was confirmed by a special provincial commission set up in 1927, the

---

[19] Poggi, *Le fognature*, 66–7, Galbani, 'L'Ufficio tecnico', 183; U. Massari, 'La deviazione del fiume Olona secondo il tracciato del Piano Regolatore (Legge 12-7-1912, n. 866) e la sistemazione del Lambro meridionale', *Atti del sindacato provinciale fascista ingegneri di Milano*, 2, 1929.

[20] Büschenfeld, *Flüsse und Kloaken*, 51 ff.

[21] This differed from what was happening, for example, in Germany, see Büschenfeld, *Flüsse und Kloaken*, 285 ff; U. Gilhaus, "*Schmerzenskinder der Industrie". Umweltverschmutzung, Umweltpolitik und sozialer Protest im Industriezeitalter in Westfalen 1845–1914* (Paderborn, 1995), or in Britain, see B.W. Clapp, *An Environmental History of Britain since the Industrial Revolution* (London, 1994); see also, for France, G. Massard-Guilbaud, 'La régulation des nuisances industrielles urbaine (1800–1940)', *Vingtiéme Siècle*, 64, 1999.

tendency was to favour the fast dispersal of industrial waste in a way returning to a separate channeling, at least for industrial areas.[22]

In reality the dispersal of the 'denser and more putrid' water would only have been a temporary solution as the problem would have merely repeated itself on a wider scale. In effect Milan's problem was to avoid its territory being crossed by canals full of floodwater and the industrial waste of its surrounding communes. In their turn, the surrounding communes now experienced contamination between the collection and drainage of water that thirty years before had induced Milan to reorganize its own water circuits. The consortiums born in the communes of the city's Northern hinterland at the end of the 1920s to control industrial discharges into the canals and streams of the area had quickly realized that 'the situation is serious and is becoming more serious every day' and they had therefore begun, on the one hand to build aqueducts and sewers in order to prevent the contamination of the aquifer that provided water for their wells, and on the other, to construct a network of drainage channels which should have collected industrial waste and discharged it, avoiding Milan, into the Lambro. The first objective was in part successful: from 1924 to 1934 the communes with aqueducts had risen from 38 to 92 (109 in 1937) and in 1934 only 43 of the 274 communes of the province had a complete sewer and another 64 an incomplete sewer (for 20 per cent and 35 per cent of the population). The second objective remained unrealized due to the seriousness of the situation, the number of water courses, and the size of the territory.[23]

Towards an Environmental Crisis

By the second half of the 1930s the whole water system of the territory was entering into a visible crisis. The network of rain and floodwater irrigation and outflow canals was in a state of disarray and extremely

---

[22] Poggi, *Le fognature*, 81–6, 100, 692; ACM Ac, II, c.31, n. 16922.

[23] Provincia di Milano, *L'opera dell'amministrazione nel 1927* (Milan, 1928 and the following years); C.A. Ragazzi, 'Acque non canalizzate e acque industriali a Milano', *Atti del sindacato provinciale fascista ingegneri di Milano*, 1, 1933; C. Ruggiero, 'Ultimi progressi nella diluizione delle acque urbane', ibid., 5, 1933; G. Bellincioni, 'Approvvigionamento idrico e smaltimento dei rifiuti', in *Atti del primo convegno lombardo di igiene rurale* (Milan, 1934); G. Manfredi, 'Censimento acquedotti e fognature della Lombardia', in *Atti del convegno interprovinciale*; M. Belloni, 'Il contributo dell'amministrazione provinciale di Milano al miglioramento delle comunicazioni ed al risanamento dei comuni rurali', in Istituto nazionale di urbanistica, *Atti del I congresso nazionale d'urbanistica. I/2: Urbanistica rurale* (Rome, 1937).

inefficient. There were two principal reasons for this: the reclamation of land for agricultural purposes and the expansion of the built-up area had reduced the soil's capacity to absorb water and many canals were partially blocked by dams that harnessed water for irrigation, and were in any case in a bad state of repair. Clearly the intensification of land-use for construction and farming had altered the delicate functional equilibrium of the rural canal network. Serious consequences ensued and continual and extensive flooding and the spread of malaria in the countryside to the north and south of Milan were only the most significant and harmful. To these problems of managing the water network, the extensive pollution of surface and to a degree underground water resources also has to be added. This was brought on by the inadequacy of the sewerage systems of the villages and small towns to the north of Milan as well as the uncontrolled disposal of industrial waste.

To technicians involved, it was clear that the situation was becoming unsustainable and a series of solutions were put forward. In essence, these proposed the further drainage of moist soils and the reorganization of the canal network in order to keep the irrigation and floodwater draining canals separate and to join the canals to the North with those to the South of the city. In addition, it was necessary to complete the city sewerage system and, as far as pollution was concerned, to add an artificial to the biological purification basin of the *marcite* as well as to catalogue all the watercourses in order to decide which ones should be used for industrial waste.[24] Clearly, these proposals demonstrated a new awareness of the complexity of the whole water system. In fact it was openly argued that there was a need to act in an integrated and programmed way on all these different fronts. It is also clear that the proposals aimed at the reorganization of the Milanese water network in terms of structure and functionality. The final aim was that of maximizing the exploitation of resources (not just water) and therefore the principal criteria applied were the drainage of as wide areas as possible, the increase in the flow of water in the canals to foster a more rapid circulation of water, and the disposal of industrial and organic residues in the latter. Overall, these were methods that had been used for the half century since the reorganization of the Milanese water system had begun, but they were now to be applied not only to the city but to the whole area involved in the urban and industrial development.

The reorganization that had begun in the 1880s had transformed the

---

[24] E. Campini, 'La bonifica idraulica della pianura lombarda fra Adda – Ticino – Po', *Atti dei sindacati provinciali fascisti ingegneri di Lombardia*, 6–7/8, 1936; Belloni, *Il contributo*.

city's water system. This had been made possible through the application of technology, in particular construction, mechanics and electromechanics. The objectives attained had been exponentially to increase the availability of water and of land for industries, transport, housing and services. This had been achieved by separating surface water from the ground, by mechanically moving vast quantities of water, and by introducing a marked hierarchy between different kinds of water usage in favour of those that were needed for urban and industrial development.

In the space of a few decades this reorganization had been achieved and had resulted in the city possessing a 'modern' and stable water network that worked reasonably well. However, it was precisely its completion in the 1930s that confirmed the shifting of its imbalances and difficulties outside the city into the territorial water system. The imbalances had also been accentuated by the contemporary industrial and urban development in a much wider area and, to a degree, by the rationalization of farming. The construction of the 'modern' water system had been dominated by a mechanistic approach that considered the character of natural and hydro-resources and the complex eco-system of which they were a part, in a dangerously reductionist manner. For these reasons, the human exploitation of water resources clashed with the natural water reproduction cycle both at the chemical-physical and biological level as well as at the water catchment basin and higher level.

In conclusion, the incorporation of water in the urban industrial area of Milan in the decades of industrialization did not lead to the setting up of a sustainable system for the management of natural resources. Rather it laid the basis for an environmental crisis[25] – at such a high level of pollution that it would hamper greatly the very exploitation of natural resources – that would hit the territory two decades later, after a further and intense bout of industrialization and urbanization.

---

[25] For an example of the historiographical use of the concept of 'environmental crisis', see M.V. Melosi, ed., *Pollution and Reform in American Cities, 1870–1930* (Austin, 1980); see also M.V. Melosi, *Effluent America*, 140 ff.

CHAPTER TEN

Constructing Urban Infrastructure for Multiple Resource Management: Sewerage Systems in the Industrialization of the Rhineland, Germany

Ulrich Koppitz

Introduction: About Resource Identification

Urban resource management is a highly sophisticated economic approach, aiming at sustainability or sustainable growth.[1] From this perspective, management performance should be analysed over a period of decades, which can only be done retrospectively, making particular use of concepts derived from ecological economy.[2] Environmental history, especially that part of the discipline concerned with pollution, often focused on a single environmental medium – air, soil or water, viewed as the natural resource at risk.[3] Resource management presupposes the identification or rather definition of this single resource, almost necessarily at the expense of attention to other resources, however. In contrast to urban pollution problems, careless or illegal action or unwanted side effects seem to be of minor importance in resource management when long term planned intentional activities prevail and are likely to result in the construction and utilization of special institutions or infrastructure.

---

[1] E. Kula, *Economics of natural resources, the environment and politics*, 2nd. ed. (London et al., 1993), 31–6. The author is very much indebted to the understanding and help of the editors who made it possible to arrive at an English version of this article finally.

[2] A most promising research project in long-term material flow accountancy for Paris in the 19th century is in progress, see the contribution by S. Barles in this volume. The historical approach in ecological economy is not only suitable for a reconstruction of earlier material flows and their heritage, but also for extensive testing of methods responsible for environmental acceptability analysis.

[3] F.-J. Brüggemeier and Th. Rommelspacher, *Besiegte Natur: Geschichte der Umwelt im 19. und 20. Jahrhundert* (München, 1987).

One of the most persistent elements of urban infrastructure are sewerage systems.[4] This paper attempts to analyse such systems from a resource management perspective. First, we ask which kind of resource management concepts could have been driving forces behind the planning, building and operation of sewerage systems in the era of industrialization and urbanization. According to primary and secondary sources, at least five vital issues need to be discussed: the management of water, waste, human and animal faeces, health and urban space as resources. Thereafter, evidence is provided from a case study of Düsseldorf in the German Rhineland.

Water Management

'Water for the cities' is a classic issue in urban resource management,[5] in terms of the quantity as well as the quality or pollution of supply. The amount of water pumped by central waterworks into a city like Berlin around 1900 outweighed any other kind of goods and was slightly larger than either the supply for private enterprises or the volume attributable to precipitation. The total amount of 'waste-water', can only be approximately calculated.[6]

Water history has become a field in its own right.[7] However, this contribution deliberately looks at the issue of urban waste-water

---

[4] M. Strell, *Die Abwasserfrage in ihrer geschichtlichen Entwicklung von den ältesten Zeiten bis zur Gegenwart* (Leipzig, 1913).

[5] N.M. Blake, *Water for the Cities: A History of the Urban Water Supply Problem in the United States* (Syracuse, NY, 1956).

[6] T. Weyl, *Versuch über den Stoffwechsel Berlins. Bearbeitet mit Unterstützung des Magistrats von Berlin* (Berlin, 1894): Central water supply amounted to 24,000 kg per capita and year (in 1890), compared to 200 kg beer and wine, 84 kg milk and some 330 kg of other foodstuff. In the same year the area of Berlin received some 32 thousand million litres precipitation of which 20,6 thousand million litres should have been discharged by sewers. The municipal waterworks delivered 35,4 thousand million litres altogether, and the output of private decentralized water supply was estimated at about 22 thousand million litres. On the other hand, some 51 thousand million litres of sewage were pumped to the sewage farms. On a larger scale, e.g. for Austria, W. Hüttler and H. Payer, 'Der Wasser-Stoffwechsel', in M. Fischer-Kowalski et al., eds, *Gesellschaftlicher Stoffwechsel und Kolonisierung von Natur. Ein Versuch in sozialer Ökologie* (Amsterdam et al., 1997), 95–110.

[7] With the conferences in Aberystwyth and Bergen and the foundation of the International Society for Water History at the latest, see http://www.iwha.net, and of the discussion network H-Water, search www.h-net.org; and with fascinating aspects in cultural history, e.g. U. Borsdorf, ed., *Wasser-Fälle – an Rhein und Maas* (Bottrop, 2002).

management from a number of different angles, focusing on the
decisions discussed when modern waterworks and sewerage systems
began to offer greater technical possibilities, including the 'invention of
waste-water'.[8] Typically, in Germany, municipal waterworks were
installed decades before corresponding sewerage systems were
constructed.[9] In spite of fundamental uncertainties, the calculation of
sewage flow – according to a simplistic paradigm of 'flow hydrology'[10]
which neglected phenomena such as stormwater outlets or groundwater
transfer[11] – was developed as an instrument of scientific research as well
as administrative water management.[12] This taxed the discharge of

---

[8] U. Koppitz, Theorien und Praktiken der Indirekteinleitung und die
Klärschlammfrage – bei Einführung der Schwemmkanalisation und überhaupt', in J.
Lange and E. Schramm, eds., *Das Management von Fäkalien und Flüssigabfällen aus
Haushalten – historische Perspektiven auf ein Problem der Gegenwart* (Frankfurt
a.M., 1996), 39–46: S. Barles, 'L'invention des eaux usées: l'assainissement de Paris,
de la fin de l'Ancien Régime à la seconde guerre mondiale', in C. Bernhardt and
G. Massard-Guilbaud, eds, *Le démon moderne: La pollution dans les sociétés
urbaines et industrielles d'Europe* (Clermont-Ferrand, 2002), 129–56.

[9] J. Vögele, Sozialgeschichte städtischer Gesundheitsverhältnisse während
der Urbanisierung (Berlin, 2001), 253–57; Vögele, J., Urban Mortality Change
in England and Germany, 1870–1910 (Liverpool, 1998), 150–59; a
comprehensive statistics in H. Salomon, *Die städtische Abwasserbeseitigung in
Deutschland*, 3 vols (Jena, 1906–11); Klette, 'Tiefbau', in R. Wuttke, ed., *Die
deutschen Städte*, vol. 1 (Leipzig, 1904), 370–419.

[10] A critique of the prevailing flow hydrology and drainage paradigm was
already published in the mid-19th century: A. Dieck, *Die naturwidrige
Wasserwirthschaft der Neuzeit, ihre Gefahren und Nachtheile, wie solche in
Folge der durch sie erzeugten Übel den Völkern in sich steigerndem Grade
bevorstehen, mit einer Schätzung der Schäden, welche die deutsche Nation,
wegen nicht genügender Ausnutzung der Dung-, Trieb- u. Tragkraft des Wassers
für Landwirthschaft, Gewerbe, Industrie, Schiffahrt und Handel heute schon
erleidet* (Wiesbaden, 1879).

[11] For England H. Cook, 'Groundwater Development in England',
Environment and History, 5, 1999, 75–96; for Germany scattered data were
published by the contemporaries according to Pettenkofer's soil and
groundwater theory in the journal Zeitschrift für Biologie, e.g. M. Pettenkofer:
'Typhus und Cholera und Grundwasser in Zürich', *Zeitschrift für Biologie*, 7,
1871, 86–103.

[12] S. Laakkoonen and P. Lehtonen, 'A quantitative analysis of discharges into
the Helsinki urban sea area in 1850–1995', *European Water Management*, 2,
1999, 30–40; I. Douglas, R. Hodgson and N. Lawson, 'Materials flows through
200 years of industrial history: the case of Manchester', in M. Fischer-Kowalski
and V. Winiwarter, eds, '*Nature, Society, History: Long Term Dynamics of Social
Metabolism*' (conference CD, Vienna, 1999); with special regard to salt freight
calculations and the concept of limiting values see J. Büschenfeld, 'Visionen des
Fortschritts: Grenzwerte in der Gewässerschutzdebatte um 1900', in: H.-L.
Dienel, ed., *Der Optimismus der Ingenieure. Triumph der Technik in der Krise
der Moderne um 1900* (Stuttgart, 1998), 77–128; J. Büschenfeld, *Flüsse und*

waste water attributable both to mining companies and municipal sewage in heavily industrialized regions like the Ruhr-valley.[13]

Waste and Manure Management

In line with the concept of the 'search for the ultimate sink' and the mentality associated with this idea, it is the merit of research in environmental history[14] that sewerage systems have been described as a means of transporting waste matter and a neutralizing vector of urban-environmental risk into rivers and hinterland.[15] In Germany, a similarly sceptical view concerning health risk versus health benefits was taken by the Royal Medical Council of Prussia already in the late 1870s. The medical expert Rudolf Virchow declared that modern sewerage or traditional systems could likewise meet all hygienic needs if properly employed and that the issue was mainly a question of transportation costs.[16]

Kloaken. Umweltfragen im Zeitalter der Industrialisierung, 1870–1918 (Stuttgart, 1997); and the publications by S. Barles e.g. in this volume.

[13] U. Gilhaus, *'Schmerzenskinder der Industrie'. Umweltverschmutzung, Umweltpolitik und sozialer Protest im Industriezeitalter in Westfalen 1845–1914* (Paderborn, 1996), 236–74; B. Olmer, *Wasser – historisch. Zur Bedeutung und Belastung des Umweltmediums im Ruhrgebiet 1870–1930* (Frankfurt a.M., 1998); M. Weyer von Schoultz, *Stadt und Gesundheit im Ruhrgebiet 1850–1929. Verstädterung und kommunale Gesundheitspolitik am Beispiel der jungen Industriestadt Gelsenkirchen* (Essen, 1994); Th. Kluge and E. Schramm, *Wassernöte. Zur Geschichte des Trinkwasssers*, 2nd edn (Cologne, 1988); for Britain cf. J. Sheail, 'The Sustainable Management of Industrial Watercourses: An English Historical Perspective', *Environmental History*, 2, 1997, 197–215.

[14] J.A. Tarr, *The Search for the Ultimate Sink: Urban Pollution in Historical Perspective* (Akron, Ohio, 1996); M. Melosi, *The Sanitary City. Urban Infrastructure in America from Colonial Times to the Present* (Baltimore/London, 2000), 90–99. For the principle of 'tout à l'égout' see J.A. Tarr and G. Dupuy, eds, *Technology and the rise of the networked city in Europe and America* (Philadelphia, 1988); J.A. Tarr and G. Dupuy, 'Sewers and cities: France and the U.S. compared', *Journal of the Environmental Engineering Division, Proceedings Am.Soc.Civ.Engin.*, 108, 1982, 327–38.

[15] Cf. S. Neri Serneri, 'Water pollution in Italy: the failure of the hygienic approach 1890–1960s', in C. Bernhardt and G. Massard-Guilbaud, eds, *Le démon moderne: La pollution dans les sociétés urbaines et industrielles d'Europe* (Clermont-Ferrand, 2002), 157–78; J. Lange and E. Schramm, eds, *Das Management von Fäkalien und Flüssigabfällen aus Haushalten – historische Perspektiven auf ein Problem der Gegenwart* (Frankfurt a.M., 1996).

[16] R. Virchow, *Canalisation oder Abfuhr? Eine hygienische Studie* (Berlin, 1869); H. Eulenberg, ed., *Gutachten der königlichen wissenschaftlichen Deputation für das Medizinalwesen in Preussen über die Canalisation der Städte* (Berlin, 1883).

In another sophisticated approach indebted to environmental economics, yet also reaching in its intellectual origins as far back as Justus von Liebig,[17] sewerage systems were and are blamed for wasting vital resources, especially manure.[18] The installation and maintenance of large sewage farms[19] to recycle nutrients was based on calculations of urban metabolism, and fertilizer was at least not deliberately wasted when sewage farms were installed or when sludge from treatment plants was sold to farmers. Compared to traditional manure management, however, sewage farms were clearly designed as a rationalized transportation system and implied shortcomings in distribution and intensity of agricultural use.[20] During fallow periods, and particularly during frosty weather, a constant flow of sewage served no useful purpose, and notoriously under-funded sewage farms soon became 'over-fertilized' and contaminated. This obvious deterioration of agricultural resource management could only be seen as a compromise, where urban resources as cleanliness, urban aesthetics and modern civilization prevailed.[21]

---

[17] V. Winiwarter, 'Where did all the waters go?', in C. Bernhardt, ed., *Environmental problems in European cities in the 19th and 20th Centuries* (Münster, 2001), 106–119, 112 sq.; J. von Simson, 'Die Flußverunreinigungsfrage im neunzehnten Jahrhundert', *Vierteljahrschrift für Sozial- und Wirtschaftsgeschichte*, 65, 1978, 370–90; E. Schramm, *Im Namen des Kreislaufs. Ideengeschichte der Modelle vom ökologischen Kreislauf* (Frankfurt a.M., 1997).

[18] N. Goddard, 'A mine of wealth': the Victorians and the agricultural value of sewage', *Journal of Historical Geography*, 22, 1996, 274–90; J. Sheail, 'Town Wastes, agricultural sustainability, and Victorian sewage', *Urban History*, 23, 1996, 189–210; E. Mårald (1999), 'Everything Circulates: Agricultural Chemistry and Recyling Theories in the Second Half of the Nineteenth Century', *Environmental History*, 8, 2002, 65–84; N. Goddard/J. Sheail, 'Victorian sanitary reform: where were the innovators', in C. Bernhardt, ed., *Environmental Problems in European Cities in the 19th and 20th Centuries* (Münster, New York, 2001), 87–103; and again, the works published by S. Barles, e.g. in this volume.

[19] Cf. the papers by N. Goddard and by S. Barles in this volume; for Germany see A. Dix, 'Kontaminierte Landschaften – Rieselfelder in Westfalen im 19. und 20. Jahrhundert', in K. Ditt, R. Gudermann and N. Rüße, eds., *Agrarmodernisierung und ökologische Folgen. Westfalen vom 18. bis zum 20. Jahrhundert* (Paderborn et al., 2001), 261–86.

[20] E.g. E. Heiden, A. Müller and Karl von Langsdorff, *Die Verwerthung der städtischen Fäcalien* (Hannover, 1885).

[21] 'Cleansing the towns': B. Luckin, 'Pollution in the city', in M. Daunton, ed., *The Cambridge Urban History of Britain*, vol. III: 1840–1950 (Cambridge, 2000), 207–28, here 213–17.

Public Health Management

In contemporary as well as modern literature, sewerage systems[22] tended to be regarded as a part of 'sanitary infrastructure' and complementary to water supply as a 'necessary evil'. Urban history as well as the history of medicine and public health supported this view and praised the foresight of the sanitary movement.[23] However, more critical research revealed a struggle for professional control between different disciplines[24] and highlighted the fact that unclear hygienic concepts lay behind these massive infrastructural investments:[25] According to classic humoralism, stagnant matter was likely to cause ill-health and had to be removed before smell and miasmatic gases could develop or the soil be polluted. Apart from these traditional localist views, Max Pettenkofer – the first German professor of Hygiene – demanded after his research into the Bavarian cholera epidemics of 1854, that the groundwater table in settlement areas should become

[22] For the history of technology cf. J. von Simson, 'Water Supply and Sewerage in Berlin, London and Paris: Developments in the 19th Century', in H.-J. Teuteberg, ed., *Urbaniserung im 19. und 20. Jahrhundert* (Köln, Wien, 1983), 429–40; John von Simson, *Kanalisation und Städtehygiene im 19. Jahrhundert* (Düsseldorf, 1983); E. Sickert, 'Kanalisationen im Wandel der Zeit', in Vereinigung für Abwasser, Abfall und Gewässerschutz, ed. *Geschichte der Abwasserentsorgung. 50 Jahre ATV* (Hennef, 1999), 17–36.

[23] E.g. B. Witzler, *Großstadt und Hygiene: kommunale Gesundheitspolitik in der Epoche der Urbanisierung* (Stuttgart, 1995), defined almost everything as 'sanitary' which was dealt with in the ambitious handbooks for hygiene, see T. Weyl, ed., *Handbuch der Hygiene*, 10 vols (Jena, 1896–1901); cf. R. Millward and F. Bell, 'Choices for town councillors in nineteenth-century Britain: investment in public health and its impact on mortality', in S. Sheard and H. Power, eds, *Body and city: histories of urban public health* (Aldershot, 2000), 143–65; P. Hennock, 'The urban sanitary movement in England and Germany, 1838–1914: a comparison', *Continuity and Change* 15, 2000, 269–96.

[24] Especially engineering, chemistry, medicine, cf. e.g. the paper by L. Lestel in this volume; S. Barles, *La ville délétère: médecins et ingénieurs dans l'espace urbain, xviiie–xixe siecle* (Seyssel, 1999); E. Houwaart, *De hygienisten: artsen, staat & volksgezondheid in Nederland 1840–1890* (Groningen, 1991).

[25] A. Labisch, *Homo hygienicus: Gesundheit und Medizin in der Neuzeit* (Frankfurt a.M., 1992); J. Vögele, 'Die Entwicklung der (groß)städtischen Gesundheitsverhältnisse in der Epoche des Demographischen und Epidemiologischen Übergangs', in J. Reulecke and A. zu Castell Rüdenhausen, eds., *Stadt und Gesundheit. Zum Wandel von 'Volksgesundheit' und kommunaler Gesundheitspolitik im 19. und frühen 20. Jahrhundert* (Stuttgart, 1991), 21–36; cf. A. Labisch and J. Vögele: 'Stadt und Gesundheit. Anmerkungen zur neueren sozial- und medizinhistorischen Diskussion in Deutschland', *Archiv für Sozialgeschichte*, 37, 1997, 396–424.

fixed at a rather low level.[26] In a popularizing lecture, Pettenkofer –
following British example – estimated the amount of money which could
be saved if the population of a city were to become more healthy and he
used this sum to argue for investments in sanitary infrastructure which
would enhance human health.[27]

In Germany there was a crucial period between 1875 and about
1900, when the Prussian government banned emerging combined sewer
systems if cities did not install sufficient sewage farms or purification
plants. The latter were still undergoing fundamental technological
modification.[28] Yet towns and cities preferred to keep on building
sewerage systems without treatment facilities and to modernize
cesspools and hydraulic transport systems via the use of horses and
carts. This amounted to a modified version of the separate system[29]
over a lengthy period of time. Indeed, it would endure until a
compromise was reached with a cheap end-of-pipe approach.

During the nineteenth century, many competing etiological concepts
warned of health risks associated with sewerage systems. Within the
classic miasmatic view, the fear of sewer gas prevailed, contagionist and
bacteriological perspectives focused on river pollution and tried to arrive
at threshold values for germs in waterworks intakes.

The epidemiological effects of the development of sanitary
infrastructure have been subject to many scientific analyses and still lack

---

[26] M. Pettenkofer, *Untersuchungen und Beobachtungen über die
Verbreitungsart der Cholera nebst Betrachtungen über Maßregeln, derselben
Einhalt zu thun* (München, 1855); M. Pettenkofer: *Boden und Grundwasser in
ihren Beziehungen zu Cholera und Typhus. Erwiderung auf Rudolf Virchows
hygienische Studie 'Canalisation oder Abfuhr'* (München, 1869); M.
Pettenkofer, 'Zum gegenwärtigen Stand der Cholerafrage', *Archiv für Hygiene*,
4, 1886, 249–354, 397–546, *Archiv für Hygiene*, 6, 1887, 1–84, 129–233,
303–58, 373–441 and *Archiv für Hygiene*, 7, 1887, 1–82; C.-E. A. Winslow,
The conquest of epidemic disease, a chapter in the history of ideas (Madison,
1980).
[27] M. Pettenkofer, *Ueber den Werth der Gesundheit für eine Stadt*
(Braunschweig, 1876); cf. A. Thakkar-Scholz, '*Der Wert des Menschen*', MD
thesis Düsseldorf, 1998; J. Vögele and W. Woelk, 'Der Wert des Menschen in
den Bevölkerungswissenschaften', in R. Mackensen, ed., *Bevölkerungslehre und
Bevölkerungswissenschaften vor 1933* (Opladen, 2002), 121–33; M. Weyer-von
Schoultz, *Max von Pettenkofer – eine Biographie*, in preparation.
[28] Vereinigung für Abwasser, Abfall und Gewässerschutz, ed., *Geschichte der
Abwasserentsorgung. 50 Jahre ATV* (Hennef, 1999); C. Hamlin, 'Muddling in
Bumbledom: On the Enormity of Large Sanitary Improvements in Four British
Towns, 1855–1885', *Victorian Studies*, 32, 1988, 55–83.
[29] J.A. Tarr, 'The separate vs. combined sewer problem: a case study in urban
technology design choice', reprinted in D. Smith, ed., *Water Supply and Public
Health Engineering* (Aldershot, 1999), 289–320.

certitude when areas with or without sewerage are compared.[30] For major cities in Germany, sewerage construction started in the 1870s and 1880s and was accompanied by a steady decrease in mortality, especially from gastro-intestinal diseases like typhoid fever, which was considered an indicator of the quality of housing conditions.[31] Contemporary literature proudly presented these developments in graphical form and they were hailed as evidence for the beneficial effects for urban sanitary improvement.[32] The same trends, however, may be detected in small towns or even rural communities, where sewerage systems were rare until the early 1900s.[33]

Table 10.1 Typhoid fever mortality in Prussian communities (per 10,000 living)[34]

Year	large towns	medium towns	small towns	small rural communities
1876	6.0	6.4	8.1	6.6
1881	3.2	5.1	6.5	5.4
1891	1.4	2.3	2.4	1.9

Urban Real Estate Management

In the case of Frankfurt upon Main, the most prosperous city in Germany, where many high-profile and at the same time antagonistic proponents of sanitary infrastructure in Germany lived and where a sewerage system had

[30] J. Vögele, *Urban Mortality Change in England and Germany, 1870–1913* (Liverpool, 1998), 150–80; J. Vögele, *Sozialgeschichte städtischer Gesundheitsverhältnisse während der Urbanisierung* (Berlin, 2001).
[31] J. Vögele, 'Typhus und Typhusbekämpfung in Deutschland aus sozialhistorischer Sicht', *Medizinhistorisches Journal*, 33, 1998, 57–79.
[32] Cf. e.g. A. Spiess, *Die hygienischen Einrichtungen von Frankfurt am Main* (Frankfurt a.M., 1888), 29, graph repr. B. Witzler, *Großstadt und Hygiene* (Stuttgart, 1995), 254; T. Weyl, *Die Einwirkung hygienischer Werke auf die Gesundheit der Städte mit besonderer Rücksicht auf Berlin* (Jena, 1893).
[33] In 1907, hardly 1 per cent of the Prussian communities with fewer than 2,000 inhabitants had sewerage access, H. Matzerath, *Urbanisierung in Preußen 1815–1914* (Stuttgart, 1985), 339.
[34] Vögele, *Urban Mortality Change*, table 23, after W. Kruse, 'Die Verminderung der Sterblichkeit in den letzten Jahrzehnten und ihr jetziger Stand', *Zeitschrift für Hygiene und Infectionskrankheiten*, 25, 1897, 113–67: 139; J. Vögele, 'Différences entre ville et campagne et évolution de la mortalité en Allemagne pendant l'industrialisation', *Annales de démographie historique*, 1996, 249–68.

been constructed before a modern waterworks,[35] critics argued that the
prevailing goal for these municipal initiatives was the development of a
new bourgeois suburb in a marshy area, the splendid West-end.[36]

Moreover, the administrative and economic implementation of
municipal sewerage systems, mostly undertaken by authorities
responsible for public streets, convey the impression that, at least for
contemporaries, this part of water management was mainly interpreted
as land management. This was scarcely surprising when compared to
agrarian water management with its focus on land and production
rather than on water resources in their own right.

Artificial drainage was fundamental to sewerage systems and was
often ignored because of its seeming triviality. However, it was vital to
eliminate the perceived environmental 'chaos' that prevailed in marshy
areas, and although more and more waterproof sewers were constructed
in the nineteenth century, the effect of drainage remained.[37] This was
because excavations irreversibly destroyed the upper aquifers.
Groundwater drainage is essential. The transportation of different kinds
of waste water – from that attributable to precipitation to highly toxic
chemicals – is not necessarily carried out by means of a sewerage system
but is subject to the way in which waste water is defined and managed.
The draining powers of sewerage systems may have been their main
advantage over other systems of waste water management, for example
Liernur's hydraulic pipe or various carriage systems.

With respect to urban resource management, it could be argued that
sewerage systems were developed to physically construct the most

---

[35] William Lindley senior and junior, the constructor Philipp Holzmann, the
physician Varrentrapp, and the engineer Charles T. Liernur, who developed a
pneumatic system, lived in Frankfurt: cf. the comprehensive study by T. Bauer,
*Im Bauch der Stadt: Kanalisation und Hygiene in Frankfurt am Main 16. – 19.
Jahrhundert* (Frankfurt a.M., 1998).

[36] Kluge and Schramm, *Wassernöte* (1st edition, Aachen 1986), 56; following
this critical approach M. Rodenstein, *'Mehr Licht, mehr Luft' –
Gesundheitskonzepte im Städtebau seit 1750* (Frankfurt a.M., 1988), 90sq., and
M. Gather, 'Städtehygiene und groß-städtische Entsorgung in Deutschland vor
1914 – Das Beispiel der frühen kommunalen Umweltplanung in Frankfurt am
Main', in: K. Wolf and F. Schymik, eds., *Frankfurt und das Rhein-Main-Gebiet.
Geographische Beiträge aus Anlass des 75-jährigen Bestehens der J.W. Goethe-
Universität* (Frankfurt a.M., 1990), 131–73.

[37] About the relationship of man and nature regarding reason and chaos, i.e.
drainage and swamps: B. Herrmann and M. Kaup, eds, *'Nun blüht es von End'
zu End' all überall' – Die Eindeichung des Nieder-Oderbruches 1747–1753*
(Münster u.a. 1997); S. Barles, *La ville délétère: médecins et ingénieurs dans
l'espace urbain, xviiie-xixe siecle* (Seyssel, 1999), 163–82, 304–26; J. Radkau,
Natur und Macht: Eine Weltgeschichte der Umwelt (München, 2000); C.
Colten, ed., *Transforming New Orleans and its environs* (Pittsburgh, 2002).

important and expensive of all urban resources[38] – land, dry ground – for buildings, roads and circulation. An effective demand for infrastructure usually went hand in hand with land development and this is where the revenue to fund these vast investments was to be found.[39] In turn, this acted as a control over the rampant development of urban industrialism.[40] The financing and administration of sewerage systems has always been linked to authorities responsible for public streets.[41] The impact of ubiquitous supply systems on town planning cannot be underestimated, and indeed this may explain why these services were undertaken by municipal authorities and their specialists and workforces whom they employed.[42]

Evidence from a Case Study: Düsseldorf on Rhine 1875–1905

These different issues of resource management can be traced using Düsseldorf as a case-study. The latter was the rapidly urbanizing capital of the most industrialized district of the Prussian Rhine Province with a

---

[38] Municipal land 'funds' also played a crucial role in financing cities, Hans Böhm, 'Bodenpolitik deutscher Städte vor dem Ersten Weltkrieg', in K.H. Kaufhold, ed., *Investitionen der Städte im 19. und 20. Jahrhundert*, (Cologne, 1997), 63–94.

[39] J. Wisotzky and M. Zimmermann, eds, *Selbstverständlichkeiten. Zur Genese städtischer Infrastruktur in der Großstadt Essen* (Essen, 1997).

[40] Comparative analyses of different urban areas lead to similar results as comparative analyses of different towns in terms of innovation and diffusion, J.C. Brown, 'Public Reform for Private Gain? The Case of Investments in Sanitary Infrastructure: Germany, 1870–1887', *Urban Studies*, 26, 1989, 2–12; J.C Brown, 'Wer bezahlte die hygienisch saubere Stadt? ', in J. Vögele and W. Woelk, *Stadt, Krankheit und Tod. Städtische Gesundheit während der Epidemiologischen Transition* (Berlin, 2000), 237–57.

[41] Some reformers with special emphasis on water management complained about this tradition, e.g. E. Koch, *Die städtische Wasserleitung und Abwässerbeseitigung volkswirtschaftlich sowie finanzpolitisch beleuchtet* (Jena 1911), who found that only the city of Mannheim established direct financial links between waterworks and sewerage; other waterworks did also pay subsidies, yet more often for other municipal purposes than the water discharge systems.

[42] Cf. e.g. M. Gandy, 'The Paris sewers and the rationalization of urban space', *Transactions of the Institute of British Geographers*, 24, 1999, 23–44, J.A. Peterson, 'The Impact of Sanitary Reform upon American Urban Planning, 1840–1890', *Journal of Social History*, 13, 1979, 83–103; S.K. Schultz and C. McShane, 'Sewers, Sanitation and City planning in late nineteenth-century America', *Journal of American History*, 65, 1978, 389–411; S. Galishoff, 'Drainage, Disease, Comfort, and Class: A history of Newark's sewers', *Societas – a Review of Social History*, 6, 1976, 121–38.

population of over 100,000 in 1883.[43] Compared with uniform water management systems in England, the homeland of industrialization and the sanitary movement, medium-sized German towns usually convey an impression of simply adopting inadequate urban infrastructure. A closer analysis of the reluctance, if not opposition, to certain resource management and sanitary systems can detect other, more hidden but nevertheless systematic, strategies corresponding to differing hierarchies of values.

After the failure of a project to make the polluters pay for the construction of a private canal to control industrial pollution,[44] the internationally renowned expert William Lindley developed a general outline for a sewerage system in 1872.[45] According to this plan, a couple of modern sewers were first built parallel to the Düssel brook in order to protect municipal parks and boulevards from river pollution. A few factories offered to construct quite lengthy private connections. But further sewerage projects were abandoned in 1876 because of high costs.

This core sewerage system, with its provisional outlet into the Rhine only some 100m. downstream from the old town, could not be used for human faeces. This was because the Prussian state – reflecting British experience and legislation[46] – had prohibited allowing untreated sewage into rivers in 1875.[47]

---

[43] J. Vögele, 'Düsseldorf – Eine gesunde Stadt? Zur Entwicklung der Sterblichkeit in Düsseldorf im 19. und frühen 20. Jahrhundert', *Düsseldorfer Jahrbuch*, 69, 1998, 193–209; Düsseldorf is situated on the right bank plain of the lower Rhine in between the watersheds of the rivers Ruhr and Wupper; M. Weyer-von Schoultz, 'Düsseldorf – eine Industriestadt?', *Düsseldorfer Jahrbuch*, 69, 1998, 159–91; as a basic source, see E. Beyer, *Die Fabrik-Industrie des Regierungs-Bezirks Düsseldorf vom Standpunkt der Gesundheitspflege* (Oberhausen, 1876), about Eduard Beyer A. Labisch, 'Die Montanindustrie in der Gewerbeaufsicht des Regierungsbezirks Düsseldorf. Ein lokalhistorischer Beitrag zur Frage, warum im 19. Jahrhundert in Preußen, bzw. in Deutschland zwar eine Gewerbeaufsicht, aber kein Gewerbemedizinaldienst entstand, in Jos Massard et al., eds, *L'homme et la terre. Actes du 13e Congrès Benelux d'Histoire des Sciences* (Echternach, 1996), 41–72; in general: Hugo Weidenhaupt, ed., *Düsseldorf. Geschichte von den Ursprüngen bis ins 20. Jahrhundert*, 3 vols (Düsseldorf, 1988), and F.-W. Henning, *Düsseldorfs und seine Wirtschaft* (Düsseldorf, 1981).

[44] Municipal Archives Düsseldorf II 540–48, II 1453–5.

[45] W. Lindley, 'Bericht des Ingenieurs W. Lindley an den Oberbürgermeister Hammers über die Canalisation der Stadt Düsseldorf', *Correspondenz-Blatt des Niederrheinischen Vereins für öffentliche Gesundheitspflege*, 1, 1872, 220–23; H. Seeling, 'England siegt. William Lindley in Düsseldorf: Pionier technischer Hygiene und des Umweltschutzes', *Das Tor*, 48, 1982, 8–10.

[46] H. Eulenberg, ed., *Gutachten der königlichen wissenschaftlichen Deputation für das Medizinalwesen in Preussen über die Canalisation der Städte* (Berlin, 1883); cf. L.E. Breeze, *The British Experience with River Pollution, 1865–1876* (New York et al., 1993); B. Luckin, *Pollution and Control: a Social History of the Thames in the nineteenth century* (Bristol, 1986).

[47] J. von Simson, 'Die Flußverunreinigungsfrage im neunzehnten Jahrhundert', *Vierteljahrschrift für Sozial- und Wirtschaftsgeschichte*, 65, 1978,

Although the sewerage plan by Lindley included a large sewage farm on a nearby heath, this part of the scheme, which attempted to introduce a more sustainable system of resource management, was never carried out because of costs which were allegedly too high. However, the town did buy large portions of this land in the following decades – in due course the airport would be located at this site.[48] Instead of implementing Lindley's plan, Düsseldorf improved its horse-and-cart transport system based on private cesspools by modern hydraulic pumping equipment. It was now forbidden to discharge faeces or hot or acid water into the new sewerage system. Over the ensuing decades factory waste-water tanks gradually disappeared.

This separate system of faeces removal and water discharge seemed to have worked quite well; there was only one major problem remaining: a zone of marshy land in the former fortification foreland to the east of the town, criss-crossed by railway tracks and far from rivers as well as the new sewage works. Here, roads were extremely bad, construction sites frequently flooded and buildings were wet.[49] A new railroad system and major industrial zone were planned in this area, which was characterized by an absence of official municipal control.[50] The

---

370–90; T. Kluge and E. Schramm, *Wassernöte. Zur Geschichte des Trinkwasssers*, 2nd edn (Cologne, 1988); T. Bauer, *Im Bauch der Stadt: Kanalisation und Hygiene in Frankfurt am Main 16. – 19. Jahrhundert* (Frankfurt a.M., 1998).

[48] The town bought up military training grounds in the heath called Golzheimer Heide. H. Rademacher, *Beeinflussung einer Stadtplanung durch industrielle und gewerbliche Entwicklung: Eine historisch-geographische Untersuchung der Planungen der Stadt Düsseldorf in den Jahren 1854–1914* (Frankfurt a.M. et al., 1994).

[49] Cf. the most comprehensive account – concealing most conflicts however – by C. Geusen, 'Die Kanalisationsanlagen Düsseldorfs', in Th. Weyl, ed., *Die Assanierung von Düsseldorf* (Leipzig, 1908), 31–71; more concise with the same tenor: *Düsseldorf im Jahre 1898. Festschrift den Theilnehmern an der 70. Versammlung deutscher Naturforscher und Ärzte dargereicht von der Stadt Düsseldorf* (Düsseldorf, 1898); Architekten- und Ingenieurverein Düsseldorf, ed., *Düsseldorf und seine Bauten* (1904, reprint Düsseldorf, 1990); Otto Brandt, *Studien zur Wirtschafts- und Verwaltungsgeschichte der Stadt Düsseldorf im 19. Jahrhundert* (Düsseldorf, 1902); J. Krawinkel, 'Geschichtliches über Düsseldorfs Entwässerung', *Jan Wellem*, 3, 1928, 167–72; H. Meydenbauer, *Düsseldorf im Ausstellungsjahre 1902. Festschrift* (Düsseldorf, 1902).

[50] H. Rademacher, *Beeinflussung einer Stadtplanung durch industrielle und gewerbliche Entwicklung: Eine historisch-geographische Untersuchung der Planungen der Stadt Düsseldorf in den Jahren 1854–1914* (Frankfurt a.M. et al., 1994), blamed the municipal administration for having neglected the Eastern quarters Flingern and Lierenfeld, but as G. Massard-Guilbaud dealing with Clermont-Ferrand and the impressive Michelin factory pointed out in this volume, abstinence of public planning constraints was most attractive to industrial development.

administration employed the former district government official
Gerhardt Frings to work out Lindley's project in detail and once again
begin sewerage construction.[51]

During the election campaign of 1883, the sewerage system provided
a focus for the first genuinely local campaign, but strong objections from
houseowners overwhelmed any progressive argument. Thus all parties
and the town council openly rejected these and alternative plans, as well
as the pneumatic system which was offered by Charles T. Liernur.[52]

Nevertheless, the town administration implemented the sewerage
system in a telling manner: with new streets constructed for urban
industrial needs, pipes and sewers were built first. However, the use of
the infrastructure was reserved for the drainage of heavily used streets.
As a concession to houseowners' protests, nobody was forced to connect
to the sewerage system and, to the astonishment and anger of the
administration, almost nobody did. Running into financial difficulties in
1885, the mayor managed to make connection a necessary condition for
obtaining a building permit. Investors who could afford to build new
houses or factories, thus competing with older buildings, were more
inclined to undertake modernization, and this process of selection and
succession in a period of rapid urban growth of the city and the number
of new buildings, eventually led to a change in the collective mentality
of landowners and majorities both in the town and the council[53] (see
Table 10.2).

The growth of the sewerage system was uneven and more advanced
in newly built areas. In districts suffering from sanitary shortcomings
environmental inequality continued to prevail.

Interpretation of the growth of this particular specific sewerage
system is highly informative not least since its gravitational conduits are
prone to more practical constraints than other forms of infrastructure.
For example, the direction of flow or the diameters of some sections

[51] G. Frings, 'Die Kanalisation von Düsseldorf, *Gesundheits-Ingenieur*,
11–12, 1889, 11–17.

[52] H. Berg, *Entgegnungen auf den Gutachten des Hrn. Baurath Hobrecht
und des Hrn. Regierungs-Baumeister Frings* (Düsseldorf, 1883); B. Ladd, 'City
planning and social reform in Cologne, Frankfurt and Düsseldorf, 1866–1914',
PhD thesis (Yale, 1986), 165 sq.; B. Ladd, 'Die Anfänge der Parteipolitik in der
Düsseldorfer Stadtvertretung 1870–1914', *Düsseldorfer Jahrbuch*, 61, 1988,
243–57; A. Kuntz, ed., *Düsseldorf vor 100 Jahren* (Düsseldorf, 1982).

[53] About 40 per cent of houses with data of their age and at least a quarter
of all houses in Duesseldorf 1901 had been constructed after 1885, J. Feig, *Die
Grundstücks- und Wohnungszählung vom 1. Dezember 1905* (Düsseldorf,
1907), appendix 21 [table 26]; for municipal bylaws cf. C. Ottermann,
*Düsseldorfer Bürgerbuch. Sammlung der Ortsstatuten, Polizei-Verordnungen
. . .*, 3 vols (Düsseldorf, 1905–1910).

Table 10.2 Sewerage constructions in Düsseldorf, 1870–1913[54]

Year	Sewerage events	New sewers (m)	Houses connected (total)	New buildings (annual)
1873	no modern sewer	0		332
1874	parallel to brook	ca. 3,000		507
1875		ca. 3,000		427
1876	construction abandoned	ca. 1,000	30	288
1877		0	38	238
1878		0	46	234
1879		600	60	241
1880		0	68	272
1881		0	71	294
1882	Rhine flood	0	86	350
1883	sewers abolished	?	84	366
1884	new streets only	2,145	102	515
1885	new houses only	4,682	126	486
1886		?	160	510
1887		3,435	?	534
1888		6,238	?	411
1889		6,835	?	426
1890	houses after 1875 obligatory	5,752	1,278	443
1891		5,295	1,652	668
1892		15,439	2,052	573
1893		7,476	2,790	878
1894		10,367	3,563	713
1895	connection fee introduced	8,524	4,748	580
1896		9,929	5,573	707
1897		8,733	6,218	507
1898		10,427	7,032	?
1899		11,663	8,573	344
1900		14,288	8,573	550
1901		24,788	9,421	589
1902		9,345	10,029	883
1903	purification plant (riddle)	11,984	10,682	862
1904	W.C. connections obligatory	6,651	11,400	656
1905		9,016	11,936	782

[54] E. Hüsgen, 'Die finanzielle Entwicklung der Stadt Düsseldorf von 1850–1913', Würzburg Univ., PhD thesis 1921, table 45 supplemented with figures from the corresponding administrative reports: Bericht über den Stand und die Verwaltung der Gemeindeangelegenheiten der Stadt Düsseldorf.

could not be altered without affecting major parts of the whole system, and a strictly regular growth of these tree-like structures from the outlet to the ever more far-flung and branched pipes could be taken as a norm from the technical viewpoint. Thus, as the irregular growth and shape of a tree can be interpreted, spatial disparities in terms of the fulfilment of or deviation from the original plan and schedule can be defined more clearly than in other areas of urban social geography and measured in contrast to the norm down to the final yard or year. For example, for no evident technical reason the sewerage reached the Citadellstrasse more than twenty years after the Königsallee although the latter was about twice as far from the outfall into the Rhine.[55]

Following final negotiations with the Prussian state, a simple mechanical riddle wheel apparatus was installed in 1904 and this served as the only sewage treatment plant for decades. After that, the installation of water closets and their connection to the sewers was not only permitted but soon became obligatory.[56] In addition, an ever-larger volume of water was used to flush the sewage regularly. In 1907, the total accumulated expenditure on sewerage systems was about thirteen million marks, of which some four million had already been paid by houseowners. The municipality and the waterworks authority regularly contributed only between twenty and thirty per cent of annual maintenance costs.[57]

---

[55] Cf. Fritz Dross, 'Zum Rothen Ochsen auf der Citadelle. Geschichte eines Hauses, seiner Menschen und ihrer Umgebung', *Düsseldorfer Jahrbuch*, 67, 1996, 17–184 and Günther Zebisch, *Die Städtebauliche Entwicklung der Königsallee in Düsseldorf*, Dr.Ing.-thesis (Aachen, 1968); a systematic analysis of these phenomena, positive or negative project achievements in certain areas, is in progress; the impression is that the results found in comparisons between cities are mirrored by results between different functional city districts; cf. J.C. Brown, 'Economics and infant mortality decline in German towns, 1889–1912: household behaviour and public intervention', in S. Sheard and H. Power, eds., *Body and city: histories of urban public health* (Aldershot, 2000), 166–93; J.C. Brown, 'Wer bezahlte die hygienisch saubere Stadt?', in J. Vögele and W. Woelk, *Stadt, Krankheit und Tod. Städtische Gesundheit während der Epidemiologischen Transition* (Berlin, 2000), 237–57.

[56] J. Paul, 'Der Rhein als Klärbecken für städtische Abwässer: Abwasserpolitik in Köln und Düsseldorf seit dem 19. Jahrhundert', *Geschichte im Westen*, 1995, 135–48.

[57] O. Most, *Die Gemeindebetriebe der Stadt Düsseldorf* (Leipzig, 1909), 129.

Conclusion

In conclusion, sewerage systems were designed for several reasons. In public debates the high-sounding motives invariably came to the fore: in this discourse, sanitary reform seemed to have gradually pushed aside worries about sustainable resource management.[58] In the nineteenth century, sanitary reforms had been triggered by idealistic visions, but in most cases they could not be implemented in a market economy or without major modification. Infrastructural projects were put in place as multifunctional tools to enhance economic performance, much as other reforms were praised in hygienic terms: here the translocation of graveyards as well as industrial areas or the demolition of fortifications were frequently mentioned.[59] Despite severe spatial discrepancies in terms of resource allocation, municipalities never ceased to seek to implement infrastructure for everyone and ultimately did not exclude any area of legal settlement. Finally, sewerage infrastructure was installed on a very large scale even when arguments were marshalled against such developments. Keeping up with international standards seemed to gain an economic value in its own right in the twentieth century.

In the decisive years in the late nineteenth century, however, stepwise implementation of infrastructure and allocation of resources were often based on a variety of strategies in urban development and the free market economy. The implementation of a sewerage system in Düsseldorf as a means of combating urban industrial pollution was greatly reduced within a few years – when the construction in itself seemed sufficient and the costs appeared too high. After that, private landlords lost interest in sanitary reform, but the city administration

---

[58] A critical evaluation of the frequent implementation of combined sewerage with rather ineffective sewage treatment plants after 1900 in Germany, see e.g. E. Schramm, 'Kommunaler Umweltschutz in Preußen (1900–1933): Verengung auf Vollzug durch wissenschaftliche Beratung?', in J. Reulecke and A. zu Castell Rüdenhausen, eds., *Stadt und Gesundheit. Zum Wandel von 'Volksgesundheit' und kommunaler Gesundheitspolitik im 19. und frühen 20. Jahrhundert* (Stuttgart, 1991), 77–89.

[59] U. Koppitz, 'Räumliche Organisation preußischer Städte im 19. Jahrhundert zwecks Funktionalität und Gesundheit', in J. Vögele and W. Woelk, *Stadt, Krankheit und Tod. Städtische Gesundheit während der Epidemiologischen Transition* (Berlin, 2000), 259–74; a similar multiple resource management is to be traced in rural agrarian types of land development, e.g. malaria control measures could only be introduced if they fitted into general projects of agricultural reform, cf. D. Henley, 'Malaria past and present: the case of North Sulawesi, Indonesia', *Southeast Asian Journal of Tropical Medicine and Public Health*, 32, 2001, 595–607.

continued to build sewers for different reasons. In this sense, demand for sewage disposal went hand in hand with a booming real estate market.

As, in general, a piece of land adjacent to a watercourse was more productive and valuable, the economic value of an estate fully connected to urban water management systems came to be valued more highly. Quantity and reliability of water supply were very important for every urban estate. Seeking the advantages of water connection without the disadvantages of moisture and flood risks, housing developments were to be built on dry ground, which was considered the most important urban resource of all: in search for an 'ultimate urban resource', real estate ownership and development determined access to all other urban resources.

CHAPTER ELEVEN

Towards the Socialist Sanitary City: Urban Water Problems in East German New Towns, 1945–1970

Christoph Bernhardt

Introduction

When in 1989 the socialist system in Eastern Europe collapsed, ecological crisis and the longterm decline of cities played a key role in triggering popular rebellion of the citizens against the state. At that time, dust emission of more than 60 tons per sq.km per year were recorded in big East German cities such as Berlin, Halle and Leipzig. The Elbe river transported about 200 tons of arsenic and the same quantity of lead per year, and extremely polluted areas like the 'silver sea' near the Wolfen chemical company and the radioactively polluted region around Aue in Saxony were symbols of environmental degradation.[1] The situation was not much better in other socialist countries and especially in the Soviet Union, even if detailed information is difficult to obtain for these countries as a result of the suppression of environmental data.[2]

Some of the major polluters during this period such as heavy industry and chemical plants have been clearly identified, notably in the report of the Commission of the German Parliament on the *Socialist Unity Party-Dictatorship in Germany* and other publications.[3] But what has not

---

[1] C. Jordan, 'Umweltzerstörung und Umweltpolitik in der DDR', in 'Enquete-Kommission, Aufarbeitung von Geschichte und Folgen der SED-Diktatur in Deutschland', ed., *Machtstrukturen und Entscheidungsmechanismen im SED-Staat und die Frage der Verantwortung*, vol. II.3, (Baden-Baden, 1995), 1770–90.

[2] R. Worobjow, 'Umweltbelastungen in europäischen Städten und Regionen der Russischen Föderation', in *Europa Regional*, 5, 1997, 38–51, here 39.

[3] For a general survey of the environmental situation in the territory of the GDR, see Jordan, Umweltzerstörungen; G. Würth, *Umweltschutz und Umweltzerstörung in der DDR* (Frankfurt a. M., 1985), 170, and *DDR-Handbuch*, ed. by Bundesministerium für innerdeutsche Beziehungen (Köln, 1985), 1369–80.

been analysed up to now is how urban environmental and water problems developed during the socialist period and the role they played when compared with industrial pollution. At least something is known about the poor state of the water infrastructure in old industrial centres and cities like Leipzig, which was the centre of East German opposition in 1989. Here, the committee *Initiative zur Rettung Leipzigs* (Initiative for the Salvation of Leipzig) presented a catastrophic picture of the socialist period. A third of Leipzig water pipes were suffering, the municipal department for underground construction stated, from 'serious damages' but would have had to remain in operation for another three hundred years.[4] The Leipzig *Volksbaukonferenz* (Building Conference of the People) held in January 1990 concluded that the underground infrastructure was even worse maintained than the overground buildings and could not meet 'the needs of a modern city'.[5] The Minister for Building and Housing, Baumgärtel, admitted that 'the development in the whole region and its surroundings has caused serious ecological problems'.[6]

What is even less well known are the environmental effects of the programme of urbanization across the whole GDR in which numerous new towns and settlements were constructed. Nor is it clear whether the situation in urban water provision and sewerage was worsening or improving, as was the case in a number of Western European countries from the 1970s onwards.[7] An answer to this question is also of major interest from a more general perspective: new towns and housing estates played a key role in sustaining mass loyalty to the socialist system, and as it will be argued here, sanitary standards were an important element of that political mechanism. This article will therefore try to contribute, in a similar style to other recent research into the East German state, to the debate on the specific socialist 'culture of legitimacy'[8] and ask if sanitary modernization in the context of housing policy served as an instrument to stabilize the socialist system. It will also focus on the

---

[4] Sewerage pipes had not been cleared of mud or repaired for an exceptionally long period. Initiativgruppe, *1. Volksbaukonferenz Leipzig 1990*, Statement D. Kolbe, 143.

[5] Ibid., Statement M. Körner, 187.

[6] Ibid., Statement G. Baumgärtel, 31–2.

[7] C. Bernhardt and G. Massard-Guilbaud, 'Ecrire l'histoire de la pollution', in C. Bernhardt and G. Massard-Guilbaud, eds, *Le Démon Moderne. La pollution dans les sociétés urbaines et industrielles d'Europe* (Clermont-Ferrand, 2002), 9–32, here 10.

[8] T. Lindenberger, 'Die Diktatur der Grenzen. Zur Einleitung', in T. Lindenberger, ed., *Herrschaft und Eigen-Sinn in der Diktatur. Studien zur Gesellschaftsgeschichte der DDR (Zeithistorische Studien, vol. 12)* (Köln, 1999), 13–44.

extent to which the socialist regime was able to manage for some time and to some extent the environmental crisis. These mechanisms can be studied within the context of the famous new towns situated at the Oder river in which an attempt was made to realize a socialist urban vision. The intention is also to evaluate the achievements, deficits and driving-forces in the urban-environmental history of the water sector during the socialist epoque and thereby identify key aspects and turning-points in the socialist pathway within the context of urban environmental history.

Urbanization and Water Problems in a Postwar Socialist Society

At the end of the second world war newly established socialist governments in the East European states had to meet two major challenges: cities, regions and industries, many of which had been horrifically destroyed, had to be reconstructed and the socialist regime stabilized by means of economic policy, legislation and social policy. To realize these overall objectives, parallel to the reconstruction campaigns, a policy of massive industrialization and urbanization was initiated, in line with the model developed in the Soviet Union since the 1930s.[9] The lower Oder region, which will be looked at more closely here (Figure 11.1), was to become a model region for this policy, since it had been designated by the East German Socialist Unity Party SED (*Sozialistische Einheitspartei Deutschlands*) as the location for new heavy industries and new towns. These were to compensate, as a first step, for iron and steel imports from the West that had been stopped following the division of Germany in 1949. From the early 1950s onwards in Eisenhüttenstadt and, later on, in Schwedt two new large heavy industrial combines and corresponding 'new towns' were created.

Industrialization involved a break in the style of regional development according to which a formerly agrarian region was transformed into an agro-industrial district. Between 1955 and 1987 industrial product in the district increased by two thousand per cent.[10] The city of Eisenhüttenstadt grew from around 7,000 in 1950 to 53,000 inhabitants in 1988, Schwedt from less than 10,000 inhabitants in 1960 to nearly 53,000 in 1988. The old city of Frankfurt (Oder) which was declared a district capital in 1952 and was to become a microelectronic centre from

[9] H. Bodenschatz and C. Post, eds, *Städtebau im Schatten Stalins. Die internationale Suche nach der sozialistischen Stadt in der Sowjetunion 1929–1935*, (Berlin, 2003); G.M. Lappo and F.W. Hönsch, eds, *Urbanisierung Rußlands (Urbanization of the Earth, vol. 9)* (Stuttgart, 2000).

[10] Autorenkollektiv, *Der Bezirk Frankfurt. Geographische Exkursionen* (Gotha/Leipzig, 1971), 17.

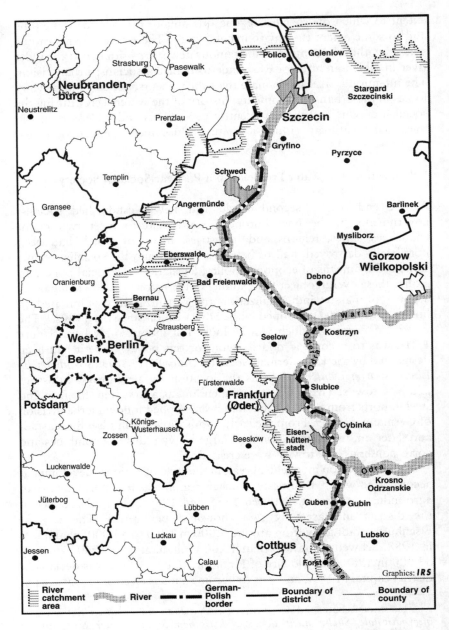

Figure 11.1   The German-Polish border region along the Oder river
(administrative boundaries before 1989)

the 1970s onwards, grew from 53,000 in 1950 to around 87,000 in 1988.[11]

As a consequence, from the outset a massive increase in the use of water by industries and private households was to be expected, and the government was deeply concerned about the capacity of available natural resources to meet these needs.

Table 11.1 Potential water resources and water consumption in selected European states c. 1980

State	Potential Water Resources (bill. m³/a)	Water Consumption (bill. m³/a)	Rate of Consumption (in %)
USSR	3,150.0	61.5	1.9
Italy	150.0	15.6	10.4
Poland	55.0	5.8	10.5
France	183.0	24.0	13.1
FRG	93.0	14.0	15.0
CSSR	30.0	4.6	15.3
GDR	18.5	7.0	37.8

Source: G. Würth, *Umweltschutz*, 229.

The rate of water consumption in relation to the potential water resources was very high compared to other European countries (see Table 11.1). This caused political and ideological problems and forced the authorities fundamentally to reform prewar water legislation as early as 1952. More than 2,500 local and regional associations involved in various fields of water management in the GDR were amalgamated by the 'Verordnung über die Organisation der Wasserwirtschaft' on 1st January 1953. This was a new centralized state-managed system of 15 large regional water management enterprises (the so-called 'Z' enterprises).[12] In order to ensure optimal water use, these enterprises were organised according to river catchment areas. Two major reforms in 1958 and 1963/64 completed this radical transformation of the highly decentralized traditional German system which was based on numerous small associations. In 1964, pre-existing municipal water works and sewerage associations were amalgamated in 'people's own enterprises

---

[11] *Statistisches Jahrbuch der DDR* (Berlin 1989), 3.
[12] Verordnung über die Organisation der Wasserwirtschaft, *Gesetzblatt*, 1952, 792; H. van der Wall and R.A. Kraemer, *Die Wasserwirtschaft in der DDR*, (Berlin, 1991), 7–20.

water provision and sewage treatment' (*VEB Wasserversorgung und Abwasserbehandlung/WAB*).[13] This centralization led to 'a weakening of the local administration which lost nearly every power that it had previously held in relation to water management'.[14] Furthermore, as early as 1952 a general reform had deprived local governments of most of their rights within the venerable German tradition of municipal self-government. From now on cities would only be allowed to maintain urban water infrastructure while district authorities would be responsible for all major investment.[15]

In fact, these reforms were highly ambivalent: motivated by interests of more efficient resource exploitation and fears of water scarcity the changes deprived local authorities of all their rights. At the same time the implementation of river basin authorities and the institutional fusion of waterworks and sewerage plants established modern water management structures which converged in some ways with those in Great Britain and France.[16]

Among the various fields of water management the socialist government gave priority to the modernization of water supply. While practically all towns with more than 5,000 inhabitants were already equipped with central waterworks, the situation was much worse in small towns and rural areas. In 1958 only 26 per cent of towns with less than 5,000 inhabitants possessed such utilities. The figure for villages in rural areas of the northern districts was only 6 per cent.[17] These proportions did not change substantially until the late 1960s but by that date the situation in general had improved. By 1966 the population connected to central waterworks had grown to 78 per cent in the GDR. The district of Frankfurt/Oder lagged behind with an average of 63.4 per cent and only 56 per cent in the rural areas. Whilst some counties like Beeskow (26.6 per cent) and Seelow (46.6 per cent) were even less

---

[13] 'Anordnung über die Bildung der VEB Wasserversorgung und Abwasserbehandlung vom 23.03.1964', *Gesetzblatt*, III, 20, 10 Apr. 1964, 206–207.

[14] Van der Wall and Kraemer, *Die Wasserwirtschaft*, 57.

[15] See H. Bartsch, 'Aufgaben und Struktur der örtlichen Verwaltung', in K. König, ed., *Verwaltungsstrukturen der DDR* (Baden-Baden, 1991), 109–34, here 109–11. I have provided further details on local administration in the GDR in C. Bernhardt, 'Planning urbanisation and urban growth in the socialist period: The Case of East-German New Towns, 1945–1989', *Journal of Urban History*, special issue ed. by R. Morris et al., forthcoming (2005).

[16] On river basin management in France after 1964 see Internationale Kommission für die Hydrologie des Rheingebietes, *Der Rhein unter der Einwirkung des Menschen – Ausbau, Schiffahrt, Wasserwirtschaft*, (Lelystad, 1993), 24.

[17] Würth, *Umweltzerstörung*, 232.

well resourced, urban areas, like the cities of Frankfurt/Oder (97.1 per cent), Eisenhüttenstadt (95.2 per cent) and Schwedt (92.5 per cent) were clearly privileged.[18]

These differentials indicate that the regime's sanitary campaigns had been quite successful. Table 11.2 shows that the rates of connection were constantly raised so that at the end of the socialist period around 90 per cent of the East German population were provided with centrally supplied water. In the field of sewerage serious attempts were made, too, but with significantly less effect: connection rates of 69.1 per cent for sewerage and no more than 52 per cent for treatment plants show that the clearing of waste water could not keep up with a rapid increase in consumption. In a more general sense this means that water supply construed as a central component of quality of life was given major importance while, despite a large-scale investment programme, environmental policy continued to lag behind.

Table 11.2 Central water supply, sewerage and waste water treatment in GDR (in % of Population)

Year	Central Water Supply	Sewerage	Sewage Works
1945			27.0
1950	57.0	49.0	31.0
1955	71.6		
1960	76.2	56.3	36.9
1961	72.4	52.8	35.0
1965	78.7	58.6	39.0
1970	80.7	60.4	42.7
1975	85.2	64.2	46.9
1980	89.1	68.6	52.0
1981	89.9	69.1	52.4

Source: G. Würth, *Umweltschutz*, 233.

Towards 'full comfort housing' in socialist neighbourhoods: water supply and sanitary standards in Eisenhüttenstadt

The modernization of water supply systems and sewerage as shown in Table 11.2 indicates a clear contrast to the decline of water infrastructure in the old industrial centres. These improvements were

---

[18] Brandenburgisches Landeshauptarchiv, Rep. 601 Nr. 10334, 97, Anlage 6.

realized despite serious financial shortages. A closer look at the model
town of Eisenhüttenstadt, proudly proclaimed as the 'first socialist city
in Germany', can show how this policy was realized at the local level
and identify the driving forces behind this process. Eisenhüttenstadt was
built up since 1950 following the concept of constructing building
blocks for 'socialist neighbourhoods'. These so-called *sozialistische
Wohnkomplexe* (WK), seven of which were built for around 4,500
inhabitants each (see Figure 11.2), represent a kind of typology and a
museum for the changing paradigms of socialist building policy.[19] They
also show very clearly the key role of water infrastructure and sanitary
standards in socialist urban development.

The building blocks in the first WK, which was constructed between
1950 and 1955, offered workers' hostels during the period in which the
new town was being completed. The dominant form was that of the low
standard small apartments. Warm water and heating were provided by
coal stoves, gas stoves were used in kitchens.[20] At that time, urban
infrastructural technology was under-developed: for example, a large
public building like the municipal theatre was heated by a steam
locomotive.[21] Low housing standards caused massive protests on the part
of workers so that socialist leader Walter Ulbricht, who visited the town
in 1952, forced the planners to build better-equipped and designed
accommodation. Moreover, in reaction to nationwide and violent protests
of June 17, 1953, the regime decided to stop the expansion of the
Eisenhüttenstadt steel works and increase the number and enhance the
standard of mass housing.[22] As a consequence, the next developments,
the so-called 'workers palaces' of the WK II, were dominated by 80 sq.m
three-room-apartments. This proved to be a very elevated standard in the
history of working-class housing both in the GDR and possibly in the rest
of Europe. Gas, hot water for bathing and for washing clothes and kitchen
utensils were widely combined with modern furniture.[23]

With the transition from the 'national building tradition' to the
'industrialized building' in 1955, the regime began to give high priority
to rationalized prefabrication of houses. Planners of the East German

[19] R. May, *Planstadt Stalinstadt. Ein Grundriß der frühen DDR – aufgesucht in Eisenhüttenstadt* (Dortmund, 1999).
[20] Stadt Eisenhüttenstadt, *Bauaktenarchiv (EHS-BA)*, Mappe 'Block 46'.
[21] A. Ludwig and S. Retzlaff, 'Die Stadt beginnt zu leben. Zeit der Provisorien', in Arbeitsgruppe Stadtgeschichte, ed., *Eisenhüttenstadt: 'Erste sozialistische Stadt Deutschlands'* (Berlin, 1999), 92–100.
[22] I. Apolinarski and C. Bernhardt, 'Entwicklungslogiken sozialistischer Planstädte am Beispiel von Eisenhüttenstadt und Nova Huta', in H. Barth, ed., *Grammatik sozialistischer Architekturen. Lesarten historischer Städtebauforschung zur DDR* (Berlin, 2001), 51–66, 62.
[23] EHS-BA, *Akte Stalinstadt/1794*, Block 46a.

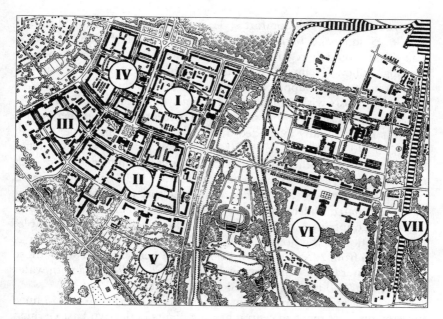

Figure 11.2   The new town of Eisenhüttenstadt (Plan from 1953)

Building Academy who developed these projects for Eisenhüttenstadt had to take local public opinion into account. The local population called massively, as socialist socio-political institutions like the *Nationale Front* reported, for advanced sanitary standards. 'The population gave special importance to the spatial relation of kitchen and bathroom' and called for separated water closets, large bathrooms and bath tubs as well as for bidets.[24]

As a consequence, so-called 'full-comfort' standards, including a central hot water supply and gas, were maintained and even improved in the context of a high degree of standardization, rationalization and cost reduction in the housing sector. When, in 1955, architect Herbert Schriewer from the *Bauakademie der DDR* (German Building Academy) developed a pioneering '0-series of large block building systems' for Eisenhüttenstadt, he considerably reduced the size of habitations down to 46 sq.m for a three-room apartment but also managed to install gas, a central hot water supply, central heating, and a telephone. In a block in Georgij-Dimitroff-Street built in 1957 three-room apartments were

---

[24] Herbert Schiweck, 'Ein Typenprojekt für Großblockbauweise', in *Deutsche Architektur* 8/1956, 344–9, here 349.

constructed in this full-comfort style, but kitchens were still no larger than 6.95 sq.m and bathrooms measured no more than 3.94 sq.m.[25] This trend should be regarded as a key element in East German socialist housing policy. Technical standards in the fields of water supply, bathrooms and gas supply were enhanced despite the overall objective of reducing costs within the context of a drive for rationalization.

As a result of this national strategy, the percentage of apartments with hot water was rapidly expanded during the 1960s from 18 per cent in 1960 to 90 per cent in 1970. In terms of newly constructed accommodation in the GDR, the proportion of units provided with central heating rose from nine to 65 per cent.[26] The role that this rapid modernization played within the socialist 'culture of legitimacy' cannot be overestimated. Indeed, a similar pattern may also be detected in other socialist countries. In Moscow, to take a prominent example, modernization of the housing stock raised the percentage of dwellings with a bath from 22.0 per cent in 1940 to 97.3 per cent in 1980, of those with hot water from 52 per cent in 1966 to 88.2 in 1984 and with water closets from 73.0 per cent in 1940 to 99.5 per cent in 1984.[27]

Moreover, in the period of sharp financial restriction after 1955 huge investments were made in central heating plants in the two East German 'model' new towns of Eisenhüttenstadt and Hoyerswerda. In internal debates in the Ministry of Construction experts of the Building Academy justified these investments as being of 'high national economic value' even though they admitted that they were 'very costly'.[28] The principal guideline for planners and the building industry, *Der Sozialistische Wohnkomplex* from 1959, which became obligatory for future projects all over the GDR, underlined the specific economic value of a central heating infrastructure with detailed calculations, arguing that 'central heating provision is not a luxury'.[29] Consequently, according to the planners' calculations for the *Wohnkomplex*, investments for networks of public water supply systems, central heating and waste water represented a considerable portion of aggregate capital investment.[30]

---

[25] Ibid.; EHS-BA, Nr. 22/57: Kapazitätsberechnung des Entwurfbüros vom 23.5.1957.

[26] Deutsche Bauakademie, *Organisation und Gestaltung von Wohngebieten* (Deutsche Bauakademie zu Berlin, 1972), 12.

[27] T.J. Colton, *Moscow: Governing the Socialist Metropolis* (Harvard, 1995), 488.

[28] Bundesarchiv Lichterfelde (BA LI), DH 2, II/07-5/11, Manuskript 'Vorläufige Kostenrichtzahlen für den Städtebau' 8.

[29] *Der Sozialistische Wohnkomplex* (Berlin, 1959) 47.

[30] For Wohnkomplex VII see the calculations in Archiv Institut für Regionalentwicklung und Strukturplanung, Begutachtung Neubaugebiete, Eisenhüttenstadt WK VII, 1. Bauabschnitt, 2f.

In Eisenhüttenstadt the period of central heating as 'standard' began in 1957 when the first urban central heating plant started production. From the 1960s onwards all newly built apartments provided central heating and hot water. We can observe the same trend in Moscow, where in 1940 only 46 per cent but in 1984 99.5 per cent of all dwellings had access to central heating.[31] The Eisenhüttenstadt central power plant was fuelled by coal. Waste water was, as a result of strict functional and spatial segregation, collected separately according to industrial and residential designation. Domestic waste water was pumped from the centre of the town to the waste water plant south-eastwards up in the Diehlo hills and diverted to nearby sewage farms. Separate sewers for domestic waste water and rainwater were introduced for financial reasons but also had positive effects in environmental terms.[32]

To some degree the huge investment in infrastructure and particularly in the field of water supply and waste water technology for the new towns resulted from their privileged position on the socialist policy agenda. In a more general sense, these policies expressed the high value accorded to hygienic standards within socialist ideology and the regime's strategy to achieve political loyalty by means of the provision of large housing programmes. Moreover, new towns and industries urgently needed such investment since they could only exist and expand by attracting workers from other places and motivating them to become long-term residents who would be willing to lay down family roots. The regime tried to achieve this aim by granting privileges in terms of a high standard of living, high wages, modern social infrastructure and access to consumer goods.[33] Among these arguments the technical standard of housing, gas, electricity, and washing facilities became the most attractive features in the new communities.

The dream of a 'clean warm home' was a clinching factor for immigrants. The attraction of Eisenhüttenstadt, Schwedt and the other East German new towns and housing estates depended heavily on these social, architectural and residential innovations.[34] Oral history research in the early 1990s with Eisenhüttenstadt immigrants who had come in very large numbers from rural areas, retrospectively confirms these

---

[31] Colton, *Moscow*, 488.

[32] Ludwig and Retzlaff, 'Die Stadt', 92.

[33] See EKO Stahl GmbH, ed., *Einblicke. 50 Jahre EKO Stahl* (Eisenhüttenstadt, 2000), 104.

[34] P. Springer, 'Vom Verschwinden der Zukunft: Stadthistorische Überlegungen zum Utopieverlust in der sozialistischen Stadt Schwedt', in H. Timmermann, ed., *Deutsche Fragen: Von der Teilung zur Einheit* (Berlin, 2001), 452–64, 457.

conclusions: 'Many had not seen a bath before',[35] 'it was only a two-room-apartment, not very large, but with an elevator, and refuse disposal facilities, a built-in cupboard, a washing machine in each individual house, and we immediately got a telephone',[36] 'these were the reasons which made us decide to move: yes, out of a stove-heated apartment, into the centrally heated apartment!'[37] If, as leading scholars like Hannemann have argued, large public building programs had always served as a means of strengthening legitimacy for the socialist regime,[38] advanced sanity standards were the main instrument of that policy.

Water for Industry: The Case of the SCHWEDT Petrochemical Company

Water consumption by domestic households increased from 11 per cent in 1958 to 15.6 per cent in 1980, but industry (66.2 per cent in 1980) greatly exceeded the demands of domestic households and agriculture (18.2 per cent).[39] Central governmental economic policy forced the 15 administrative districts in East Germany to develop a mono-industrial profile and this led to specific kinds of water and environmental problems. Thus, the brown coal district *Braunkohlebezirk Cottbus* to the south of Frankfurt/Oder saw gigantic transformations in the landscape and the natural water system and suffered seriously from the lowering of the water table and from massive air pollution.[40] Things were different in the district of Frankfurt/Oder. Here, big drainage works were executed in the agricultural sector, whereas the chemical company of Schwedt consumed large quantities of water and, in the long run, ever more damagingly polluted the environment. However, the morphology of watercourses remained relatively unchanged.

In the debates of the 1950s about where to locate the new combines, Eisenhüttenstadt and Schwedt had been chosen mainly because of the

[35] D. Semmelmann, G. Prengel and U. Krüger, ed., *Eisenhüttenstädter Lesebuch*, (Berlin, 2000), 41.
[36] Ibid., 103.
[37] Ibid., 79.
[38] C. Hannemann, *Die Platte. Industrialisierter Wohnungsbau in der DDR*, (Braunschweig/Wiesbaden, 1996), 85/86, 101/02.
[39] Würth, *Umweltschutz*, 230.
[40] See C. Bernhardt, 'Von der "Mondlandschaft" zur sozialistischen "Erholungslandschaft"? Die Niederlausitz als Exerzierfeld der Regionalplanung in der DDR-Zeit', in G. Bayerl and D. Maier, eds, *Die Niederlausitz vom 18. Jahrhundert bis heute: Eine gestörte Kulturlandschaft?* (Münster, 2002), 301–23.

surrounding network of waterways, the existence of canals to Berlin, to the Baltic sea and the river Elbe (see Figure 11.1). What was even more important in spatial terms was the key role of water for the industrial needs of chemical production and cooling. These latter factors determined the location of the plant within close proximity to the Oder river. As a popular journal stated: 'The Oder can deliver fresh water and receive cleaned waste water'.[41]

But as soon as the project was made public in 1958 the state and neighbouring downstream riparian interests in Poland initiated a massive diplomatic intervention. Poland was determined to protect the quality of drinking water in the large Polish city of Szeczin which was some fifty kilometres downstream from Schwedt. Polish intervention proved moderately successful, and this despite the fact that downstream interests usually find themselves outgunned by their neighbours upstream.[42] As a result of complex negotiations, the Petrochemical Combine (*Petrochemisches Kombinat, PCK*) equipped itself with the most up-to-date water treatment technology that could be obtained in the GDR. This integrated mechanical, chemical and biological treatment systems and additional technologies to strengthen the self-cleansing capacity of the river. The city, also, was equipped with a modern water infrastructure, including a biological water treatment plant and new waterworks.[43]

The East German water administration claimed that the sewerage technology used for PCK represented 'the world's most advanced standard in the field of raw oil waste water treatment'. Ten per cent of aggregate investment on the plant had been spent on waste-water treatment with the result that water had been emitted cleaner than it had been on entry into the system.[44] The extraordinary sensitivity of environmental issues and the far-reaching achievements of waste-water treatment in the case of Schwedt – compared to other East German regions – had also been made possible by the highly distinctive upstream-downstream riparian situation. Poland was also in a position of an upstream riparian (see Figure 11.1), and Polish industries and residential developments in the Polish upstream riparian

[41] H.W. Brunn, 'Tabak+Erdöl=Schwedt', in *Natur und Heimat,* 1960, 259–64, here 263.

[42] J. Barandat, ed., *Wasser – Konfrontation oder Kooperation. Ökologische Aspekte von Sicherheit am Beispiel eines weltweit begehrten Rohstoffs* (Baden-Baden, 1997).

[43] BLHA Rep. 601 Nr. 3520; H. Glade, *Zwischen Rebenhängen und Haff. Reiseskizzen aus dem Odergebiet* (Leipzig, 1976), 100.

[44] The Head of the Central Bureau for Water management, Rochlitzer, cited in Würth, *Umweltschutz,* 238.

regions played their own part in massively polluting the Oder river. As a consequence, Poland was in a position to offer, as a compensation for waste water treatment in Schwedt, programmes in the fields of flood prevention and waste water treatment upstream. Last but not least, the raw oil for PCK had to be imported to Schwedt by transit through Poland.

The Water Crisis of the Early 1970s

The examples of Eisenhüttenstadt and Schwedt can be read as a 'partial success story' for socialist policy that was developing parallel to constant environmental degradation and the decline of water infrastructure in old industrial regions and cities like Leipzig, Berlin or Halle. But during the 1960s urbanization and industrialization led to a serious over-exploitation of water resources. In quantitative terms total water consumption in the GDR was estimated to have increased from around 4.7 billion cbm. in 1958 to 7.7 billion cbm. in 1980.[45] As for the Schwedt petrochemical combine the first plans in around 1960 worked on the assumption of quantities of between 4000 and 5000 cbm/h. for production and cooling, which would be taken from wells and the Oder lateral canal. Already in 1966 water consumption had exploded because of the rapid expansion of PCK up to around 2,900m³/h. for production and another 34,500m³/h. for cooling.[46]

The water consumption of private households displayed the same trend. Technical guidelines calculated an average water need of 170 litres per day per inhabitant for habitations with central heating and hot water provision, a bath and a wc, while accommodation with no central heating or hot water needed about 130 litres. Households in old buildings heated by coal with a wc but no bath consumed no more than 80 litres. In contrast, single family houses, of which only a relatively small number were built in socialist countries, needed as much as 200 litres or more per day per inhabitant.[47] In West German publications the consumption in new socialist housing estates was estimated, because of their advanced sanitary standards, to reach 400 litres in hot summer periods.[48] Experts in the East German Building Academy calculated that in new residential areas with advanced sanitation standards water

[45]   Ibid., 230.
[46]   BU LI DK 4, Nr. 422; BLHA, Rep. 601 Nr. 7665.
[47]   O.E. Fischer and R. Scheer, *Gas- und Wasserinstallation* (Berlin, 1975), 237.
[48]   *DDR Handbuch*, Vol. 2, 1464.

consumption and waste water volumes would be up to three times higher than in older building stock.[49]

To meet this demand the GDR initiated an ambitious programme to build 125 new dams and storage basins that doubled storage up to a volume of 1.4 billion cbm. in 1985:[50] by around 1980 'nearly every water course above a certain size had been integrated in its upper section, where there was little pollution, into a system of linked drinking and commercial water supply'.[51] But this did not prevent serious water shortages that particularly affected the Halle-Leipzig region. In the lower Oder region with its wealth of natural watercourses and late industrialization and urbanization such a critical point was only reached by 1970, when the whole region suffered from serious water shortage. Reports from district authorities noted 'irregularities in the water provision' around Eisenhüttenstadt, overexploitation of water resources in the area of Straussberg east of Berlin and an emergency situation in the town of Bad Freienwalde, where a hospital and a Soviet military camp were cut off from the central water systems and had to be supplied by mobile tanks. Around the city of Beeskow south east of Berlin emergency interventions were necessary to prevent massive problems threatening the downstream capital of Berlin. Furthermore, in Frankfurt/Oder a 50-million mark waterworks did not work properly because of technical problems. In due course, the central authorities and party leaders intervened and replaced the managers of the plant.[52]

This water shortage also affected industrial and energy production which lacked cooling capacity. An example here was the power plant at Finkenherd south of Frankfurt/Oder. Moreover, water resources of the Oder region were directed to Berlin which was given priority in critical periods of water scarcity. To guarantee sufficient drinking water and to 'stabilize water flow in the capital of GDR' a special plan was developed in 1971 for a 'controlled lowering' of the water table of lakes in the surrounding districts of Cottbus, Frankfurt/Oder and Potsdam. Moreover, the transportation of water from the Oder watershed to the Spree watershed on which Berlin depended was intensified. For the regional and central water authorities guaranteeing sufficient water for the capital was a matter of prestige and political standing. Therefore, the

---

[49] B. Hunger et al., eds, *Städtebauprognose DDR. Städtebauliche Grundlagen für die langfristige intensive Entwicklung und Reproduktion der Städte*, (Berlin, 1990), 86.

[50] See *DDR-Handbuch* Vol. 2, 1464 for a table on the important dams built in the GDR.

[51] Würth, *Umweltschutz*, 230.

[52] See the various reports of district authorities in BHLA, Rep. 601, Nr. 8346.

Central Office for water management developed another more detailed plan for 'prevention and security' of water supply during the Eighth Party Congress of the governing Socialist Unity Party (SED) in June 1971.[53] Even if during the 1970s campaigns to lower water consumption in the GDR had some effect, water shortages continued to be a major problem in East German and Polish towns until the end of the socialist period.[54]

The situation was even worse in the field of waste water treatment and sewerage. Central water authorities stated in the early 1960s that the major chemical plant of Buna emitted organic wastes into the relatively small river Saale in quantities equivalent to the waste from a city of 2.3 million inhabitants.[55] Even advanced technology like that implemented in PCK could not cope with the rapid expansion of industry which caused numerous serious problems in terms of water and soil pollution. PCK, for example, was one of 'some major enterprises which are emitting massively polluted waste water' in the region of Schwedt.[56] In fact, even powerful state authorities were not able or willing to act against environmental damages caused by big plants. Administrative procedures in cases of expansion of production examined environmental arguments like water pollution, but decisions were clearly dominated by the interests of individual enterprises. Plants like PCK were responsible for the monitoring of their waste water for which they had to collect and evaluate data to be presented to the authorities whenever they were asked for information of this kind. But in fact toxic substances like prussic acid, polymers, heavy metals such as Cadmium, PCB, and many others constantly polluted the river as well as its floodplains. Right up until the present, pollution around Schwedt is much more serious than in other German rivers and river regions.[57]

The situation was to some extent different in the field of the urban sewerage systems. As shown above, waste water treatment plants were constructed 'considerably slower than in the field of water supply'.[58] But some progress was made and the portion of the population that was connected to centralized sewerage was significantly increased.[59] With

[53] Ibid.
[54] *Die Welt*, 23 Mar. 1984.
[55] Rochlitzer, cited in Würth, *Umweltschutz*, 236.
[56] BHLA, 601, Nr. 8346.
[57] BHLA 601/7665; Landesumweltamt Brandenburg, ed., *Untersuchungen der Oder zur Belastung der Schwebstoff- bzw. Sedimentsphase und angrenzender Bereiche* (Potsdam, 1998), 42, 93, 148.
[58] Würth, *Umweltschutz*, 232.
[59] The capacity of all municipal waste-water treatment plants was more than quadrupled from 901,000 cbm/d (1949) to 4.1 million cbm/d (1965). Official

regard to standards of living in the new towns these achievements indicated, as official propaganda put it, a change from the 'housing town' to the 'complete city'.[60]

But many of the plants worked poorly and lacked biological treatment techniques. In 1970 only 16.7 per cent of all municipal waste-water plants provided biological procedures. Hazards like the one in the waste-water treatment plant of Frankfurt/Oder in 1971 were a constant threat for drinking water quality. Water scarcity and pollution caused numerous problems. Thus the water of 8 per cent of all East-German waterworks showed a contamination by nitrate above the critical threshold of 40mg/l in 1975. The central water authorities estimated that the health of 4 per cent of all East German babies (ca. 12,000 each year) was threatened by nitrate in drinking water. In 1970, the vast majority of all water courses were classified as 'category III or IV'. This meant that they 'were either absolutely unsuited to be used for drinking or productive purposes or only by costly cleaning of the water'.[61] At the end of the 1970s even official handbooks admitted that waste water emissions from industry and excessive chemical fertilization in agriculture had caused a 'continuing and progressive degradation of the water quality of lakes'.[62]

Conclusion

By looking closely at general trends and some of the 'best practices' in socialist urban water policy a more detailed and ambivalent picture emerges than the catastrophic one that currently still dominates the literature. In contrast to the water infrastructure in old industrial regions considerable modernization was made in the fields of urban water infrastructure and management in other regions. This was especially true for some of the newly developing industrial regions and new towns. Depriving the cities of their traditional rights of self-government, introducing more efficient administrative structures and modernizing life-styles and sanitary standards was integral to the socialist

---

sources underlined that between 1949 and 1965 the capacity of water treatment plants in the GDR rose by 90 per cent and the proportion of the population served by sewerage systems had been increased to 72.2 per cent. Institut für Wasserwirtschaft, ed., *Ökonomik der Wasserwirtschaft in der Deutschen Demokratischen Republik* (Berlin, 1982), 27.

[60] Ibid., 233; Ludwig and Retzlaff, 'Die Stadt', 92–100.

[61] Würth, *Umweltschutz*, 214, 276, 234; BHLA, 601, Nr. 8346.

[62] Institut für Wasserwirtschaft, ed., *Ökonomik der Wasserwirtschaft*, 42. In the district of Frankfurt/Oder many lakes were listed as 'endangered' (category III) or prohibited for leisure activities (worst category IV) BLHA, Rep. 601, Nr. 10334.

programme. In some ways the regime perpetuated an old and powerful vision of public health and a socialist 'sanitary city'.[63]

This interpretation should not be misread as a whitewashing of the urban environmental record during the socialist period. Only if the ambivalent character of socialist policy is adequately revealed will it be possible to identify the potentials of legitimacy that the regime was mobilizing through a policy of 'sanitary welfare' which included an externalization of negative environmental effects. It was in fact the breakthrough of a socialist consumer society which stabilized the system from the 1960s onwards.[64] This breakthrough showed, as has been demonstrated through the example of water supply at the 'micro' level of the socialist new town of Eisenhüttenstadt, a dialectic dynamic. The regime found itself under intense pressure from urban residents to either introduce modern sanitary standards or risk losing the masses' loyalty.

When, alarmed by massive problems of water scarcity and pollution at the end of the 1960s, the East German regime started a second campaign of institutional reform and environmental policy it seemed to act according to the same logic as a number of western countries.[65] But these reforms failed because the government continued a traditional policy of forced industrialization with the result that, in contrast to western countries and cities, environmental degradation was not halted or diminished but actually dramatically increased. The 'socialist pathway' in urban environmental and water policy finally revealed that it was structurally unable to undertake substantial environmental modernization. As a result, from around 1970 it was doomed to 'death by stagnation'.[66]

---

[63] See the concluding remarks of Melosi, 423 in M. V. Melosi, *The Sanitary City. Urban Infrastructure in America from Colonial Times to the Present* (Baltimore 2000), and Robert Millward, 'The political economy of urban utilities', in M. Daunton, ed., *The Cambridge Urban History of Britain*, vol. II 1840–1950 (New York, 2000), 315–50, here 324.

[64] For the state of research on water consumption with regard to consumer society, see G. Bayerl, 'Konsum, Komfort und Netzwerke. Die Versorgung mit Wasser', in R. Reith and T. Meyer, ed., *'Luxus und Konsum' – eine historische Annäherung (Cottbuser Studien zur Geschichte von Technik, Arbeit und Umwelt, vol. 21)* (Münster, 2003), 129–58, esp. 133–9.

[65] The two most important reforms in the field of environmental policy around 1970 were the '*Landeskulturgesetz*' from 1970 and the creation of a Ministry for environmental protection and water management in 1971. For a survey, see *DDR Handbuch* Vol. 2, 1376–1380. For France, see M. Flonneau, 'Entre morale et politique, l'invention du "Ministère de l'Impossible"', in C. Bernhardt and G. Massard-Guilbaud, eds, *Le Démon Moderne*, 109–28, for Italy, see S. Neri Serneri, 'Water pollution in Italy: The failure of the hygienic approach, 1890s–1960s', in ibid., p. 157–78.

[66] In C. Bernhardt, 'Von der "Mondlandschaft"' I have reconstructed some major 'socialist environmental discourses', achievements and defeats between the 1950s and the 1970s.

CHAPTER TWELVE

Experts and Water Quality in Paris in 1870

Laurence Lestel

In the second half of the nineteenth century, for Paris, as indeed for all major European cities, the supply of drinking water was a matter of great concern. Two factors combined to make this so: Paris' rapidly growing population and the manifestly worsening quality of river water. 'During the last twenty years, the deterioration and corruption of watercourses has progressed rapidly. A large number of rivers, hitherto very pure, have become foul spillways. All watercourses in the department of Seine have successively become infected', Gérardin wrote.[1] Everywhere, the deterioration of flowing water, equally apparent in London, Brussels or Berlin, had the same cause: sewers pouring industrial and domestic waste water into it. This situation drew the attention of governments and, in France in the 1860s, gave rise to lively discussions at the *Académie des Sciences* and the *Académie de Médecine*. It made sense 'to take note of the composition of Seine water upstream and downstream of Paris, the impairments that it suffers on passing through the city and the suburban boroughs, [. . .] and of the effect of these impairments on the salubrity of water distributed to the populace'.[2] The initial problem was the quality of drinking water supplied to the inhabitants of Paris: was it adequate to meet demand without causing infectious diseases among a population as yet rather defenceless against them, some 20 years before the revolution brought about by Pasteur in the 1880s? But the debate went beyond the issue of public health: it was occasioned by the growing capacity of Paris' water supply and sewerage systems. Although they stood as symbols of modernity and of the city's improved hygiene, they were not without negative aspects, as evidenced by the marked worsening of water quality in the Seine since the 1840s. The first part of this paper will recall the

---

[1] A.C. Gérardin, *Rapport sur l'altération, la corruption et l'assainissement des rivières* (Imp. Nationale, 1874), 2. All quotes from French sources have been translated by the author. See also M.G. Grimaud, 'Des rivières et de leurs rapports avec l'industrie et l'hygiène des populations', *Comptes-rendus de l'Académie des Sciences*, 58, 1864, 955–9.

[2] 'Etudes sur les eaux potables', *Annales du Conservatoire des Arts et Métiers*, 5, 1864, 60–61.

state of water in Paris in the latter half of the nineteenth century, both
from the perspective of supply and from that of its corollary, the disposal
of polluted water, and will include a description of analyses performed at
that time on river water to test for hardness and for oxygen content.

Uncertainty then prevailed as to the causes of waterborne diseases.
Lead was one alleged culprit among many others blamed for a series of as
yet inexplicable epidemics. In June 1873, E. de Laval, an engineer from the
Ecole des Mines, submitted to the Municipal Council of Paris a petition
signed by 907 doctors, hospital pharmacists, professors and others calling
for a ban on lead pipes to supply water for human consumption. This
marked the start of the 'lead war', leading to the publication of 14 entries
in less than a year in the Proceedings of the *Académie des Sciences*, where
such experts as Eugène Belgrand, the engineer in charge of Paris' water
supply, Jean-Baptiste Dumas, the most influential chemist at that time, or
Joseph Fordos, pharmacist in chief at the Charité hospital, conjectured as
to the action of water on lead pipes. In the second part of this paper we
shall describe the part played in the battle for and against lead by these
experts. Modest though this was, the point at issue was clearly
environmental in nature: the question of the interaction between solid and
liquid substances (lead and water) was analysed in detail and the choice of
material was no longer solely to be determined by factors such as
availability and price, but with respect to the impact that the use of any
given material might have on the environment.

Water Quality in Paris in the Latter Half of the Nineteenth Century

It was under the Second Empire that a comprehensive plan to give Paris
an integrated water supply and sewerage system was drawn up. In 1853,
Haussmann engaged the engineer Belgrand to devise a modern system
capable of meeting the needs of the nineteenth century city: a supply of
water independent of local sources such as rivers and wells, frequently
contaminated, and which would allow both for rising household
consumption by the growing population, and for demand from
expanding industries, not only for more water, but for water of
consistent, continually monitored quality.[3] Drinking water – so called –

---

[3] It is not my intention here to retrace the history of water in European cities
in the nineteenth century, a subject discussed for the case of France by A.
Guillerme, 'Capter, clarifier l'eau, la distribution de l'eau dans les villes
françaises, 1800–1850', *Annales de la recherche urbaine*, 32, 1985, 32–43; J.P.
Goubert, *La conquête de l'eau* (Robert Laffont, 1986). For Paris you may refer
to the thesis of P. Cébron de Lisle, '*L'eau à Paris au XIXe siècle*', Paris University
PhD thesis, 1991.

was at that time drawn from the Canal de l'Ourcq, to the north of Paris (constructed between 1802 and 1839), and from the Seine. In 1860, work began on projects to draw water from the rivers Dhuis and Vanne, respectively, for the city's supply, the former completed in 1865, the latter in 1874, at which point ten times more water could be supplied than at the beginning of the century. The lion's share (around 60 per cent) was, however, destined for municipal use such as the spraying of streets; relatively little was supplied for private consumption as drinking water or to meet industrial needs: according to Figuier, 35 litres per inhabitant per year, which was only half the rate of consumption in London at that time.[4] Although Paris now had abundant water to draw on, never before had the water of the Seine caused so much disquiet. From successive analyses performed since the beginning of the century, the late 1840s can be seen to mark a turning point.[5] Water from the Seine, until then noted for its purity, underwent a marked deterioration, resulting both from the much larger scale of industrial activity, effluent from which had already condemned the Bièvre, and from the completion of the sewerage system. Water from the Ourcq, a heavily trafficked waterway nonetheless yielding a ready supply of drinking water, had an equally bad reputation.

The work of constructing the integrated sewerage system planned for Paris began in 1856.[6] This project involved gathering together all the capital's water in trunk ducts deep underground. These would discharge into the Seine near Clichy. At its inlets, this system collected surface (rain) water and household waste water. A prefectoral order dated 2 July

---

[4] L. Figuier, 'Industrie de l'eau', *Les merveilles de l'industrie*, vol 3 [1873–76], 318. The anthropic provision of water for Paris has been determined by Sabine Barles between 1807 and 1930. Cf. S. Barles, 'L'invention des eaux usées: l'assainissement de Paris, de la fin de l'Ancien Régime à la seconde guerre mondiale', in C. Bernhardt and G. Massard-Guilbaud, eds, *Le démon moderne* (Presses univ. Blaise-Pascal, 2002), 134.

[5] Since the early nineteenth century, analyses of Seine water followed one another at the whim of commissions which were often composed of chemists: Thénard, Hallé and Tarbé in 1816, Vauquelin in 1829 , Boutron and Henry, at the request of the Paris municipal administration in 1848. In June 1861, Félix Boudet presented a very detailed report on 'the salubrity of the Seine water viewed as drinking water' before the *Conseil d'hygiène publique et de salubrité du département de la Seine* (CHPS). It was he who was commissioned by CHPS to research lead in Seine water in 1873, following the petition sent to the city council of Paris.

[6] The question of the cleansing of Paris' water has been broadly discussed by G. Jacquemet, 'Urbanisme parisien: la bataille du tout-à-l'égout à la fin du XIXe siècle', *Revue d'histoire moderne et contemporaine*, 26, 1979, 505–48 ; S. Barles, *La ville délétère: médecins et ingénieurs dans l'espace urbain, XVIIIe-XIXe siècle* (Champ Vallon, 1999).

1867 assigned to it lavatory effluent formerly collected in 'watertight' cesspits under the houses, which were regularly emptied and their content used for manure. In November 1868, a trapped outlet under the Seine came into operation. This connected water from the left bank of the Seine to that from the right, causing further deterioration of water quality in that river. The improved distribution of water was accompanied by pollution on a scale never before experienced of the very river from which the supply of water was drawn. It was thus clearly necessary for the city authorities to acquire instruments with which to determine how far its available water resources had deteriorated.

Since the eighteenth century, samples of spring water and river water alike were examined by weighing and analysing the solid residue left after all liquid content had evaporated. It was not until 1854 that Antoine Boutron and Félix Boudet, both of them members of the *Conseil d'Hygiène du département de la Seine* (Committee for Public Hygiene and the Salubrity of the department of the Seine), first introduced in France a method of comparing water samples with one another. This had been developed in 1841 by the Scottish chemist Thomas Clark (1801–67) and was based upon the system of Gay-Lussac and Descroizilles for analysis by volume, which had already given industry the alkalimeter. Soap was added to the water sample until it formed a persistent lather, the quantity of soap required being proportional to the quantity of mineral salts in the water. In this way the *hardness* of the water could be determined, the unit of measurement being the hydrotimetric degree.[7] Table 12.1 shows some of the values obtained. 0° represents the hardness of distilled water containing no salts, by comparison with which water from the Seine, in this case measured upstream of Paris, at Ivry, or water from the Ourcq were both of acceptable hardness, unlike water at Prés-Saint-Gervais and at Belleville, which had supplied all Paris' public fountains until the early seventeenth century. This was exceptionally hard, and in the 1870s judged to be the worst that could be found.[8] These first analysts convinced the scientific community and subsequently the public at large

---

[7] A.F. Boutron-Chalard and F. Henri Boudet, 'Hydrotimétrie, nouvelle méthode pour déterminer les proportions des matières en dissolution dans les eaux de sources et de rivières', *Mémoires de l'Académie de médecine de Paris*, 1856. One French hydrotimetric degree means that 0.1 kg of soap must be added per litre of water to precipitate the calcium and magnesium salts before the formation of a lather is observed. This degree corresponds to about 0.01 g of calcium carbonate. In Britain, the units of measurement are the grain of soap and the gallon of water. One British degree is equivalent to about 1.4 French degrees.

[8] L. Figuier, 'Industrie de l'eau', *Les merveilles de l'industrie*, vol 3 [1873–76], 314.

of an inverse correlation between water hardness and water quality. But from the 1860s onwards, this criterion became untenable: having a relatively low hydrotimetric degree, the water from the Ourcq should be considered of high quality; and yet in 1870 'the corruption of the water of the Canal de l'Ourcq exceeds all bounds [. . .] Examined in the levels of Pantin, a town north of Paris, this water presents itself as a stagnant liquid, by turns yellowish, greenish and blackish in colour, and more like a stream of slurry on a farm than water from a canal'.[9] Actually, early in the twentieth century the true place of the hydrotimetric degree was found: 'The dosage for the hydrotimetric test must be deemed a convenient means of comparison, and for this reason alone its place in tables of analyses merits keeping.'[10]

Table 12.1   The first measurements of water hardness in Paris (1854–55)

Water analysed	Where sample taken	Date	Hardness (in hydrotimetric degrees)
Distilled water			0
Snow	Paris	December 1854	2.5
Rain	Paris	December 1854	3.5
Well of Grenelle	Paris	26 February 1855	4.5
Seine at Ivry docks		15 December 1854	15
Seine at Ivry docks		17 December 1854	17
Canal de l'Ourcq		25 February 1855	24.5
Prés-Saint Gervais			72
Belleville			128

In fact, there was much more concern about the organic matter being discharged from the sewers: this caused depletion of oxygen from the river, as demonstrated by Gérardin, doctor of sciences and inspector of the industrial establishments in the north of the Department of Seine. The measurement of oxygen levels in river water thus provided a relatively simple way of determining the amount of organic matter in the water and hence its purity. As Table 12.2 shows, the Seine was affected long-term between Asnières, downstream from Paris, and Poissy.

---

[9] L. Figuier, 'Industrie de l'eau', *Les merveilles de l'industrie*, vol 3 [1873–76], 155. see also E. Peligot, 'Etudes sur la composition des eaux. Recherche des matières organiques contenues dans les eaux'. *Annales du Conservatoire des Arts et Métiers*, 5, 1864, 60–103.

[10] F. Bordas, 'Eaux Potables', in Ch. Girard, ed., *Analyse des matières alimentaires* (Dunod, 1904), 13.

Table 12.2   Analysis of oxygen in Seine water in 1874 by Gérardin and Boudet[11]

Site	cc of oxygen per litre of water
Upstream from Corbeil	9
1500 m downstream	8.7
Choisy le Roi	7.5
Ivry	8
Pont de Tournelle	8
Viaduc d'Auteuil	6
Billancourt	5
Sèvres	5.4
Saint-Cloud	5.3
Asnières	4.6
Pont de Saint-Ouen	4
Saint-Denis	2
La Briche	1
Epinay	1
Argenteuil	1.4
Poissy	6
Meulan	8
Vernon	9.5
Rouen	10.5

On the other hand, metallic constituents were regarded as negligible: drains hardly discharged any and the industrial discharge of mineral substances was considered insignificant.[12] However, the scientific literature buzzed with cases of lead poisoning due to water consumption. In 1860, Lefèvre reported to the *Académie des Sciences* on cases of lead poisoning occurring on more than twenty ships on which water was kept in lead tanks. Doctor Aristide Reinvillier published his book on the poisoning of drinking water by lead in 1870, in which he hoped to prove that 'the pernicious effect of lead on the population is no less significant, nor any less serious, than that of tobacco or absinthe'.[13] Were these known cases of lead poisoning merely the tip of the iceberg, and should lead be held responsible for many cases of sickness whose

[11] L. Figuier, 'Industrie de l'eau', *Les merveilles de l'industrie*, vol 3 [1873–76], 144.

[12] C. Laboulaye, art. 'Egouts', in *Dictionnaire des arts et manufactures*, 7ème édition (1891).

[13] A. Reinvillier, *Hygiène publique – Empoisonnement des eaux potables par le plomb* (Dentu, 1870), 9.

cause had not been identified – the situation the nineteenth century rebelled against? This disquiet over the question of lead in water could explain the emergence of a veritable crusade against it in 1873.[14]

Lead in Water: a Danger to Public Health?

Faced with this situation, nineteenth century France lined up an army of experts and engineers, who deployed all their scientific knowledge to prove that the simple passage of drinking water through lead pipes installed for water distribution was not sufficient to cause lead to be dissolved in the water. A little stage management would do no harm to this superb demonstration: it was agreed that Félix Boudet, commissioned to present a report to the *Conseil d'hygiène publique et de salubrité de la Seine*, would present it at a session of this committee in November 1873, while Eugène Belgrand would similarly read his before the *Académie des Sciences*.

The problem has to be set in context: on 31 December 1873, Paris was equipped with 1,333 km of water mains made of cast iron, only 63 km were of bituminized sheet metal and a mere 3 km made of lead, not including the 4 km or so of small-diameter lead pipes.[15] So the public supply could not be called into question. But the connectors leading from the mains supply to the outlets through which water was drawn (fountains and taps in particular) were virtually all made of lead. Their length was estimated to average 40 metres for each of the 39,500 consumers of water in Paris, making the total length of lead pipes in the water supply as a whole 1,580 km.[16] The lead pipes belonged to individuals, not to the public water supply system.

The first argument put forward by the experts was that of appeal to the past and to accepted knowledge: lead pipes had existed since the time of the Romans and the public pipes had been made of lead in France until the widespread use of cast iron in the late eighteenth century. Yet 'since those remote times, no one until now had seen the slightest danger in this use of lead'.[17] Belgrand maintained that neither Pliny, a standard

[14] E. Belgrand, 'De l'action de l'eau sur les conduites en plomb', *Comptes-rendus de l'Académie des Sciences*, 77, 1873, 1055–63.

[15] Ibid., 1056. Cast iron began to replace lead at the end of the eighteenth century. Not only did its price fall considerably in the nineteenth century, but this material was also preferred by the engineers responsible for the installation of water supply systems, at the cost of the lead used by the former hydraulic engineers who were increasingly marginalized. Cf. J.P. Goubert, *La conquête de l'eau* (Robert Laffont, 1986), 57 and A. Guillerme, *Bâtir la ville* (Champ Vallon, 1995), 242.

[16] Ibid., 1057.

[17] Ibid., 1056.

reference for the description of hazardous technology in the Roman period, nor Frontin, nor any of the historians of ancient times had ever mentioned the slightest poisoning from the use of lead pipes. He omitted to refer to the book by Reinvillier which showed that, on the contrary, Galen, in 130 AD, had already condemned the use of lead for conveying drinking water.[18] Nor did he quote Mathieu Orfila who, in his *Leçons de médecine légale*, reported as a long-known fact that 'water that had been transported via lead aqueducts or has fallen from roofs covered in this metal, can retain in solution large enough amounts of this poison to cause serious accidents'.[19] Besides, it had been known with certainty since 1809 that distilled water *attacked* lead, consequently producing white lead.[20] The publication by Guyton de Morveau[21] was abundantly quoted in nineteenth century articles and it was common practice that demonstrations be carried out in public. Thus Besnou saw this experiment on the peculiar action of distilled water on lead for the first time in 1830, in a course by M. Chatelain, first pharmacist-in-chief of the Navy in Brest.[22] But this attack on lead depended on the mineral purity of the water. It was the hydrotimetric degree which was seen as most relevant for measuring the capacity for reaction between lead and water: in flasks containing different kinds of water (a public experiment by Dumas), only distilled water immediately attacked lead, rainwater contained traces of it, and the water from the Ourcq, from the Seine and from wells were too rich in calcium salts for any noticeable attack on lead in the Paris pipes.

The second argument was that of its great durability: aside from the fact that this was the same material that had been used since Roman times, the ancient pipes were a direct proof that lead resisted the ravages of time. Indeed, if these pipes had been attacked by water, traces of corrosion would have been visible, which was not the case. A pipe from the suburb of Saint-Antoine, installed there in 1670, at the same time as the pump of the Notre-Dame bridge, showed in 1873 no traces such as one might expect to find if it had become corroded over time.[23]

---

[18] A. Reinvillier, *Hygiène publique – Empoisonnement des eaux potables par le plomb* (Dentu, 1870), 16.

[19] M. Orfila, *Leçons de médecine légale*, vol 3, 2nd ed. (Bréchet, 1828), 182.

[20] L.B. Guyton de Morveau, *Annales de Chimie*, 71, 1809, 196–9.

[21] Louis Bernard Guyton de Morveau (1737–1816) lawyer and chemist. He wrote the modern chemical nomenclature along with Lavoisier, Berthollet et Fourcroy.

[22] L. Besnou, 'Action des eaux économes ordinaires et distillées, ainsi que de l'eau de mer distillée, sur le plomb et les réfrigérants en étain des divers appareils distillatoires', *Comptes-rendus de l'Académie des Sciences*, 78, 1874, 322–4.

[23] E. Belgrand, 'De l'action de l'eau sur les conduites en plomb', *Comptes-rendus de l'Académie des Sciences*, 77, 1873, 1058.

In addition it was observed that pipes became coated on the interior with a thin but tenacious crust of lime and calcium, which meant that the water passing through the pipes was not, in fact, in direct contact with the lead. This was the general state of affairs in Paris, as Belgrand could see for himself when visiting the old lead depot belonging to the maintenance works contractor for the city of Paris, M. Fortin-Hermann. The most one could say was that the new pipes, in which this protective layer had not yet formed, might produce a few transient cases of lead colic, often because they also contained dust heavily contaminated with lead during their manufacture. It was therefore advised that the water should first be allowed to run through the new pipes to rinse them out, before drinking water from them.[24] The same applied to installations which had not been in use for some time: water remaining over long periods in 'intimate' contact with lead could become contaminated with lead carbonate. This was the probable cause of the lead poisoning occurring among new tenants of houses in the *Boulevard Magenta* which had remained unoccupied for several years.[25] This was also observed by Fordos, who deliberately turned off a tap in the pharmacy of the Charité hospital for two months.[26] After this interval, the water flowing from it was cloudy. Left to stand, a deposit settled in it, which on analysis showed a high concentration of lead carbonate, while the filtered water showed virtually no lead in solution. It was enough simply to discard the water which had been standing in the pipes for a long time to retrieve lead-free water once again.[27]

To convince the people of Paris, the experiments were carried out in pipes that were markedly longer than average: one 200m. in length connecting to the *Hôtel-Dieu*, another 100m. long to the *Avenue d'Orléans*, well above the average length of 40m. for the connections. This extension of the length of the pipes, and therefore of the contact time between lead and water, did not result in any more lead being detected in the water.[28]

---

[24] H. de Parville, *Causeries scientifiques*, 13th year (1874), 311.

[25] Ibid., 311.

[26] It was at the *Hôpital de la Charité* that Tanquerel des Planches, author of the medical reference work on lead-related illnesses, cared for the sufferers of 'dry colic', the most characteristic manifestation of acute lead poisoning; cf. L. Tanquerel des Planches, *Traité des maladies de plomb ou saturnines* (Paris, 1839). In 1873, most of the lead poisoning patients were treated at the hospital of Beaujon de Clichy, which admitted workers from the neighbouring white lead factory in their hundreds.

[27] M.J. Fordos, 'Du rôle des sels dans l'action des eaux potables sur le plomb', *Comptes-rendus de l'Académie des Sciences*, 78, 1874, 1108–11.

[28] E. Belgrand, 'De l'action de l'eau sur les conduites en plomb', *Comptes-rendus de l'Académie des Sciences*, 77, 1873, 1058.

However, the debate turned upon expert argument. Félix Leblanc, who had analysed the water samples provided by Belgrand, had used the classical method of precipitation of lead sulphide by means of hydrogen sulphide:[29] this lead sulphide was slightly water-soluble, as Mayençon and Bergeret proved.[30] Thus, the water of the *Hôtel-Dieu* and the *Charité*, which had been recognized as lead-free, contained a 'marked quantity' after having remained in the connector pipes for eight to ten hours (i.e. overnight). Mayençon and Bergeret were prudent, pointing out that they had hesitated to present their results, which 'palpably differed from those reached by the most able chemists'. They therefore presented at great length their experiments on very diverse samples and then found a solution which would not cause trouble: adopting the position that even if the water did contain lead, it was nevertheless harmless to public health, 'as demonstrated by the immunity enjoyed by individuals, the pupils, the Saint-Etienne patients, in Paris and all the cities where there is a water supply'.

The most conclusive analytical method was that presented by Balard: it was recommended that the water be boiled after the addition of a few drops of tartar of ammonia, which dissolved all insoluble lead compounds (hydrate, sulphate, carbonate, phosphate, borate). Lead sulphate, easily identifiable from its characteristic colour, then precipitated out entirely.[31] However, the debate was exhausted: even if the chemical expert could now track down the slightest trace of lead in water, the subject was no longer of interest. It seemed generally accepted that the lead contained in Paris' drinking water posed no real threat, even though Fordos, the chief pharmacist of the *Charité*, continued to report a few niches where the danger reappeared.[32] In hospitals, the glass bottles destined to contain dietary or medicinal fluids were traditionally cleaned by rinsing with pure water or distilled water in the presence of lead shot, which served as an abrasive to scour the sides.

---

[29] Félix Leblanc (born 1813), mining engineer, chemist at the *Ecole Centrale*; E. Belgrand, 'De l'action de l'eau sur les conduites en plomb', *Comptes-rendus de l'Académie des Sciences*, 77, 1873, 1059.

[30] Mayençon and Bergeret, 'De l'action des eaux douces sur le plomb métallique', *Comptes-rendus de l'Académie des Sciences*, 78, 1874, 484–7.

[31] Antoine Balard (1802–76), discoverer of bromium in 1825, a teacher at the *Collège de France*, specialist in the chemistry of the marine environment, had among his students Louis Pasteur and Marcelin Berthelot, whose careers he supported; A. Balard, 'Action de l'eau sur le plomb', *Comptes-rendus de l'Académie des Sciences*, 78, 1874, 392–5.

[32] In 1873, lead poisoning patients were essentially workers in the manufacture of white lead and building painters using the latter to whiten the walls. Cf. L. Lestel, 'La production de céruse en France au XIXe siècle: évolution d'une industrie dangereuse', *Techniques et Culture*, 38, 2001, 35–66.

Similarly coopers, before pouring wine into bottles, 'used to swirl lead about in the bottles' and only rinsed them once afterwards, which was not enough to remove the lead carbonate which had formed and clung to the sides. Lead carbonate, however, dissolves in alcohol and thus in wine, which might explain as yet unexplained cases of lead poisoning.[33] Fordos thus recommended the use of iron filings instead of lead shot. Following advice from Dumas, he also suggested the addition of a little sodium carbonate to the rinsing water to slow down the oxygenation of the iron.[34]

During this time, the city of Paris, which asked these experts their point of view, accepted their results and concluded in October 1873 that there was no cause for alarm. The extent of the debate was probably beyond what it had expected, but the conclusions of these experts, underlining that the public water supply system could not be responsible for lead poisoning, convinced the Prefect of Seine that no action was necessary. To shut up further comments, the Prefect of Seine pointed out that this fuss was due to one man who had interests in a factory making lead pipes lined with tin, a technical innovation he wished to promote. Obviously, this self promotion had no connection with public health care.[35]

Conclusion

In the mid nineteenth century, the obvious deterioration in quality of Seine water through waste discharged by industry and sewage led to the adoption of new methods of analysing river water: for hardness and for presence of organic substances. The promoters of these new techniques were chemists involved in the fight against the insanitary condition of the department of Seine.

The scientists seized upon the marginal problem of the presence of lead in drinking water. By highly inefficient experimental methods, and with the help of arguments based on ancient history, they offered proof that Paris' water contained no lead. The city, which as yet had no real water monitoring laboratories, invited and accepted the results

---

[33] M.J. Fordos, 'Action de l'eau aérée sur le plomb, considérée au point de vue de l'hygiène et de la médecine légale', *Comptes-rendus de l'Académie des Sciences*, 77, 1873, 1099–1102.

[34] M.J. Fordos, 'Note sur l'emploi de la grenaille de fer pour remplacer la grenaille de plomb dans le rinçage des bouteilles', *Comptes-rendus de l'Académie des Sciences*, 78, 1874, 1411–13.

[35] *Conseil Municipal de Paris* (1873). Compte-rendu de la séance du 25 octobre 1873.

produced by these experts; all the more so since these conveniently reinforced their notion that no action was necessary.

Are we to conclude that all this agitation led nowhere? Indeed, lead was not yet recognized as an environmental problem (one must wait until the second part of the twentieth century to meet such a feeling, triggered by the use of lead in petrol). Nevertheless, this debate revealed a rise in awareness of the possible impact of the use of certain materials on the quality of those elements on which human beings depend. The aim here is still to protect man from the toxic effects of lead, but a genuine ecological preoccupation with the study of this impact had appeared: 'The engineer must, when setting up a new water distribution system, be concerned about the geological composition of the terrain, and the composition of the water, and make sure it does not fulfil the conditions required to attack lead'.[36]

The consumer, in search of the vibrios which Pasteur was later to put under the spotlight, believed briefly he had found in lead a culprit capable of producing poisoned water that was 'as clear, colourless and odourless as ordinary water'.[37] The description of its slow, pernicious effect on the consumer's health shows great concern about hidden pollution, far more complex than its more manifest forms, such as odour problems or fire hazards typically mentioned in contemporary reports. However, it was not until the late twentieth century that the heavy metal content of Seine water was systematically measured, and the question of lead in water became a sensitive subject again.

[36] H. de Parville, *Causeries scientifiques*, 13th year (1874), 316.
[37] M. Orfila, *Leçons de médecine légale*, vol 3, 2nd edn (Bréchet, 1828), 182.

CHAPTER THIRTEEN

Noise Abatement and the Search for Quiet Space in the Modern City

Michael Toyka-Seid

Noise and its effects on the human constitution are major problems in modern societies.[1] Approximately 20 per cent of the population of Germany are treated for aural disorders, and almost a third of all working diseases are connected to the creation of noise. In marked contrast to other environmental problems, noise is still on the increase. By the late twentieth century in the Rhine region near Cologne an already huge number of cars, trucks and other motor vehicles was still growing; new modes of transport like high-speed trains and the expansion of air traffic were harassing a heavily burdened population. At the same time newspaper correspondents were complaining about noisy leisure activities like downtown beach volleyball tournaments or the 'acoustic pollution' of open air concerts. But disturbing noise, caused by industry, traffic, neighbours, children and the like are not only omnipresent. They must also be seen as an intricate and multifarious sensual phenomenon – perhaps one reason why the issue has not figured prominently either in recent environmental campaigns or in environmental history.[2] When the minister of Bonn's cathedral complained about the large number of public events on the open space in front of the Church his plea for more quietness was rejected in a letter to the editor in the local press: 'His ringing of the bells does not help to reduce noise on the Cathedral place either!'[3] And when embittered residents of Cologne airport organized an Anti-Noise-March to the private home of the Prime Minister of North-Rhine/Westphalia in Bonn, the police ordered them to stop: the Samba-

---

[1] A.L. Bronzaft, 'Noise pollution: a growing world problem', in P.J. Thompson, ed., *Environmental Education for the 21st Century* (Frankfurt/M., 1997), 99–108; M. Schulzke, 'Rrruhe! Menschen im Lärm – krank, erschöpft, ruhelos', *Psychologie heute*, 22, 1995, 44–9.

[2] The changing and sometimes perplexing conceptions of the 'auditory community' of early modern towns are described in D. Garrioch, 'Sounds of the City: the soundscape of early modern European towns', *Urban History*, 30, 2003, 5–25.

[3] *Generalanzeiger Bonn*, 26 April 2001.

group *Rabatz* (Row) was alleged to be playing too loudly for this quiet residential area![4]

The subject of this paper is the effect of noise and acoustic pollution on urban societies and the reactions of individuals and of society as a whole to this environmental problem.[5] It will be argued that the amount of noise has dramatically expanded since the early stages of the industrial revolution. The constant din of urban life has affected labour productivity, caused aural and mental disorders and led to arguments about the level of noise the modern urbanite should have to endure. The reasons for the rather hesitant reaction to a major environmental problem of the modern city by politicians, public administrators and experts in the late nineteenth and early twentieth centuries are numerous. Perhaps other problems needed more urgent action, perhaps they seemed to be more readily soluble and measurable.[6] But the main problem, of course, was and still is the question as to what should be considered to be 'unnecessary' or 'unbearable' noise.[7] When the term 'noise' (*Lärm*) eventually found its way into a German encyclopaedia in the 1930s, the article only attempted to find a working definition of the phenomenon; what constituted noise was left to the feeling of the 'average human'.[8]

In the first part of this paper I shall briefly describe some early attempts to come to terms with noise generated by steam-driven machines. The breakthrough of the industrial revolution had brought new levels of noise, especially in rapidly growing urban industrial regions. Soon the fight against 'noise nuisance' became the task of administrators, experts and doctors, but also of lawyers and judges. They had to decide how much noise an inhabitant of the modern industrial city could be expected to endure. At the same time, the urban elite tried to establish standards by which it could keep the local environment noise-free. Quietness, defined as absence of noise, became a scarce and sought-after resource in urban environments. But there was another side to the coin, which will figure more prominently in the second part of this paper. Like fuming chimneys, unremitting noise

---

[4] Generalanzeiger Bonn, 24 May 2002.

[5] For an early attempt to write the history of sound and noise, see R.M. Schafer, *The Tuning of the World* (New York, 1977).

[6] For the contemporary debates about the relevance of environmental problems, see in another context F. Uekötter, 'Die Kommunikation zwischen technischen und juristischen Experten als Schlüsselproblem der Umweltgeschichte. Die preußische Regierung und die Berliner Rauchplage', *Technikgeschichte*, 66, 1999, 1–31.

[7] For an examination of the changing idea of 'noise', see P. Bailey, 'Breaking the sound barrier: a historian listens to noise', *Body and Society*, 2, 1966, 49–66.

[8] *Der Große Brockhaus*, Vol. 11 (Leipzig, 1932), 137.

rapidly became a significant component of the modern age, loathed by sufferers, causing physical and mental illnesses, but at the same time symbolizing progress and economic success. While politicians and health reformers combined to fight noise which had to be endured by factory workers,[9] authors and newspaper editors became used to or were converted to the idea of the never-sleeping city and the ubiquitous bustle of new metropolises.[10] Since those years noise has remained a Janus-faced symbol of the modern city, as vociferously condemned as warmly welcomed: fittingly, perhaps, when Simon and Garfunkel reminded us of the 'Sounds of Silence' in Central Park in 1982, a roar of thousands of enthusiastic fans answered back. The final part of this paper will concentrate on the years after the second world war, the period which experienced hitherto unprecedentedly high levels of noise. A glimpse of the small numbers of individuals and organizations which continue to wage the 'fight against noise' and some thoughts about the reasons for the minimal response to these demands will conclude the paper.

Industrial Noise and Middle Class Concerns

It was not difficult for the enterprising brothers Torley to get permission to start their ironworks in the little village of Wald in the Prussian Rhine province in the 1870s. Only when in 1886 a new postmaster moved into the growing industrial settlement did problems arise. The new neighbour filed a complaint against the noise and the vibrations caused by the Torleys' steam hammer and gained the support of the government of the province. Members of the Prussian parliament, the *Haus der Abgeordneten*, were indignant; the representative Pleß from the Roman Catholic *Zentrum* party declared: 'In the community of Wald a steam hammer is not unusual; the noise caused by such a hammer is well known. . . . The neighbours, who have moved to Wald, knew, which kind of noise is caused by those industries; they knew it, when they moved to Wald, and I think they have no reason to complain.' Must the entrepreneur, as another representative insisted, put feather-cushions under the hammer to soften the noise?[11]

---

[9] For example, ten years work in a iron-bending firm resulted in a loss of hearing of about 90 per cent; K. Saul, '"Kein Zeitalter seit Erschaffung der Welt hat so viel und so ungeheuerlichen Lärm gemacht" . . . Lärmquellen, Lärmbekämpfung und Antilärmbewegung im Deutschen Kaiserreich', in G. Bayerl et al., eds, *Umweltgeschichte. Methoden, Themen, Potentiale* (Münster, 1996), 187–217, 189.

[10] A. Endell, *Die Schönheit der großen Stadt* (Stuttgart, 1908).

[11] Quoted in F.-J. Brüggemeier/M. Toyka-Seid, eds., *Industrie-Natur. Lesebuch zur Geschichte der Umwelt im 19. Jahrhundert* (Frankfurt/M., 1995), 167–8; all translations from the German in this paper by the author.

Occurrences such as the Wald episode were not exceptional in the years of German high industrialization.[12] Sanitary engineers, medical experts, architects and planners were eagerly trying to single out cases for the new *Lärmplage* (noise nuisance) and ways to cope with this 'resource' of silence. The problems they faced were numerous. The most important was the question of how to measure noise. Whereas the consequences could easily be seen and described, more especially with regard to aural deficiencies of labourers working in factories, the sheer scale of the urban environmental problem could only be estimated. Only in the 1920s would noise become measurable with the introduction of a new unit of measurement, the phon.

Like other environmental and sanitary 'nuisances' connected with new modes of production and their social consequences (e.g. water and air pollution, stench, health hazards, overpopulation), the problem of industrial noise in Prussia and later in the German Empire was initially treated in the context of pre-industrial legislative regulation. The definition of *Ortsüblichkeit* (the environmental standard considered to be typical for a certain region) was the usual measure for the quantity of pollution urban residents had to endure. But the situation was not reliable for factory owners. In 1869 the Prussian Minister of Commerce refused to introduce special permission for noise-generating business enterprises. Fifteen years later the High Court allowed a complaint by a neighbour against the nightly noise of a printing works: the noise generated by the printing machines, so the Court was told, caused damage to the rights of the owner. Although the traditional definition of 'noise nuisance' was extended by this decision, a new legislative framework to regulate the problem was not established.

One reason for this omission was dispute among the experts. The late nineteenth century may have been a 'nervous' time and noise one of the worst stress-causing agents, as Joachim Radkau has put it.[13] Lawyers, politicians, medical men, and business inspectors could not agree on the real importance of noise nuisances. It was a tricky question: did an excess of noise cause nervousness? Or were modern 'urbanites' – and no one doubted, that inhabitants of cities were more liable to nervous diseases

---

[12] Klaus Saul has collected a whole bunch of court cases mainly from the last quarter of the 19th century which shows that the noise question was an important part of the contemporary sanitary and hygienic debate; K. Saul, 'Kein Zeitalter', 191–2, and by the same author: 'Wider die "Lärmpest". Lärmkritik und Lärmbekämpfung im Deutschen Kaiserreich', in D. Machule et al., eds, *Macht Stadt krank? Vom Umgang mit Gesundheit und Krankheit* (Hamburg, 1996), 151–92.

[13] J. Radkau, *Das Zeitalter der Nervosität. Deutschland zwischen Bismarck und Hitler* (München, 1998), 208.

because of their daily dose of noise and vibrations[14] – so distressed because of the anxieties of city life? This implied that they had become oversensitive to every kind of sound. And: what constituted an 'average' urban individual, which was postulated in a High Court decision in 1896 and which was to become a common point of reference in German civil law?

The nervousness of modern urbanites played a major role in the public discussion at the beginning of the twentieth century. But whereas people like the philosopher Theodor Lessing, who in 1908 founded the first and not very successful *Antilärm-Verein* (Society Against Noise), indulged in elitist noise paranoia,[15] to all intents and purposes it was men (and sometimes women) of the working class who had to bear the more substantial health consequences of industrial noise. In manufacturing plants, where engines, power-driven machinery or steam hammers produced hitherto unknown quantities of noise and vibrations, the nuisance was physically felt.[16] Franz Kafka, who was not a working man himself, but visited all kinds of noisy factories while working for an insurance company and therefore knew what he was talking about, felt as though he had been thrown into the 'headquarters of noise'.[17] Most medical and hygienic handbooks of the time took note of the new health hazards and looked for remedies for the worst effects.[18] The widely read *Handbuch der Hygiene*, a multi-volume handbook dealing with all kinds of sanitary and health problems, edited by Theodor Weyl at the turn of the century, took account of health problems caused by industrial noise in its section on *Social Hygiene* as well as in an independent supplement volume dealing with urban noise and its prevention.[19] Debates and learned contributions by social

---

[14] S. Krömer, '*Lärm als medizinisches Problem im 19. Jahrhundert*', Mainz University PhD thesis, 1981.

[15] M. Lentz, '"Ruhe ist die erste Bürgerpflicht". Lärm, Großstadt und Nervosität im Spiegel von Theodor Lessings "Antilärmverein"', *Medizin in Geschichte und Gesellschaft*, 13, 1994, 81–105; R. Marwedel, *Theodor Lessing, 1872–1933* (Darmstadt, 1987).

[16] The measurement of noise pollutions is difficult and contemporary data on nineteenth century noise sources hard to find. An idea of the spectacle produced by those machinery is provided by refashioned old plants like the Gesenkschmiede Hendrichs (a company that specialized in the production of scissors) in Solingen near Cologne.

[17] 'Kafkas Fabriken', *Marbacher Magazin*, 100, 2002.

[18] E. Neisius, '*Geschichte der arbeitsmedizinischen Lärmforschung in Deutschland*', Frankfurt/M. University PhD thesis, 1989; W. Weber, *Arbeitssicherheit. Historische Beispiele – aktuelle Analysen* (Reinbek, 1988); Saul, 'Wider die "Lärmpest"', 152–3.

[19] K. Hartmann, 'Arbeiterschutz', in T. Weyl, ed., *Handbuch der Hygiene*, 4th Supplement-Vol.: Soziale Hygiene (Jena, 1904), 545–303, 586; G. Pinkenburg, 'Der Lärm in den Städten und seine Verhinderung', in: T. Weyl, ed., *Handbuch der Hygiene*, 3rd Supplement-Vol., 1st supply (Jena, 1903).

reformers and experts underline that noise in those years was perceived as not only an unpleasant, but also as a health-endangering nuisance caused by modern industry. With regard to the city, noise constituted a seemingly unavoidable ingredient and a constant threat to the environment.

It was, however, the middle classes and not the workers who were most disturbed by the new mechanical soundscape of the city – at least they expressed discontent about this encroachment on their desire for quiet. Whether or not the average noise level in the cities was actually increasing in the second half of the nineteenth century it is impossible to judge. City life had never been quiet, given the clatter of horseshoes on the paving stone streets, the ringing of bells, the noise of street musicians and street vendors and all sorts of animal sounds.[20] But there can be no doubt that the invention and dissemination of standardized consumer goods in densely populated cities reduced inner-city areas of quietness. An example worth mentioning in this context is the invention of the mass-produced piano, patronized by the educated middle classes, but despised and cursed as *Klavierpest* ('piano plague') and as a cultural *affront* by anti-noise campaigners.[21]

From Industrial Noise Endurance to Individual Noise Production

From the point of view of a historian of the environment, the years before the first world war might look like a time of social and political concern with the noise problem. This becomes even more plausible when we take into account the minimal amount of research undertaken on this subject for the interwar years. One reason for this could be that years of economic depression proved to be an unpromising period for those who championed environmental reform. An excellent example is the depression in Ruhr heavy industry in the early 1920s: as a consequence of the occupation by French troops industrial production came to a standstill. No industry meant no smoke – but also no work, no income and consequently depression and poverty. When chimneys started fuming again nobody lamented the environmental consequences. It is not surprising therefore to find that with regard to noise abatement by legal decrees or public dispute, the first half of the twentieth century was not a period of progress. But this is only part of the dilemma. What changed during those years was awareness of the problem and, even

---

[20] Pinkenburg, 'Der Lärm', 10–21.
[21] I. Wrobel (i.e. K. Tucholsky), 'Lärmschutz', *Der Kunstwart*, 27, 1913–14, 312–14.

more important, the way in which noise was being 'produced'. The first half of the twentieth century saw the development of the modern perception of noise.

Noise – meaning by now a mixture of all kinds of sounds produced by technical appliances and masses of people living and working in close proximity – became a hallmark of the city in the interwar period.[22] What had been a specific urban tendency in a few metropolises at the turn of the century[23] became part of the mental urban fabric in the urbanized world of the 1920s and 1930s. The 'golden twenties' were, as Hermann Glaser has written, 'noisy years', in more than one respect. 'The loudspeaker was the typical 'machine' of the era.'[24] It had only been about a quarter of a century since the early discoveries of the extension of electromagnetic waves by Heinrich Hertz and the invention of wireless transmission by Guglielmo Marconi. During this period broadcasting and the private radio transmitter became everyday household consumer goods. In 1921 the public broadcasting agency came on air in the United States. Already by 1924 500 stations were operating. In Germany radio entertainment started by 1923.

Radios were by no means as noisy as industrial machinery. But they added to a new generation of media which transformed the sensual climate in which men and women carried on their social and economic existence.[25] Being subjected to different forms of sounds and noises produced by mechanical devices became part of the everyday experience of urban inhabitants. What also changed were conceptions of the public and private sphere. Whereas in the early stages of broadcasting listening to the radio was a highly unusual event, and was sometimes even performed in public for popular entertainment, it soon became a part of an explicitly private sphere for the 'nervous' urbanite, a cosy island within the machinery of the city.[26] However, with increased mobility the

[22] R. Birkefeld/M. Jung, *Die Stadt, der Lärm und das Licht. Die Veränderung des öffentlichen Raums durch Motorisierung und Elektrifizierung* (Seelze, 1994).

[23] C. Zimmermann, *Die Zeit der Metropolen. Urbanisierung und Großstadtentwicklung* (Frankfurt/M., 1996).

[24] H. Glaser, *Maschinenwelt und Alltagsleben. Industriekultur in Deutschland vom Biedermeier bis zur Weimarer Republik* (Frankfurt/M., 1981), 188.

[25] I. Marßolek/A. v. Saldern, 'Massenmedien im Kontext von Herrschaft, Alltag und Gesellschaft. Eine Herausforderung an die Geschichtsschreibung', in I. Marßolek/A. v. Saldern, eds., *Radiozeiten: Herrschaft, Alltag, Gesellschaft (1924–1960)* (Potsdam, 1990), 11–38, 13.

[26] C. Lenk, 'Medium der Privatheit? Über Rundfunk, Freizeit und Konsum in der Weimarer Republik', in I. Marßolek/A. v. Saldern, eds, *Radiozeiten: Herrschaft, Alltag, Gesellschaft (1924–1960)* (Potsdam, 1999), 206–17, 207–11.

new media also became mobile. The number of complaints about inconsiderate tourists invading the quietness of the countryside with their noise-generating radios and record players steadily increased in the 1930s. Already by 1930 the Saxon Ministry of the Interior issued an instruction which forbade the use of radios and phonographs in leisure areas.[27] The advent of the radio therefore marks – together with the spread of some other consumer goods, which became common in the years between the wars – an important point of transition. Up to that point noise was mainly a concomitant of the production of industrial goods. Now it was increasingly the individual who could – by using his new, in most cases industrially produced device – become part of the 'acoustic society', making noise which was not his own responsibility but rather 'manufactured' by a new form of domestic appliance.[28]

But urban dwellers of the interwar years not only experienced far-reaching changes in the acoustic environment of their cities. The cities themselves evolved. Physical features and resources were adapted to new environmental challenges. This was substantiated by empirical data and scientific research designed to relieve inhabitants of the consequences of a loss of quietness in city life. One example was the construction industry. Emily Thomson has shown how, in the United States in the 1920s, architectural acoustics became big business.[29] Sound-absorbing materials were invented and employed, first of all in office buildings. The aim was to create healthy working conditions by preventing the accumulation and transmission of unwanted sounds. 'As the sound and pervasiveness of industry grew . . . and as the nature and landscape of city living changed, escape from the noise no longer seemed possible. Acoustic materials were thus increasingly used to eliminate noise.'[30] Another example of this more innovative approach was the attempt to create urban soundscapes in the late twentieth century. This has become a solution which has been increasingly applied to urban noise hazards.[31]

The 1920s should thus be seen as a watershed in the history of noise pollution and abatement as an environmental phenomenon. A new *Reizschwelle* (threshold of stimuli), as Ulrich Troitzsch has called it, a new

[27] *Der deutsche Rundfunk,* 30, 1930, 66.
[28] U.C. Schmidt, 'Vom "Spielzeug" über den "Hausfreund" zur "Goebbels-Schnauze" – Das Radio als häusliches Kommunikationsmedium im Deutschen Reich (1934–1945)', *Technikgeschichte,* 55, 1988, 313–28.
[29] E. Thompson, 'Listening to/ for Modernity: Architectural Acoustics and the Development of Modern Spaces in America', in P. Galison and E. Thompson, eds., *The Architecture of Science,* (Cambridge, Mass., 1999), 254–80. A good account of the range of acoustical products available in the early 1930s can be found in V.O. Knudsen, *Architectural Acoustics* (New York, 1932).
[30] Thompson, 'Listening to/ for Modernity', 266.
[31] Süddeutsche Zeitung, 13 Nov. 2002.

borderline in the way contemporaries perceived environmental problems, had been crossed.[32] While industrial noise was on the retreat, at least with regard to publicly prominent phenomena,[33] individually generated noise – which encompassed all kinds of 'consumerist noise' – became more and more prevalent. This process, taking off in the 1920s and 1930s, has still not run its full course at the beginning of the twenty-first century. The most prominent symbol of this new way of producing 'individual noise' was (and still is) the new fetish of the motor car. It is a story which has often been told and which does not need to be repeated here.[34] It is however worth mentioning that Theodor Lessing, who ended his short fight against noise shortly before the outbreak of war, had already in 1908 detected a new 'enemy' in this 'machinery for depopulation': 'Never has man moved on this earth with such noise and such a horrible odour'.[35]

If there ever has been a golden 'quiet time' in the past, it had definitely ended by the interwar period. It should however be mentioned that it was not only the rise of a consumer society, supported by the innovative potential of industry and the new organization of work, that distinguished those years from the prewar era. However, how it was that the mental and psychological order of the 1920s and 1930s came to be shaped by the experience of a technical war requires further research. Ernst Jünger's novel *In Stahlgewittern* is surely the embodiment of the experience of a literally shell-shocked war society. But it was the bustle of the great city, its excitement, dirt and noise, which without doubt had become part of popular and even of 'high' culture in the years after the great war. This was exemplified by works such as Swiss composer Arthur Honegger's *Pacific 231*, the movies *Symphonie der Großstadt* by Walter Ruttmann and *Metropolis* by Fritz Lang, or Alfred Döblin's novel *Berlin Alexanderplatz*. The experience of modern urban noises such as that attributable to the electric tram[36] had by now become a

---

[32] J. Radkau, ' Unausdiskutiertes in der Umweltgeschichte', in M. Hettling et al., eds, *Was ist Gesellschaftsgeschichte? Positionen Themen, Analysen* (München, 1991) 45–57, 48–9.

[33] H.-J. Braun, 'Lärmbelastung und Lärmbekämpfung in der Zwischenkriegszeit', in G. Bayerl and W. Weber, eds., *Sozialgeschichte der Technik. Ulrich Troitzsch zum 60. Geburtstag* (Münster et al., 1998), 251–8, 253–5.

[34] E. Bendikat, 'Städtische Umweltverschmutzung durch Verkehrsemissionen: Öffentliche Debatten und politisch-administrative Interventionen in Deutschland von 1900 bis 1939', *Archiv für Kommunalwissenschaften*, 1, 2000, 94–113.

[35] T. Lessing, *Der Lärm. Eine Kampfschrift gegen die Geräusche unseres Lebens* (Wiesbaden, 1908), 45.

[36] To quote just one of many literary examples: T. Mann, *Der Tod in Venedig* (Frankfurt/M., 1992), 18; Mann in this passage is mentioning the noise of an approaching tram in his own home town Munich.

standard topic in many novels. But not all writers welcomed the change
in their acoustic environment and the loss of peace and quiet. Theodor
Lessing commented on his first flat in Munich: 'It was the most noisy
flat I have ever lived in. . . . My bed was situated in a surf of sounds.'[37]
And the German playwright Ödon von Horváth even earned comment
by quite literally eliminating noise from his plays: thousands of
instructions for *Stille* (the stage direction for 'silence') can be found in
his literary output.[38] However, not all 'brainworkers' abhorred the new
urban soundscape. Luigi Russolo declared: 'Life in the past was
quietness. With the invention of the machine in the 19th century the
sound was born'. And noise, so the Italian futurist claimed, was not at
all bad in itself: what was needed was to compose all the sounds and
noises of the modern city, to gain a new, harmonious 'art of sound'.[39]
Admittedly futurism never gained importance as some sort of 'guiding
culture' of the era; but as a distinguishing feature of its time Russolo's
statement still keeps its place.[40]

Public action against the noise problem kept its place, although the
early enthusiasm of the anti-noise campaigners faded away. Anti-noise
organizations were common in many industrialized countries in the
years between the wars – and rather atypical in their attempt to
cooperate on an international level during a period of political tension.
The most noticeable of these societies was the American Society for the
Suppression of Unnecessary Noise, founded by Julia Barnett-Rice in
1906.[41] Quite distinct from its German counterpart, this society gained
considerable support and influence in the States, not the least because of
its pragmatic, economy-friendly approach to the question of noise
pollution. On the other hand, the weakness of most European
associations can be explained by their elitist, conservative approach to

[37] T. Lessing, *Einmal und nie wieder* (Gütersloh, 1969), 290.

[38] B. Henrichs, 'Meiner Liebe entgehst du nicht! Vom Reden und Schweigen, vom Sehnen und Würgen: Das kurze stürmische Leben des deutschen Dichters Ödon von Horváth', *Süddeutsche Zeitung* 8 December 2001.

[39] L. Russolo, 'Die Geräuschkunst', H. Schmidt-Bergmann, *Futurismus. Geschichte, Ästhetik, Dokumente* (Hamburg, 1993), 235–41, Quotation 235.

[40] A modern attempt to relive Russolo's aesthetical considerations of creating urban sound spheres was presented by A. Bosshard, 'Klangarchitektur in urbanen Räumen', www.hoerspielwoche.de/index, 15 May 2003. See also A. Mayr, 'Die Komponierte Stadt. Ein klangzeitlicher Zugriff auf den Raum', D. Henckel and M. Eberling, eds, *Raumzeitpolitik* (Opladen, 2002), 41–60.

[41] R.W. Smilor, 'Toward an environmental perspective: The anti-noise campaign, 1893–1932', in M.V. Melosi, ed., *Pollution and Reform in American Cities, 1870–1930* (London, 1980), 135–51. See also L. Baron, 'Noise and Degeneration. Theodor Lessing's Crusade for Quiet', *Journal of Contemporary History*, 17, 1982, 165–78.

the problem, which led them to cooperate with other backward-looking societies. In Britain the Anti-Noise League usually campaigned and lobbied in close collaboration with traditional amenity societies. In 1936 an official of the Anti-Noise League gave a lecture in Bristol before an audience from the Bristol Kyrle Society, a group devoted to the 'preservation of all that is old in historic Bristol'. Mr Abbott declared that it was the aim of his society 'to reduce noise and to add to the greater comfort of people living in large towns and cities. In so far as noise is an offence against beauty, our society is interested in and should endeavour to co-operate with every effort to combat the nuisance of unnecessary noises.'[42] The result was disappointing – as long as there was no common definition of what constituted 'unnecessary' noise, anti-noise societies lacked a clear-cut aim and a structured and well-organized method of achieving it. It should however be mentioned that in Germany in the 1930s one can find early traces of a new awareness of the urban acoustic environment: thus in Berlin-Schöneberg a local campaign combated noise generated by the heavy air traffic at the local airport.[43]

Reluctance and Engagement in the Fight Against Noise

Noise pollution as a theme in environmental history is highly problematic. The most common mistake is to end up with a statement such as 'since time immemorial man has had to come to terms with unpleasant noises'. Of course, there are the occasional references to the elderly Goethe standing next to a loaded cannon to immunize himself from disturbances associated with crying children and noisy neighbours. This story sounds quite similar to the snobbish outbursts of Theodor Lessing, who was fighting noise generated by people amongst whom he lived – workers' pain and possible deafness as a result of unbearable industrial noise was not the subject of this particular philosopher's complaints. Moreover, as late as 1972 Joachim Kaiser uttered a 'loud word' against noise: his subject was the 'terror' of unremitting music in supermarkets and other public places. 'The word "Silence"', Kaiser wrote, 'today sounds as outdated as "bridegroom" or the "tragedy of love".'[44] Of course Kaiser's complaint mirrored the view of the middle-classes – the real dangers

---

[42] *Annual Report Bristol Kyrle Society 1936*, 5; Bristol Record Office 33199 (14).
[43] Legal progress however remained meagre, see the leading German encyclopaedia *Der Große Brockhaus*, Vol. 11 (Leipzig, 1932), 137.
[44] *Süddeutsche Zeitung*, 17 Aug. 1972.

connected with noise probably hardly ever reached the sensitive ears of the music critic of the *Süddeutsche Zeitung* in Munich.

However, the major difference between the noise experience of Lessing or even of the Torley brothers and our own is the sheer amount of noise emitted from very different sources. In the years before the first world war the average noise level on a main thoroughfare was estimated at 50 decibels; at the end of the 1930s it was measured at 65 decibels – far beyond the limit at which noise becomes a danger to health. Since then, the increase has been a steady one, as can be seen from the annual statistical publications of the *Umweltbundesamt* (Federal Agency for the Environment). And although the noise question has never achieved the notoriety of Germany's polluted rivers, the public interest in and commitment to noise campaigns has not been inconsiderable: at the moment there are more than 30 non-governmental organizations fighting against the proposed enlargement of Frankfurt/Main airport. It should however be noted, that noise pollution and the fight for a quieter urban environment remained on the agenda of middle-class social reformers, local administrators, engineers and builders for most of the last century. However, it never achieved the prominence of other urban environmental questions. Perhaps it makes sense to concur with Alain Corbin, who reminds us of the important borderline between the spoken and the unspoken. 'The noise of motor vehicles is increasingly disappearing as a key picture in the description of cities, without our being able to pin down why it has disappeared from our perception. Is it because it is ubiquitous and no longer attracts attention, or do we deliberately keep quiet about it because it is so infinitely banal?'[45] The American composer John Cage explored the 'ins' and 'outs' of this aural borderline when he wrote his most famous piece '4'33' in 1952: a piano player entering the stage, opening the piano lid and remaining seated for more than four and a half minutes in front of the instrument without producing a single note.

There are two phases of anti-noise activity in Germany which deserve more attention than they have received in the past. The period between the wars has often been neglected by historians of the environment. In those years arguably not only the amount of noise produced but also the character of and attitude towards noise underwent a considerable change. Those years saw deliberate attempts to get rid of 'unnecessary' noise, even during the Hitler period. The second phase is the period between the

---

[45] Quoted in U.C. Schmidt, 'Urban Norms, Women, and Modern Media. German Radio after 1930', unpubl. paper, 1; in a more commonplace way this phenomena was described in an article by the German periodical 'Hobby', see Dipl.-Ing. G.W., 'Lärm. Interessante Einzelheiten, die nur wenig bekannt sind', in *Hobby*, May 1967, 68–73.

immediate aftermath of the second world war and the environmental movement of the 1970s. The first question in this context would centre on the experience of the war years. This period was marked by a mixture of extreme and frightening noise levels during aerial bombardment and unusual quietness due to lack of industrial resources towards the end of the conflict. The blackout also reduced levels of noise. In what ways did those often traumatic memories influence attitudes towards noise in the postwar period?[46] The 1950s were not only characterized by an extension and diffusion of noise, caused by the breakthrough of a consumer society in the Federal Republic of Germany,[47] but they also witnessed serious attempts to reduce the impact of these developments. Even long-time Chancellor Konrad Adenauer occasionally asked governmental specialists to think about noise abatement.[48] The growing number of non-governmental organizations which were fighting against noise began to believe that they were receiving a degree of support for their campaign for a quieter society. Most of these initiatives have not yet been investigated. A multi-party group of members of Parliament in the 1950s tried to initiate noise abatement on the national level, but proved unsuccessful and disbanded very rapidly. But there are other non-governmental organizations, small committees of specialists such as a working group in the VDI, the national organization of German engineers, or the *Deutsche Arbeitsring für Lärmbekämpfung*. The society was established in 1952. Its aim was to work as a communication platform for people suffering from noise and to convert all 'noise sinners' not yet convinced by the necessity to spare their fellow-citizens unnecessary noise.[49] 'Silence', the society proclaimed, 'is not only the first duty of the citizen, but also his first right.'[50] For more than half a century the DAL has influenced the debate

[46] The famous German conductor Joseph Keilberg in a letter from 1948 utters the conviction, that in those days it is important, even when playing classical music, to be 'economical with everything that is loud and noisy'; Süddeutsche Zeitung 21 Jun. 2003.

[47] A. Andersen, 'Das 50er-Jahre-Syndrom – Umweltfragen in der Demokratisierung des Technikkonsums', *Technikgeschichte*, 1998, 329–44

[48] F. Uekötter, '*Die lange Tradition der Umweltpolitik. Diskussion und Bekämpfung von Luftverschmutzung in Deutschland und den USA 1880–1970*', *Bielefeld University PhD thesis*, 2001, 377–8.; see also D. Klenke, *Bundesdeutsche Verkehrspolitik und Motorisierung. Konflikträchtige Weichenstellungen in den Jahren des Wiederaufstiegs* (Stuttgart, 1993), 164.

[49] *Mitteilungen des Arbeitsringes für Lärmbekämpfung*,1, 1954, 1.

[50] 'Kampf dem Lärm', *Mitteilungen des Deutschen Arbeitsringes für Lärmbekämpfung* 8 Septembre 1955, 2. The quotation goes back to the famous words of the Prussian minister Graf von der Schulenburg-Kehnert after the Prussian army had lost the battle of Jena and Auerstedt against Napoleon's troops. The original quotation did not however ask citizens to remain silent but to maintain order.

on noise in this country. Considering the progress made in those years with respect to legal decrees such as the *Technische Anleitung Lärm* (Technical Instruction for Noise) and other parliamentary initiatives to combat noise, these societies should be fully investigated by environmental historians.[51]

Further Prospects of a History of Noise Pollution

It has been argued in this paper that notwithstanding the intriguing history of noise, acoustic pollution and the fight for noise abatement in the early stages of industrialization, historians of the environment should look more closely at the recent history of noise abatement and the fight for a quieter urban environment. The modern noise problem is a child of twentieth century urbanism and consumerism. Here we can find traces and early developments in relation to the shaping of mentalities, the search for political and social solutions and the definition and implementation of administrative measures, which foreshadow contemporary environmental concerns.[52] The way noise was argued about and brought into public debate is an important part of the manner in which modern society accustomed itself to the repercussions of modernity and sought answers to new and formerly unknown threats.

Another reason why 'noise' is an important subject for environmental historians lies in the fact that, quite contrary to traditional industrial pollutions, it is not restricted to industrial areas. How noise was publicly perceived – although in a socially stratified manner – seems to indicate that 'acoustic pollution' was not necessarily seen solely as a problem of modern industrial society. How this perception worked at the local level remains an open question, as does the issue of the cultural construction of noise and noise perception: when does noise become pollution? What makes noise a polluting phenomenon? What seems obvious is that noise cannot be socially isolated. In this sense the argument of *Ortsüblichkeit* (the typical environmental standard of a certain region) did not play a major role in the debate for a lengthy period. When the mode of noise production changed from industrial emissions to individually shaped

---

[51] For a comparative perspective on NGO activities and early government responses, see B.W. Clapp, *An Environmental History of Britain since the Industrial Revolution* (Harlow, 1994), 144–5.

[52] In this sense the history of urban noise and of noise abatement in the city may fit into the broad definition of an urban environmental history presented by Martin Melosi; M.V. Melosi, 'The Place of the City in Environmental History', *Environmental History Review*, Spring 1993, 1–23, 2.

noise clusters (intensified by the high density of living in the modern city), responsibility for the reduction of the noise-plague could no longer be handed over to government or industry. The modern noise problem is to a high degree a problem of the individual 'producer' – and in this sense perhaps the most modern of the traditional environmental hazards connected with industrialization and urbanization.

Concentrating on the development of the noise question in the twentieth century thus offers a cluster of possibilities. First, it helps to avoid writing the kind of déjà vu history, which has tended to be influential during the early years of environmental historical investigation. Second, it makes it easier to find a common language, common sensibilities, impressions and ideas about a subject, which like all sensual experiences will always depend on the person who describes his or her own perceptions.[53] Third, it places the study of the history of man's more or less noisy environment in the context of the 'new' environmental history, which has not only designated the 1950s as a decisive period, but which is also trying to close the gap between a history of the environment in the age of the industrial revolution and the years of the breakthrough of the contemporary environmental movement. Noise pollution still plays a minor role in the overall debate on environmental hazards and challenges. But it is evident that the question of how to make the human environment at least a little less noisy and how to safeguard the increasingly important resource of quietness is gaining ground. The demands for a more restrictive and at the same time more innovative strategy to combat the 'noise plague' issued at 'Noise Awareness Day' 2002[54] indicate that noise abatement could play a leading role when new concepts of bargaining with emissions come to be discussed and put to the test.

---

[53] The warning, not to take the shortcut from our sensual feelings and impressions to that of former times, which may have used the same words for quite different sensations, has been given by Lucien Febvre half a century ago; quoted in R. Jütte, *Geschichte der Sinne. Von der Antike bis zum Cyberspace* (München, 2000), 20.

[54] 'Kein ausreichender Schutz gegen Lärm', *Süddeutsche Zeitung*, 24 Apr. 2002.

CHAPTER FOURTEEN

Environmental Justice, History and the City: The United States and Britain, 1970–2000[1]

Bill Luckin

Contexts

This paper explores linked issues in the historical sociology of academic knowledge. It seeks to unravel relationships between environmental activism and the shaping of national variants of environmental history.[2] Engaging with differences between recent developments in the United States and the United Kingdom, the essay suggests that, in synchronization with the onset of a more overtly urban bias among grass-roots activist movements, the environmental historical community in America evolved rapidly between the 1970s and the beginning of the new century. This thirty year period witnessed animated interaction between overtly political concerns and divisive ideological and intellectual issues – particularly in relation to race, gender, cultural relativism and postmodernism.[3] The

[1] I am very grateful to David Luckin, Chris Rootes, Joel Tarr and my fellow co-editors for their advice on earlier drafts.

[2] The European dimension should not, of course, be excluded from a survey of this kind. In this respect, a credible case can be made for arguing that, in terms of *distinctive national style*, the sub-discipline is making more rapid progress in Germany, Scandinavia and France than in Britain. For the evolution of the European discipline as a whole, see, successively, P. Brimblecombe and C. Pfister, eds, *Silent Countdown: Essays in European Environmental History* (London and Berlin, 1990); D. Schott, ed., *Energy and the City in Europe: From Preindustrial Wood Shortage to the Oil Crisis of the 1970s* (Stuttgart, 1997); C. Bernhardt, ed., *Environmental Problems in European Cities in the Nineteenth and Twentieth Centuries* (Munster and New York, 2001); G. Massard-Guilbaud, H.L. Platt and D. Schott, eds, *Cities and Catastrophes: Coping with Emergency in European History* (Frankfurt am Main, Berlin and New York, 2002); C. Bernhardt and G. Masssard-Guilbaud, eds, *The Modern Demon: Pollution in Urban and Industrial Societies* (Clermont-Ferrand, 2002); and B. Luckin, 'Pollution in the City', in M. Daunton, ed., *The Cambridge Urban History of Britain: Volume 3: 1840–1950* (Cambridge 2000), 207–208.

[3] R.J. Evans, *In Defence of History* (London, 1997), provides a succinct overview, albeit from a predominantly 'conservative' perspective, of the great debates within the historical mainstream between the 1970s and the near-present.

American community expanded rapidly in terms of numbers of practitioners and generated its own internal controversies, notably vis-à-vis the emergence of a distinctively urban-environmental as opposed to long-established agro-ecological lineage.[4] More recently, American historians have begun to engage with the concept of 'environmental justice', a term encapsulating commitment to the belief that insupportable discrepancies in quality of life experienced by inhabitants of deeply deprived inner city areas and an environmentally privileged suburbia must be rapidly and radically narrowed.[5]

However, environmental justice means different things to different people. Adherents of what is here defined as the 'wide spectrum' approach, exemplified by the work of Dolores Greenberg, believe that the concept should be brought into play to strengthen and legitimate contemporary political struggle. Scholars like Greenberg are also deeply committed to eradicating 'eco-racism', a concept based on the argument that to a far greater degree than any other socio-economically disadvantaged group it is people of colour, both historically and in the present, who have been most cynically subjected to life-threatening levels of urban degradation.[6] Here, as in other contexts, the 'class/race'

[4] See here D. Worster, 'Transformations of the earth: toward an agroecological perspective in history', *Journal of American History*, 76, 1989, 1087–1100; M. Melosi, 'The place of the city in environmental history', *Environmental History Review*, 17, 1993, 1–23; C.M. Rosen and J.A. Tarr, 'The importance of an urban perspective in environmental history', *Journal of Urban History*, 20, 1994, 299–310; W. Cronon, 'A place for stories: nature, history and narrative', *Journal of American History*, 78, 1991–92, 1347–76. These debates have been critically evaluated in B. Luckin, 'Varieties of the environmental', *Journal of Urban History*, 24, 1997–98, 510–23.

[5] There is now a massive literature on the definition, 'strengths' and 'weaknesses' of the concept of environmental justice, but see within the present context M.V. Melosi, 'Equity, eco-racism and environmental history', *Environmental History Review*, 19, 1995, 1–16 and the same author's 'Environmental justice, political agenda setting, and the myths of history', in M. Melosi, *Effluent America: Cities, Industry, Energy and the Environment* (Pittsburgh, 2001), 238–62. A creatively skeptical account is provided by C.H. Foreman Jr., *The Promise and Peril of Environmental Justice* (Washington, DC, 1998). Comprehensive theoretical overviews include D. Harvey, *Justice, Nature and the Geography of Difference* (Oxford, 1996), part 4 and R. Brulle, *Agency, Democracy and Nature: The U.S. Environmental Movement from a Critical Theory Perspective* (Cambridge, MA and London, 2000).

[6] D. Greenberg, 'Reconstructing race and protest: environmental justice in New York City', *Environmental History*, 5, 2000, 223–50. On eco-racism, see R.D. Bullard, *Dumping in Dixie: Race, Class and Environmental Quality* (Boulder, Colorado, 1990); R.D. Bullard, ed., *Unequal Protection: Environmental Justice and Communities of Color* (San Francisco, 1994); and A. Szasz, *Ecopopulism: Toxic Waste and the Movement for Environmental Justice* (Minneapolis, 1994).

dichotomy remains powerfully present in American historical and social scientific discourse. On the other hand, historians like Harold Platt deploy environmental justice in a style which clearly differentiates between past and present and largely eschews direct reference to eco-racism. Platt argues that late nineteenth century urban reformers drew on quite different ideological, linguistic and cultural resources to those used by early twenty-first-century activists engaged in the battle for local, regional and national environmental equity.[7]

Environmental history in Britain during this period remained under-developed. Numbers of practitioners were small and distanced themselves from controversial theoretical and methodological debate. At the level of political activism, British, like American, environmental movements, appeared to become increasingly involved with urban issues. But in this paper it is argued that change of this kind was more apparent than real. At the same time a deeply imbedded anti-urban-industrial ethos continued to be reflected in the preoccupations of the environmental historical community. Thus only in the 1990s would the sub-discipline generate overviews and monographs which began to do even cursory justice to key issues during the peak period of industrialization between the mid-nineteenth and early twentieth centuries.[8] We shall also note that, during that same decade, a minority within a minority of networks concerned with environmental activism, influenced by developments in the United States, began to undertake investigations into aspects of contemporary urban environmental injustice.

Might we, then, be justified in assuming that environmental activists and historians in the United Kingdom will in the future devote increased attention to the urban variable? Not necessarily: fundamental historical and cultural differences, rooted in the differing intensity of ethnic

---

[7] H.L. Platt, 'Jane Addams and the ward boss revisited: class, politics and public health in Chicago, 1890–1930', *Environmental History*, 5, 2000, 194–222. See also the same author's *Shock Cities: The Environmental Transformation and Reform of Manchester, UK and Chicago, USA* (forthcoming, Chicago, 2005).

[8] See in particular B.W. Clapp, *An Environmental History of Britain since the Industrial Revolution* (London, 1994); T.C. Smout, *Nature Contested: Environmental History in Scotland and North England since 1600* (Edinburgh, 2000) and J. Sheail, *An Environmental History of Twentieth Century Britain* (Basingstoke, 2002). It should, however, be noted that urban-industrialism necessarily constitutes a relatively minor theme in Smout's account. Sheail's study comprises a series of linked case-studies heavily influenced by administrative concerns. In many respects S. Mosley, *The Chimney of the World: A History of Smoke Pollution in Victorian and Edwardian Manchester* (Cambridge, 2001) is the most convincing monograph yet published on the urban-environmental fortunes of a single British city during the modern period. The literature as a whole is evaluated in Luckin, 'Pollution in the city', 207–28.

conflict in the two countries during the last century and a half, will probably tend to make it less likely that eco-racism will be as ardently championed in Britain as in America. As a corollary, its natural bed-mate – environmental injustice – will be likely to occupy a less prominent position in public and scholarly debate. However, this conclusion is not set in stone. For were British environmental historians finally to engage more enthusiastically with theoretical and methodological debate in the disciplinary mainstream, a much wider range of hitherto marginalized research topics, which do indeed relate to the issues of social, economic and environmental equity in the nineteenth and twentieth century city, might establish themselves. In that sense, both for activists and historians, the future remains open. Much, however, will depend on the role played by the urban historical community in Britain, and the manner in which that long-established sub-discipline reacts to environmentally focused work that has been produced since the early 1990s. If British environmental scholars have too often remained blind to the urban variable, historians of the city have thus far resisted full engagement with methodologies and findings generated by the more youthful sub-discipline.

The Founding of a Creed

The process whereby the concept of environmental justice came to be partially appropriated by a small number of historians working on the late nineteenth and early twentieth century American city, is now well documented.[9] From the later 1970s urban activists grew increasingly impatient with traditional organizations such as the Sierra Club, National Wildlife Federation and National Audubon Society. These bodies were accused of being more concerned with threatened species and the preservation of wilderness than improvement in conditions endured by city-dwellers forced to live in heavily degraded downtown neighbourhoods. Militants campaigned against toxicity-producing waste disposal policies, lead poisoning attributable to inner city highway construction and countless forms of industrial pollution. Gaining extensive media coverage in the aftermath of the much-publicized Love Canal, New York State and Warren County, North Carolina episodes in 1978 and 1982, direct action groups established local and then regional and national organizations.[10] Angry community reaction to corporate

---

[9] See Melosi, 'Equity and eco-racism' and 'Environmental history and political agenda setting'.

[10] R.D. Bullard and B.Wright, 'The politics of pollution: implications for the black community', *Phylon*, 47, 1986, 71–8.

and governmental indifference to health threats in poor neighbourhoods contributed to an enhanced sense of empowerment. In time, environmental coalesced with broader political and feminist concerns. Here eco-racism constituted a powerful rallying-cry. As John Agyeman has noted, environmental issues between the 1970s and the beginning of the new century were redefined in terms of 'justice, equity and rights'. At the same time, the term 'environment' itself underwent discursive transformation, becoming a live issue for those who saw themselves as direct successors to the civil rights movement.[11] By the late 1980s, long-established pressure groups had started to incorporate radical grass-roots strands into traditional agendas. Initially, it was argued that health-destroying pollution endured in poor communities, in which ethnic minorities were frequently over-represented, should be redistributed outwards to the suburbs. However, a minority of activists now argued that the well-tried slogan 'not in my backyard' should be replaced by 'not in anyone's backyard'. Ecological and global discourses in this sense came to be more widely articulated. As Andrew Dobson has noted, a minority of activists began to adopt increasingly holistic political attitudes towards relationships between men, women and urban nature. Nevertheless, for a majority, the idea of environmental justice remained inextricably linked to the anti-eco-racist belief that white suburbanites enjoyed an unjustifiably and, so it was argued, 'unconstitutionally' superior quality of life to that endured by people of colour living in grossly degraded inner cities and run-down suburbs.[12] Conflicts of the latter type remained local and regional rather than 'ecological' or 'global'. In addition, it was argued by academics committed to environmental justice and opposition to eco-racism that increased local awareness of triggers of pollution crises served to empower the politically powerless. In turn local conflict revealed the extent to which city, state and federal governments had manipulated political systems to conserve an inegalitarian status quo.

Meanwhile, American environmental history went through several cycles of change. Traditionally defined in agro-ecological terms, in the early 1970s the sub-discipline began to engage with the city. Inspired by

---

[11] J. Agyeman, 'Constructing environmental (in)justice: transatlantic tales', *Environmental Politics*, 11, 2002, 36.

[12] A. Dobson, *Justice and the Environment: Concepts of Environmental Sustainability and Dimensions of Social Justice* (Oxford, 1998), 23–6. The key contrast is between individual local and potentially politically explosive conflicts associated with immediate urban problems and those centred on global well-being – the supposedly conventional preoccupation of the 'non-materialist' new social movement. For context here see the paper in this volume by Jens Ivo Engels.

the pioneering research of Joel Tarr, and subsequently of Martin Melosi and William Cronon, scholars investigated urban infrastructural and ecological issues.[13] From the 1980s onwards work informed by feminist principles complemented an increasing range of publications on public water supply, sewage and garbage disposal systems. Drawing on historiographical developments rooted in the 1970s, researchers pointed to a distinctive women's role in relation to pollution, 'municipal housekeeping' and social reform.[14] In addition, in the 1980s influential urban-environmental historians engaged with issues associated with post-modernism and cultural relativism. Thus far scholars had tended to assume that mountains, prairies, plains, streets, factories, sewers and rivers were indisputably 'out there', non-problematic phenomena unambiguously available to social-scientific investigation. However, developments in cultural, critical and literary theory, and in historical geography, now implied that such confidence could not be justified. Just as travel writers return from distant lands with divergent accounts of topography, agriculture, industry, and social structure, so environmental historians might need to acknowledge that different individuals or interest groups view the 'same' landscape or city in different ways. This debate about perspective, evidence and interpretation ended in compromise. Protagonists admitted the existence of a wide diversity of perceptual and ideological stances but refused to follow a relativist route that would have implied that accounts of environmental change can *only* be culturally determined. Rather than commit themselves to this agenda, a majority of scholars in the United States opted for the idea that a wide range of different narratives should be subjected to

[13] See J.A. Tarr, *The Search for the Ultimate Sink: Urban Pollution in Historical Perspective* (Akron, Ohio, 1996); M.V. Melosi, *Garbage in the City: Refuse, Reform and the Environment 1880–1920* (College Station, Texas, 1981) and the same author's *The Sanitary City: Urban Infrastructure in America from Colonial Times to the Present* (Baltimore, 2000). W. Cronon, *Nature's Metropolis: Chicago and the Great West* (New York, 1991) has already attained classic status both within the environmental historical community and the disciplinary mainstream.

[14] The starting-point for this historiographical tendency was C. Merchant, *The Death of Nature: Women, Ecology and the Scientific Revolution* (San Francisco and London, 1979). See also S. Hoy, 'Municipal housekeeping: the role of women in improving urban sanitation practices', in M.V. Melosi, ed., *Pollution and Reform in American Cities* (Austin, Texas, 1980), 173–98; M. Flanagan, '"The city profitable, the city liveable": environmental policy, gender and power in Chicago in the 1910s', *Journal of Urban History*, 22, 1996, 163–90; A. Gugliotta, 'Class, gender, and coal smoke: gender, ideology and environmental justice', *Environmental History*, 5, 2000, 165–93; and H.L. Platt, 'Invisible gases: smoke, gender and the redefinition of environmental policy in Chicago 1900–1920', *Planning Perspectives*, 10, 1995, 67–97.

controlled interrogation.[15] The extent to which the environmental historical community in the United States was transformed by engagement in these intense theoretical and methodological interchanges should not be over-estimated. Just as many mainstream political historians in Britain ignored debates about postmodernism, cultural relativism and the linguistic and cultural turns, so many American environmental scholars ignored the 'theory wars'. At the same time, research into predominantly agro-ecological problems continued to prosper.

By the end of the twentieth century, environmental historians in America were producing very large numbers of case-studies of scientific, technological and systemic change; case-studies of communal and legal conflict over pollution of air and water; and articles and monographs on economic and cultural tension between town and country. Much of this work was set within a broadly ecological and 'systems' framework. Indeed, a case can be made for arguing that over-emphasis on the ecological variable may have played a role in persuading a small number of historians to turn, during the most recent cycle of debate, to the application of concepts derived from the environmental justice movement to the late nineteenth and early twentieth century American city.[16] The image of the city as 'system' appeared to have excluded an issue that had long preoccupied urban historians in the United States – the establishment, maintenance and deployment of political power which exerted a massive impact, either directly or indirectly, on collective quality of life and relative equity in terms of the distribution of economic social, environmental and cultural resources. Appropriation of the concept of environmental injustice, it was argued, would allow direct engagement with the issue of equality – and, more specifically, who had benefited, and failed to benefit, from improvements in the provision of urban housing and public utilities. It might also make it possible to gain a clearer understanding of how landlords, policy-makers and power brokers had so effectively spatially segregated and regulated the urban sphere. Given the interactive nature of relationships between present and past, we should hardly be surprised that an approach claiming to show how injustice had been legitimated and reaffirmed in the contemporary America city began to exert a

---

[15] See, in particular, the works cited in Cronon, 'A place for stories'.

[16] However, this should not be interpreted as implying that the major American urban-environmental 'pioneers' in the United States, and particularly Tarr, Cronon and Melosi, turned a blind eye to the issue of the distribution of power in the city. The titles cited in fn. 13 above are intimately concerned with the political variable, though within a predominantly ecological and systems-dominated paradigm.

magnet-like attraction over members of the urban environmental community.

Thus, in a persuasive article, Harold Platt draws on and modifies ideas derived from the environmental justice movement to reinterpret resistance on the part of corrupt city bosses and landlords to take action against sub-standard and disease-ridden working-class housing. Platt points to the central role played by 'public policy . . . in the degrading of the quality of life' and in spatially 'creating places [that were] below accepted standards of human health and decency'.[17] He claims to bring 'an environmental perspective to bear on urban politics that can help situate ethnicity, patronage, and machines within broader, more inclusive frameworks of analysis'.[18] Platt interrogates the intolerable conditions endured by working-class inhabitants. The key historical moment in Chicago proved to be a series of reformist investigations into a typhoid epidemic that ravaged the Nineteenth Ward in 1903 and which demonstrated that poverty-stricken areas were massively more likely than affluent suburbs to be afflicted by filth diseases. Platt argues that the strategy developed by the urban reformer Jane Addams, of 'exposing corruption by focusing public attention on carefully selected landlords and inspectors was a logical and effective way to launch the struggle for environmental justice'.[19] However, Platt acknowledges the resilience of a corrupt party machine and admits that 'politicians simply moved their base of operations from the health to the building department which became the new den of thieves for loyal patronage workers'.[20]

Dolores Greenberg's survey of the reconstruction of race and protest in New York City is informed by what is termed in this paper a 'wide spectrum' variant of the paradigm, a perspective which uses the historical chronicle of gross urban inequity explicitly to support the struggle for environmental justice in the here and now. Greenberg asserts that people of colour 'historically lacked protection of their most fundamental right – the right to life'.[21] Moreover, the legacy of slavery involved an 'inequitable distribution of well-being as old as the ecological transformation occasioned by the city's founding'.[22] Explicitly linking past to present, Greenberg insists that 'resistance movements founded on premises of social ecology articulated . . . a reform agenda that bears remarkable similarities to current advocacy'.[23]

---

[17] Platt, 'Jane Addams and the ward boss', 195.
[18] Ibid.
[19] Ibid., 208.
[20] Ibid., 213.
[21] Greenberg, 'Reconstructing race and protest', 223.
[22] Ibid., 224.
[23] Ibid., 225.

During the earlier twentieth century New York witnessed 'environmental justice efforts driven by local attachments, organized by activists from inner-city neighbourhoods, supported by informal national networks, and motivated by the common purpose to redress enmeshed social, political, economic and ecological degradation'.[24] Militants are said to have created 'a heritage of national protest for by-passing racist political processes that sustained poverty, powerlessness and unequal protection'.[25] Characterizing Harlem as an 'endangered habitat', Greenberg contends that, by the 1960s, the lessons of the past had persuaded environmental activists to participate in 'a historic first', not only in the contested district itself but 'around the world', with 'popular ecological resistance movements . . . challeng[ing] fused inequities of place, governance, and distributive justice'. Greenberg goes on to argue that 'the wider culture's integration of the reform configuration became a force for social change that encouraged politically marginalized minorities to further strengthen protests against government failure to act on their behalf'.[26] As in our own times, so in nineteenth and earlier twentieth century New York, 'everyday knowledge of inherited patterns of racism and spatial segregation shaped an awareness among people of colour of the connections between environmental and social systems governing their survival'.[27] Where Platt acknowledges the limits of the historical application of ideas derived from the environmental justice movement, Greenberg draws on urban, social and political history to bolster the struggle for urban equality in the early twenty-first century. One variant of the environmental justice paradigm, represented by the Platt article, emphasizes the extent to which non-linearity complicates attempts to make one-to-one comparisons between the struggle for better conditions in the city in the late nineteenth and early twenty-first century. The other, exemplified by Greenberg's contribution, seeks to persuade readers that the words, concepts and categories which energized radical action a hundred and fifty years ago were astonishingly similar, indeed, sometimes *directly* 'led to', the making of the environmental justice movement in the here and now.

Greenberg's criticisms of Andrew Hurley's classic study of Gary, Indiana, bring these issues into full perspective.[28] Hurley's analysis

---

[24] Ibid.
[25] Ibid., 235.
[26] Ibid., 239.
[27] Ibid., 224.
[28] A. Hurley, *Class, Race and Industrial Pollution in Gary, Indiana 1945–1980* (Chapel Hill and London, 1995). See the same author's 'Fiasco at Wagner Electric: environmental justice and urban geography in St Louis',

demonstrates that fine-grained empirical research can frequently transform key activist landmarks into temporary way-stations. In Gary, repeated redrawing of the residential map interacted with the machiavellianism of managers at US Steel to ensure that ever-shifting sectors of the population became subjected to severe levels of atmospheric pollution. Environmental reform groups were established, fragmented, and then came together again. There was little linearity: as always, the past proved itself a different and unknown country. Hurley's portrait complicates the idea of triumphalist environmental 'victory', gives as much attention to progressive 'failure' as to 'success' and highlights the extent to which scientific expertise slowly but indisputably redefined communal perceptions of the epidemiological impact of a massive urban pollution problem. As the inhabitants of the town gradually became aware of the extent of the damage inflicted on their community, increasingly sophisticated surveys of the long-term effects of uncontrolled pollution redefined the nature of risk. At the very end of Hurley's period, US Steel found itself under increasing pressure both to make recompense for the misdemeanors of the past and to conform to enhanced technical-cum-environmental standards in the future. But, even in the 1990s, 'victory' proved elusive: every step forward redefined the nature as well as the shape and thrust of protest. Hurley's study suggests that wide spectrum variants of the environmental justice paradigm oversimplify complex historical narratives. In addition to underplaying the extent to which pollution problems are repeatedly redefined in the light of new scientific knowledge, the model works against a full understanding of shifting relationships between economic and occupational structures and the dynamics of opposition to corporate and governmental malpractice. Hurley's research also underlines the fact that linearity, progressivism, and idealization of the roles of individuals may well inhibit a fully contextualized understanding of environmental conflict.[29] In a word, the wide spectrum paradigm favoured by Greenberg is better suited to the task of legitimating community empowerment in the present than explaining pollution problems in the past. This is not to denigrate social and political movements which seek to reduce appalling inequitable levels of environmental degradation. Nor does a critique of this kind deny the widespread existence and influence of eco-racism. Rather, the aim is to ask questions about the nature and public function of history

Environmental History, 4, 1997, 462–3. Greenberg criticizes Hurley for adopting a model which 'rejects the centrality of race' in favour of an interpretation focusing intensively on 'housing opportunities and political disempowerment'. See Greenberg, 'Reconstructing race and protest', 224.

[29] Hurley, *Class, Race and Industrial Pollution*.

and its role in informing and underpinning the efforts of those engaged in environmental activism and to ask whether interpretative complexity must invariably and inevitably yield to the demands of progressive ideological unity.

Environmental Activism and History in Britain Since 1970

As in the United States, environmental activism in Britain in the 1960s had long been dominated by conservative organizations such as the Council for the Protection of Rural England, the National Trust and the World Wildlife Fund. These bodies had been heavily influenced by elitist preoccupations with the preservation of a purportedly 'untouched' nature.[30] Despite the activities of the Campaign for Nuclear Disarmament, protest against weapons of mass destruction was less developed and less effectively sustained than in other parts of Europe.[31] The founding of Greenpeace and Friends of the Earth in 1970–71 and 1977 generated higher levels of direct action. The former body coordinated demonstrations against a wide range of issues such as corporate indifference towards recycling, the industrialization of the whaling industry, Britain's independent nuclear deterrent and the cruelty of the fur trade. Friends of the Earth protested against American nuclear tests in Alaska, seal culling in Newfoundland and governmental waste disposal policies.[32] Opposition to the construction of ever-larger numbers of motorways also increased during this period. Nevertheless, and despite the fact that the first European Green Party was founded in Britain in 1973, it is difficult to detect a strong association between rising memberships of environmental organizations and radical political change. In Germany, by contrast, parliamentary and extra-parliamentary protest made a significant impact on nuclear energy, toxic waste and highway construction policies.[33] However, during the 1980s, and particularly in the aftermath of the rampantly pro-car policy statement, *Roads for Prosperity* (1989), a new kind of militancy began to achieve a more prominent public profile. The Earth First! coalition held its first

[30] For an important study of the interwar origins of this idiosyncratic collective *mentalite* see D. Matless, *Landscape and Englishness* (London, 1998).
[31] F. Perkin, *Middle-Class Radicalism: The Social Bases of the British Campaign for Nuclear Disarmament* (Manchester, 1968); P. Byrne, *The Campaign for Nuclear Disarmament* (London, 1988) and I. Welsh, *The Nuclear Moment* (London, 2000).
[32] See M. Brown et al., *The Greenpeace Story* (London, 1991) and P. Byrne, *Social Movements in Britain* (London, 1997).
[33] See the contribution by Jens Ivo Engel in this volume.

annual conference in 1992 and rapidly staked a claim as an umbrella coordinator of radical community action against motorway and airport construction, quarrying, open-cast mining and experimentation with genetically modified crops. As in the United States, long established organizations now modified agendas long dominated by the preservation of nature and the protection of endangered species. In the early 1990s alternative, loosely knit groups such as the Women's Environmental Network, the Black Environment Network and the Environmental Justice Network came into being. At the very end of the century, Friends of the Earth's 'Pollution Justice Campaign' began belatedly to target specifically urban issues. Claiming that over 650 of the largest factories in the United Kingdom were to be found close to residential areas with an average annual household income of less than £15,000 (€21,500), the survey confirmed that only five such plants had been established in localities in which families earning over £30,000 (or approximately €43,000) predominated. Over 90 per cent of manufacturing plants in the London region were situated in districts characterized by below average household income while in the North East more than four fifths of large-scale manufacturing units were to be found in areas in which a majority of households earned no more than £5,000 (or approximately €7,010) a year.[34] This was the context within which new radical groups emphasized that traditional conservationist bodies had represented the interests of '[the] well-off, [the] white [and] middle-class'.[35] Appealing to 'community groups, networks, national and local organizations, schools and committed individuals', the Environmental Justice Network echoed the conclusions of the Friends of the Earth factory report and told its six hundred affiliates that the 'poorest communities suffer the worst environments'.[36] To urban and environmental historians, these findings are, of course, unsurprising, indeed very nearly trivial. But that may be to miss the point. The significance of the report was its insistence that issues of this kind, which had thus far been wholly ignored both by British environmental movements and environmental historians, must finally be confronted.

Despite minority interventions of this kind, early twenty-first century British environmental protest movements have continued to be heavily

---

[34] C. Church, 'The quiet revolution: 10 years since Agenda 21. Measuring the impact of community-based sustained development in the UK. Shell Better Britain Campaign'. http:// www.sbbco.co.uk/reports. It should be noted that the exceptionally low incomes cited for the poorest sectors of the urban communities cited in this paragraph clearly exclude individual and family state benefits.

[35] Ibid.

[36] Ibid.

influenced by predominantly rural values. Thus a recent quantitative breakdown of themes dominating protests between 1988 and 1997 reveals that broadly non-urban almost certainly outnumbered broadly urban targets. The most 'active' sector was transport, with demonstrations against new motorways accounting for the bulk of interventions in this sphere. Spurred on by quality of life issues in towns threatened by the ubiquitous culture of the private car, demonstrations of this kind were nevertheless underwritten by an intense desire to defend traditional village life, and intimately related to arcadian, anti-materialist and New Age ideals.[37] The environmental status of the city remained peripheral. The culture of an 'untouched' countryside, closely related to the continued political and cultural influence of the British upper and upper middle classes as well as to the fact that so many members of the 'first industrial nation' sought solace in a rural and arcadian 'vision of England', continued to predominate. The heritage and tourist industries also played a powerful and culturally reinforcing role.

What of British environmental history? In sharp contrast to events in the United States, between the 1970s and the 1990s the sub-discipline remained in a state of suspended animation, largely oblivious to theoretical and methodological controversy within the disciplinary mainstream. Neither the 'limits to growth' debate of the 1970s nor the worldwide emergence of ecological discourses precipitated the formation of a specifically historical academic community.[38] In the small numbers of places in which it was practised the sub-discipline tended to be undertaken by geographers, geologists, climatologists and environmental scientists.[39] However, scholars working on the early modern period – pre-eminently Keith Thomas – published pioneering and invaluable studies of pre-modern attitudes towards nature.[40]

[37] C. Rootes, 'Environmental protest in Britain, 1988–1997', in B. Seel, M. Paterson and B. Doherty, eds, *Direct Action in British Environmental Protest* (London, 2000), 34.

[38] However, within the social scientific community precisely the converse appears to have been the case. See, for example, P.R. Ehrlich and A.H. Ehrlich, *Population, Resources, Environment: Issues in Human Ecology* (San Francisco, 1970) and C. Freeman and M. Jahoda, eds, *World Futures: The Great Debate* (London, 1978).

[39] Many of these texts have adopted a wide lens *longue duree* approach. See, for example, I.G. Simmons, *An Environmental History of Britain: From 10,000 Years Ago to the Present* (Edinburgh, 2001). For a representative example of activist-ecological history, see C. Ponting, *Green History of the World* (Harmondsworth, 1992).

[40] K. Thomas, *Religion and the Decline of Magic: Studies in Popular Beliefs in Sixteenth and Seventeenth Century England* (London, 1971) and the same author's *Man and the Natural World: Changing Attitudes in England 1500–1800* (Harmondsworth, 1984). See, also, among a cluster of books

Institutionally marginalized by economic, social and urban history, research into the environmental tended to be inhibited by long-standing barriers between 'science' and 'non-science' and the widely held belief that work in this field could only be undertaken by scholars whose major expertise was technical and scientific rather than historical.[41]

There may be another kind of explanation for the relative backwardness of environmental history in Britain in the period before approximately 1990. In the late 1970s it had been persuasively argued that the long-running 'standard-of-living' debate would only be settled when larger numbers of researchers engaged with the issue of quality of life in the new industrial society.[42] Only a handful of historians took up the challenge and as a result broadly environmentally-oriented studies of individual towns remained thin on the ground.[43] However, in due course demographic historians and historical epidemiologists began to investigate the extent to which inequalities may have been directly or indirectly linked to a maldistribution of urban resources and utilities. Such work has, inter alia, identified overcrowding as a key variable in relation both to the transmission and increased virulence of micro-organisms responsible for the dissemination of specific diseases. Indeed, British scholars are now moving towards a point at which cause of death data can be used to illuminate historically elusive environmental variables. At the same time, environmental evidence is being deployed to

---

concerned with the 'nature of nature', Peter Coates, *Nature: Western Attitudes since Ancient Times* (London, 1998). Keith Thomas's general approach was brilliantly extended into the nineteenth century by J. Obelkevich in *Religion and Rural Society: South Lindsey, 1825–1875* (Oxford, 1976).

[41] The seminal texts underlying the 'two cultures' debate were C.P. Snow, *The Two Cultures and the Scientific Revolution* (New York, 1959) and F.R. Leavis, *Two Cultures: The Significance of C.P.Snow* (London, 1962).

[42] G.N. von Tunzelmann, 'Trends in real wages 1700–1850, revisited', *Economic History Review*, 32, 1979, 49.

[43] Key aspects of the 'urban sector' would in due course be investigated by A.S. Wohl, *Endangered Lives: Public Health in Victorian Britain* (London, 1983) and J. Hassan, *A History of Water in Modern England and Wales* (Manchester, 1998). See also for studies of individual cities, Mosley, *Chimney of the World* and B. Luckin, *Pollution and Control: A Social History of the Thames in the Nineteenth Century* (Bristol and Boston, 1986). Revealingly, and very much in line with the thrust of the general argument presented in this paper, important British urban environmental studies have also been published by American historians. Pre-eminent among these is C. Hamlin, *Public Health and Social Justice in the Age of Chadwick: Britain, 1800–54* (Cambridge, 1998). But see also D.H. Porter, *The Thames Embankment: Environment, Technology and Society in Victorian London* (Akron, Ohio, 1998). The extent to which Hamlin's conception of 'justice' within a nineteenth century urban context coincides with or diverges from contemporary American activist definitions is an intriguing issue.

throw light on the spatial incidence of bacteriologically and virally distinctive infections.[44] In addition, numerous studies of infant mortality have explored the roles played by class, occupation and locality in determining death rates among the youngest members of the community. Fine-grained analysis of individual household level data has made it possible to identify interactions between housing, incidence of breast-feeding and disposal of domestic waste.[45] It might therefore be hypothesized that the cultural space occupied by environmental history in the United States has been partially appropriated in Britain by demographic and epidemiological history.

Transatlantic Contrasts

Only an arch-British patriot would deny that over the last thirty years environmental history has been dominated by American initiative and American innovation. Breaking with the preoccupation with wilderness studies, a pioneering group of scholars during the 1970s began to investigate urban networks and infrastructure. Engaging somewhat later with theoretical and methodological debate within the disciplinary mainstream, the new community revealed itself to be open to issues of gender. More recently, a small number of historians have begun to explore the potential of the environmental justice paradigm. In Britain, on the other hand, the environmental historical community failed to expand, a state of affairs that may have been related to the dominant values underlying environmental activism, the failure, for whatever reason, of interested academics to make crucial connections between present and past, the pre-existing supremacy of economic, social and urban history and the institutionalized explosion of demographic, medical and epidemiological research.[46] During this period dominant strategies among environmental organizations ranged from the non-confrontational, through public demonstrations to one or another form

---

[44] See R. Woods and J. Woodward, eds, *Urban Disease and Mortality in Nineteenth Century England* (London, 1984); R. Woods and J. Shelton, *An Atlas of Victorian Mortality* (Liverpool, 1997); and R. Woods, *The Demography of Victorian England and Wales* (Cambridge, 2000).

[45] For incisive bibliographical orientation see A. Hardy and S. Szreter, 'Urban fertility and mortality patterns', in Daunton, ed., *Cambridge Urban History Volume 3*, 637–9. N. Williams, 'Death in its season: class, environment and the mortality of infants in nineteenth century Sheffield', *Social History of Medicine*, 5, 1992, 71–94 proved to be a ground-breaking study.

[46] A key institutional factor here has undoubtedly been the very significant support given to these sub-disciplines by the highly influential Wellcome Trust, which is by far the largest grant-giving body of its kind in Europe.

of direct action.[47] However, the most influential, though invariably occluded, *leitmotif* continued to be either openly or tacitly rural. Even the intensification of radical protest during the 1990s has been more heavily influenced by preoccupation with the preservation of village culture than the now fully publicized plight of economically and socially excluded minorities in otherwise unprecedentedly affluent towns and cities. In the United States political activism will undoubtedly ensure that the wide-spectrum environmental justice paradigm becomes increasingly influential.

Continuing to live out the contemporary repercussions of a deeply troubled racial past, and possessing a legal system which encourages citizens to seek equity through the courts in every sphere of communal life, America habitually looks, in its unending quest for the 'good' society, to a quite different set of mediating institutions than have evolved in Britain. In this sense, the environmental justice movement, and eco-racism, could only have attained political and cultural prominence in a nation, which has experienced and continues to live with the multiple legacies of the civil rights movement.[48] Will these traditions and linked ideological concerns enable protagonists of the wide-spectrum paradigm to formulate convincing diagnoses of the inequalities of the urban past? Or will the inherently present-centred nature of this powerful ideology, exemplified by Greenberg's recent contribution, obscure the inherently non-linear historical processes that it seeks to clarify? The question remains open. But in Britain it is to be hoped that environmental historians will finally engage with sociological, ideological and methodological controversy, move closer to the disciplinary mainstream, and focus as intensively on the city – and inequality in the city – as on the countryside.

---

[47] Rootes, 'Environmental protest in Britain'.

[48] Agyeman, 'Constructing environmental (in)justice'. However, it cannot be too strongly emphasized that sometimes openly, sometimes at a subterranean level, racism – and particularly the much discussed phenomenon of 'institutional racism' – is alive and kicking in the United Kingdom. Precisely how this problem should be defined and related to explicitly urban, environmental and historical contexts lies beyond the scope of this paper.

CHAPTER FIFTEEN

'In Stadt und Land': Differences and Convergences between Urban and Local Environmentalism in West Germany, 1950–1980

Jens Ivo Engels

The success of modern environmentalism, following the 'ecological revolution' of the early 1970s, has long attracted the attention of social and political scientists. Recently, historians have also discovered this field of research. Modern environmentalism has frequently been analysed as part of the so-called 'new social movements' phenomenon, a concept which seeks to incorporate and interpret women's, peace, and other organizations advocating 'direct action'. These are stated to be heterogeneous, lacking a precise ideological world view and dedicated to limited and concrete goals. In addition, new social movements are characterized as anti-hierarchical. Novel forms of protest, and particularly civil disobedience, are deployed.[1]

However, the idea of a new social movement has strong normative implications, with protagonists interpreting the existence of such groups as a sign of increasing political commitment. They are also presented as models of participatory action in modern western society. Such evocations strongly resemble self-characterizations presented by the members of these movements. Moreover, three decades after their first

---

[1] On 'new social movements': K.W. Brand, D. Büsser and D. Rucht, *Aufbruch in eine andere Gesellschaft. Neue soziale Bewegungen in der Bundesrepublik* (Frankfurt a.M./New York, 1986); A. Melucci, 'The New Social Movements. A Theoretical Approach', *Social Science Information*, 19, 1980, 199–226; D. Rucht, *Modernisierung und neue soziale Bewegungen. Deutschland, Frankreich und USA im Vergleich* (Frankfurt, 1994). Recent approaches: D. McAdam, J. McCarthy and M. Zald, eds, *Opportunities, Mobilizing Structures, and Framing. Comparative Applications of Contemporary Movement Theory* (Cambridge, 1996); A. Mertig and R. Dunlap, 'Environmentalism, New Social Movements, and the New Class. A Cross-National Investigation', *Rural Sociology*, 66, 2001, 113–36. Critical account: M. Greven, 'Charismatische Herrschaft und Vertrauen in Neuen Sozialen Bewegungen', *Vorgänge*, 160, 2002, 4–16.

emergence, political systems in western societies have not in fact greatly changed. The prevailing model of representative democracy has not been replaced by direct democracy or a grassroots model of political representation. The claim that new social movements have broadened the social range of political action also rests on shaky foundations. Thus, there is evidence that a majority of activists have been members of those same middle-class groups that have traditionally dominated the political process. Moreover, the concept must be interpreted within the context of fundamental socio-cultural change during the late 1960s and early 1970s. It is ill-equipped to explain environmental action during earlier periods. In this respect, recent studies have begun to point to the importance of environmental protection activities in the era before the 'ecological revolution'.[2] The modern movement needs to be analysed within the context of a 'pre-ecological' era.[3]

The new social movement paradigm is strongly linked to Ronald Inglehart's 'post-materialism'.[4] This latter concept is based on the hypothesis that environmental protection became increasingly attractive among western publics in the years after 1970. Motives are claimed to have been non-material and altruistic. Political protest against the establishment and unconventional social behaviour became increasingly widespread. However, these changes should not be exclusively interpreted in terms of values, but rather as a combination of shifting

---

[2] R.H. Dominick, *The Environmental Movement in Germany* (Bloomington, 1992); F.J. Brüggemeier, *Tschernobyl, 26. April 1986. Die ökologische Herausforderung* (München, 1998); K. Hünemörder, *Die Frühgeschichte der globalen Umweltkrise und die Formierung der deutschen Umweltpolitik (1950–1973)* (Stuttgart, 2004); F. Uekötter, *Von der Rauchplage zur ökologischen Revolution. Eine Geschichte der Luftverschmutzung in Deutschland und den USA 1880–1970* (Essen, 2003).

[3] Cf. S. Chaney, *'Visions and Revisions of Nature: From the Protection of Nature to the Invention of the Environment in the Federal Republic of Germany, 1945–1975'*, University of North Carolina at Chapel Hill PhD thesis 1996; J.I. Engels, *Ideenwelt und politische Verhaltensstile von Naturschutz und Umweltbewegung in der Bundesrepublik 1950–1980* (forthcoming).

[4] R. Inglehart, *The Silent Revolution. Changing Values and Political Styles Among Western Publics* (Princeton, 1977); R. Inglehart, *Culture Shift in Advanced Industrial Society* (Princeton, 1990). Critics in P.R. Abramson, 'Postmaterialism and Environmentalism. A Comment on an Analysis and a Reappraisal', *Social Science Quarterly*, 78, 1997, 21–23; S. Cotgrove and A. Duff, 'Environmentalism, Values, and Social Change', *British Journal of Sociology*, 32, 1981, 92–110; M. Klein and M. Potschke, 'Gibt es einen Wertewandel hin zum "reinen" Postmaterialismus? Eine Zeitreihenanalyse der Wertorientierungen der westdeutschen Bevölkerung zwischen 1970 und 1997', *Zeitschrift für Soziologie*, 29, 2000, 202–16; E.H. Witte, 'Wertewandel in der Bundesrepublik Deutschland (West) zwischen 1973 und 1992', *Kölner Zeitschrift für Soziologie und Sozialpsychologie*, 48, 1996, 534–41.

life-styles and evolving modes of cultural expression.[5] In addition, it would be misleading to depict earlier generations as 'materialists' exclusively concerned with attaining economic and social security.[6] There is another empirical argument against linking postmaterialism to environmentalism – action of the latter kind is for the most part the result of multiple motivations, combining economic and non-economic aspects.

Since 'grand theory' concepts such as 'postmaterialism' and 'new social movements' suffer from a number of weaknesses, this paper seeks other categories within which to frame and describe the development of modern environmentalism. It aims to avoid over-simplification and implicitly normative judgements and is linked to empirical findings in relation to the 1970s and earlier decades.

The contribution is concerned with the relationship between urban and rural environmental activism in West Germany between the 1950s and the 1980s. Focusing initially on the 1970s, it examines socio-geographic phenomena, namely the purported cultural opposition of large centres and the provinces. On the one hand 'urban' is compared with 'local', 'provincial' and 'rural' environmentalism. On the other, the notion of 'local' refers both to the countryside as well as to small geographical locations, ranging from villages to minor towns in suburbanized regions. Boundaries between the urban and the local are, of course, difficult to establish. However, this is possibly less important than the fact that this chapter is concerned above all with convergence. This very process will be highlighted through the deployment of ideal types.

The paper analyses environmental action by making use of the idea of 'convergence'. This is a secular process of modernity, which encompasses a wide range of political, economic, social and cultural phenomenona. Convergence is a process which *includes* all spheres, and is not simply a 'colonization' of peripheries by (urban) centres.

---

[5] On the conception of 'culture' as a mode of communication, K. Rohe, 'Politische Kultur und ihre Analyse. Probleme und Perspektiven der politischen Kulturforschung', *Historische Zeitschrift*, 250, 1990, 321–46; T. Mergel, 'Überlegungen zu einer Kulturgeschichte der Politik', *Geschichte und Gesellschaft*, 28, 2002, 574–606.

[6] Cf. for instance the important discussions during the 1950s about the cultural, psychological and medical costs of industrialization: A. Schildt, *Moderne Zeiten. Freizeit, Massenmedien und 'Zeitgeist' in der Bundesrepublik der 50er Jahre* (Hamburg, 1995).

Convergence Between Rural and Urban Spaces and their Images After the Second World War

In the second half of the twentieth century, several factors minimized differences between life in cities and the countryside in West Germany. Structural change within the western economies and their agrarian markets, technical development and formal rural politics stimulated the mechanization and specialization of agriculture as early as the 1950s. Nevertheless, the profitability of this sector continued to decline, to the extent that local and national authorities had to look for alternative roads to growth. Official policy favoured the establishment of commercial and industrial enterprises outside urban centres. An important tool here proved to be the improvement of infrastructure. New roads enabled businesses to establish themselves in small towns and in the countryside. Flourishing private transport made it possible for the rural population to find work within an ever-widening radius.[7]

The massive increase of private transport facilities in the 1960s favoured a counter-current: members of the middle-classes reinforced the growth of suburban settlement and the emergence of dormitory towns.[8] As R.P. Sieferle has noted, suburban sprawl is one of the main factors evening out structural differences between the urban and the rural, resulting in what he terms a 'total landscape'.[9] As a consequence, environmental problems tended to become more similar in the two spheres.

In the late 1950s, conservationists and specialists in landscape protection gradually became interested in the urban condition. This reorientation was part of a larger change. Looking for new opportunities to stir up public interest and gain political support, major figures in the movement decided to move the human quality of life to the top of the agenda. Nature conservation and landscape protection should no longer simply protect animals and the countryside as ends in themselves. They must also be oriented towards generalized social improvement.[10]

---

[7] D. Münkel, ed., *Der lange Abschied vom Agrarland. Agrarpolitik, Landwirtschaft und ländliche Gesellschaft zwischen Weimar und Bonn* (Göttingen, 2000); K. Ditt, R. Gudermann and N. Rüße, eds, *Agrarmodernisierung und ökologische Folgen* (Paderborn, 2001).

[8] P. Exner, 'Vom Bauernhof zur Vorstadt. Metamorphosen der Landgemeinde nach 1945', in C. Zimmermann, ed., *Dorf und Stadt* (Frankfurt a.M., 2001), 245–67; Th. Fliege, 'Zwischen Einkaufszentren und Umgehungsstraßen. Das Land im Suburbanisierungsprozeß am Ende des 20. Jahrhunderts', in C. Zimmermann, ed., *Dorf und Stadt*, 273–88.

[9] R. P. Sieferle, *Rückblick auf die Natur. Eine Geschichte des Menschen und seiner Umwelt* (München, 1997), 186–92, 206–13.

[10] See for instance the proceedings of the 3rd conference of German Nature Protection Commissioners in 1949 at Bad Schwalbach; *Verhandlungen Deutscher Beauftragter für Naturschutz und Landschaftspflege*, 3, 1949, 29–32.

Since its earliest days, conservation had been based among the urban middle-classes and ideologically opposed to life in towns. In Germany, the idea of 'homeland protection' (*Heimatschutz*) had been dominant until the middle of the century. It had advocated conservation of the rural world, arguing that landscape and the rural way of life implied a 'healthy' relationship to the soil. The city was claimed to have lost this quality and was therefore argued to be doomed to social unrest and cultural decline.[11]

After the second world war, conservationists began to accept the fact that a majority of the West German population lived in towns and cities. On the one hand, aesthetic and cultural considerations continued to provide an ideological framework. Criticism of 'mass society' and pathological depictions of urban centres as 'cancerous ulcers' retained their influence until the 1970s.[12] But questions of public health and pollution gained increasing importance.

Within German conservationism, two major solutions were proposed. From 1956 onwards, the 'Nature Conservation Park Society' (*Verein Naturschutzpark*) campaigned successfully for a new approach.[13] It proposed to send urban residents to the countryside in order to improve health and advocated the development of a system of rural holiday areas – the latter suggestion followed the example of the American and British National Park programmes.[14] Other groups envisaged changes in the character of city life.[15] Based on long-established Garden City ideas, this agenda proposed to make towns more like the countryside, or, rather, an idealized notion of the countryside. It recommended the creation of more green space and tidiness, a separation of residential, commercial and industrial areas and low housing densities. In addition, it was characterized by a mix of cultural criticism and 'pre-environmental' concerns. Some experts argued that everyone ought to have a small garden or at least a balcony devoted to plants and window boxes. This assumed that contact with plants, birds and the soil – with 'nature' – would enable humans to establish permanent social ties and enjoy 'genuine' happiness. Other thinkers proposed community health

---

[11] W. Oberkrome, *Teure Heimat. Nationale Konzeption und regionale Praxis von Naturschutz, Landesgestaltung und landschaftlicher Kulturpolitik. Westfalen-Lippe und Thüringen 1900 bis 1960* (Münster, 2004).

[12] On the 1970s cf. several articles in the periodical of BUND called *Natur und Umwelt*.

[13] See the periodical *Naturschutzparke. Mitteilungen des Vereins Naturschutzpark e.V.*

[14] Cf. D. Evans, *A History of Nature Conservation in Britain* (London, 1997); C. Spehr, *Die Jagd nach Natur* (Frankfurt a.M., 1994).

[15] Cf. the periodical *Hilfe durch Grün*, ed. *Arbeitsgemeinschaft für Garten- und Landschaftskultur*, published since 1952.

solutions, and emphasized the positive effect of urban greenery on the local climate, air quality and noise reduction.[16]

In 1961 a group of urban planners, gardening experts, and landscape conservationists published a *Green Charter of the Mainau*. Emphasizing that the foundations of human life were now endangered by pollution, the charter advocated technological, economic and 'natural' adjustments. It invited the authorities to work for the development of a healthy life worthy of human beings living both in cities and the countryside.[17] Over the next few years, the Charter served as a guideline to the newly established German Council on Landscape Protection (*Deutscher Rat für Landespflege*). The Council developed schemes to improve the environmental situation not only in agrarian localities, but also in urban and industrial centres. In so doing, it helped to pave the way for the emergence of environmental protection as a wide-ranging concept.

Together with the triumph of the idea of 'environmental protection' in the 1970s, conceptions of urban and rural space were transformed. Thus conservationists discovered urban and industrial areas as man-made habitats, harbouring species-rich flora and fauna. In contrast to urban planning experts who wished to design cities in styles influenced by rural values, younger biologists became aware that nature could be found in the city. Conceptions of nature thus came to be adapted to the needs of urban activists. At the same time, the public became increasingly aware of the fact that rural areas had themselves been radically modified by human intervention. Landscape protection specialists had long known this to be the case. However, conservationists had refused to modify a dominant conception of the countryside as 'unsullied nature'.[18] Traditional conceptions of a 'natural' landscape versus an 'artificial' city lost their persuasiveness.

Strategies and Motivations in 'Provincial' and 'Urban' Environmental Protest

In terms of differences between urban and rural protest, the most important issues proved to be political style and social structure. Here we shall discuss national and regional conservation associations that should

---

[16] For instance E. Kühn, 'Sonderschau "Hilfe durch Grün" im Rahmen der Gruga 1952 Essen'; in: *Hilfe durch Grün* 1,1952, 25. Critics in O.W. Haseloff, 'Großstadt als Umwelt des Menschen', in P. Vogler and E. Kühn, eds, *Medizin und Städtebau*, 2 vol. (München, 1957), vol. 1, 317–32.

[17] Deutsche Gartenbau-Gesellschaft, ed., *Grüne Charta von der Mainau – mit Kommentar* (Bonn, 1961).

[18] S. Körner, *Das Heimische und das Fremde* (Münster, 2000).

be assigned neither to the urban nor the rural sphere. Rather, the focus is on grassroots activities. Provincial conservation and anti-pollution movements between 1950 and 1970 were influenced by NIMBY assumptions. Protest focused on specific threats to local interests – large-scale industrial disamenity, motorways and dangers to wildlife. In most of these cases, a combination of economic, public health and to a lesser extend 'ecological' factors pushed residents into action. The same was true with respect to urban phenomena such as the protest against the Oer-Erkenschwick power plant in the Ruhr-Basin during the 1950s.[19]

By the 1970s the landscape of environmental action had changed. However, this was more prominent in cities than in the countryside. In provincial localities, environmentalism continued to be predominantly motivated by local concerns, although activists now used arguments which highlighted the global dimension of environmental destruction. The anti-nuclear movement at Wyhl in south-west Germany (c. 1973–75) claimed to fight atomic energy in that locality 'and elsewhere', but local support decreased as the construction of the plant became less likely.[20] In cities, however, several one-issue-movements evolved into citizens' groups addressing different environment-related issues. The Karlsruhe 'Citizens' Action Group for Environmental Protection in the Central Upper Rhine Region' (*Bürgeraktion Umweltschutz Zentrales Oberrheingebiet*) was rooted in protest against the extension of an oil refinery.[21] After a successful campaign in 1972, the group maintained its existence, and addressed further large-scale projects such as motorway construction. This same action group established an information service on environmental problems in the Karlsruhe region. In the same year, it started a research project on air quality. Other themes, including organic gardening, were developed. Between 1970 and 1972 similar groups came into being in almost every large town in West Germany. Many did not begin as protest movements in the narrower sense. Rather, they were founded by citizens anxious to improve their immediate environment in cooperation with urban authorities.

In the early years, these citizens' groups acted less as protest organizations than auxiliaries to official planning and development boards. However, with the passing of the years, rhetoric changed. Citizens' groups began to express disappointment with bureaucratic

---

[19] R. Weichelt, 'Das Kraftwerk der Zeche Ewald Fortsetzung in Oer-Erkenschwick'; *Vestische Zeitschrift*, 90/91, 1991/92, 315–38.

[20] J.I. Engels, 'Südbaden im Widerstand. Der Fall Wyhl', in K. Kretschmer and N. Fuchsloch, eds, *Wahrnehmung, Bewußtsein, Identifikation* (Freiberg, 2003).

[21] On 'Action Group', see its periodical *Der Umweltschutz*.

procedures, denouncing unwillingness on the part of the authorities to acknowledge the validity of citizens' claims. Eventually, relations with urban institutions deteriorated and public subsidies were withdrawn.[22]

Provincial protest rarely flourished without the support of local elites or major socio-political forces such as professional associations, clubs or municipal agencies. In terms of reaction to environmental problems there are two possible scenarios – consensus or conflict. When a whole population found itself threatened by polluting industry, for instance, and could expect to gain economic advantage from such enterprises, consensus was assured. Even when ad hoc protest associations were founded, their activities were based on existing institutions – a district council or even a choral society.[23] Local loyalty ruled out vertical loyalty. Branches of political parties might join a protest even when ordered not to do so by the same party's state board.

The alternative scenario was of a provincial environmental protest generated by conflicting interests. The construction of a motorway, for instance, often divided local residents, with one group expecting economic gain as a result of improved infrastructure, and others being afraid of pollution and the loss of natural habitats. Supporters were frequently local businessmen, backed by district representatives hoping to increase tax yields. At the other extreme, farmers' associations, forestry officials and representatives of hunting organizations attempted to articulate their differing interests, sometimes supported by conservationists. In an area dominated by the tourist trade, hoteliers and restaurant owners tended to vote against large-scale projects.[24] The

---

[22] *Bürgerinitiative Umweltschutz Hannover* as documented in the periodical *Umwelt-Depesche*.

[23] See for instance the activities of *Notgemeinschaft Kleinblittersdorf und Umgebung e.V.* representing citizens and local village administrations on the banks of Saar river, fighting during the 1950s a coal-fired power station situated just on the other side of the border on French territory, Communal Archives of Kleinblittersdorf. Almost the same is true in the case of Wyhl, J.I. Engels, 'Gender Roles and German anti-nuclear Protest. The Women of Wyhl', in C. Bernhardt and G. Massard-Guilbaud, eds, *Le démon moderne. La pollution dans les sociétés urbaines et industrielles d'Europe* (Clermont-Ferrand, 2002), 407–24.

[24] Cf. conflicting local interests in the following cases: Expressway near Eltville (c. 1960–75), Bundesarchiv Koblenz, B 108/18717–18719; B 108/53539–53541. Construction of Motorway 91 (c. 1973–80) as related by E. Hoplitschek, *Der Bund Naturschutz in Bayern* (Berlin 1984). Resistance against Pfälzerwald-Autobahn (c. 1980), Bundesarchiv Koblenz, B 342/886. See also T. Zeller, *Straße, Bahn, Panorama* (Frankfurt a.M., 2002). On tourist trade M. Frese, 'Tourismus und Landschaftsbild. Zielvorstellungen und Erwartungen des Tourismusgewerbes in Westfalen zwischen Kaiserreich und Bundesrepublik', in K. Ditt, R. Gudermann and N. Rüße, eds, *Agrarmodernisierung und ökologische Folgen* (Paderborn, 2001), 603–26.

struggle against motorway No. 91 in western Bavaria near Feuchtwangen in the 1970s was thus designed to coordinate the collection of signatures and the signing of manifestos. This was not a grassroots movement. Rather, it had been established by members of the Bavarian Nature Conservation Association. The *real* core of opposition comprised an informal but nevertheless vigorous alliance of farmers', fishermens', forestry, hunting and conservation associations.

However, large-scale projects affected more than the immediate local world. State or even federal authorities, interest groups and politicians were also involved. Therefore, activists and their opponents sought to create alliances drawn from different decision-making levels. At Eltville near Wiesbaden in the 1960s an expressway was planned which would have menaced a romantic Rhine riverside promenade. Local activists built up a coalition with the Federal Ministry of Transport. The latter selected an alternative route traversing vineyards. However, the Hesse state authorities decided to go ahead with the original plan in order to protect the interests of winegrowers and landowners.[25] In the motorway 91 case, Bavarian conservation and farmers' associations at state level played an important role. A combination of influences and alliances crossing vertical as well as horizontal networks decided whether or not a specific project would be completed. It would therefore be misleading to conceive these processes in terms of a simple model of centre versus periphery.

Sociological research on new social movements has emphasized the presence of a well-educated, younger middle-class generation. Evidence from urban environmental groups, however, suggests that during the early years middle-aged individuals predominated. It was only in the mid-1970s that the younger generation took control.[26] Nevertheless, the existence of urban environmental groups addressing a variety of different issues such as ecological urban planning, toxic waste and bikers' concerns highlights the three main principles of middle-class engagement: First, there was an intention to participate in local politics without becoming involved in party politics. Second, there were quality-of-life issues, related to health and physical well-being. Finally, and to a lesser extent, there was the idea of creating new forms of sociability and leisure-time activities, stimulating the foundation of information centres and the encouragement of public discussions and 'environmental parties'.[27] The environmental movement cannot be distinguished from a

---

[25] Bundesarchiv Koblenz, B 108/18717–18719; B 108/53539–53541.

[26] Cf. *Umwelt-Depesche*.

[27] See presentation of Berlin citizens' group 'Knesebeckstraße' in the periodical *Zitty* 22, 1978. Reprinted in W. Beer and W. Spielhagen, eds., *Bürgerinitiativen, Modell Berlin* (Berlin, 1978).

flourishing sub-political culture involving different groups addressing a large number of issues concerning urban life. These considered themselves to be parts of a substantial movement concerned with social modernization via socio-political grassroots counter-currents.[28]

However, there are many exceptions to this depiction of differences between urban and provincial environmentalism. Suburbanization led to social change, so that a large number of middle-class activists now lived in provincial locations. Gerhard Thielcke was a biologist at the ornithological station at Radolfzell (Lake Constance). At the end of the 1970s, he became president of one of the most important national conservation associations. In 1973 he established at Radolfzell one of the most dynamic cells of what would become the Baden-Würtemberg state branch of the 'Nature and Environment Protection Association' (BUND). Thielcke campaigned for various regional environmental issues, and changed local political behaviour by using public opinion and the regional press to exert pressure on local administrations.[29]

Convergence Through the 'Ideological' Framework

Germany's environmental debate was shaped by federal politics. In 1970 the government published an environmental protection programme, announcing a large number of legislative and administrative measures to reduce pollution.[30] This helped to publicize the concerns of non-governmental organizations in relation to nature protection. During the next few years, the issue of environmental protection became one of the most important topics in German political life. By the end of the decade, discontent reached a point at which activists found it possible to establish a new political force – the Green Party.

'Ecology' now became one of the key notions in environmental discourse. Within a few years, this term had been transformed from a mere biological concept into a political category. As early as 1970 or 1971, conservationists criticized state-sponsored technical environmental protection as incomplete if it did not take into account human interaction with the biosphere.[31] They claimed that it would not

[28] On Berlin Beer and Spielhagen, *Bürgerinitiativen*; on Frankfurt R. Hartel, 'Blütenträume zwischen Skyline und Beton. Konflikthafte gesellschaftliche Naturverhältnisse und alternative Bewegungspolitik in Frankfurt am Main 1971–1990', *Archiv für Frankfurts Geschichte und Kunst*, 67, 2001, 249–309.

[29] On Thielcke Reichelt, *Wach sein*, 189–90, 207, 214.

[30] E. Müller, *Innenwelt der Umweltpolitik* (Opladen, 1986); H.-P. Vierhaus, *Umweltbewußtsein von oben*. (Berlin, 1994).

[31] Chaney, 'Visions', 389.

be sufficient to fight isolated pollution problems. Humanity must change its attitude towards nature and its value systems. Activists castigated anthropocentrism, and demanded that society accept the existence of nature in its own right. However, these debates revitalized agrarian romanticism, which postulated the existence of a rural life that provided a better and 'softer' alternative to urban-industrial life-styles.

Many problems were common both to the urban and rural sphere. During the 1970s traffic problems, for example, became a major unifying topic for environmental movements. Roads and motorways threatened urban green space as well as rural landscapes. Cars symbolized Germany's postwar wealth and played an important role in the country's creation of an image of modern consumer society.[32] All this represented an attractive target for environmental criticism. Furthermore, public health experts became aware, from the mid 1960s onwards, that air and water pollution were not limited to a specific region, but constituted global phenomena transgressing political and geographical borders. Polarities between countryside and town were no longer central.[33]

Another important factor contributing to the ideological convergence of rural and urban environmentalism was the debate over atomic energy. Numerous nuclear power plants were to be constructed in the countryside. As a consequence, local residents became deeply concerned. Such projects shifted what may be termed the social costs of industrialization from town to country. In the mid-1970s atomic energy became the major target of all those critical of the modern industrial world, the state's role in economic management and an alleged lack of democracy in West German society. Little wonder that rural protesters built alliances with urban environmental groups.

When town-based activists joined rural protests, different attitudes towards life-styles emerged. This was because generational and socio-cultural change occurred in the cities before catching on in the countryside. Young and well-educated urban environmentalists often behaved in a way that rural populations found hard to accept. During the Wyhl anti-nuclear protest, for example, urban women aspiring to full political participation, and young men with long hair and leftist political views produced a degree of mistrust and caused serious communication problems. Despite such differences concerning motivation, social structure, gender role, political style, rhetoric and even political aims, the anti-nuclear movement established a loose but

---

[32] D. Klenke, 'Freier Stau für freie Bürger'. Die Geschichte der bundesdeutschen Verkehrspolitik (Darmstadt, 1995); cf. Zeller, Straße.

[33] Brüggemeier, Tschernobyl; Hünemörder, Frühgeschichte; Uekötter, Rauchplage.

common ideological framework. This was grounded in opposition to atomic power, the denunciation of an official unwillingness to consider community objections and alleged interconnections between political and economic interests as driving-forces of the nuclear programme. When conflicts between local and urban activists endangered joint action, activists conjured up founding myths thereby focusing on the unifying force of the 'cause'.[34]

Convergence Through Organizational Change

There was another important factor which strengthened connections between urban and non-urban environmental action during the 1970s: centralization of citizens' groups and, in some instances, decentralization of the traditional conservation movement.[35]

Over the preceding decades, nature protection associations had not backed every local resistance movement. Groups fighting hydroelectric power stations in the south of Bavaria were supported by organizations such as the 'German Conservation Ring' (*Deutscher Naturschutzring*) and the regional 'Bavarian Nature Conservation Association' (*Bund für Naturschutz in Bayern*).[36] However, in other cases, national societies refused to support local movements when they judged it politically ill-timed to do so or when local activists refused to subordinate themselves to long-established representatives of conservation. At the time, national bodies in the field tended to be cautious. Conservationists feared that they might lose political credit if they campaigned too aggressively, and claimed that their organizations did not embrace explicitly 'political' aims. Advocates of a conservative social ideology, they criticized political life for being dominated by groups who lobbied politicians, exerted pressure on the authorities and represented what were termed 'particular interests'. According to their own self-perception, they gave primary attention to general welfare. Successes were gained through confidential negotiation with official representatives. In addition,

---

[34] Engels, 'Women'.

[35] This is not to say that there had only been centralized organizations in conservation. In fact, conservation *milieu* had been made up by a huge number of local and regional *Heimatschutz-* or *Wander*-associations. However, the agendas and strategies of most local organizations owed very much to the politics defined by the leaders of the national umbrella organizations; on *Heimatschutz*, W. Oberkrome, 'Heimatschutz und Naturschutz in Lippe und Thüringen 1930–1960. Strukturen und Entwicklungen', in M. Frese and M. Prinz, eds, *Politische Zäsuren und gesellschaftlicher Wandel im 20. Jahrhundert* (Paderborn, 1996), 419–38.

[36] Dominick, *Movement*, 127–30.

conservationists' organizations were strongly interconnected, with leading positions being held by a relatively closed group of social peers. They were mistrustful of the 'not informed' – newcomers who spoke up for the rights and interests of local bodies.

As a consequence, local campaigners sometimes were forced to mobilize their resources without the support of big, traditional organizations. Tactics, ideological framing and prospects of success differed greatly. Sometimes, however, local movements gained successes without the backing of these long-established peer group leaders.[37]

During the 1970s, traditional conservationists attempted to capitalize on new social forces supporting environmental protest. In 1975, a number of prominent conservationists and ecologists centred around Bernhard Grzimek, Horst Stern, Bodo Manstein and Hubert Weinzierl founded the 'German Environment and Nature Protection Association' (*Bund für Umwelt- und Naturschutz in Deutschland*, BUND).[38] They had been disappointed by the failure of the traditional conservation movement to act quickly, and by their unwillingness or incapacity to cooperate with environmentalism. The founders' basic idea was to establish a central board which would act as a pressure group. It would need to be strong enough to influence federal politics and compete with interest groups representing farmers and industry. Replicating the political structure of the Federal Republic, the new body would be organized along state lines which should represent the local groups. In 1975, the national board could only call on groups in South Germany. The well-organized and long-established Bavarian Nature Conservation Association constituted BUND's main pillar. In Baden-Württemberg, a state branch had been founded only a few months earlier, combining provincial groups in the Lake Constance and Baar regions as well as a Freiburg urban environmental association. In some states, the new coordinating body cooperated with existing groups, but in others, state associations and local groups had to be artificially established. The genesis of BUND was therefore marked by a mix of centralized control and convergence of provincial and small urban groups into a nationwide holding organization. The first years proved difficult because of endless quarrels about how financial resources should be distributed between

---

[37] One of the most striking examples is the 'Knechtsand affair' in the mid-1950s, Bundesarchiv Koblenz B 116/5514, Niedersächsisches Hauptstaatsarchiv Hannover, Nds. 50 Acc. 96/88 and Nds. 60 Acc. 37/85.

[38] On BUND see A. Wolf, *Die Analyse der Reformfähigkeit eines Umweltverbandes am Beispiel des Bund für Umwelt und Naturschutz Deutschland e.V. (BUND)*, Technical University of Berlin PhD thesis 1996 and BUND Archives conserved at *Bundesarchiv Koblenz* B 342; Archives of BUND-Landesverband Baden-Württemberg; BUND's periodical *Natur und Umwelt*.

state associations and the central board. In the longer term a combination of local and national, urban and provincial forces proved highly successful. Although BUND's founders addressed conservation topics, city-based members' contributions extended the sphere of activity into the area of 'technical' environmental protection. They all agreed on an ideological framework consisting of 'ecology' and unconditional opposition to atomic energy. However, at times some of BUND's most prestigious representatives expressed conservative ideas that were in sharp conflict with the beliefs of leftist or 'alternative' members.

Another example demonstrating the convergence of ecological protest is the BBU, the 'Federal Association of Citizens' Initiatives Active in Environmental Protection' (*Bundesverband Bürgerinitiativen Umweltschutz*). It was founded soon after the emergence of the first citizens' groups in 1972. The BBU was a loose union of member organizations, and aimed to be represented at a national level. Federal officials played a role in bringing together the 15 founding citizens' groups. BBU never established a centralized structure and only possessed a very small administrative apparatus. In 1980, BBU leaders were unable to list the precise number of bodies they were supposed to represent, estimating it at roughly a thousand.[39] The organization had no direct influence over its members. Nevertheless, success in the 1970s indicates that citizens' groups were anxious to locate local activities within a national framework. BBU rhetoric and activities were more radical than those of a majority of individual member organizations. During the emergence of a nationwide debate over nuclear power, however, the leadership strengthened its ideological influence, providing members with a portfolio of persuasive arguments. In addition, BBU played an important role in arguing for the cause of non-violent protest.[40]

The Importance of Expertise

BBU and BUND, the two major representatives of the German environmental movement during the 1970s, were neither exclusively provincial nor exclusively urban phenomena. They became driving-forces as a result of the converging rhetoric and strategy of urban and rural environmental activists. Ecological discourse provided many local groups with globalized legitimation. In addition, such organizations needed scientific expertise if they were to prevent the construction of nuclear power stations or motorways that threatened urban green space.

---

[39] T. Ellwein, M. Leonhard and P.M. Schmidt, *Umweltschutz-verbände in der Bundesrepublik Deutschland* (Konstanz, 1983), 199.

[40] Archives of BBU at Bonn and the periodical *BBU-aktuell*.

German public works planning law requires public hearings, which enable concerned citizens to articulate their interests. When groups wished to make a coherent case, they needed the help of technical experts.[41] In this sense, many activists looked upon the environmental and anti-nuclear movements as learning curves which enabled participants to take part in the political process and play a role in the protection and development of the environment.[42] Both BBU and BUND sponsored 'AKs', or working groups. These consisted of members who collected scientific information about water pollution, traffic, energy, communication or public relations. These bodies looked upon themselves as think-tanks, which provided fellow-campaigners with tactical information – how to win a lawsuit – and strategic perspectives on ecological reform. They developed close relationships with academics and often were located in university towns.[43] They also transmitted city-based scientific, technical and legal knowledge to other urban centres and provincial movements.

Nevertheless, by the end of the 1970s, transmission of expert knowledge had moved beyond the stage at which towns 'instructed' provincial areas. In some cases, activists in hot-spots like Wyhl gained specialized skills because such methods had been derived from the experience of local action. From 1977 onwards, 'solar energy fairs' were organized by a local branch of BUND in rural Sasbach in South West Germany. Choosing this location reflected the emergence of a 'cell' of experts in the Upper Rhine valley, and was intended to demonstrate that 'alternative technology' need not be tied to industrialized centres. Environmental action and expertise in the 1970s can be conceptualized as a networking system. Nevertheless, urban groups remained in a privileged position, because they possessed a larger proportion of educated personnel and larger financial resources. Only a few rural groups published their own periodical.[44] However, a large number of urban organizations issued a newsletter.[45] As long as the central boards

---

[41] On 'experts', R. Hitzler, 'Wissen und Wesen der Experten', in id., A. Honer and C. Maeder, eds, *Expertenwissen* (Opladen, 1994), 13–30; D. Rucht, 'Gegenöffentlichkeit und Gegenexperten', *Zeitschrift für Rechtssoziologie*, 9, 1988, 290–305; B. Schumacher, ed., *Der Experte. Aufstieg einer Figur der Wahrheit und des Wissens* (Zürich, 2001).

[42] W. Beer, *Lernen im Widerstand* (Hamburg, 1978).

[43] Cf. '*Arbeitskreis Wasser im BBU*', situated at Freiburg, and BBU '*AK Verkehr*' at Berlin.

[44] See e.g. '*Was wir wollen*' edited by the citizens' groups fighting against Wyhl nuclear power station.

[45] E.g. *Umwelt-Depesche* by *Bürgerinitiative Umweltschutz Hannover*, *Der grüne Hammer* by several groups at Hamm, *Der Umweltschutz* by *Bürgeraktion Umweltschutz Zentrales Oberrheingebiet* at Karlsruhe.

of environmental groups were unable to afford to employ professional staff, decentralized structures continued to function. However, even BBU, a strong advocate of grassroots action, sponsored the founding of *Öko-Institut* ('Ecological Institute') which became the first and one of the most influential think-tanks concerned with ecological development.[46]

As differences between the urban and rural world decreased in the second half of the twentieth century, environmental problems and protest converged. Internationally prominent ecological concepts, which were becoming increasingly culturally central from the early 1970s onwards, provided a new ideological and scientific framework. This proved to be highly flexible, enabling town-based as well as local activists to articulate their apprehension about a wide range of problems. Nevertheless, differences between provincial and urban protest can be detected with respect to socio-political and socio-cultural issues. Provincial protest appears to have been more 'pragmatic', whereas city-centred environmentalism included a larger number of counter-cultural elements. However, environmental movements helped to build up multiple relationships between residents of both geographic spheres. In addition, the very nature of large-scale projects such as nuclear power stations and motorways forced planners and their opponents to interact at many different levels. It is unhelpful to conceive the convergence of the environmental movement in terms of a simple model of a provincial periphery being heavily influenced by a town-based centre. This was not how things happened. Rather, provincial and town-based activists interacted with one another and bridged and blurred differences between the two spheres.

---

[46] *Alternativen. Anders denken, anders handeln. Zum Selbstverständnis der Bürgerinitiativbewegung*, ed. Öko-Institut (Freiburg, 1978).

CHAPTER SIXTEEN

Path Dependence and Urban History: Is a Marriage Possible?

Martin V. Melosi

The impact of a variety of technologies and infrastructures on the growth of cities is a central concern of urban environmental history. The implementation of new urban technologies, however, was not automatic, coincidental, nor inadvertent, but an intentional effort by decision makers to confront existing problems faced by cities as they extended upward and outward in the nineteenth and twentieth centuries.

Path dependence is an important approach for exploring the role of decision making on the development and impact of specific technologies or technical systems. The theory focuses attention on the means by which choices are made, the connection of those choices to future options and sequences of events, and to outcomes. The use of path dependence reinforces the idea that a variety of externalities influence the adoption of technologies. It can help historians turn from concentrating so heavily on a singularly past-centred perspective to a present-centred perspective that devotes significant attention to results as well as constraints on outcomes. This is especially useful if historians are interested in the policy implications of their work.

Social scientists, especially economists, began exploring path-dependence theory in the mid-1980s. Although definitions vary, simply put, path dependence exists 'when the present state of a system is constrained by its history'.[1] The theory has been applied to a variety of technologies, institutions, and policies. In a larger context, path dependency has challenged neoclassical economics by stressing the importance of institutions (institutional economics) and through the suggestion that historical events affect present choices (evolutionary economics).[2] Economic historian Paul A. David has argued that 'the

---

[1] P.A. Gorringe, 'Path Dependence – Causes, Consequences and Policy,' in Grimes, Arthur, et al., eds, *Economics for Policy: Expanding the Boundaries: Essays by Peter Gorringe* (Wellington, NZ, 2001).

[2] See D.J. Puffert, 'Path Dependence in Economic History', November, 1999, Internet www.vwl.uni-muenchen.de/ls_komlos/pathe.pdf, based on 'Pfadabhangigkeit in der Wirtschaftsgeschichte', in Herrmann-Pillath, Karsten,

future of economics as an intellectually exciting discipline lies in its becoming an historical social science'.[3] Given that economics, and other social sciences, have been dominated by a strong behaviourist philosophy built upon quantitative methodologies, some saw the notion that *history matters* as a radical departure. From David's perspective '[H]ow could there be anything new or radical in the idea that particular sequences of events in the past have had enduring effects upon current conditions?'[4] For historians, path dependence is quite reasonable, given our own sense of causation and the importance of sequencing events to determine change over time. The radicalism of path dependency, however, lies not so much in its fundamental claims, but in its challenge to social science orthodoxy in the wake of the cliometric revolution.

The debate over path dependency is interesting in its own right. That debate has also been useful in helping to explore the intrinsic value of the theory for historians, including urban historians. A central question – and an ironic one – is: why borrow such an idea from colleagues in the social sciences, who borrowed it from us in the first place? This paper explores the scope of path dependence as developed by its advocates and criticized by its detractors, and reflects upon its value to the study of urban history. Paul David's 1985 article, 'Clio and the Economics of QWERTY', brought widespread attention to path dependency. David illustrated the theory through a case-study on the adoption of the QWERTY standard English language typewriter keyboard in the 1870s.[5] The QWERTY had been designed to reduce the mechanical jamming of the keys and was quickly adopted by many office managers. Other keyboards, notably the Dvorak Simplified Keyboard introduced in the late 1930s, appeared to be faster and more efficient, but the QWERTY had long since dominated the market. In David's view, a small – or accidental – historical event had 'locked-in' the QWERTY technology and essentially eliminated its competitors.[6] While the article

---

Lehmann-Waffenschmidt, and Marco, eds, *Handbuch zur evolutorischen 'O'konomik* (forthcoming). See also L. Magnusson and J. Ottosson, eds, *Evolutionary Economics and Path Dependence* (Cheltenham, UK, 1997), 1–2.

[3] P.A. David, 'Path-Dependence: Putting the Past into the Future of Economics', Technical Report No. 533 (Stanford, CA, Dec. 1988): abstract.

[4] Ibid., 6.

[5] The name of the keyboard was derived from the first six letters on the top row of the keys.

[6] P.A. David, 'Clio and the Economics of QWERTY', *American Economic Review*, 75, May, 1985, 332–7. See also David, 'Understanding the Economics of QWERTY: The Necessity of History', in W.N. Parker, ed., *Economic History and the Modern Economist* (New York, 1986); David, 'Path Dependence and the Quest for Historical Economics: One More Chorus of the Ballad of QWERTY', University of Oxford Discussion Papers in Economics and Social

garnered substantial attention and stimulated additional study of path
dependence, defenders of neoclassical economic theory were
unconvinced by David's argument and questioned the QWERTY case in
particular and the path dependency theory in general.[7] But as Douglas
J. Puffert – a student of David's – perceptively noted, 'David defined
path dependence as a dynamic feature of an allocation process, whether
or not the resulting allocation is efficient. Many readers of his article,
however, interpreted path dependence primarily as a source of market
failure through lock-in to a suboptimal technology.'[8] In essence,
supporters and critics were often debating different issues.

In a recent article, and in response to critics, David defined the
concept of path dependence as 'a property of contingent, non-reversible
dynamical processes, including a wide array of biological and social
processes that can properly be described as "evolutionary"'. He added
that 'the policy implications of the existence of path dependence are
shown to be more subtle and, as a rule, quite different from those which
have been presumed by critics of the concept'.[9] These alterations in his
definition were meant to suggest that *history matters* in economic
processes, but not always in the same way. In addition, the concept of
historical *lock-in* should not be taken too literally, but viewed as 'a vivid
way to describe the entry of a system into a trapping region – the basin
of attraction that surrounds a locally (or globally) stable equilibrium'.[10]
Thus *lock-in* is not rigidly inflexible, but the result of making choices in
the past that constrain options in the present or future.

David utilized path dependence theory to question economic
orthodoxy. 'Indeed, for too long', he stated, 'it has seemingly been our
collective educational purpose to extirpate from the minds of neophyte
economists all but the most fundamental human intuitions about the
role of the past in present (economic) affairs'.[11] 'Path dependence, at
least to my way of thinking', he also stated, 'is therefore about much
more than the processes of technological change, or institutional
evolution, or hysteresis effects and unit roots in macroeconomic growth.

History, No. 20, 1997; David, 'Path-dependence and Predictability in Dynamic
Systems with Local Network Externalities: A Paradigm for Historical
Economics', in D. Foray and C. Freeman, eds, *Technology and the Wealth of
Nations: The Dynamics of Constructed Advantage* (London, 1993).
    [7] A well-known rebuttal is S.J. Liebowitz and S.E. Margolis, 'The Fable of
the Keys', *Journal of Law and Economics*, 33, 1990, 1–25.
    [8] Puffert, 'Path Dependence in Economic History', 2.
    [9] P.A. David, 'Path Dependence, Its Critics and the Quest for "Historical
Economics"', 1, Internet, www-econ.stanford.edu/faculty/workp/swp00011.pdf.
    [10] Ibid., 10.
    [11] P.A David, 'Path-Dependence: Putting the Past into the Future of
Economics', 9.

The concepts associated with this term have implications for epistemology, for the sociology of knowledge, and cognitive science as well.'[12] While David set a foundation for path dependence and attracted an initial firestorm of criticism, others have attempted to refine the theory and broaden its applicability within the field of economics as well as in the other social sciences. Particularly noteworthy is the work of W. Brian Arthur, Douglass C. North, and Paul Pierson. Among his contributions to refining path dependency, Arthur has been particularly noteworthy in the area of increasing returns economics, by demonstrating how small historical events can be amplified by positive feedbacks. This approach stands in opposition to conventional economic theory that emphasizes diminishing returns, that is, economic actions that produce negative feedbacks resulting in a state of equilibrium for prices and market shares resulting in stabilizing the economy.[13] Arthur and others found this latter approach to defy reality in several cases. Under increasing returns, multiple outcomes are possible. As a consequence, tracing the way in which small events accrue to cause a particular system to move to one particular outcome instead of another becomes important.[14] In examining choices made among technologies, Arthur noted that 'modern, complex technologies often display increasing returns to adoption in that the more they are adopted, the more experience is gained with them, and the more they are improved'.[15] When technologies compete for a market, therefore, 'insignificant events' may give one an initial advantage for adoption. The technology may then improve more than the others, and thus appeal to a wider group of adopters, and so on. In this scenario the technology that by chance gained an early lead may 'corner the market' of adopters, and other technologies may become 'locked-out'. Such an approach highlights two new properties in the adoption process: *historical lock-in* of a given technology (inflexibility) and path dependence (non-ergodicity). Arthur admitted that not all technologies enjoyed increasing returns with adoption, but he believes that it might be useful to determine to what degree the actual economy might be locked-in to inferior technology paths. This perspective, of course, is in direct opposition to the concept of diminishing returns, where small events cannot determine outcomes and where a laissez-faire approach leads to

---

[12] P.A. David, 'Path Dependence, Its Critics and the Quest for "Historical Economics"', 16.

[13] W.B. Arthur, *Increasing Returns and Path Dependence in the Economy* (Ann Arbor, 1994), 1.

[14] Ibid., 28.

[15] W.B. Arthur, 'Competing Technologies, Increasing Returns, and Lock-In by Historical Events', *Economic Journal*, 99, March, 1989, 116.

the success of a superior technology. Arthur's increasing returns approach challenges those assumptions.[16]

Arthur's focus on modern technologies, however, does not take ample account of an institutional context for path dependence. Nobel laureate Douglass North clearly added that dimension to the theory: 'History matters. It matters not just because we can learn from the past, but because the present and the future are connected to the past by the continuity of a society's institutions.'[17] North regards institutions as 'the rules of the game in a society or, more formerly, are the humanly devised constraints that shape human interaction'. His concern is that there is no analytical framework to integrate institutional analysis into economics or economic history.[18] North is particularly sensitive to the gulf between neoclassical theory and its concern over 'the allocation of resources at a moment of time', and how much of 'a devastatingly limiting feature' that is to historians 'whose central question is to account for change over time'. 'Moreover', he adds, 'the allocation was assumed to occur in a frictionless world, that is, one in which institutions either did not exist or did not matter'.[19] North made clear that institutional analysis could make the US economic history (in this case) 'a truly historical story', and much of that history he believed was path dependent – 'simply by nature of constraints from the past imposing limits on current choices and therefore making the current choice set intelligible'. Focusing on the process of economic growth, he postulated that the primary source of economic growth is 'the institutional/organizational structure of a political economy'; and that economic growth is dependent on 'stable political/economic institutions. Furthermore, the 'belief systems of societies and the way they evolve' is the 'underlying determinant of institutions and their evolution'.[20] Understanding the nature of path

---

[16] Ibid., 117, 123, 126–8. See also Arthur, 'Competing Technlogies and Economic Prediction', *Options*, (Laxenburg, Austria, 1984), 10–13; Arthur, 'Self-reinforcing Mechanisms in Economics', in P.W. Anderson, K.J. Arrow and D. Pines, eds, *The Economy as an Evolving Complex System* (Redwood City, CA, 1988); Arthur, 'Path Dependence, Self-reinforcement, and Human Learning', *American Economic Review*, 81, 1991, 133–58; Arthur, 'Competing Technologies: An Overview', in G. Dosi, C. Freeman, R. Nelson, G. Silverberg, and L. Soete, eds, *Technical Change and Economic Theory* (London, 1988), 590–607; Arthur, 'Positive Feedbacks in the Economy', *Scientific American*, 262, 1990, 92–9.

[17] D.C. North, *Institutions, Institutional Change and Economic Performance* (Cambridge, 1990), vii.

[18] Ibid., 3.

[19] Ibid., 131.

[20] D.C. North, 'Some Fundamental Puzzles in Economic History/Development', in W.B. Arthur, S.N. Durlauf, and D.A. Lane, eds, *The Economy as an Evolving Complex System II* (Reading, MA, 1997), 224–5.

dependence, he concluded, 'is the key to understanding the success or failure of economies in altering their competitive positions'.[21] North also observed the ability of several actors to influence outcomes within an 'institutional matrix' through, among other things, a variety of increasing returns, through inducing incremental change, and through informal constraints such as the transmission of values.[22] A theory of institutional change incorporating path dependence, he concluded, can become a central feature in understanding economic growth.

Political scientist Paul Pierson has been influential in utilizing path dependence to analyse politics, political institutions, and decision making. In a recent article, he explored path dependence as a social process 'grounded in a dynamic of "increasing returns"'. Like Arthur and others, he argued that increasing returns processes 'are likely to be prevalent' and can provide a strong framework for developing the study of historical institutionalism.[23] He is particularly interested in developing path dependence theory with more rigour and beyond the 'loose and not very helpful assertion' that *history matters*. Utilization of an increasing returns process to elaborate path dependency is especially important because in this process 'the probability of further steps along the same path increases with each move down that path'. In addition, he is interested in exploring a narrow conception of path dependence (social processes that exhibit increasing returns is one approach) so that the theory does not suffer 'concept stretching' in which different types of temporally linked sequences are identified under a single banner.[24] Pierson is aware that applying tools of economic analysis to politics can be 'treacherous' unless applied carefully and systematically. He believes that doing so produces salutary outcomes because 'The political world is unusually prone to increasing returns'.[25] He is particularly concerned that in identifying initial causes influencing future patterns, the object of study needs to become the critical juncture or 'triggering events' which set development along a certain path. In addition, he cautioned that path dependent analyses need not presume that a particular alternative is

[21] Ibid., 228.

[22] North, *Institutions, Institutional Change and Economic Performance*, 137–8.

[23] P. Pierson, 'Increasing Returns, Path Dependence, and the Study of Politics,' *American Political Science Review*, June 2000, 1. See also 'Not Just What, but When: Timing and Sequence in Political Processes', *Studies in American Political Development*, 14, 2000, 72–92; S. E. Robinson, 'You Can't Get There from Here: Path Dependence, Evolutionary Economics, and Public Agencies', (Paper presented at the Scientific Study of the Bureaucracy Conference, College Station, Texas, February 2–3, 2001), 2.

[24] Ibid., 3.

[25] Ibid., 18.

permanently locked-in. With these caveats, he strongly asserts that increasing returns arguments may produce exciting results in political science.[26] Skeptics of path dependency have challenged vigorously this analytical tool and, in turn, questioned the heightened assaults on neoclassical theory. For those interested in applying path dependence to a variety of historical problems, the critiques are valuable for an array of pertinent issues requiring further consideration. The best-known criticism of path dependence comes from economists Stan J. Liebowitz and Stephen E. Margolis. The primary thrust of their argument is that path dependence merely presents a false claim of market failure. They suggest that economists have found imperfections in free markets, and that improvement was difficult, but also that alleged market imperfections may prove later not to exist at all. Moreover, there may not be realistic means to overcome supposed market imperfections and ways may be found to improve upon independent decision making (by firms and individuals) which is how resources are allocated in a free market.[27]

In defining path dependence, Liebowitz and Margolis assume that the theory 'spilled over' to economics from other fields or disciplines – in physics and mathematics in the form of chaos theory (a non-linear model 'with sensitive dependence on initial conditions') and from biology via contingency ('the irreversible character of natural selection'). In comparing chaos theory and path dependence, they suggest that in chaos theory 'small events or perturbations tend to cause a system to evolve in very different ways but the system never settles down in any repeatable path or fixed equilibrium'. In the case of path dependence in economics, the view that minor initial perturbations are important is imported from chaos theory, 'but has grafted this on to a theory where there are a finite number of perfectly stable alternative states, one of which will arise based on the particular initial conditions'. Perpetual disequilibrium is thus missing from path dependence.[28] Defence of

---

[26] Ibid., 19, 22–3. Others have made a distinction between *trajectories* and *turning points*. The former are 'interlocked and interdependent sequences of events' whereas the latter are 'events that have the potential to redirect trajectories along new paths'. Trajectories are inertial, but turning points can switch trajectories to new paths. See L.A. and D. Harrison, 'Technological Trajectories and Path Dependence', 4, Internet www.bath.ac.uk/imp/pdf/18_AraujoHarrison.pdf.

[27] S.J. Liebowitz and S.E. Margolis, *Winners, Losers & Microsoft: Competition and Antitrust in High Technology* (Oakland, CA, 1999), 1.

[28] S.E. Margolis and S.J. Liebowitz, 'Path Dependence', May 28, 2001, 1, Internet, www.pub.utdallas.edu/~liebowitz/palgrave/palpd.html. See also Liebowitz and Margolis, 'Path Dependence, Lock-In, and History', Internet, www.utdallas.edu/~liebowitz/paths.html.

traditional market mechanisms led Liebowitz and Margolis to dismiss David's claims of path dependence as demonstrated in his various case studies, including the QWERTY example. Liebowitz and Margolis assert that David's evidence is shaky, especially the notion that QWERTY became the standard because of the lack of sufficient challengers. They question the assumptions that the Dvorak keyboard was inherently superior, and that the sustaining influence of the QWERTY clearly indicated a market failure. Their critique challenges David's historical data and also his drift away from neoclassical theory to make the case for market failure. They conclude that 'what credence can possibly be given to a keyboard that has nothing to accredit it but the trials of a group of mechanics and its adoption by millions of typists? If we use only sterilized models of markets, or ignore the vitality of the rivalry that confronts institutions, we should not be surprised that the historical interpretations that result are not graced with truth.'[29] In a rather clever condemnation of path dependence – again relying heavily on an unwavering reliance on neoclassical economics – Liebowitz and Margolis developed taxonomy of path dependence. A minimal form – or first-degree path dependence – is an element of 'persistence or durability' in a decision with no apparent harm done at a later time. In second-degree path dependence, past conditions lead to outcomes that are 'regrettable and costly to change', but where an individual failed to predict the future perfectly because of imperfect information. Third-degree path dependence – the strongest form – suggests that known feasible and preferable alternatives exist at the time the initial decision was made and thus an error that arises was avoidable. Their conclusion is that first-, and second-degree path dependence are common, have always been a part of economic thought, and that traditional theories of neoclassical economics can explain them. Third-degree path dependence – the kind associated with the critics of neoclassical theory – does not exist in the real world. Such argumentation effectively dismisses path dependence.[30] In the concluding chapter of their recent book, *Winners, Losers & Microsoft*, Liebowitz and Margolis conclude 'our message is simple: Good products win. Whether they are lowly mousetraps or high-tech networks, better products prevail in the marketplace. People choose what they want, and what they want survives, at least for a while. Surviving products are imitated and become the norm. . . . Eventually, when something decidedly better comes along, there is a transition to the new product.'[31] And as Liebowitz was quoted as saying in a 1998 email

---

[29] Liebowitz and Margolis, *Winners, Losers & Microsoft*, 39.
[30] Ibid., 49–56.
[31] Ibid., 235.

exchange: 'Finally . . . there is the claim that path dependence enhances the value of economic history. We think not.'[32]

To a large extent, Liebowitz and Margolis are defending methods of neoclassical economic theory against an interloper. It is quite acceptable that path dependence (and economic history in general) be used as a tool for understanding some past actions, but when it is also used as a way of explaining and influencing the present, critics – especially in economics – fall back on disciplinary orthodoxy. As Puffert suggested, '[M]any neoclassical economists view history as little more than a source of data for testing theories. At the most, they restrict the role of history to determining the fundamental, a priori, 'exogenous' parameters that presumably then determine a unique equilibrium – such parameters as institutions, technology, factor endowments, tastes, and information.'[33] To be fair, of course, it must be added that economists and historians do not always ask the same questions, although they may have, as economic historian G.R. Hawke stated, 'overlapping rather than identical interests'. He perceptively noted, 'historians frequently use expressions like "understanding the past in its own terms", while economists want to employ concepts developed more recently in their studies of past societies. The point might be described as a conflict between "past centred" and "present centred" studies.'[34] Hawke point outs that the difference is one of degree, but the difference often exists nonetheless. Since his 1985 article, David has explained and refined his views on path dependence on several occasions. Ultimately, he has promoted some basic precepts of causation that historians should find easily compatible with their own views: 'effects follow causes in temporal succession' and 'there are outcomes which simply cannot be achieved – or, are extremely unlikely to arise – except through some particular dynamic of intervening events'.[35] In many respects, path

[32] Email, John Conover, December 14, 1998, Internet www.johncon.com/john/correspondence/981214003911.12734.html. Others support Liebowitz and Margolis with similarly strong language. In a review of *Winners, Losers & Microsoft* appearing in *Regulation*, 23, emeritus professor of mineral economics Richard L. Gordon noted: 'Liebowitz and Margolis are overly polite in dealing with the fundamental problem of the path-dependence model: its reliance on a long chain of improbable assumptions to prove that markets can sustain bad choices.'

[33] Puffert, 'Path Dependence in Economic History', 1.

[34] G.R. Hawke, *Economics for Historians* (Cambridge, 1980), 3.

[35] Ibid., 12–13. Causation is central to historians' thinking, so much so that, as one study suggests, 'historians continuously use causal language. In fact, they are the only cognitive discipline in which it is correct to emphasize the types of causation present in ordinary, undisciplined, common-sense discourse'. See P.K. Conkin and R.N. Stromberg, *Heritage and Challenge: The History and Theory*

dependence puts a different name – and at times a different perspective – on a process that is basic to historical inquiry. Indeed, it is a concept originally borrowed from the discipline of history itself. What appears most useful about path dependence for historians, however, is not just the reconfirmation of historical causation, but a shift in focus from past to present, that is, greater attention to outcomes of past events rather than simply tracking change over time, which often emphasizes the look back as opposed to the look ahead or the impact of choices made. In this sense, critiques like that of Liebowitz and Margolis are valuable in forcing proponents of path dependence to provide more precise definitions of the theory. As economic historians Lars Magnusson and Jan Ottosson have argued, '. . . Liebowitz and Margolis are certainly right in that if "path dependency" is to serve as anything more than a catchword for sweeping criticism of neo-classical economics, it is important that we try to be more specific regarding its theoretical status'.[36] For the purposes of historians, Liebowitz's and Margolis's argument too narrowly focuses on market failure, inefficiency, and good and bad (mistaken) technical choices. In some respect, the argument makes a priori judgement, not necessarily questioning that choices lead to particular paths, but that results that produce inferior outcomes do not correspond to actual market forces. 'Better products prevail in the marketplace.' They seem to accept a distinction made by others that choices can be *past dependent*, rather than *path dependent*. In other words, they question the sequencing of events that lead to what they argue are improbable outcomes.[37] Yet, how can any outcome that is either *past* or *path* dependent not be influenced by what came before? Specifically, with respect to superior/inferior technologies, Liebowitz and Margolis seem to miss the point that what Arthur and others are talking about are *characteristics* of technologies rather than simply technologies themselves.[38]

---

of History (Arlington Heights, IL, 1989), 170. For more on historical causation and conceptions of time, see 171–91; A.J. Lichtman and V. French, *Historians and the Living Past: The Theory and Practice of Historical Study* (Arlington Heights, IL, 1978), 44–72, 249–54; R.F. Berhofer, Jr., *A Behavioral Approach to Historical Analysis* (New York, 1969), 211–69; D.H. Fischer, *Historians' Fallacies: Toward a Logic of Historical Thought* (New York, 1970), 164–86.

[36] Magnusson and Ottosson, *Evolutionary Economics and Path Dependence*, 3.

[37] Something may be *past dependent*, the argument goes, if events within a specific system can be predicted on the basis of the state of the system at a later time, independent of how the system arrived at that time. See Araujo and Harrison, 'Technological Trajectories and Path Dependence', 2.

[38] Pierson, 'Increasing Returns, Path Dependence, and the Study of Politics', 8.

It is not the point of this paper – nor is it within the expertise of the writer – to enter the rather extensive and detailed debate over the value of path dependence within the field of economics, or whether path dependence undermines neoclassical economics and offers a major epistemological breakthrough in the field.[39] This discussion hardly does justice to a thorough discussion of market forces, network effects, diminishing returns, increasing returns, and so forth. More simply, rather than taking on that large task or even questioning the more narrow notion of whether an inferior technology could succeed in a market economy, for example, it is argued here that path dependence may be useful for historians in addressing questions from a slightly different vantage point. What are the constraints placed on a current generation because of choices made in the past? What are the limits of a chosen path, as opposed to what is or is not changeable? What are the implications of particular choices and potential lock-ins on practice and policy? What kinds of impacts are possible with path-dependent actions? In many respects, these are qualitative issues, but the kinds of issues that complement traditional uses of historical causation in understanding technologies, institutions, and politics, useful to urban historians. Again, 'market failure' seems to be a very narrow way to judge the value of path dependence. Historians tend to think in degrees of change, rather than absolutes. It seems that a major virtue of path dependence is to determine how future choices are constrained or limited rather than how they are precluded. *Lock-in* need not be a permanent condition, nor is it the best issue for historians to track. Choices are made, what are their consequences? Is there a substantial impact on the sequencing of events because of initial choices? These seem to be more useful question for historians rather than debating whether initial choices grow out of 'insignificant' or 'small' events or even random actions. 'Insignificant', 'small', or 'random' have to be evaluated and based on outcomes. Something is hardly insignificant if it produces a significant outcome. To repeat what was stated earlier, path dependence can help historians turn from concentrating so heavily on a singularly past-centred perspective to a present-centred perspective that devotes significant attention to results as well as constraints on outcomes. This is especially useful if historians are interested in the policy implications of their work.

In my recent book, *The Sanitary City*, I attempt to use path dependency to help explain why choices made in American cities about

---

[39] However, it might be useful at some future date to consider the impact of path dependence theory on the Kuhnian notion of paradigms. Path dependence suggests evolutionary change, while Thomas Kuhn made a case for paradigm shifts in science – an idea that has been broadly applied to many fields. See Thomas Kuhn, *The Structure of Scientific Revolutions* (Chicago, 1962).

water supply, waste-water, and solid waste systems in the early- to mid-nineteenth century constrained choices available in the late-twentieth century.[40] (Some reviews rightly noted that my use of path dependence for solid waste systems was less convincing than for the other two.) Among other things, I argued that decisions to seek city-wide water supply and waste-water systems in the nineteenth century were influenced by several factors, including a growing desire by major cities to gain increasing control over revenues and services in the name of *home rule*; dissatisfaction with private approaches to service delivery that either failed to live up to expectations or weakened the ability of cities to control their own affairs; rapid population growth that produced a scale of demand for such services that no longer could be adequately provided by individuals themselves; for water supply in particular, the fear of fire; and an abiding dread of epidemic disease that could affect the whole city and its hinterland. In the wake of these converging issues in the nineteenth century, city leaders sought to provide water supply and waste-water services (however, these services did not appear simultaneously – water supply had the greatest priority.) Strongly informing choice was the 'sanitary idea' that had migrated from England in the 1840s. The notion that disease was caused by filth – or miasmas and smells emanating from putrefying waste – held sway in the United States until the bacteriological revolution became widely accepted in the twentieth century, purporting that disease was contagious and was caused by microscopic agents – or bacteria – and not from environmental causes like miasmas and putrefaction. The miasmatic theory of disease led to the conclusion that disease could be reduced and indeed eliminated through environmental sanitation. This meant, in the case of water supply, developing a technical system that carried *clean* water (determined largely through the senses) through pipes to home and businesses throughout the city. For effluents originating in the home or in businesses, pipes could likewise evacuate and deposit liquid wastes elsewhere – most typically into nearby rivers and streams or into the ocean. In essence, these early technologies of sanitation were nothing more than elaborated transportation systems for water and waste-water, but conformed to the thinking about disease eradication prevalent at the time.

Through these practices, several forms of epidemic disease showed sharp declines, due in part to these closed systems. But disease itself was not eradicated; in some cases displaced from one location to another or not confronted at all. Yet bad science had led to relatively effective

---

[40] *The Sanitary City: Urban Infrastructure in America from Colonial Times to the Present* (Baltimore, John Hopkins University Press, 2000).

technology – at least within the context of the nineteenth century. Future additions to the systems – filters, treatment facilities, chlorination equipment – emerged in the wake of the bacteriological revolution and took careful account of the communicable nature of epidemic diseases and placed increasingly less reliance on environmental sanitation. Despite the significant breakthrough in the understanding of diseases, the basic systems changed little from their origins in the nineteenth century in the sense that they were highly centralized, capital intensive systems focusing on access to *pure* water supplies and contending with forms of point pollution. In the later years of the twentieth century, however, pollution problems became increasingly complex – more pollution from run-off (non-point pollution) and ground-water contamination. These forms of pollution were not easily addressed with large-scale fixed systems that were incapable of capturing run-off from a variety of sources and directly addressing groundwater sources of pollution. This change in context – along with a growing sensitivity to a range of ecological perspectives which made our understanding of the environment more sophisticated, but more complex as well – indicated that our technologies of sanitation derived from the nineteenth century were not up to the task of protecting cities from current health hazards as they were believed to be years before. Choices made earlier in the path clearly constrained future options for no other reason than that the existing infrastructure was too extensive, too costly to replace, or resistant to change.

The weakness of my assessment was not discussing viable alternatives to the existing systems or outlining carefully the available policy options. Frankly, this is something I intended to do in a series of articles after the book was written; believing that the primary thrust of the study was to provide the historical underpinnings for some future discussion of these questions. In some respects, as well, the book did not deal explicitly with the theory of path dependence much after the introduction, since I assumed that the issues were implicit in the narrative. The possible weaknesses of my presentation with respect to path dependence theory, however, do not undermine the value of the theory to historical scholarship – in this case urban history. Path dependence theory focused my attention on the means by which choices are made by decision makers, the connection of those choices to future options and sequences of events, and to outcomes. The use of the theory clearly reinforces the idea that a variety of externalities influence the adoption of technologies, but I am not convinced that the proper way to frame the questions is to rely on the assumption that choices result essentially from *historical accidents* or *insignificant events*. Many decisions are made without the ability to predict outcomes or to appreciate potential alternatives. Context is extremely important. The miasmatic theory was not an historical accident or an insignificant event. It was made significant because of its timing and the related issues and concerns that produced the desire to develop new technologies of sanitation in the nineteenth century. It is no little comfort that some economic historians, economists, political scientists, and other social scientists believe that *history matters*. It is for historians to help demonstrate what the phrase actually means in practice. Employing path-dependence theory – or at least experimenting with it – can advance that effort.

Index

La Capria, Raffaele 97
La Rochelle 93
Labour government 91
land use policy 87, 108, 128–9, 166,
    176; *see also* expropriations,
    urban planning
land zoning *see* zoning
landfill 45
landscape 63–4
    alteration of 76–7
    architects of 89
    perception of 105
    protection *see* conservation
Lang, Fritz 223
Latham, Baldwin 138, 148
Laurentian region 68
Laval-des-Rapides 70, 75, 77
Laval-sur-le-Lac 71–3
Lavoisier, Antoine Laurent de 60
Le Play, Frédéric, 86
lead 21, 185, 204, 208–14
    lead colic 211
    lead pipes 204
    lead sulphide, sulphate 212
    see also heavy metals, pollutants
Leipzig 85, 186, 199
leisure
    facilities 70, 73
    places for 67, 76
Lesser 88
Lessing, Theodor 219, 223–5
Liebig, Justus 60, 172
Liebowitz, Stan J. 268–70
*Ligue française du coin de terre et du
    foyer* 85, 87
lime sulphate 116; *see also* fertilizer
Lindley, William 178
Lloyd George 85
Local Government Act 144
London 94
Loos, Adolph 89
Love canal 233
Luxembourg 87

McNeil, John 4, 106
mafia *see Camorra*; *see also* corruption
Magnusson, Lars 271
malaria 166; *see also* epidemic
Manstein, Bodo 258
manure 34, 36, 38, 40, 51, 171; *see
    also* fertilizer; sewage; waste
marcite 153, 162, 166; *see also*

Achères; Beddington grounds;
    sewage, farming, irrigation;
Margolis, Stephen E. 268–70
Marseille 47
measurement
    of noise 22, 216, 218, 226; *see
        also Ortsüblichkeit*
    of water quality *see* water,
        analysis
mechanization 54–5
Meisner Rosen, Christine 3
Melosi, Martin 2–3, 10, 235
metabolism, *see also* ecological,
        system of exchange
    social metabolism 10–12, 26
    urban metabolism 9–10, 13, 17,
        28–47
metals *see* heavy metals
miasmatic theory 12, 25, 137,
        173–4, 273; *see also* scientific
        analysis, knowledge
Michelin 17, 120–31
Migge 88
Milan 18, 149–67
    hydraulic system 150, 153
Mile, Alfred Auguste 37
Montfaucon 36; *see also* waste,
        management, disposal
Montferrand 121, 125
Montréal 63–79
mortality
    rate 122, 132, 136, 243–4
    statistics, tables 138
Moscow 194
motor car as a source of nuisance 223
Mulhouse 84
municipal
    incorporation 75, 148, 154
    policy 107, 111, 116–17, 122,
        128–9, 176, 180

Nantes 17, 114–20, 130
Naples 16, 101–12
National Federation of City Farms
    94
National Hay Association 57
National Trust 240; *see also*
        conservative organizations
nature
    as a resource 103
    colonization of 10–11, 63–4,
        70–71, 76